DATE DUE

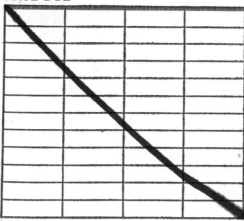

DISPASSIONATE JUSTICE

A Synthesis of the Judicial Opinions of Robert H. Jackson

DISPASSIONATE JUSTICE

*A Synthesis
of the Judicial Opinions
of Robert H. Jackson*

GLENDON SCHUBERT
York University

The Bobbs-Merrill Company, Inc.
Indianapolis and New York

To Frank August Schubert, my son,
with the wish that he may become
learned in the law
and
wise in politics

PREFACE

This book is about American political life, seen from the perspective of a justice of the United States Supreme Court. In writing the series of essays brought together in this volume, Robert Houghwout Jackson had several goals in view. His immediate aim was to construct as cogent and persuasive an argument as possible to justify his own position, in relation to the positions of his colleagues, in the decision of Supreme Court cases. His longer-range objective was to influence the thinking of a large number of other persons—lower court judges, lawyers, law professors, congressmen, businessmen, and future members of the Supreme Court itself—about the issues of public policy raised by these cases. In order to realize both his proximate and his ultimate goals, and also as a reflection of his own taste and character, Jackson took considerably more than ordinary pains to say what he had to say in a way that would excite the interest and rouse the feelings of his readers.

Throughout his career as a lawyer (in both private and public practice) and as a judge, Jackson maintained close ties with the organized bar. He identified strongly and positively with his profession, and many of his opinions—as well as most of his extramural writing—reflect his deep interest in the interests of lawyers. His continuing preoccupation with the practice of law made him an authentic spokesman for the legal profession, in his judicial utterances. More than any other Supreme Court justice in this century, Robert Jackson was the voice of the bar, speaking from the bench.

I have called the book *Dispassionate Justice* because this was the ideal against which Robert Jackson measured the performance of his brethren on the Supreme Court. A recurrent theme of his opinions is the failure of his colleagues to live up to the high standards of judicial neutrality, in regard to the conflicts of value that were at stake in their decisions, suggested by Jackson as the norm that ought to govern all judicial decision-making. Yet he himself was no judicial automaton; quite to the contrary, Bob Jackson was a very human person. And the emotional language which colors his opinions reveals him to have been a not unpassionate judge.

This very dissonance between the ideal and the actual in adjudicative behavior, which is characteristic of Anglo-American legal systems, adds importance to Jackson's judicial writing. For he was no seminal thinker breaking new ground at the intellectual frontiers of the legal profession. He is of interest, instead, because of the faithfulness with which he mirrored, in his writing, the ideas which predominated among American lawyers of his generation. Those ideas have undergone particularly rapid

change during the years since Jackson's death in the mid-fifties; and many
of the most cherished beliefs of his generation already have slipped out
of present consciousness into the subliminal influences of intellectual
history. The problems with which he was concerned, however, largely
remain as the social and economic issues that confront the political decision makers of today. So we read Robert Jackson as the poet of the faith
of our fathers, brought to bear upon the fundamental questions of public
policy that face us.

The themes that Jackson discusses in his opinions are, therefore,
quite familiar to us. As he himself described it, he was concerned with
civil liberties from the points of view of both the right of the individual
to be free of arbitrary and unnecessary governmental restraint and the
right of the majority to protection against threats to order and security
raised by extreme social deviants and political fanatics. Like most of us,
Jackson valued both individual freedom and social stability. To him, property rights were a special legal way of thinking about certain aspects of
individual freedom. He favored upholding the authority of legislatures to
regulate private property to achieve goals important to the common interests of a larger public; but he favored also the restraint of the administrators who were responsible for bringing those legislative goals into effect.
The initiative in public policy-making, Jackson thought, ought to lie with
Congress and the President, rather than with the Supreme Court or
other judges. On the other hand, in the federal relationship between the
national and state governments, and among the states, it was, he believed,
appropriate for the courts to play a more creative role, protecting the national market (as he called it) from state interference, and building a
national legal system in those policy enclaves (such as the field of divorce law) where the possibility of effective political solution seemed
remote.

In regard to both civil liberties and the separation of powers, therefore, Jackson argued that courts could be expected to accomplish relatively little. He reserved his most scathing criticism for those colleagues
whom he perceived to be "libertarian activists," seeking to use the Supreme Court as an instrument for the establishment of national policies
promoting particular civil liberties or novel socioeconomic policies. Only
the people, through party and electoral processes, could or should attempt
to make fundamental changes of this sort. For judges to attempt the
task was to corrupt the democratic political process. However, Jackson
did not seem to consider it inconsistent to advocate a more expansive
judicial role in the building of a national system of law to supplant some
of the demonstrated inadequacies of our federal constitutional system,
particularly in regard to the protection of property rights.

Since the very beginnings of our constitutional polity, judicial politics has been a major process of policy making in the United States. The father figure of the judge making wise laws for loyal citizens is a primary political image—and a basic social myth—which permeates the historical American culture much as it did the imaginary culture of Plato's *Republic*. Plato's guardians were an elite trained from childhood for their role of authority; American judges represent a single learned profession of men who monopolize the important roles in the courts which constitute the stages for the drama of judicial politics. A political scientist may be expected, therefore, to want to understand the judicial process better, and to explain more fully to his fellow citizens how the legal profession, through this self-delegated representational system, declares the law for the rest of us. The programmer controls the range of possible results that an electronic computer can report, and the substantive analyst with data and a problem to solve gets answers from the machine only through the agency of computer programmers. Lawyers are the programmers of the decision-making apparatus for judicial policy making, and judges and other officials constitute its component parts. At the control board of the computer sit the justices of the United States Supreme Court.

The dominant force that shaped Jackson's thinking, and his life and way of living into late middle age, was the small American town of the turn of the century. He grew up during the Progressive era in American politics, and he stood fast in the faith of the Bryans and La Follettes long after these architects of his political ideology had passed from the scene. Like most other Americans of his own age, Jackson had no college education, and he probably was fortunate to have completed high school. His father raised, raced, and traded horses; and farmers rather than college graduates or professional men were his father's and mother's forebears. His own learning and educational tastes were entirely consonant with the great Chautauqua Institute which dominated the intellectual horizons of the countryside in which he grew up. These were the wellsprings of his political thinking; and the wonder is not that they reappear so clearly in the opinions that he wrote as a judge—but rather that he succeeded so well in sublimating these primordial values during the half dozen or so years of his political apprenticeship as a New Dealer, a Washington bureaucrat, and F.D.R.'s brightest young legal eagle. That he did is mute testimony to the strength of the consuming political ambition that possessed him as he climbed closer to positions of really significant power—the Presidency—and prestige—the Chief Justiceship.

Jackson's judicial career is the story of the denouement and dissolution (in no small measure masochistic) of his political ambitions. For most small-town lawyers, to become a Supreme Court Justice would mark the apex of one's aspirations for office and public preferment; but for Bob Jackson, it was only second best to his just deserts as rewards would be apportioned in a polity which dispensed dispassionate political justice. So he was not a happy lawyer-on-the-bench; he was a sardonic judge, and hence a confirmed critic of both his colleagues and his times. But the devil who drove him made Jackson a more interesting writer than it is likely he otherwise would have been.

The judicial opinions reproduced in this book are taken from the official *United States Reports* of the decisions of the Supreme Court. Cases are cited in the usual fashion followed by lawyers and political scientists: volume number; U.S. (designating the series, *United States Reports*); the page on which the case begins; and the page, if different, on which Jackson's opinion begins, or the page or pages to which specific reference is made. Mere references to precedent decisions usually have been deleted from Jackson's opinions, because few such citations would be familiar or meaningful to readers. Most of the original footnotes have been eliminated, and those that have been retained have been renumbered. The footnotes are Justice Jackson's unless the symbol "[Ed.]" follows a footnote. Omissions are denoted in the usual way by ellipses. Most of Jackson's shorter opinions included here are reproduced in full; longer ones have been abbreviated, but in such a way as to preserve the flavor and substance of his arguments.

The advice of Professors David Danelski of Yale University and Walter Murphy of Princeton University aided me in revising an earlier draft of the manuscript. For assistance during the early stages of selecting and analyzing opinions, I am particularly indebted to several former graduate students in political science at Michigan State University, including George Kantrowitz, Steighton J. Watts, and James E. Holton. My research was supported by a series of annual All-University Faculty Research Grants from Michigan State University, by the Penrose Fund of the American Philosophical Society, and by the former Bureau of Social and Political Research of Michigan State University. For the typing and reproduction of the final drafts of the manuscript, I am indebted to Mrs. Amy Shinoki and to the University of Hawaii's Social Science Research Institute. Robert DeVoursney and Mark Lerner, graduate students in political science at the University of North Carolina, Chapel Hill, and York University, respectively, assisted me in the preparation of the index. My wife and younger children long since have adjusted to life with father when he is working on another book so I owe them no special debt of gratitude—only the incalculable and continuing obligation of and for love, companionship, and friendship.

Glendon Schubert
Toronto
October 1968

CONTENTS

1 PERSONALITY

A. LEGAL IDEOLOGY

Robert Houghwout Jackson was an eloquent spokesman for the pattern of beliefs and feelings characteristic of the political ideology of the American lawyer. More than any other Supreme Court justice of the twentieth century, Jackson was a lawyer's lawyer. A colleague who worked with him during the five years before Jackson's death wrote that "in my opinion he is one of the dozen truly great judges of the Court. He had deep convictions about the business of government and none understood its ramifications better. But best of all he was a lawyer judge."[1] Law is the profession that, more than any other in the American polity, both trains the actors and writes the scenario for the key roles in our political drama. The legal profession dominates all American political life, but the bar exercises monopolistic control over the American judiciary.

Jackson himself once pointed out that "Custom decrees that the Supreme Court shall be composed only of lawyers, though the Constitution does not say so. Those lawyers on the bench will hear only from lawyers at the bar."[2] In a speech to the New York Bar Association, delivered on January 29, 1937 (just a week before Roosevelt's own speech attacking the Court), Jackson identified himself as "the New Dealer on your program," and then went on to say that "Lawyer prestige rests on judicial supremacy in government. Only by our monopoly of the high Court can we hold society to those technical legal patterns which only counselors at law can weave or unravel. But lawyer control of the high Court rests only on public sufferance and tradition. The framers of our Constitution did not see fit to make provision that the membership of the Supreme Court must be only lawyers. They deliberately left it open to men of other learnings than the law. But from the very beginnings we have kept it packed with lawyers, and now lawyers feel a vested interest in holding all the seats on the Court for themselves."[3] Fortunately, leavening and liberalizing influences are also at work in American politics so that in practice the per-

---

[1] Mr. Justice Sherman Minton in a letter dated March 19, 1957, to and quoted by Eugene C. Gerhart, *Robert H. Jackson: Lawyer's Judge* (Albany: Q Corporation, 1961), pp. 102-103.

[2] Robert H. Jackson, *The Struggle for Judicial Supremacy: A Study of a Crisis in American Power Politics* (New York: Random House, Inc. 1941), p. 291.

[3] "Lawyers and Government," *Congressional Record*, LXXXI, Part 9, 75th Congress, 1st Session (Washington: Government Printing Office, 1936), Appendix, p. 124.

formance differs in many important ways from the lawyers' script. The
legal point of view nevertheless remains central in the values that constitute the political ideology of American society.[4] Legal ideology looks backward; hence in almost any situation of political choice, legal arguments
tend to subserve stability (which represents the preeminent and fundamental value of law to society), and to promote accommodations of
conflicting present interests by means of political compromises more appropriate to yesteryear. Jackson himself noted that "The entire philosophy,
interest, and training of the legal profession tend toward conservatism. . . .
[I]t is much concerned with precedents, authorities, existing customs, usages, vested rights, and established relationships. Its method of thinking,
accepted by no other profession, cultivates a supreme respect for the past,
and its order. . . . No lawyer sufficiently devoted to the law to know our
existing rules, the history of them, and the justification for them, will depart from them lightly. The contribution of legal philosophy to the balance of social forces will always be on the conservative side."[5]

The predominant values in legal ideology are poor guides to solutions
to the many novel problems that are certain to arise out of changes already in process and that will confront the two million young Americans
born every year. But most social problems are only partly—or seemingly—
new. The making of public policy, whether one thinks of the process as
legislative or administrative or adjudicative or something else, involves
many recurring conflicts in values, in patterns of perceptions and evalua-
tions that change but slowly. Therefore, the values dear to lawyers and the
law even a generation ago are significant in our public search for solutions
to today's social problems.

Jackson believed strongly in the virtues of *nineteenth*-century liberalism and individualism,[6] and he became that rare bird among twentieth-
century American politicians—a verbally sensitive, often brilliant,
exponent of modern conservatism. "He was," as Norman Redlich has said,
"judicial liberalism personified, 1937 style. Regrettably, he also typified

---

[4] See Hugo Wolfsohn, "Ideology Makers," in *Australian Politics: A Reader*, ed. Henry
Mayer (Melbourne: F. W. Cheshire, 1966), Chapter 4; Glendon Schubert, "Judges and
Political Leadership," in *Political Leadership in Industrialized Societies*, ed. Lewis J. Ed-
inger (New York: John Wiley & Sons, Inc., 1967), Chapter 8.

[5] Jackson, *The Struggle for Judicial Supremacy*, pp. 313-314. "I, for one," he said, "do
not complain that the contribution of the courts and of the legal profession to the balance
of social forces should be on the conservative side." From a speech at Carnegie Hall on
March 24, 1937, on the month-old Court-packing proposal, as quoted in Eugene C. Gerhart,
America's Advocate: Robert H. Jackson (Indianapolis: The Bobbs-Merrill Company, Inc.,
1958), p. 115.

[6] "I am by temperament," he said, "an individualist" (as quoted by Gerhart, *Lawyer's
Judge*, p. 107).

the failure of that type of liberalism to meet the challenge of the cold war."[7] His biographer has recorded that

> Jackson's political philosophy of independence was developed in his law practice in western New York. All his life he treasured a picture Frank Mott [the attorney under whom he served his apprenticeship] had taken out of the old humor magazine, *Life*. It portrays a lone man seated at his desk studying. There are books strewn about him, an old-fashioned oil lamp is on the desk, a globe stands in one corner of the room. Over the head of the young man a phantom hand holds a laurel wreath. The caption beneath the picture is a line from Kipling's poem "The Winners"—"He travels fastest who travels alone." Jackson kept that picture near his desk, even while on the Supreme Court, as a symbol.[8]

For over seven years the same cartoon adorned the walls of various offices in the Department of Justice. One of Jackson's assistants there commented that "Neither the execution nor Mr. Kipling's thought was exceptional; all that was exceptional was the fact that this reticent man would hang a memory on the wall for all to see."[9] But, as Jackson himself observed, "A person gets from a symbol the meaning he puts into it, and what is one man's comfort and inspiration is another's jest and scorn."[10] The comfort that he himself must have derived from homiletic images is revealed by his frequent retelling of

> ... the old story of the stone-cutters who were asked what they were doing. The first workman gave the uninspiring, but very practical reply, "I am earning a living"; the second workman, without lifting his eyes from his immediate work, said, "I am cutting this stone"; but the face of the third lighted up as he said, "I am building a cathedral."[11]

Evidently, this anecdote is on about the same level of profundity as the Kipling maxim, or the scrapbook jottings of Elbert Hubbard, the Sage of

---

[7] "The Court and the Cold War," *Nation* CLXXXI (September 24, 1955), 265. Similarly, J. A. C. Grant has pointed out in regard to the justice who was closest ideologically to Jackson that: "It has been said of Holmes that he survived into his own generation. It may yet be written of Frankfurter that he was appointed as his was passing into history. He came to the Court beautifully equipped to carry on the Holmes-Brandeis opposition to judicial activism in the economic field. In twenty-three years on the bench, he had occasion to write just one such opinion. He came totally ill-equipped, emotionally as well as from his sense of values, to meet the challenge of a new era." From "Felix Frankfurter: A Dissenting Opinion," *UCLA Law Review*, XII (1965), 1042.

[8] Gerhart, *America's Advocate*, p. 48.

[9] Warner W. Gardner, "Robert H. Jackson, 1892–1954: Government Attorney," *Columbia Law Review*, LV (1955), 439.

[10] *West Virginia State Board of Education* v. *Barnette*, 319 U.S. 624, 632–633 (1943), and Chap. 2A, *infra*.

[11] Robert H. Jackson, "The Law Above Nations," *American Journal of International Law*, XXXVII (1943), 305. The same story appears at several other places in his writing, for example, "The American Bar Center: A Testimony to Our Faith in the Rule of Law," *American Bar Association Journal*, XL (1954), 22.

East Aurora who was such a dominant figure in the intellectual life of southwestern New York during Jackson's youth.

Jackson was straightforward in his opposition to contemporary political liberalism. The liberal members of the Court in his day—most conspicuously Black, Murphy, and Douglas—were his personal and political enemies, as well as opponents in the policy-making work of the Court. In his posthumous valedictory he remarked:

> A cult of libertarian judicial activists now assails the Court almost as bitterly for renouncing power as the earlier "liberals" once did for assuming too much power. This cult appears to believe that the Court can find in a 4,000-word eighteenth-century document or its nineteenth-century Amendments, or can plausibly supply, some clear bulwark against all dangers and evils that today beset us internally. This assumes that the Court will be the dominant factor in shaping the constitutional practice of the future and can and will maintain, not only equality with the elective branches, but a large measure of supremacy and control over them. I may be biased against this attitude because it is so contrary to the doctrines of the critics of the Court, of whom I was one, at the time of the Roosevelt proposal to reorganize the judiciary. But it seems to me a doctrine wholly incompatible with faith in democracy, and in so far as it encourages a belief that the judges may be left to correct the result of public indifference to issues of liberty in choosing Presidents, Senators, and Representatives, it is a vicious teaching.[12]

In fact, during the thirteen years of Jackson's membership the Supreme Court was never dominated by a libertarian majority. During his early New Deal years as a Washington lawyer, it had been dominated by a conservative majority of judicial activists (as he himself so eloquently charged).[13] But in either case the Court's function was that of a continuing national debating society; and Robert Jackson, as much as any of his colleagues, sought to influence his countrymen on a variety of unfolding issues of public policy. In other political cultures, other institutions perform an equivalent function; but in the United States the justices of the Supreme Court play this essential role of openly debating public policy. The President rarely has an adversary of equal stature with whom to debate national issues except quadrennially in election campaigns. And the significant debates in Congress go on behind the scenes; rarely do the formal deliberations on the House or Senate floors command the attention of a national audience. The news media focus on occasional committee hearings and investigations, where the procedures and the size of the forums tend more to resemble those of an appellate court—such as the Supreme Court—than those of either house of the Congress.

---

[12] Robert H. Jackson, *The Supreme Court in the American System of Government* (Cambridge: Harvard University Press, 1955), pp. 57–58. Regarding Jackson's use of the phrase "libertarian judicial activists," see C. Herman Pritchett, *Civil Liberties and the Vinson Court* (Chicago: The University of Chicago Press, 1954), Chap. X.

[13] Jackson, *The Struggle for Judicial Supremacy*, Chaps. III–V.

Jackson was a great lawyer who personified to an unusual degree both the vices and virtues of the legal profession. His skill as an advocate brought him within that select circle of men who have been considered suitable for both the Presidency and the Chief Justiceship, the two most prestigious, and probably most important, political roles in America. Only William Howard Taft actually has held both offices, and Charles Evans Hughes is the only other person who has come close to doing so. Earl Warren is probably the best contemporary example of a lawyer-politician who was considered a possibility for either position. Even the number of candidates who (like Jackson) "also ran" for both jobs is not large.

Jackson failed to rise above the secondary level of political leadership partly because of certain characteristics which he shared with his profession—characteristics which, though legal virtues, were political vices. Looking back upon the critical years for Jackson's political preferment, a lawyer associate who knew him well remarked, "his bent was to plow old pastures in a new way, not to leap fences and attack virgin soil. He was a professional man, and neither a planner nor a dreamer. It was his job to defend, not to formulate policies."[14] Certain misfortunes of timing also affected the fall of his political star, just as earlier and luckier breaks had accompanied its rise. From start to finish, Jackson's political career was a function of his inclusion among F.D.R.'s entourage: Roosevelt's decision to seek a third term denied to Jackson the Presidency; Roosevelt's desire to attract Republican support accounted for his first denial, to Jackson, of the Chief Justiceship; and Roosevelt's death resulted in the second and final denial, to Jackson, of the center chair on the Court. From this point of view, Jackson's career in Washington was dependent upon what best served the interests of Roosevelt's dominant political career.

Certain personal qualities of Jackson the man were also involved, however, in the calling of the third strike against his ambitions for political advancement. Among his personal virtues were sociability, candor, eloquence, and wit; his vices were pride, jealousy, and—although it is not usually so considered today—ambition. At what was by any objective criterion the very summit of his professional success as a lawyer and as a man, he yielded to disappointment at the frustration of his political ambition for the Chief Justiceship and committed what was most certainly political suicide by dispatching the cable from Nuremberg publicly attacking his colleague Hugo Black, at the close of his work at the war crimes trials in June 1946.[15] This denouement occurred when two-thirds

14 Gardner, "Government Attorney," 438.
15 For further discussion of these events, see pp. 16-17, *infra*.

of his judicial career still lay ahead of him; thereafter, he increasingly became a spokesman for more conservative values. Alan F. Westin has observed that:

> Beginning about 1946 . . . Jackson began to feel increasingly uncomfortable in the New Deal position. In his speeches and opinions he began to challenge the idea of a constitutional difference between human and property rights for purposes of judicial review, or of "preferred" civil liberties which should receive special treatment.[16]

And Max Lerner has described the changes in the overtones and undertones of expression that accompanied the shift in content noted by Westin:

> [T]he ever more frequent ironic smile that plays about his lips, and has become almost settled there, reveals his role. On a Court full of individualists he is the supreme one. . . . [Since his return from Nuremberg] the edge of outrage and contempt has been added to an already sharp style. To read his opinions is to delight in the literary result while mourning the personal bitterness and frustrations that give rise to it.[17]

As eloquent in writing as in speech, Jackson was the most fluent advocate of judicial conservatism of the past several decades. From his last public address, delivered at the dedication of the American Bar Center building in Chicago less than a year before his death, came the text inscribed over its main entrance: "A Cathedral to testify to our faith in the rule of law."[18] His ideas remain important because of the manner, often provoking and never dull, in which he articulated them, and because they are so very orthodox. He expressed what was surely at the time, and probably still is, the consensus of the American bar on the basic issues of social, economic, and political policy that flowed through the Court during his participation in its decisions. In reading Jackson we are reading the opinions of Everyman of the law, although better said than the average lawyer would phrase them.

B. LITERARY STYLE

Oliver Wendell Holmes, Jr., and Benjamin Nathan Cardozo are widely recognized as the outstanding men of letters among Supreme Court justices since John Marshall. Unlike Jackson, both Holmes and

[16] Book review by Alan F. Westin, *Commentary,* XXII (July, 1956), 23.

[17] Max Lerner, "The Supreme Court," *Holiday,* VII (1950), 73.

[18] Jackson, "The American Bar Center," 22. He had spoken at much greater length on the common wellsprings of law and religion (in the Old Testament, among the Romans, at common law, and in America) at the dedication of two consistory windows for the National Cathedral in Washington. Jackson, "Law and Lawgivers," *Alabama Lawyer,* XII (1951), 93-98.

Cardozo were celebrated as great judges in the common-law tradition[19] and as chief justices of distinguished state supreme courts. Both had written widely read books about law *before* they joined the Supreme Court, but at about the same age (62) as that at which Jackson's own work as a justice was terminated. Unlike Jackson, each was for his own day an outstandingly liberal justice.

Jackson, quite unlike Holmes and Cardozo,[20] was a very conventional legal thinker. Nonetheless, Holmes and Cardozo were his models of judicial excellence. In at least one respect, that is, in the quality of his writing,[21] both in his judicial opinions and speeches and in occasional articles and books, he can be said to rank as their rival.

It is true that Felix Frankfurter, a student[22] and disciple of Holmes, succeeded literally to the position that had been occupied since 1902, first by Holmes and then by Cardozo. But few would be so lacking in candor to make other than invidious comparisons between the pithy prose of Holmes[23] or the rhythmic cadences of Cardozo[24] and the verbal produc-

19 Karl N. Lewellyn, *The Common Law Tradition: Deciding Appeals* (Boston: Little, Brown and Company, 1960).

20 Glendon Schubert, *Judicial Behavior: A Reader in Theory and Research* (Chicago: Rand McNally & Company, 1964), pp. 9-27.

21 "Not every judge is a Bleckley or a Holmes, Stone, or Jackson; yet each brings his own particular style to the task [of writing opinions]." Griffin B. Bell, "Style in Judicial Writing," *Journal of Public Law*, XV (1966), 219. According to Edward Dumbauld, "If the wit and clarity so characteristic of Justice Holmes is to be found in the writings of any of his successors on the Supreme Court bench it is in those of Robert H. Jackson." *Proceedings of the American Society of International Law, 1955* (Washington: American Society of International Law, 1955), p. 118. John P. Frank has said that "For the consistent capacity to turn a nice phrase, Justice Jackson has never been matched. . . . Jackson's longer passages are outstanding prose." *Marble Palace* (New York: Alfred A. Knopf, Inc., 1958), Chap. VII ("The Law as Literature"), and Appendix, pp. 130-143 and 295-302, at pp. 141-142. And Jackson's colleague, Sherman Minton, in a letter to Gerhart on March 19, 1957, indulged in what is certainly hyperbole when he wrote that Jackson "had a facility for expression unsurpassed by any man who ever sat on the Court." From Gerhart, *Lawyer's Judge*, p. 104.

22 Felix Frankfurter, *Mr. Justice Holmes and the Supreme Court* (Cambridge: Harvard University Press, 1938).

23 One of Holmes' many virtues was brevity, which Jackson attributed to Holmes' life-long practice of writing his opinions in longhand while *standing* at a desk about the height of a draftsman's. See Gerhart, *Lawyer's Judge*, pp. 109-110.

24 For his not unself-conscious statement of some standards of taste, see Cardozo's essay "Law and Literature" in his book of the same title (New York: Harcourt, Brace & World, Inc., 1931), pp. 3-40. Jackson fits fairly well, of course, into a combination of two of the six types of opinions categorized by Cardozo, who said that an "opinion will need persuasive force, or the impressive virtue of sincerity and fire, or the mnemonic power of alliteration and antithesis, or the terseness and tang of the proverb and the maxim. . . . [Two] types [of opinions] which run into each other by imperceptible gradations [are] the

tions of the Court's expert in legal needlepoint. It was clearly Jackson, and not Frankfurter, who fell heir to the Court's Muse.

Frankfurter was nevertheless the colleague closest to Jackson in voting and in shared opinions (however great the differences in their prose styles), and he had an exceptional opportunity to observe Jackson at close range, not only throughout his activity as a Supreme Court justice but also earlier when Jackson was first Solicitor General and then Attorney General. Thus, he had observed Jackson's verbal behavior both before and on the bench of the Supreme Court. And Frankfurter has explained what it was that made Jackson's style so different:

> To an unusual degree in the history of the Court, Justice Jackson wrote as he felt. In his case the style was the man. . . . He belonged to what might be called the naturalistic school [of opinion writers]. He wrote as he talked, and he talked as he felt. The fact that his opinions were written talk made them as lively as the liveliness of his talk. . . . No man who ever sat on the Supreme Court, it seems to me, mirrored the man in him in his judicial work more completely than did Justice Jackson.[25]

Certainly this was true of his nonjudicial writing. With the exception of one book, *The Struggle for Judicial Supremacy*, and a very few articles, almost everything that Jackson ever published was initially given (or was intended to be) as a speech.

Like many other American lawyer-politicians who have taught themselves to write, Jackson's knowledge of the classics of English and American literature was unusual.[26] Despite his example, his colleagues did not

---

laconic or sententious and the conversational or homely. There has been no stage of our legal history in which these methods have been neglected. The Year Books are full of wise saws and homely illustrations, the epigram, the quip, the jest. Perhaps this is but a phase of that use of the maxim or the proverb which is characteristic of legal systems in early stages of development. . . . If the maxim has declined in prevalence and importance, now that the truths of the law have become too complex to be forced within a sentence, there has been no abatement of recourse to the laconic or sententious phrase, to drive home and imbed what might otherwise be lost or scattered. . . . Next door to the epigram is the homely illustration which makes its way and sinks deep by its appeal to everyday experience. In the wielding of these weapons, the English judges have been masters. The precept may be doubtful in the beginning. How impossible to fight against it when the judge brings it down to earth and makes it walk the ground, the brother of some dictate of decency or of prudence which we have followed all our lives." *Ibid.,* pp. 9, 17-18. See also B. H. Levy, *Cardozo and the Frontiers of Legal Thinking: With Selected Opinions* (Port Washington: Kennikat Press, 1965).

[25] Felix Frankfurter, "Mr. Justice Jackson," *Harvard Law Review,* LXVIII (1955), 938-939. "His speech," Frankfurter added in another eulogy, "breaks through the printed page. He was one of those rare men whose spoken word survives in type." From "Robert H. Jackson, 1892–1954: Foreword," *Columbia Law Review,* LV (1955), 437.

[26] And subject to the continuing guidance of his high school English teacher, Mary Willard. See Gerhart, *America's Advocate,* pp. 32-33.

adorn their opinions with references to Milton and Scott, to Emerson and William James.[27] In constructing his opinions, however, he did not rely upon either literary allusion or legal embellishment. As Philip Halpern, a justice of the Appellate Division of the New York Supreme Court, has explained:

> He had a reservoir of learning, from which he drew gracefully and effortlessly. But the most marked quality of his judicial and nonjudicial writing was not the ability to borrow an apt quotation or to find an idea well expressed by one who had written before him; it was the ability to think brilliantly in original and bold fashion and to express his thoughts in forceful and eloquent English of a style inimitably his own. His writing was pithy and pungent; yet he never sacrificed clarity of thought for a well-turned phrase. He was a master of the paradox; he had a great love of alliteration and his antithetical statements were gems. Yet his wit never descended to the frivolous; it always added a barb to the telling point. His wit was especially telling when turned upon himself or his Court. . . .[28]

He relied always upon direct, straightforward, and relatively simple prose. In the appraisal of the committee of the bar that prepared his official eulogy:

> He wrote with a trenchant, concrete, Saxon style of great beauty and vigor, nurtured chiefly on the King James version of the Bible and on Shakespeare. He contributed to the literature of the Court elements of freshness, clarity and originality that will never be forgotten.[29]

The principal complication of his writing consisted of his fondness for epigrammatic juxtaposition of ideas, as exemplified by his observation that "When the Court moved to Washington in 1800, it was provided with no books, *which probably accounts for the high quality of early opinions.*"[30] He used the device of the epigram as the *coup de grâce* to

---

[27] "He is the best stylist on the Court," said one with better qualifications than most to make such a judgment, "and his opinions make the best literature, especially when he taunts his colleagues with some allusion to Byron or Demosthenes, and drives home his point by reducing their position to an absurdity." Max Lerner, "The Supreme Court," *Holiday,* VII (February, 1950), 73.

[28] Philip Halpern, "Robert H. Jackson, 1892–1954," *Stanford Law Review,* VIII (1955), 4.

[29] "Memorial Proceedings of the Bar and Officers of the Supreme Court," 349 U.S. xxxv (April 4, 1955).

[30] Jackson, *The Supreme Court,* p. 30. Emphasis added. "There is a story," he had written as Solicitor General, in one of his many addresses to the American Bar Association, "that Justice Miller of the Supreme Court observed that one of the great factors in early American law was ignorance. . . . The judges, having only the Constitution and the debates and the Federalist to rely on, were apt to do the right thing. Their successors, with the benefit of several hundred volumes of U.S. Reports, cannot be so sure. Yet the several hundred volumes must be taken account of, and so ignorance no longer suffices for a judge." "Back to the Constitution," *American Bar Association Journal,* XXV (1939), 745.

implement his "sense of the jugular." (The phrase belongs to Holmes, who also possessed the instinct.) As Gordon Dean, his friend and associate at the Nuremberg war crimes trials, put it, "Robert Jackson had the unusual capacity to strike to the heart of the matter and to clothe the truth therein discovered with words so vivid and so forceful that one never lost sight of it."[31] Speaking with particular reference to Jackson's performance at the war crimes trials, Dean described his "clear and simple Anglo-Saxon words, arranged frequently in an epigrammatic form but always chosen to bring to light the truth he feared might otherwise lie hidden. They were the words best designed to strip from logic its dullness and make it exciting and memorable.[32] And Professor Paul Freund, Jackson's sometime assistant in the Department of Justice and a connoisseur of fine writing by judges, expressed what is no doubt the prevailing opinion of his lawyer colleagues:

> However much one analysis of his judicial work may differ from another, there will be no disagreement about its artistry. He had style to delight, grace and power of expression to captivate. His was an Elizabethan gusto for the swordplay of words. If his style was like pearls, they were occasionally—as was said of the style of a Scottish judge, surely a forbear —pearls dissolved in vinegar. He wrote for the lawyers he knew, with an eye fixed on what was practicable in the outcome and accessible in the sources, but his opinions have held withal a rare fascination for students of the law, and this they will not cease to hold so long as sagacity wrapped in wit has power to move the inquiring mind.[33]

C. POLITICAL CAREER

Robert Jackson's death marked the end of an era in American judicial politics, because he left behind as a minority those remaining of his colleagues who had joined with him, during the preceding decade and a half, to constitute the Roosevelt Court.[34] He was a rather short man of great charm, immense vitality, and intense ambition who chose to dress (according to one old friend) "like Beau Brummell." A life-long Democrat and early New Dealer, he was "the President's lawyer" who argued the

[31] "Proceedings before the Supreme Court of the United States, April 4, 1955," *In Memory of Robert Houghwout Jackson* (Washington: privately printed, 1955), p. 43.

[32] *Ibid.*, p. 44.

[33] *Ibid.*, p. 52.

[34] C. Herman Pritchett, *The Roosevelt Court: A Study in Judicial Politics and Values, 1937–1947* (New York: The Macmillan Company, 1948).

Administration's case before the Supreme Court[35] in the terms immediately enveloping the Court-packing episode of 1937—a dispute in which Jackson was, of course, intimately involved. His service as Associate Justice of the United States Supreme Court spanned the epoch of World War II and the cold war.[36]

Jackson was a self-made small-town lawyer and country gentleman who, at 42, went to Washington to work for the remaining two decades of his life. On his arrival, early in 1934, there was little to suggest that, in the span of half a dozen years, this yearling government lawyer would be a leading contender for both of the most important political offices in Washington: the Presidency and the Chief Justiceship. He had never held elective public office; and, prior to 1933, his experience in government employment (other than local) was limited to membership on an investigatory commission authorized by the New York State Legislature. Even this appointment was due to his Bar Association contacts. Indeed, the natural question to have raised at this time would have been: Why should he leave Jamestown? He had worked hard and successfully in the community for twenty-one years, and he liked the role and life of a country squire.[37]

Jackson was born on the same Pennsylvania farm as his father and grandfather. The homestead had been worked by his great-grandfather as

---

[35] One who observed him closely in that role has commented that: "Solicitor General Jackson was free to give concentrated personal attention to his own work [including] the argument of cases to the Supreme Court. Just as he would not interfere with his subordinates, so he expected and wanted no help from them to do his work. As he prepared for argument there came no requests for a digest of the record, no requests for consultation or advice on the presentation. It was his job and he did it—alone, thoroughly, quickly and with superlative skill. He was the most effective . . . advocate I have seen." Gardner, "Government Attorney," 441.

[36] Brief biographical sketches of Jackson can be found in William L. Ransom, "Associate Justice Robert H. Jackson," *American Bar Association Journal*, XXVII (1941), 478-482; *Current Biography 1940* (New York: The H. W. Wilson Company, 1941), pp. 427-429; *Current Biography 1950* (New York: The H. W. Wilson Company, 1951), pp. 273-275; William W. Bishop, Jr., "Robert Jackson," *American Journal of International Law*, XLIX (1955), 44-50; and in the report of the "Memorial Proceedings of the Bar and Officers of the Supreme Court," 349 U.S. xxvii-li (April 4, 1955). Among the obituary notices are those of *Life*, XXXVII (October 18, 1954), 24; *Newsweek*, XLIV (October 18, 1954), 51; and *Time*, LXIV (October 18, 1954), 24. *America's Advocate*, the biography by Eugene Gerhart, emphasizes Jackson's nonjudicial career as a lawyer in Washington and at Nuremberg.

[37] Professor Arthur E. Sutherland of the Harvard Law School has written that, as a lawyer practicing in Rochester (New York), he "looked to Robert Jackson's career in Jamestown as 'the best possible life of the practicing lawyer.'" *Stanford Law Review*, VIII (1952), 2.

the first settlement in the township.[38] Jackson, himself, has described the importance to his ideology as a judge of what he considered to be the "truly democratic" social and economic aspects of his rearing:

> My early life was spent entirely among rural folk and the tradesmen who lived in the small towns dependent on the countryside. My relatives and friends, my clients and jurors were from them. *That their views and attitudes and their manner of life impressed me early and deeply and profoundly influence my present outlook and attitude to life I should be the last to deny.* . . . Such a life is an isolationist life, possible only for the self-reliant and self-sufficient and developing those traits above all others. . . . From early youth to extreme age every sanction, economic and social, favored hard work, long hours, and thrift. . . . That kind of existence has largely passed and I am from the last generation to have had that experience and to have felt that kind of influence of Democracy.[39]

His great-grandfather, Elijah Jackson, was described as a "stiff Democrat" who was identified with a group of "generally intense partisans of General Andrew Jackson." His grandfather, Robert R. Jackson, "was a Democrat throughout his life, [who] boasted to young Robert of having voted for Franklin Pierce and for every Democratic candidate for President from that time down to Woodrow Wilson." In "a community that was intensely and sometimes bitterly Republican," his father, William Eldred Jackson, "remained an outspoken Democrat";[40] so did Robert H. Jackson.

Robert was a self-educated man who studied law primarily under the apprenticeship system. He never attended college and he was never graduated from law school. His formal education beyond high school was limited to attendance at the neighboring Chautauqua Institute and a single year at the Albany Law School. Albany was not then, and is not now, reckoned among the great national law schools; Jackson went there "because some of Jamestown's leading lawyers were Albany Law men, and

[38] For a delightful example of his literary style in one of his few articles that did *not* reproduce a speech, see Robert H. Jackson, "Falstaff's Descendants in Pennsylvania Courts," *University of Pennsylvania Law Review*, CI (1952), 313-332. In this he recounts the tale of a hoary local litigation with roots in the days of Prince Hal.

[39] *In Memory of Robert Houghwout Jackson*, as quoted by John Lord O'Brian, p. 25. (Emphasis in the original.) And he confided to his biographer that: "My philosophy perhaps would more or less be the philosophy that a man would have to develop if he practiced law for the relatively small industries of a community like Jamestown." Gerhart, *Lawyer's Judge*, p. 107.

[40] At the time when Jackson's appointment to the Court was announced, a fellow New York lawyer wrote that: "Understanding of his outlook on public questions would be aided by an appreciation of the atmosphere of rugged independence, free discussion, and keen solicitude for the rights and welfare of the individual, which pervaded his city and county, so profoundly influenced by the presence of the Chautauqua Assembly, with its great public platform to which the leaders of public thought came and spoke. . . . [H]e shared his home town's habit of courage and outspoken action in behalf of independent thinking." Ransom, "Associate Justice Robert H. Jackson," 481.

because the city was the seat of state government."[41] Evidently the year at Albany was sufficient for his own purposes and those of the local community in which he planned to practice, for he soon became an active leader in first the local, and then the state and national bar associations. It was through his bar association work that he came to the attention of Governor Franklin Roosevelt.[42] Through this association began the process of his metamorphosis, from the pastoral life he had chosen, to the turmoil of the nation's capitol during the first year of the New Deal.

There were four events of special significance in Jackson's career as a Supreme Court Justice: (1) Roosevelt's third-term decision, (2) the appointment of Stone rather than Jackson as Chief Justice in 1941, (3) Jackson's experience as Chief Prosecutor at Nuremberg, and (4) the appointment of Vinson rather than Jackson as Chief Justice in 1946.

(1) It was James Farley's own presidential ambitions that punctured a trial balloon which, if successful, might have made Jackson Governor of New York in 1938 and therefore a front-runner for the Democratic nomination in 1940 (assuming that Roosevelt had stepped down at that time).[43] Instead, Jackson remained in the post of Solicitor General during 1938 and 1939. His brilliant performance in this role kept him in the public eye, and after his promotion to the position of Attorney General on January 4, 1940, he remained a highly available prospective candidate[44] until Roosevelt's third-term decision foreclosed the Presidency to him, at least for the time being.

[41] Gerhart, *America's Advocate*, p. 34.

[42] Gerhart, *America's Advocate*, pp. 55-59. Typical of Jackson's writing at this time are such articles as "Compulsory Incorporation of the Bar from the Country Lawyer's Standpoint," *New York Law Review*, IV (1926), 316-20, "The Future of the Bar," *Lincoln Law Review*, III (1930), 41-44, and "An Organized American Bar," *American Bar Association Journal*, XVIII (1932), 383-386.

[43] Herbert Corey, "A Man with a Flexible Future," *Nation's Business*, XXV (September, 1937), 75-76, 78, 119: "Robert H. Jackson," *Fortune*, XXVI (March, 1938), 78-80; Wesley McCune, *The Nine Young Men* (New York: Harper and Brothers, 1947), pp. 180-181, 186; Gerhart, *America's Advocate*, Chap. 9: "The New York Governorship Bubble."

[44] "Jackson was first on the dopesters' list of men to be groomed to succeed Roosevelt, should he not run for his third term in 1940. Moreover, most of them wanted him to be first on the list." McCune, *The Nine Young Men*, pp. 180-181. See also Marquis W. Childs, "The Man Who Has Always Been a New Dealer," *Forum*, CIII (March, 1940), 148-154. None other than his loyal lieutenant, Bob Jackson, had thrown F.D.R.'s hat in the ring, for a third term, in an Andrew Jackson Day speech at Cleveland: "Young Hickory," *Time*, XXXV (January 15, 1940), 11. What appears in retrospect to have been the most dazzling fairy stories were reserved, appropriately enough, for children, as in the political tip that "most observers say that the President would declare himself out of the race for good if he were sure the Democrats would nominate Jackson." "Roosevelt's Man," *Senior Scholastic*, XXXVI (March 25, 1940), 10.

(2) Even then, there still remained the Chief Justiceship, and when the elderly Hughes announced his retirement early in June, 1941, Jackson was widely acclaimed as the leading Democratic candidate and Roosevelt's own preference for the job. And why not? To many, Jackson symbolized the legal changes wrought by the New Deal; he came from the right circuit (but so did Stone!); and he was the recent author of a book that argued trenchantly for judicial acquiescence in the policy changes brought about by the Roosevelt Administration.[45] That acceptance had already become an accomplished fact as the aftermath of the Court-packing episode, which was due in no small measure to Jackson's own efforts as Solicitor General and Attorney General. Moreover, the President was obligated to Jackson for the right kind of legal advice on some critical issues such as the Court-packing plan, the destroyer deal, and the seizure of the North American Aviation plant[46]—although this business of advisement, too, was a reciprocal process.[47]

The timing of Jackson's candidacy was unfortunate, however, because Roosevelt needed to build in the public mind an image of himself as a symbol of national unity in the face of impending war. This required Jackson, for the second time in as many years, to postpone his personal ambitions in favor of F.D.R.'s self-image as the indispensable leader of the American people in a crusade for freedom. So the Chief Justiceship went to Republican Stone, and Jackson had to settle for an Associate Justiceship.[48] There was talk at the time that Stone would retire after a

[45] Jackson, *The Struggle for Judicial Supremacy.*

[46] See Jackson's testimony on the "Reorganization of the Federal Judiciary," United States Senate Committee on the Judiciary, *Hearings on S. 1392: Part I* (75th Congress, 1st Session; Washington: Government Printing Office, 1937), pp. 37-64; *Youngstown Sheet and Tube* v. *Sawyer,* 343 U.S. 579, 645n.14, 648-650 (1952); and McCune, *The Nine Young Men,* pp. 183-184.

[47] Robert H. Jackson, "A Presidential Legal Opinion," *Harvard Law Review,* LXVI (1953), 1353-1361.

[48] Alpheus T. Mason, *Harlan Fiske Stone: Pillar of the Law* (New York: The Viking Press, Inc., 1956), pp. 563-568, especially 567; Eugene Gerhart, *America's Advocate,* Chaps. 15 and 16. In his eulogy of Charles Evans Hughes, published in the same month in which Stone was promoted to the center chair and Jackson himself was appointed to the most junior position, on the extreme left wing of the bench (*i.e.,* on the right from the point of view of the audience), Jackson took advantage of the opportunity not only to praise Caesar but also to interject a face-saving caveat: "[Hughes'] established position in public opinion gave the country a sense of steadiness, in spite of rapid movement, and an assurance that he was leading in the direction of amendment of doctrine rather than toward destruction of institutions. The Chief Justice was himself a symbol of stability as well as of progress. . . . It was this kind of assurance that made the succession of Harlan F. Stone to the Chief Justiceship not only appropriate but well nigh inevitable if the interest of the Judiciary as an institution were to be fostered." Robert H. Jackson, "Judicial Career of Chief Justice Hughes," *American Bar Association Journal,* XXVII (July, 1941), 408-409.

year or so, thus clearing the way for Jackson's promotion. Apparently, Jackson believed that Roosevelt had promised him the job as soon as it became vacant again; but Stone claimed never to have been consulted on any such question, and his own plans did not envisage an early retirement from his new position.[49] In any event, Jackson joined the Court not as a man whose greatest ambition had been gratified, but rather as one twice frustrated whose expectations of an early elevation to the position of Chief, which would provide a more adequate opportunity for the display of his undoubted talents, had been aroused before he ever took his seat on the Court.[50]

(3) The four years of American participation in World War II drew to a close; Roosevelt died, to be followed shortly by Hitler; and Stone remained Chief Justice, with no apparent intention of vacating his office. In the spring of 1945, Harry Truman looked like anything but a candidate for reelection in 1948; and when he offered Jackson the opportunity to assume a leading role in the portending trials of the so-called Axis war criminals—a position which was certain to thrust its incumbent into the spotlight of worldwide, to say nothing of national, attention—Jackson was quick to accept, notwithstanding that both he and the President knew that Chief Justice Stone was very much opposed to having members of the Court take on such extrajudicial assignments.[51]

Jackson was a brilliant success in the role of Chief Prosecutor, and he looked upon this experience as the crowning achievement of his career.[52] Although he had been an outspoken critic of the legitimation of Executive and military lawlessness by enshrouding these in the facade of the judicial process, he soon became the leading apologist for the new "historic precedent," and wrote and spoke widely in justification of the war crimes trials in which he had been a major protagonist.[53]

[49] Mason, *Harlan Fiske Stone,* p. 593.

[50] McCune, *The Nine Young Men,* pp. 185-186.

[51] Mason, *Harlan Fiske Stone,* pp. 714-719.

[52] "It was, perhaps, the greatest opportunity ever presented to an American lawyer," he wrote in his principal opinion justifying his role at Nuremberg. This document makes quite clear how obviously proud he was of the record of his accomplishment in Germany. "Justice Jackson's Final Report to the President Concerning the Nuremberg War Crimes Trial," *Temple Law Quarterly,* XX (1946), 338-344, at 344. See also his preliminary accounting at the end of his first month on the job, "Report to the President on Trials for War Criminals," *New York Times* (June 8, 1945), 4:1-8.

[53] Jackson, *The Case Against the Nazi War Criminals: Opening Statement for the United States of America* (New York: Alfred A. Knopf, Inc., 1946); *The Nürnberg Case* (New York: Alfred A. Knopf, Inc., 1947); "The Nuremberg Trial: An Example of Procedural Machinery for Development of International Substantive Law," *David Dudley Field, Centenary Essays,* Alison Reppy, ed. (New York: New York University Press, 1949), pp. 314-324; "United Nations Organization and War Crimes," *Proceedings of the American*

(4) To return from Nuremberg to his seat on the Court would have been, in any circumstances, anticlimactic; but it seems clear that the news of Stone's death on April 22, 1946, as the war crimes tribunal's work drew to a close, led Jackson to expect a triumphant return to the Court as its new Chief Justice. He had sacrificed his presidential aspirations (unless, of course, his party should turn to him in 1948); he had awaited Stone's retirement for five years; he had earned the right to the job. Moreover, many thought he was the best qualified man to be Chief Justice and he himself believed that Roosevelt had promised the position to him. This meant that Roosevelt's running mate, who had ridden F.D.R.'s coattails to the Presidency, was obligated to carry through on the outstanding commitments of the Roosevelt Administration. As Jackson must have perceived the matter, it was, in every sense, a debt of honor.

His disappointment at Vinson's nomination was understandably intense.[54] This was especially so because he attributed Truman's failure to select him to the underhanded politicking of his libertarian colleagues under the leadership and due to the personal spite of Hugo Black, who was a rival candidate for the center chair. Jackson had to remain at Nuremberg while the fateful decision was being made. He was cut off from direct personal contact with both his supporters and his opponents, and the rumors that reached him, based in part at least upon Washington gossip and the "inside stories" of political columnists, necessarily gave him a distorted view of the events, however true his worst suspicions may have been in fact. It has been suggested that Jackson reacted to the situation like any G.I. who receives a letter from home telling him of the infidelity of his wife.[55] Although an understanding of his viewpoint makes his behavior seem less incredible, the fact remains that his chosen course of action constituted what is perhaps the greatest breach of judicial ethics

---

Society of International Law, 1952 (Washington: American Society of International Law, 1952), 196-204; and his introduction to Whitney R. Harris, *Tyranny on Trial* (Dallas: Southern Methodist University Press, 1954), especially at p. xxxiii. Fourteen other speeches and articles are cited in "Mr. Justice Jackson," *Stanford Law Review*, VIII (1955), 74-76. See also his "The Significance of the Nuremberg Trials to the Armed Forces," *Military Affairs*, X (Winter, 1946), 2-15. A more dispassionate and balanced appraisal is provided by Telford Taylor, "Robert H. Jackson, 1892-1954: The Nuremberg Trials," *Columbia Law Review*, LV (1955), 488-526.

[54] As his biographer has commented, "not once, but twice, he missed by the narrowest margin being appointed Chief Justice of the United States." Gerhart, *Lawyer's Judge*, p. 105.

[55] Arthur M. Schlesinger, Jr., "The Supreme Court: 1947," *Fortune*, XXXV (January, 1947), 78 (quoted in Pritchett, *The Roosevelt Court*, pp. 28-29). For a pro-Jackson view of the affair, see Gerhart, *America's Advocate*, pp. 258-265. A countervailing bias is provided by John P. Frank, *Mr. Justice Black: The Man and His Opinions* (New York: Alfred A. Knopf, Inc., 1949), pp. 124-131.

and blow to the prestige of the Court ever committed by one of its own members.

While the nomination of Vinson was before the Congress awaiting Senatorial confirmation, Jackson announced to the press on June 10, 1946 (the last day the Supreme Court was in session for the 1945 term and the eve of his departure from Nuremberg for a Scandinavian vacation), that he had sent a long cable to the Judiciary Committees of both the House and the Senate exposing to the world—in view of the role he was then playing—his side of the "feud" which, as he said, had split the Supreme Court.[56] Jackson must have realized that his cable could only hasten Vinson's confirmation. It certainly cast the die against Jackson's ever again being considered for either the Chief Justiceship or the Presidency.[57] When Jackson did return to the Court it was to play out the denouement of his career. The pinnacle was now behind him, and he could look forward to nothing more challenging than a continuance of his service as an Associate Justice.

D. JUDICIAL BEHAVIOR

The ups and downs in Jackson's political fortunes have an interesting bearing upon his behavior as a justice.[58] As one might expect, his verbal and voting support for civil liberties were positively and significantly correlated, although his overall voting record showed less sympathy for civil libertarianism than did his opinions. In relation to his colleagues, Jackson consistently was a moderate in his political liberalism, that is, in his

[56] *The New York Times* (June 11, 1946), 2:3-6; *United States News*, XX (June 21, 1946), 81-82. The story is told in chapter 5G, *infra*. See also *New York Times* (June 11, 1946), 1-2; *United States News*, XX (June 21, 1946), 15-16; McCune, *The Nine Young Men*, pp. 45, 164-170, 178-179; Pritchett, *The Roosevelt Court*, pp. 26-29; Merlo J. Pusey, *Charles Evans Hughes*, Vol. II (New York: The Macmillan Company, 1951), p. 802; Robert J. Steamer, *The Constitutional Doctrines of Mr. Justice Robert H. Jackson* (Ph.D. dissertation, Cornell University, 1954; University Microfilms No. 9802, Ann Arbor, Michigan), pp. 30-34.

[57] At the time that his cable was dispatched, there was speculation that he might leave the Court to run for Governor of New York—and then the White House in 1948? See *The New York Times* (June 11, 1946), p. 2:3.

[58] This paragraph, and the three that follow it, are a slight revision of the concluding pages of my "Jackson's Judicial Philosophy: An Exploration in Value Analysis," *American Political Science Review*, LIX (1965), 962-963, and they rely, of course, upon the evidence presented in that article.

voting on civil liberty issues. After the end of World War II, he manifested a slight but not significant tendency toward greater political conservatism, which apparently was quite independent of the swings of the
Court toward greater (1946–1948 Terms) and toward lesser (1949–
1953) political liberalism.

The issue to which Jackson was most deeply attached, however, was
economic policy, and a very high and significant correlation exists between
his opinion and his voting behavior in this regard. Renowned as an economic liberal at the time of his appointment to the Court, he maintained
this image, in both his opinions and his voting, only during his first four
terms. After the war, his behavior changed sharply and significantly to
strong and consistent support of economic conservatism; and throughout
his last eight terms on the Court, he vied with Frankfurter for the bottom
position in the rank order of the justices in voting in support of economic
liberalism (*i.e.*, in his support for unions, the fiscal claims of injured
workmen, governmental regulation of business, and economic underdogs
generally). Moreover, his rate of dissent in behalf of economic conservatism doubled during this later period.

Jackson *argued* in support of economic liberalism in dissenting opinions just as often—indeed, a bit more often—than he supported economic
conservatism in majority opinions which he wrote for the Court. In his
voting, however, he frequently upheld the conservative position when in
the majority, while dissenting only thrice (and then, only during the 1952
Term) in support of economic liberalism during his entire period of service on the Court; so Jackson was no more prepared to dissent in behalf
of economic liberalism in his "liberal" period than he was during his
"conservative" period. Given his own sophisticated sensitivity to the political implications of dissenting behavior (*infra*), consider that he was
unwilling ever to dissent, *even once,* in support of the position that we
can assume would have furthered his political ambitions, during the time
when such a display of conspicuous economic liberalism might have
done him the most good, politically speaking. I attribute his failure so to
behave, with such rationality, to a consistency with his own most strongly
rooted attitude; and this was economic conservatism. Therefore, Jackson's change in his opinions to greater support for economic conservatism,
and his reinforcing dissenting behavior, reflected not a conversion to a new
view of political economy, but rather a more conspicuous display of the
beliefs of his forefathers, his youth, and his manhood prior to his entry
into political office.

His espousal of economic liberalism and relatively low rate of dissent
during the war years were generalized characteristics of his judicial behav-

ior, in addition to being specifically related to each other. The same was true of his economic conservatism and much higher rate of dissent *after* the war. Jackson's economic liberalism was a necessary function of his political career; and the collapse of his political ambitions after his return from Nuremberg best explains both his manifest reversion to what had been his latent economic conservatism, and his increasing dissidence. With life tenure as an associate justice, he had nothing more to lose; and so he wrote and voted in support of the value that was most fundamentally related to both his political ideology and his legal career before he went into politics.

The ideas that were most important to Bob Jackson, and that are also central elements in the cognitive orientation toward public policy of the American lawyer, are set forth at some length in the selection, in this book, of his best opinions as an Associate Justice of the United States Supreme Court. During his dozen years as a judge, Jackson participated in close to 20,000 decisions of the Court; but nine-tenths of these were refusals to review judgments of lower courts, and opinions rarely are written to justify either the jurisdictional decisions of the Court, or the votes of individual justices, in such cases. (Only one of the opinions of Jackson that we shall examine was of this sort, and it came under exceptional circumstances in a decision to *grant* jurisdiction.[59]) There remained over two thousand decisions "on the merits" of the issues presented (as lawyers phrase the matter) in which the Court did purport to resolve issues of social, economic, political, and legal policy, and in which Jackson took part. Of these, over half entailed disagreement sufficient to provoke dissenting votes from one or more of the justices, and Jackson himself was a dissenter in about a fourth of these split decisions of the Court, some two hundred and fifty all told. He wrote a total of over three hundred opinions as a justice,[60] and about a sixth of these, fifty-three, are presented here.

I believe this collection is representative of Jackson's style, of his best judicial writing, and of the scope and content of his thinking. However, it does not provide a representative sample, in a statistical sense, of Jackson's judicial opinions, because I have deliberately preferred to follow humanistic rather than scientific criteria in deciding what to include here, since my objective is to encourage others to read what Jackson had to say. (I have ventured elsewhere a more scientific analysis of his opinions,[61] upon which I have of course relied to the extent that I could do so con-

---

[59] *Hirota* v *MacArthur*, 335 U.S. 876 (1948), and Chap. 9D, *infra*.

[60] A list of his opinions appears in "Mr. Justice Jackson," *Stanford Law Review*, VIII (1955), 60-71.

[61] "Jackson's Judicial Philosophy," 940-963.

sistently with the present objective.) The most important differences between the present collection and the universe of his opinions relate to
substance, on the one hand, and to form, on the other.

In the first place, this sample is biased by the emphases which it gives
to the kind of policy issues which are discussed. Over half of the opinions
herein focus upon issues of civil liberties, and there are about a third more
of them than there are of opinions which discuss primarily issues of
economic policy; in his opinions in the reports, the balance lies in the
opposite direction. Moreover, he tends to argue by what seems in this
sample to be a pronounced margin (of about three to two) in favor of
civil liberties; but in general, the ratio was about fifty-fifty. Hence the
emphasis suggested by this sample is somewhat misleading, in that it
might seem to imply that Jackson was both more interested in, and more
sympathetic to, civil liberties, than in fact was true of his opinions taken
as a whole.

In the second place, there is an even greater distortion in the format
of his opinions: this collection includes far too many dissents and concurrences, and far too few opinions in which Jackson served as majority spokesman for the Court, to be even crudely representative of his
opinion behavior as a judge.[62] Of course this result was no accident. The
reason for taking so many opinions in which Jackson spoke for himself
alone, or at most for one or two others as well, is twofold. Group or joint
opinions necessarily are always products of a compromise in points of view;
so I have picked the opinions which best represent Jackson's own ideas.
And by the same token, the justice who dissents or concurs, particularly
when he does so alone, is much less inhibited than is the majority spokesman in his freedom to indulge in more impassioned rhetoric; for he is
not checked by the necessity of obtaining the agreement of others (or at
least, of so many others) to what he wishes to say, and neither need he
be directly concerned about the immediate consequences that can be
expected to flow from his utterance—or at least, he need not be so concerned to nearly the same degree as the spokesman for those who exercise
"the power of decision" in a case. The point has been well expressed by
Jackson's avowed mentor, Cardozo:

> Comparatively speaking at least, the dissenter is irresponsible. The spokesman of the
> court is cautious, timid, fearful of the vivid word, the heightened phrase. He dreams of an
> unworthy brood of scions, the spawn of careless *dicta,* disowned by the *ratio decidendi,* to
> which all legitimate offspring must be able to trace their lineage. The result is to cramp and

[62] The distribution for all of his opinions, by these categories, is: for the Court, 149
(47%); dissenting, 113 (35%); concurring, 53 (17%); memorandum and other, 4 (1%).
The corresponding distribution for the sample is: for the Court, 4 (8%); dissenting, 29
(55%); concurring, 19 (36%); and memorandum, 1 (2%).

paralyze. One fears to say anything when the peril of misunderstanding puts a warning finger to the lips. Not so, however, the dissenter . . . . For the moment he is the gladiator making a last stand against the lions. The poor man must be forgiven a freedom of expression, tinged at rare moments with a touch of bitterness, which magnanimity as well as caution would reject for one triumphant.[63]

In his own valedictory, immediately after quoting Cardozo as above Jackson hastens to add:

There has been much undiscriminating eulogy of dissenting opinions. It is said they clarify the issues. Often they do the exact opposite. The technique of the dissenter often is to exaggerate the holding of the Court beyond the meaning of the majority and then to blast away at the excess. So the poor lawyer with a similar case does not know whether the majority opinion meant what it seemed to say or what the minority said it meant. Then, too, dissenters frequently force the majority to take positions more extreme than was originally intended . . . [and] there is nothing good, for either the Court or the dissenter, in dissenting per se. Each dissenting opinion is a confession of failure to convince the writer's colleagues, and the true test of a judge is his influence in leading, not in opposing, his court.[64]

There is no doubt much truth in what both Cardozo and Jackson say, but they also explain why dissenting opinions tend to make for more interesting reading than do opinions of the Court. Certainly this was true in Jackson's case.

From the point of view of distribution through time, there is little or no distortion in the sample. He tended to write as well as to dissent relatively more frequently during the years immediately after his return to the Court from the year's leave of absence in Europe, and the present collection similarly includes more opinions from this middle period, than from either his initial or his concluding years on the Court. Almost all of the chapters herein include opinions drawn from all three periods of his tenure.

The criteria that I have followed, in selecting opinions, are these: (1) style and literary merit; (2) typicality of Jackson's views; and (3) coverage of all of the major issues with which he was concerned. In applying the first criterion I have followed my own taste, although I have been guided also by the opinions of a panel of other persons who undertook

---

[63] Benjamin N. Cardozo, "Law and Literature," *Yale Review*, XIV (1925), 715. Speaking in the same vein, Walter F. Murphy has ventured the opinion that: "Ironically, part of the difficulty in understanding Jackson lies in his marvelous ability to weave words. He had not only a talent for translating law into literature, but also a penchant for fashioning sentences into weapons with which to flay his opponents. . . . Jackson's wry and pungent style, his bitingly sarcastic and often *ad hominem* remarks, brought out his dissents with a force that was sometimes overwhelming. But, on the whole, this great literary gift did not bring out his central ideas in stark relief." "Mr. Justice Jackson, Free Speech, and the Judicial Function," *Vanderbilt Law Review*, XII (1959), 1019-1020.

[64] Jackson, *The Supreme Court in the American System of Government*, pp. 18-19.

to read and comment upon a much larger number of Jackson's opinions, from which the present selection was drawn. In applying the second and third criteria, I have had the advantage of being able to draw upon the findings of several earlier studies.[65]

Of course, the particular situations that Jackson discussed in these opinions have been replaced. Today we have the Vietnam war instead of World War II. Until recently we were favored with the late American Nazi leader George Lincoln Rockwell, instead of fascist spokesmen Father Terminiello and Gerald L.K. Smith. Jackson worried about the relatively mild civil unrest provoked by Jehovah's Witnesses and the relatively remote danger of insurrection fomented by the Communist Party, but such experiences as Watts and Newark suggest that the lion in the streets is now an Adam Powell or a Stokely Carmichael and that his roar is for black power. It might, indeed, be suggested that Jackson's premature death precluded his participation in the most significant sectors of constitutional policy making by the Supreme Court during the past generation—the civil rights issue during the fifties, and reapportionment during the sixties.

Jackson had virtually nothing to say that can be identified directly as personal opinion in any of the major decisions on civil rights. He joined in the majority opinion in the white primary decision[66]; he disqualified himself from participating in the restrictive covenant cases[67] because, according to newspaper gossip at the time, his own country estate, Hickory Hill, in suburban McLean, Virginia,[68] was subject to a racial restriction on ownership and sale; and he joined in the unanimous majorities of the higher education and school segregation decisions[69] for which the opinion

[65] Particularly Pritchett, *The Roosevelt Court*, and his *Civil Liberties and the Vinson Court* (Chicago: The University of Chicago Press, 1954) ; and my own *The Judicial Mind: Attitudes and Ideologies of Supreme Court Justices, 1946–1963* (Evanston: Northwestern University Press, 1965), and "Jackson's Judicial Philosophy." Other discussions of Jackson's ideology are cited in the second footnote at pages 940-941 of the latter article. Gerhart's *Lawyer's Judge* is primarily a doctrinal analysis of Jackson's opinions. The best of the prior studies that focus upon a particular facet of Jackson's ideology is Walter F. Murphy's "Mr. Justice Jackson, Free Speech, and the Judicial Function," *Vanderbilt Law Review*, XII (1959), 1019-1046. Of greater interest for its methodological aspirations than for its substantive findings is James M. Shellow's, "An Analysis of Judicial Methodology: Selected Opinions of Justice Robert H. Jackson," *Marquette Law Review*, XLV (1961), 103-116.

[66] *Smith* v. *Allwright*, 321 U.S. 649 (1944).

[67] *Shelley* v. *Kraemer*, 334 U.S. 1 (1948) ; *Hurd* v. *Hodge*, 334 U.S. 24 (1948).

[68] A dozen years after Jackson's death, the occupant of Hickory Hill was another Presidential aspirant, Robert F. Kennedy.

[69] *Sweatt* v. *Painter*, 339 U.S. 629 (1950) ; *McLaurin* v. *Oklahoma State Regents*, 339 U.S. 637 (1950) ; *Brown* v. *Board of Education*, 347 U.S. 483 (1954) ; *Bolling* v. *Sharpe*, 347 U.S. 497 (1954).

of the Court was in each case written by the Chief Justice. The only opportunity that he might have had to take a position on the question of equality in political representation was missed because of his absence in Nuremberg. His participation would have been critical to the outcome of this particular decision,[70] conceivably with the result that the reapportionment revolution would have been accelerated by sixteen years. But there are two other major fields in which policy making by the Supreme Court seems likely to continue for some time to be of crucial importance. These are political dissent, and the rights of criminal defendants. On both of these subjects, Robert Jackson had a great deal to say.

Certainly not all credit can go to the United States Supreme Court for the social chaos which, together with associated economic and physical factors of internal decay and environmental pollution, are rapidly making vast enclaves of American megalopoli unfit for human habitation. Awareness of similar developments in Tokyo, London, and elsewhere should dispel any naive notion that our Supreme Court is to blame for the ills that beset urban concentrations in industrialized countries; but the question remains whether, in the political role that it does play in this country, the Supreme Court supports political and social policies which aggravate the problems that, from quite independent causes, have arisen and seem certain to continue to flourish. Liberals generally applaud the changes that the Supreme Court has encouraged by decisions which (1) postulate some minimal procedural rights for citizens who are compelled to testify as witnesses before legislative investigating committees; (2) have cut through the independent but supporting hypocrisies of Catholicism and Puritanism, by approving public dissemination of information about birth control; and (3) place upon police and prosecutors greater restraints (at least, in principle) to minimize the conviction of the innocent, whose availability happens to satisfy parochial demands for either premature closure in the solution of crimes, or the repression of members of minority groups. Conservatives, on the other hand, look about upon a country in which they see bearded youths smoking pot, carrying signs, and preaching against the government's policy on Viet Nam; they also hear advocates of racism openly preach (while their followers practice) riot, arson, and plunder in the metropolitan satrapies where racists rule; and conservatives are appalled that murderers, rapists, and the criminally insane become conspicuous recidivists, the while police and trial courts alike fail to achieve the strict standards of rectitude which now are prerequisites for the successful detention of criminal defendants and for the incarceration of convicted felons. The problem, from the conservative

[70] *Colegrove* v. *Green*, 328 U.S. 549 (1946).

point of view, is that legal sophistication[71] seems to be spreading at an alarming rate among the many socially maladjusted individuals who, when brought to account for their deviations, interpose claims to a panoply of constitutional rights and liberties—claims to freedom of speech and political dissent, equal protection of the laws, and due process of law —which they say have been guaranteed to them by decisions of the Supreme Court.

As a matter of fact, the Supreme Court was dominated by conservative majorities for a hundred and seventy-two years and throughout Robert Jackson's tenure as a justice. It has only been since 1962, with the appointment of Arthur Goldberg, that a solid majority, sympathetic to political liberalism and civil liberties, has existed. The chances in favor of further liberalization of the rights of political dissent and of criminal defendants seem excellent. But such changes will not come painlessly, and they will entail social costs. Although, in comparison to the colleagues with whom he was associated, Jackson held a relatively moderate position on such issues as these, the views that Jackson expressed then would place him clearly as one of the most conservative members of the contemporary Court. (Such was the position, incidentally, in which Felix Frankfurter found himself less than five years after Jackson had died.) So we can interpolate for the changes in the milieu that have taken place since Jackson wrote, by assuming that his arguments in favor of the suppression of ideas, and of the rights of society to be protected from criminality, are what would be said today by an articulate political conservative, if there were (and there is not) such a justice on the Court.

On questions of economic policy, however, Jackson was, like Frankfurter, a conservative at the time he wrote. Here he represented a point of view which it is probably politically impossible to replicate on the Court. That is to say, it is very unlikely that Lyndon Johnson or any person likely to succeed him in the foreseeable future—and I assume here that Barry Goldwater and Robert Welch are too remote as probabilities to consider seriously—would find it politically expedient to appoint to the Supreme Court a person with beliefs as conservative economically as those of either Jackson or Frankfurter. Jackson's remarks about economic policy are, therefore, less relevant to today's problems, excepting perhaps as a reminder of the extent to which the relevant range of alternatives open to debate has shifted to the left during the past three decades. This is an aspect of the legacy of the New Deal to which Jackson did make a contribution, both in his administrative roles prior to, and in his decisions as a judge in the years immediately following, his appointment to the Court.

---

[71] See, for example, Anthony Lewis, *Gideon's Trumpet* (New York: Random House, 1964); and Abraham S. Blumberg, *Criminal Justice* (Chicago: Quadrangle Books, 1967).

Jackson's own conceptualization of the issues before the Court was pristinely conventional.[72] He believed in the separation of powers,[73] and in federalism, and he believed that these architectonic principles of the constitutional document provided the most appropriate bases for describing and analyzing relationships among the actors in the real world, whose conflicts of interest passed in " review before the Court. The Bill of Rights was, he thought, an afterthought to the Constitution itself; and he often argued, both on and off the bench, that judges could make little of an enduring contribution toward the extension of civil rights and liberties, because only through the manipulation of political processes could such values be assured.[74]

An independent and systematic examination of Jackson's opinions indicates that for him certain values were not only linear but unidirectional as well. He often preached to his colleagues the virtue of candor, and the available evidence suggests that such advice was no mere lip service.[75] Those well qualified to appraise him agree that candor was a hallmark of his personality and not merely an embellishment of his writing.[76] He was

[72] Jackson, *The Supreme Court in the American System, passim.*

[73] "Judgments within the powers vested in courts by the Judiciary Article of the Constitution," he would say, "may not lawfully be revised, overturned, or refused faith and credit by another Department of the Government." On the other hand, "The Supreme Court cannot review the constitutional acts of equal and coordinate branches of the government." And especially in the field of foreign affairs, "it should be the scrupulous concern of every branch of our Government not to overreach any commitment or limitation to which any branch has agreed." In his last writing, he explained that "The Supreme Court often is required to arbitrate between [the executive and the legislative branches] because litigation in one form or another raises questions as to the legitimacy of the acts of one branch or the other under the doctrine of separation of powers." *Ibid.,* p. 62. Shades of *Marbury* v. *Madison!*

[74] "I know of no modern instance in which any judiciary has saved a whole people from the great currents of intolerance, passion, usurpation, and tyranny which have threatened liberty and free institutions. . . . No court can support a reactionary regime and no court can innovate or implement a new one . . . and it is my belief that the attitude of a society and of its organized political forces, rather than its legal machinery, is the controlling force in the character of free institutions." *Ibid.,* pp. 80-81. Commenting upon this statement, in his review of the book, Fred Rodell has remarked that "What Jackson forever failed to learn . . . was precisely the potentially great and freedom-defending role of 'The Supreme Court in the [italics added] *American* System of Government.' " "Justification of a Justice," *Saturday Review,* XXXVIII (July 16, 1955), 18. (The emphasis is Rodell's.) Another reviewer characterized Jackson's book as a brief for judicial passivism: Norman Redlich, "The Court and the Cold War," *Nation,* CLXXXI (September 24, 1955), 265.

[75] A good and very typical example of his candor is his discussion of the basis for the deprecatory lay image of the legal profession. Robert H. Jackson, "The Lawyer: Leader or Mouthpiece?" *Journal of the American Judicature Society,* XVIII (1934), 70-75.

[76] "He had 'impish candor,' " said Frankfurter, "to borrow one of his own phrases. Candor, indeed, was one of his deepest veins." Felix Frankfurter, "Mr. Justice Jackson," *Harvard Law Review,* LXVIII (1955), 938.

open and direct in manner and in speech, as well as in writing—often to
the point of being brutally frank. He also made frequent, usually derogatory, references to his judicial colleagues. Probably these were not meant
to be taken too seriously, and were only part of the game of advocacy that
he continued to play with them while he filled the role of a judge. Frankfurter, the colleague with whom he was perhaps on best terms and certainly the one with whom he found himself in ideological agreement
most often, recalled that:

> Mr. Justice Brandeis said that Jackson should be Solicitor General for life. The function
> of an advocate is not to enlarge the intellectual horizon. His task is to seduce, to seize the
> mind for a predetermined end, not to explore paths to truths. There can be no doubt that
> Jackson was specially endowed as an advocate.[77]

The central theme in Frankfurter's own writing, both before and after he
joined the Supreme Court, was the role of the judge. In the case of Jackson, the image with which he was preoccupied as a judge was the same
as the role that he had lived during the three preceding decades, that of the
passionate advocate, not that of the dispassionate judge. Jackson was glad
to leave his seat on the bench for a leading position at the bar of world
opinion, in which he could play once again the role he loved best. When
he returned to his place on the Supreme Court in 1946, it was because there
were no more worlds of legal advocacy left to be won.[78] All that remained
was to argue the cases with his colleagues, in his opinions as in their con-
ferences.

In addition to questions of civil liberties and those of economic policy,

---

[77] *Ibid.*, 939.

[78] Nuremberg was not only a gambit but a gamble as well, and it proved to be a very
poor one from the point of view of facilitating Jackson's longer-range political goals. As a
journalist, reflecting the opinion of the time, wrote only a year after the event: "It will be
supposed as long as nothing to the contrary is unearthed that Jackson would have been the
Chief Justice if he hadn't been away on the Nuremberg mission." McCune, *The Nine Young
Men*, p. 185. Had Jackson foregone the temptation to play the role of advocate before an
international audience with the world as a stage, it is more than possible that he could have
avoided antagonizing the incumbent Chief Justice. Moreover, he could have kept in better
touch with his own sources of political support at the time when Stone suddenly died and
the choice of a successor had to be made. Most importantly, Jackson would have been on
the scene in the main ring in Washington—and not off-stage in a side show, playing the
role of Siegfried in a latter-day performance of *Die Götterdämmerung* in a then recently
bombed but ancient "palace of justice" amidst the rubble of the walled medieval town of
Nürnberg. (For details on the staging of this Teutonic morality play, see Gerhart, *America's
Advocate*, pp. 351-354, and the photograph facing p. 386.) The wisdom of hindsight is
certainly to be preferred to unwisdom; and in this case it seems most probable that Robert
Jackson's best chance of becoming Chief Justice lay in sticking out the duration of the war
on the home front and in continuing to do his job, to the best of his ability, as an associate
justice of the Supreme Court.

the most common themes of his opinions include: judicial review of decision making by Congress and the Administration, federal centralization, centralization as between the Supreme Court and lower courts, activism and restraint by the Supreme Court in policy making, and expressions of sympathy or antipathy toward litigants. His overall tendencies were to argue: deference to the two "political branches of the government"; in behalf of states rights; deference to lower courts; and restraint in supreme Court policy making; but negative deference toward litigants.[79] The highest degree of association was between his political liberalism, (that is, his verbal support of civil liberties) and his economic conservatism. This is the central link in his ideological structure. His support of states rights tended to be associated with remarks favorable to civil liberties and with judicial review of decision making by Congress and the Administration. He usually spoke favorably of litigants when the situational context was one of civil liberties, economic conservatism, or states rights. Support for civil liberties often was accompanied by remarks favoring Supreme Court review of the decisions of lower courts. This was natural, because almost without exception, civil liberties questions that are appealed to the Supreme Court occur in cases where the decision immediately below is adverse to the civil liberties claimant. Jackson's most frequent references, however, were to activism and restraint—especially, of course, to the latter —in policy making by the Supreme Court; but such remarks bore almost no significant relationship to his support for any of these other values.[80] The most reasonable inference from this evidence is that talk about judicial activism and restraint served, at least for Jackson, only as one of the tactics of effective judicial advocacy; activism and restraint had no definite substantive content for him.

We can appraise the organization of Jackson's opinions, in the present collection, in relation to the preceding description of the more general structuring of his attitudes. The next three chapters (2-4) all focus upon civil liberties issues. Chapter 2 includes a group of opinions that are favorable to claims of political and religious liberty, and Chapter 3 a group that are unfavorable. His opinions in Chapter 4 discuss, partly sympathetically and partly not, claims of criminal defendants. Chapter 5 focuses upon issues of economic policy. Unlike the balance in his overall statements pro and con this value, all except one of the eight opinions in this chapter argue for economic conservatism. The result is less a distortion of his views than might appear at first blush, however, because

79 Schubert, "Jackson's Judicial Philosophy," 949-950.

80 *Ibid.*, 951. For a contrary view, see D. J. Simpson, "Robert H. Jackson and the Doctrine of Judicial Restraint," *U. C. L. A. Law Review,* III (1956), 325-359

Jackson's *voting*, as distinguished from his verbal behavior, was predominantly quite conservative. Moreover, as noted earlier, there was a sharp break in both his voting and opinion behavior if we compare the four years before with the eight years after his absence at Nuremberg. The direction of his decisions was clearly liberal prior to his absence, and it was just as clearly (and even more strongly) conservative after his return. So the presentation of a group of opinions that are overwhelmingly conservative in tone is no misrepresentation of his articulation of his economic views during the latter and longer period of his service as a judge. Chapter 6 includes half a dozen opinions that discuss, mostly favorably, judicial review of decision making by the Presidency, regulatory commissions, and administrative agencies. The first three of these opinions purport to justify votes that were economically conservative; the latter three opinions rationalize votes that upheld claims of civil liberties. Almost all of the opinions in these five chapters (2-6) involve also the expression on Jackson's part variously of a great deal of empathy, or of very substantial hostility, toward the litigants concerned.

Chapter 7 deals with activism and restraint in Supreme Court policy making, and in most of these opinions, as in his opinions generally, he argued for restraint. Several of these opinions also discuss judicial review and urge deference toward Congress but the opposite in cases involving administrators. Chapter 8 includes opinions that tend to be somewhat more sympathetic to federal centralization (and somewhat less sympathetic to decentralization in judicial policy making) than is true of his opinions in general. Chapter 9 focuses upon Jackson's attitude toward the professional roles of lawyers and judges. This is a subject that appears to have been of fundamental importance in his legal ideology, but it is discussed—his usually derogatory, and apparently projective, cracks at his colleagues aside—with such relative infrequency that they were not included in the more systematic analysis of my earlier article. Chapter 10 presents a brief summary of Jackson's ideology as a judge as evidenced by the opinions included herein.

The above comparison indicates that the scope of these opinions includes all the issues that the systematic analysis denoted as important, but that there are some differences in emphasis between the content of the sample and that of the universe. Such differences are an unavoidable consequence of my decision to give overriding preference to literary over statistical merit.

2 LIBERTY

In most of the cases that we shall examine in this chapter, Jackson voted to uphold some petitioner who claimed that he could not rightfully, that is, "constitutionally" be compelled to express—through speech, or other symbolic behavior—his beliefs and faith, political or religious. Pillars of the church or community do not often stand in court on their constitutional right of freedom of belief: they do not often need to go to law to assert or maintain such a claim. Therefore, the parties to the cases below include such persons as a Jehovah's Witness, sundry apostolic messengers of a faith-healing cult, and an athiest. From Jackson's point of view, these persons sought to defend a *passive* right to internalize and accept certain (typically, non-majoritarian) values, without having to divulge them, or to suffer punishment or deprivations for their nondisclosure. Whether this is a fair, or necessarily the best, way to conceptualize the issues in these cases is beside the point; it is the way Jackson saw them. For him, the negative side to freedom of speech (namely, the right to remain silent) and the passive aspect of freedom of religion (namely, the right to believe) were much more deserving of protection by the Supreme Court than their affirmative and activist counterpart, the right to speak and thereby to proselyte in behalf of one's beliefs, irrespective whether the content of the latter be religious, political, economic, or social. Hence, little girls should not be forced to bow down before graven images; visionaries should not be forced to defend their hallucinations; union leaders should not be asked to abjure belief in an abstract right of revolution as a condition of their employment; taxpayers should not be forced to contribute to the operating costs of evangelizing for particular paths to salvation, and parents should not be compelled to have their children educated under schemes whereby the public schools are used to support such activities. The only petitioner in this chapter who raised an activist claim of an affirmative right to proselyte was union mogul R. J. Thomas; and for reasons that I shall explain, Jackson used him as a surrogate for the entrepreneurial class of employers who Jackson felt were denied access to the Court by his colleagues, and thereby were in no position to plead directly their own claim to freedom of speech vis-a-vis their employees.

"Where the secular ends and the sectarian begins in education," Jackson remarked, "is a matter on which we can find no law but our own prepossessions." If we grant this premise, it is hardly surprising to find him

29

concluding, in his judicial valedictory on the subject, that the opinion of the Supreme Court, rationalizing its decision in a case which raised this issue, would "be more interesting to students of psychology and of the judicial processes than to students of constitutional law." It is, of course, arguable that all judicial opinions are of at least equal interest to students of the psychology of the judicial process, as they are to students of constitutional law; but for Jackson to have made this concession—which can hardly be said to reflect his settled view on the question of the relative importance of legal versus behavioral analysis of the Supreme Court[1]— indicates the extent to which he found his own values in disagreement with those of most of his colleagues in all three of these decisions relating to the commingling of the sacred and the profane in education. On the other hand, it is not surprising if Jackson and his colleagues *did* rely upon their prepossessions rather than upon legal precedents to decide these cases. How could they possibly do otherwise? The issue was quite literally unprecedented.

The Supreme Court had celebrated its sesquicentennial and World War II was over before the Court undertook, for the first time, to interpret the first ten words of the Bill of Rights, the establishment clause of the First Amendment to the United States Constitution. The general assumption, throughout our history as a nation since the Bill of Rights was proposed by the First Congress, has been that the relevant issue of constitutional policy was what usually is called the requirement for the separation of church and state. But state-supported churches were gone by the time of the adoption of the ancillary Fourteenth Amendment, and there never has been anything remotely resembling a national church in the United States; therefore, the occasional questions that reached the Supreme Court concerning "freedom of religion" all related to the other (the "free exercise") religious clause of the First Amendment (*Barnette* and *Ballard, infra*).[2]

In the early twentieth century, in Gary, Indiana, a movement to articulate with the public schools a variety of private schemes for religious indoctrination began as an alternative to what was considered to be the failure of Sunday School, and similar in-church programs of religious education, to attract and hold young people. By the mid-forties some two million public school pupils were directly involved in such programs in more than two thousand different communities. Because of this, within a

---

[1] See both the method and the content of Jackson's posthumously published *The Supreme Court in the American System of Government* (Cambridge: Harvard University Press, 1955).

[2] Leo Pfeffer, *Church, State, and Freedom* (Boston: Beacon Press, 1953); Alvin W. Johnson and Frank H. Yost, *Separation of Church and State in the United States* (Minneapolis: University of Minnesota Press, 1948).

time span of less than half a dozen years the Supreme Court decided several cases on the question of the separation of school and church. To what extent would the Supreme Court as then constituted give its imprimatur to the integration of religious with secular education? To what extent would the Court approve the use, by dominant local interest groups, of public funds and public school facilities to advance the parochial educational goals and policies of private sects?

The three most important decisions came in the latter part of Jackson's tenure. In these cases the Vinson Court gave, in substantial measure, its blessing to the modus vivendi that had found expression in the status quo in thousands of local communities throughout the country. It did seem for a brief interval following *McCollum* (the second of these three decisions) that the Court was going to play a more activist role in positing limits to the integration of church and public education, but the actual changes resulting from that decision were slight.[3] Moreover, the Court quickly reversed its field in *Zorach*, the third decision. A decade was then to elapse before the Court turned to this general policy sector again, when a much more liberal majority of justices of the Warren Court made even more controversial decisions about prayers and bible-reading in public schools,[4] than in the three cases with which Jackson was concerned.

A. THE FLAG SALUTE

WEST VIRGINIA STATE BOARD OF EDUCATION V. BARNETTE
319 U.S. 624 (June 14, 1943)

"One who belongs to the most vilified and persecuted minority in history is not likely," wrote Frankfurter, "to be insensible to the freedoms guaranteed by our Constitution. Were my purely personal attitude relevant I should wholeheartedly associate myself with the general libertarian views in the Court's opinion, representing as they do the thought and action of a lifetime. But as judges we are neither Jew nor Gentile, neither Catholic nor agnostic. We owe equal attachment to the Constitution and are equally bound by our judicial obligations whether we derive our citizenship from the earliest or the latest immigrants to these shores." Thus began what is perhaps Frankfurter's best-known dissent from what also is

[3] Gordon Patric, "The Impact of a Court Decision: Aftermath of the McCollum Case," *Journal of Public Law*, VI (1957), 455-463.

[4] Lucius J. Barker and Twiley W. Barker, Jr., *Freedom, Courts, Politics: Studies in Civil Liberties* (Englewood Cliffs: Prentice-Hall, Inc., 1965), Chap. 1.

probably Jackson's most famous opinion for the Court. Frankfurter, one
of the later immigrants, landed on Ellis Island in the 1890's at the age of
twelve to hear English spoken for the first time; Jackson, per contra, was
the product of gilt-edged pioneer stock. His paternal line, which included
the first white settler in the Pennsylvania township in which he was born a
century later, was Scotch-Irish. A Dutch maternal line descended directly
from Pieter Hagawout who arrived in Nieuw Amsterdam about 1660.

It was not usual for Frankfurter and Jackson to disagree, especially
in a case raising issues of civil liberty; but this decision was uncommon
in other respects as well. Jackson participated in dozens of cases involving
claims of members of the Jehovah's Witnesses sect, and this was his only
opinion in their defense. This is also the only opinion in which Jackson
espoused, no doubt, with strong urging from Chief Justice Stone, the doctrine that civil liberties premised upon First Amendment claims are in a
preferred constitutional position. His customary argument, quite to the
contrary, was that no particular constitutional liberties could be elevated
to a preferred status without thereby automatically relegating other
equally fundamental ones to a *deferred* position.[5] Finally, there are relatively few instances in which Jackson was willing to argue for a position
more sympathetic to civil liberties than such reputedly more libertarian
justices as Douglas and Black. Among those few instances are two other
cases which we shall encounter in this chapter (*Ballard* and *Everson,
infra.*).

Some dozen months before Jackson was seated, Harlan Stone had
been the only dissenter against Frankfurter's opinion for the Court that
supported "the brutal compulsion which requires a sensitive and conscientious child to stultify himself in public"[6] by enforced participation in a
group flag-salute ritual, even though Jehovah's Witnesses children such as
Lillian Gobitis were taught to believe, as a religious tenet, that the national flag is a "graven image," and obeisance to it would be certain to
bring down, and directly upon them personally, the wrath of a jealous God
Almighty.[7] As Pritchett has pointed out, "It is not irrelevant to note that
this decision came in June, 1940, at a time when the Germans were over-
running France and the Low Countries, and American security was challenged as it had not been for one hundred and twenty-five years."[8] The
effect of *Gobitis* was to encourage a number of states, including West

[5] *Brinegar* v. *United States,* 338 U.S. 160, 180 (1949), and Chap. 9A, *infra.*

[6] Robert E. Cushman, "Constitutional Law in 1939–1940," *American Political Science
Review,* XXXV (1941), 271.

[7] *Minersville School District* v. *Gobitis,* 310 U.S. 586 (June 3, 1940).

[8] C. Herman Pritchett, *The Roosevelt Court* (New York: The Macmillan Company,
1948), p. 95.

Virginia, to tighten up their requirements for patriotic education. But the three most "libertarian" members of the anti-libertarian *Gobitis* majority —Murphy, Douglas, and Black—experienced increasing misgivings which they voiced in the exceptional form of an explicit disavowal of their former stance. Not only did they recant; their statement was in context gratuitous, and they solicited an opportunity to correct their mistake, by saying that: "Since we joined in the opinion in the Gobitis case, we think this is an appropriate occasion to state that we now believe that it . . . was wrongly decided."[9] Because they could count on Stone, who by now was the Chief Justice, to join them, this group already had the four votes necessary to grant jurisdiction in any new case that raised the same issue as *Gobitis*. The *Barnette* case, in which the Witnesses succeeded in inducing a three-judge federal district court to disregard *Gobitis* and enjoin West Virginia's new flag-salute requirement, was duly docketed by the Witnesses on December 16. The appointment of Wiley Rutledge on February 15, 1943, assured a favorable majority for a decision on the merits, so Jackson's doubtless welcome, if surprising, support[10] made the new anti-flag salute majority a safe one and thus provided the icing for the cake.

When *Barnette* overruled *Gobitis* on June 14, 1943—Flag Day, no less—World War II was far from over. Jackson was designated by Chief Justice Stone to write the opinion of the Court (which was joined in by Rutledge, Murphy, and Stone, as well as by Jackson), whereas separate concurring opinions were written by Black, Douglas, and Murphy. But Frankfurter's opinion for the Court in the *Gobitis* precedent was only three years old when it was interred and, to some extent, ridiculed by his customary ideological ally, Jackson. It is no wonder that Frankfurter's protest was the more anguished. For Frankfurter, the defense of *Gobitis* was a matter of both "traditional" and "personal" *stare decisis;*[11] and it is not unlikely that the latter obligation was the more deeply felt of the two. Did the Court's only foreign-born member have a greater need to demonstrate his patriotism, in the month that the invasion of Sicily was

[9] *Jones* v. *Opelika,* 316 U.S. 584, 624 (June 8, 1942). Stone dissented independently but Jackson joined the anti-Witness majority in this decision, which upheld a municipal license tax on the door-to-door peddling of pamphlets by the Witnesses.

[10] On May 3, 1943, Rutledge had joined Murphy, Douglas, Black, and Stone in a pro-Witness reversal, upon reargument, of what a year earlier had appeared to be the Court's decision on the merits: see *Jones* v. *Opelika,* 319 U.S. 103, in which Jackson dissented with the Frankfurter-Roberts-Reed group. It is clear that the substitution of Rutledge for Byrnes accounts for the change in the Court's position in these two decisions.

[11] See the discussion of this distinction in Reed C. Lawlor, "What Computers Can Do: Analysis and Prediction of Judicial Decisions," *American Bar Association Journal,* XLIX (1963), 337-344.

begun, than the scion of Uri Jackson, a Connecticut farmer who six generations earlier had served during the Revolution as a corporal of the militia?

Nor was Frankfurter alone in his discomfiture; at least two of the other five remaining members of the *Gobitis* majority were also troubled by the unabashed language now employed by the new and novel quadrumvirate of Stone, Jackson, Murphy, and Rutledge. It is all right to overrule *old* precedents, because this proves that the Court is keeping the lag between law and life within appropriate bounds; it is even proper to overrule recent precedents *sub silentio,* because this makes it possible to maintain the myth that the law is a seamless web; but to decide the same issue in opposite ways, candidly and openly and in such a short period of time, makes it appear that overrulings are occasioned by changes in the personnel of the Court. Thus embarrassed by Jackson's forthright activism, two of the "libertarians" felt impelled to enter conservative caveats to water down the Court's militant liberalism. Black and Douglas stated that *Gobitis* was not wrong in principle, but merely in application to its particular facts; and they warned sternly that the protection of the First Amendment is not absolute, and certainly does not obviate the necessity for laws to protect society from grave and immediate danger. Frankfurter's own dissent emphasized that the evils of judicial legislation were a greater danger to democracy than was posed by nondiscriminatory legislation which happened to conflict with the bizarre views of a particular minority group. This legislation was not intended to regulate religious beliefs; and any such slight and incidental effect, such as this, that it might have, was no reason for judges to substitute their notions about public education for those of local school boards.

The flag-salute issue had no direct relevance to the successful prosecution of the war. Perhaps, for that very reason, it functioned as a catharsis for those justices who were frustrated by an overriding need to substitute libertarian restraint for libertarian activism for the duration. Nevertheless, Jackson's opinion includes passages that rank among the great paeans to human liberty and freedom of the mind.

MR. *JUSTICE JACKSON delivered the opinion of the Court:*

Following the decision by this Court on June 3, 1940, in *Minersville School District* v. *Gobitis,* 310 U.S. 586, the West Virginia legislature amended its statutes to require all schools therein to conduct courses of instruction in history, civics, and in the Constitution of the United States and of the State "for the purpose of teaching, fostering and perpetuating the ideals, principles and spirit of Americanism, and increasing the knowledge of the organization and machinery of the government." Appellant Board of Education was directed, with advice of the State Superintendent of Schools, to "prescribe the courses of study covering these subjects" for public schools. The Act made it the duty of private, parochial and denominational schools to prescribe courses of study "similar to those required for the public schools."

The Board of Education on January 9, 1942, adopted a resolution containing recitals taken largely from the Court's *Gobitis* opinion and ordering that the salute to the flag become a "regular part of the program of activities in the public schools," that all teachers and pupils "shall be required to participate in the salute honoring the Nation represented by the Flag; provided, however, that refusal to salute the Flag be regarded as an act of insubordination, and shall be dealt with accordingly."

The resolution originally required the "commonly accepted salute to the Flag" which it defined. Objections to the salute as "being too much like Hitler's" were raised by the Parent and Teachers Association, the Boy and Girl Scouts, and the Red Cross, and the Federation of Women's Clubs. Some modification appears to have been made in deference to these objections, but nó concession was made to Jehovah's Witnesses. What is now required is the "stiff-arm" salute, the saluter to keep the right hand raised with palm turned up while the following is repeated: "I pledge allegiance to the Flag of the United States of America and to the Republic for which it stands; one Nation, indivisible, with liberty and justice for all."

Failure to conform is "insubordination" dealt with by expulsion. Readmission is denied by statute until compliance. Meanwhile the expelled child is "unlawfully absent" and may be proceeded against as a delinquent. His parents or guardians are liable to prosecution, and if convicted are subject to fine not exceeding $5 and jail term not exceeding thirty days.

Appellees, citizens of the United States and of West Virginia, brought suit in the United States District Court for themselves and others similarly situated asking its injunction to restrain enforcement of these laws and regulations against Jehovah's Witnesses. The Witnesses are an unincorporated body teaching that the obligation imposed by law of God is superior to that of laws enacted by temporal government. Their religious beliefs include a literal version of Exodus, Chapter 20, verses 4 and 5, which says: "Thou shalt not make unto thee any graven image, or any likeness of anything that is in heaven above, or that is in the earth beneath, or that is in the water under the earth; thou shalt not bow down thyself to them nor serve them." They consider that the flag is an "image" within this command. For this reason they refuse to salute it. . . .

The freedom asserted by these appellees does not bring them into collision with rights asserted by any other individual. It is such conflicts that most frequently require intervention of the State to determine where the rights of one end and those of another begin. But the refusal of these persons to participate in the ceremony does not interfere with or deny rights of others to do so. Nor is there any question in this case that their behavior is peaceable and orderly. The sole conflict is between authority and rights of the individual. The State asserts power to condition access to public education on making a prescribed sign and profession and at the same time to coerce attendance by punishing both parent and child. The latter stand on a right of self-determination in matters which touch individual opinion and personal attitude....

There is no doubt that, in connection with the pledges, the flag salute is a form of utterance. Symbolism is a primitive but effective way of communicating ideas. The use of an emblem or flag to symbolize some system, idea, institution, or personality, is a short cut from mind to mind. Causes and nations, political parties, lodges and ecclesiastical groups seek to knit the loyalty of their followings to a flag or banner, a color or design. The State announces rank, function, and authority through crowns and maces, uniforms and black robes, the church speaks through the Cross, the Crucifix, the altar and shrine, and clerical raiment. Symbols of State often convey political ideas just as religious symbols come to convey theological ones. Associated with many of these symbols are appropriate gestures of acceptance or respect: a salute, a bowed or bared head, a bended knee. A person gets from a symbol the meaning he puts into it, and what is one man's comfort and inspiration is another's jest and scorn....[12]

It is also to be noted that the compulsory flag salute and pledge requires affirmation of a belief and an attitude of mind. It is not clear whether the regulation contemplates that pupils forego any contrary convictions of their own and become unwilling converts to the prescribed ceremony or whether it will be acceptable if they simulate assent by words without belief and by a gesture barren of meaning....

It was said that the flag-salute controversy confronted the Court with "the problem which Lincoln cast in memorable dilemma: 'Must a government of necessity be too *strong* for the liberties of its people, or too *weak* to maintain its own existence?' " and that the answer must be in favor of strength. *Minersville School District* v. *Gobitis, supra,* at 596.

We think that these issues may be examined free of pressure or restraint growing out of such considerations.

It may be doubted whether Mr. Lincoln would have thought that the strength of government to maintain itself would be impressively vindicated by our confirming power of the State to expel a handful of children from school. Such over-simplification, so handy in political debate, often lacks the precision necessary to postulates of judicial reasoning. If validly applied to this problem, the utterance cited would resolve every issue of power in favor of those in authority and would require us to override every liberty thought to weaken or delay execution of their policies.

Government of limited power need not be anemic government. Assurance

---

[12] Jackson's argument anticipates by some two decades a central theme of anthropologist Edward T. Hall's *The Silent Language* (New York: Doubleday & Company, Inc., 1959). [Ed.]

that rights are secure tends to diminish fear and jealousy of strong government, and by making us feel safe to live under it makes for its better support. Without promise of a limiting Bill of Rights it is doubtful if our Constitution could have mustered enough strength to enable its ratification. To enforce those rights today is not to choose weak government over strong government. It is only to adhere as a means of strength to individual freedom of mind in preference to officially disciplined uniformity for which history indicates a disappointing and disastrous end.

The subject now before us exemplifies this principle. Free public education, if faithful to the ideal of secular instruction and political neutrality, will not be partisan or enemy of any class, creed, party, or faction. If it is to impose any ideological discipline, however, each party or denomination must seek to control, or failing that, to weaken the influence of the educational system. Observance of the limitations of the Constitution will not weaken government in the field appropriate for its exercise. . . .

The Fourteenth Amendment, as now applied to the States, protects the citizen against the State itself and all of its creatures—Boards of Education not excepted. These have, of course, important, delicate, and highly discretionary functions, but none that they may not perform within the limits of the Bill of Rights. That they are educating the young for citizenship is reason for scrupulous protection of Constitutional freedoms of the individual, if we are not to strangle the free mind at its source and teach youth to discount important principles of our government as mere platitudes.

Such boards are numerous and their territorial jurisdiction often small. But small and local authority may feel less sense of responsibility to the Constitution, and agencies of publicity may be less vigilant in calling it to account. The action of Congress in making flag observance voluntary and respecting the conscience of the objector in a matter so vital as raising the Army contrasts sharply with these local regulations in matters relatively trivial to the welfare of the nation. There are village tyrants as well as village Hampdens, but none who acts under color of law is beyond reach of the Constitution. . . .

The very purpose of a Bill of Rights was to withdraw certain subjects from the vicissitudes of political controversy, to place them beyond the reach of majorities and officials and to establish them as legal principles to be applied by the courts. One's right to life, liberty, and property, to free speech, a free press, freedom of worship and assembly, and other fundamental rights may not be submitted to vote; they depend on the outcome of no elections.

In weighing arguments of the parties it is important to distinguish between the due process clause of the Fourteenth Amendment as an instrument for transmitting the principles of the First Amendment and those cases in which it is applied for its own sake. The test of legislation which collides with the Fourteenth Amendment, because it also collides with the principles of the First, is much more definite than the test when only the Fourteenth is involved. Much of the vagueness of the due process clause disappears when the specific prohibitions of the First become its standard. The right of a State to regulate, for example, a public utility may well include, so far as the due process test is concerned, power to impose all of the restrictions which a legislature may have a "rational basis" for adopting. But freedoms of speech and of press, of assembly, and of worship may not be infringed on such slender grounds. They are susceptible of restriction only to prevent grave and immediate danger to interests which the State may lawfully protect. It is important to note that while it is the Fourteenth Amendment which bears directly upon the State it is the more specific limiting principles of the First Amendment that finally govern this case.

Nor does our duty to apply the Bill of Rights to assertions of official authority depend upon our possession of marked competence in the field where the invasion of rights occurs. True, the task of translating the majestic generalities of the Bill of Rights, conceived as part of the pattern of liberal government in the eighteenth century, into concrete restraints on officials dealing with the problems of the twentieth century, is one to disturb self-confidence. These principles grew in soil which also produced a philosophy that the individual was the center of society, that his liberty was attainable through mere absence of governmental restraints, and that government should be entrusted with few controls and only the mildest supervision over men's affairs. We must transplant these rights to a soil in which the *laissez-faire* concept or principle of non-interference has withered at least as to economic affairs, and social advancements are increasingly sought through closer integration of society and through expanded and strengthened governmental controls. These changed conditions often deprive precedents of reliability and cast us more than we would choose upon our own judgment. But we act in these matters not by authority of our competence but by force of our commissions. We cannot, because of modest estimates of our competence in such specialties as public education, withhold the judgment that history authenticates as the function of this court when liberty is infringed. . . .

Struggles to coerce uniformity of sentiment in support of some end thought essential to their time and country have been waged by many good as well as by evil men. Nationalism is a relatively recent phenomenon but at other times and places the ends have been racial or territorial security, support of a dynasty or regime, and particular plans for saving souls. As first and moderate methods to attain unity have failed, those bent on its accomplishment must resort to an ever-increasing severity. As governmental pressure toward unity becomes greater, so strife becomes more bitter as to whose unity it shall be. Probably no deeper division of our people could proceed from any provocation than from finding it necessary to choose what doctrine and whose program public educational officials shall compel youth to unite in embracing. Ultimate futility of such attempts to compel coherence is the lesson of every such effort from the Roman drive to stamp out Christianity as a disturber of its pagan unity, the Inquisition, as a means to religious and dynastic unity, the Siberian exiles as a means to Russian unity, down to the fast failing efforts of our present totalitarian enemies. Those who begin coercive elimination of dissent soon find themselves exterminating dissenters. Compulsory unification of opinion achieves only the unanimity of the graveyard.

It seems trite but necessary to say that the First Amendment to our Constitution was designed to avoid these ends by avoiding these beginnings. There is no mysticism in the American concept of the State or of the nature of origin of its authority. We set up government by consent of the governed, and the Bill of Rights denies those in power any legal opportunity to coerce that consent. Authority here is to be controlled by public opinion, not public opinion by authority.

The case is made difficult not because the principles of its decision are obscure but because the flag involved is our own. Nevertheless, we apply the limitations of the Constitution with no fear that freedom to be intellectually and spiritually diverse or even contrary will disintegrate the social organization. To believe that patriotism will not flourish if patriotic ceremonies are voluntary and spontaneous instead of a compulsory routine is to make an unflattering estimate of the appeal of our institutions to free minds. We can have intellectual individualism and the rich cultural diversities that we owe to exceptional minds only at the price of occasional eccentricity and abnormal attitudes. When they are so harmless to others or to the state as those we deal with here, the price is not too great. But freedom to differ is not limited to things that do not matter much. That would be a mere shadow of freedom. The test of its substance is the right to differ as to things that touch the heart of the existing order.

If there is any fixed star in our constitutional constellation, it is that no official, high or petty, can prescribe what shall be orthodox in politics, nationalism, religion, or other matters of opinion or force citizens to confess by word or act their faith therein. If there are any circumstances which permit an exception, they do not occur to us now.

We think the action of the local authorities in compelling the flag salute and pledge transcends constitutional limitations on their power and invades the sphere of intellect and spirit which it is the purpose of the First Amendment to our Constitution to reserve from all official control. . . .

B. THE TRUE BELIEVER

UNITED STATES V. BALLARD
322 U.S. 78 (April 24, 1944)

Once when the parties to a case before the Supreme Court switched positions completely from the ones that they had argued below, Jackson remarked that the parties had "changed positions as nimbly as if dancing a quadrille."[13] Knowledgeable readers of the Court's opinions during the years of World War II might well have inferred that in this, the first *Ballard* case, the justices themselves had joined the dance. (Alternative images of a game of musical chairs or a Mad Tea Party come readily to mind.)

This case began as one of many federal mail-fraud prosecutions in a city notorious for the eccentrics whom it nurtures. The defendants were several surviving "I Am" cultists, associates both spiritual and temporal of the late faith-healer and "ascended master" Guy W. Ballard, alias Jesus, George Washington, Saint Germain, and Godfre Ray King. With the consent of counsel for the Ballards as well as that of the government, the trial judge had withdrawn the question of whether the beliefs and promises of the Ballards were "true" or "false." This left the jury to decide whether the Ballards had knowingly and wilfully made representations *which they well knew and believed* to be false. The jury, therefore, had decided the "fact question" whether the Ballards were mendacious hypocrites, on the assumption that if the Ballards did not believe their own preachings, they obviously were using the mails to defraud, and the question of the "objective" truth or falsity of their doctrines was irrelevant. Among the many items which counsel for the Ballards assigned as error, on the appeal of their convictions, was the claim that the jury should have been required to decide whether the Ballards were "in fact," and irrespective of their own beliefs, teaching false doctrine.

The conviction of the Ballard cronies was reversed and they were granted a new trial by the circuit court of appeals. The Solicitor General asked the Supreme Court to reinstate the jury verdict, which is precisely what three dissenters, Chief Justice Stone, Frankfurter, and Roberts wanted. A majority, consisting of Rutledge, Murphy, Douglas, Black, and Reed, agreed that the circuit court of appeals must be reversed, but for the very different reason to quash the new trial and to direct the circuit court of appeals to consider the other constitutional claims that had been urged by the defendants.[14] Jackson alone favored the more extreme liber-

---

[13] *Orloff* v. *Willoughby*, 345 U.S. 83, 87 (1953).

[14] The lower court rejected these other constitutional claims; and when the case came back to the Supreme Court a couple of year later, the same majority who controlled the disposition of the case in the first *Ballard* decision now directed the dismissal of the indictment, on the new ground that the trial court had discriminated against women in trying the Ballards before an all-male jury, since females were eligible to serve as jurors in the California state courts. Jackson, of course, concurred, adhering to his opinion in the first decision; he also, however, noted his agreement, except as to outcome, with the dissenting opinions of Frankfurter, and Burton (vice Roberts) who, together with Stone, held out for conviction. *Ballard* v. *United States,* 329 U.S. 187 (December 9, 1946).

tarian solution of affirming the acquittal of Saint Germain's "divine messengers."

Even the most renowned of the Court's commentators have been puzzled by Jackson's seemingly ultra-liberal stance in this decision. Corwin suggested that Jackson took "leave of common sense to indulge some high-flown doubts that were evidently suggested to him by a perusal of William James's *The Will to Believe*."[15] There is some internal evidence in the opinion which suggests that, when this case was discussed in conference, or perhaps in chambers, some of his more agnostic brethren made remarks that were offensive to Jackson's religious sensibilities: some who knew him well claimed that he was a "deeply religious" man, and he himself once pointed out that he chose to send his children to private denominational schools.[16] Yet it might still seem incongruous that he selected the duplicity of this Lilliputian sect as the foundation for his strongest plea in behalf of freedom of religious belief. We can note, however, that the Ballards presented no great threat to organized society in general, and virtually none to the affluent upper class whose interests in particular were homologous with Jackson's. So for Jackson the decision offered a neat opportunity to outflank his reputedly more libertarian colleagues in the very field where they usually chose to wage ideological battle.

MR. JUSTICE JACKSON, dissenting.

I should say the defendants have done just that for which they are indicted. If I might agree to their conviction without creating a precedent, I cheerfully would do so. I can see in their teachings nothing but humbug, untainted by any trace of truth. But that does not dispose of the constitutional question whether misrepresentation of religious experience or belief is prosecutable; it rather emphasizes the danger of such prosecutions.

The Ballard family claimed miraculous communication with the spirit world and supernatural power to heal the sick. They were brought to trial for mail fraud on an indictment which charged that their representations were false and that they "well knew" they were false. The trial judge, obviously troubled, ruled that the court could not try whether the statements were untrue, but could inquire whether the defendants knew them to be untrue; and, if so, they could be convicted.

---

[15] Edward S. Corwin, *The Constitution and What It Means Today*, 8th ed. (Princeton: Princeton University Press, 1946), p. 194; quoted in Pritchett, *The Roosevelt Court*, p. 101.

[16] *Zorach* v. *Clauson*, 343 U.S. 306, 324 (1952), and *infra*. His biographer identifies Jackson as an Episcopalian. Eugene C. Gerhart, *Robert H. Jackson: Lawyer's Judge* (Albany: Q Corporation, 1961), p. 115.

I find it difficult to reconcile this conclusion with our traditional religious freedoms.

In the first place, as a matter of either practice or philosophy I do not see how we can separate an issue as to what is believed from considerations as to what is believable. The most convincing proof that one believes his statements is to show that they have been true in his experience. Likewise, that one knowingly falsified is best proved by showing that what he said happened never did happen. How can the Government prove these persons knew something to be false which it cannot prove to be false? If we try religious sincerity severed from religious verity, we isolate the dispute from the very considerations which in common experience provide its most reliable answer.

In the second place, any inquiry into intellectual honesty in religion raises profound psychological problems. William James, who wrote on these matters as a scientist, reminds us that it is not theology and ceremonies which keep religion going. Its vitality is in the religious experiences of many people. "If you ask what these experiences are, they are conversations with the unseen, voices, and visions, responses to prayer, changes of heart, deliverances from fear, inflowings of help, assurances of support, whenever certain persons set their own internal attitude in certain appropriate ways." If religious liberty includes, as it must, the right to communicate such experiences to others, it seems to me an impossible task for juries to separate fancied ones from real ones, dreams from happenings, and hallucinations from true clairvoyance. Such experiences, like some tones and colors, have existence for one, but none at all for another. They cannot be verified to the minds of those whose field of consciousness does not include religious insight. When one comes to trial which turns on any aspect of religious belief or representation, unbelievers among his judges are likely not to understand and are almost certain not to believe him.

And then I do not know what degree of skepticism or disbelief in a religious representation amounts to actionable fraud. James points out that "Faith means belief in something concerning which doubt is still theoretically possible." Belief in what one may demonstrate to the senses is not faith. All schools of religious thought make enormous assumptions, generally on the basis of revelations authenticated by some sign or miracle. The appeal in such matters is to a very different plane of credulity than is invoked by representations of secular fact in commerce. Some who profess belief in the Bible read literally what others read as allegory or metaphor, as they read Aesop's fables. Religious symbolism is even used by some with the same mental reservations one has in teaching of Santa Claus or Uncle Sam or Easter bunnies or dispassionate judges. It is hard in matters so mystical to say how literally one is bound to believe the doctrine he teaches and even more difficult to say how far it is reliance upon a teacher's literal belief which induces followers to give him money.

There appear to be persons—let us hope not many—who find refreshment and courage in the teachings of the "I Am" cult. If the members of the sect get comfort from the celestial guidance of their "Saint Germain," however doubtful it seems to me, it is hard to say that they do not get what they pay for. Scores of sects flourish in this country by teaching what to me are queer notions. It is plain that there is wide variety in American religious taste. The Ballards are not alone in catering to it with a pretty dubious product. The chief wrong which false prophets do to their following is not financial. The collections aggregate a tempting total, but individual payments are not ruinous. I doubt if the vigilance of the law is equal to making money stick by over-credulous people. But the real harm is on the mental and spiritual plane. There are those who hunger and thirst after higher values which they feel wanting in their humdrum lives. They live in mental confusion or moral anarchy and seek vaguely for truth and beauty and moral support. When they are deluded and then disillusioned, cynicism and confusion follow. The wrong of these things, as I see it, is not in the money the victims part with half so much as in the mental and spiritual poison they get. But that is precisely the thing the Constitution puts beyond the reach of the prosecutor, for the price of freedom of religion or of speech or of the press is that we must put up with, and even pay for, a good deal of rubbish.

Prosecutions of this character easily could degenerate into religious persecution. I do not doubt that religious leaders may be convicted of fraud for making false representations on matters other than faith or experience, as for example if one represents that funds are being used to construct a church when in fact they are being used for personal purposes. But that is not this case, which reaches into wholly dangerous ground. When does less than full belief in a professed credo become actionable fraud if one is soliciting gifts or legacies? Such inquiries may discomfort orthodox as well as unconventional religious teachers, for even the most regular of them are sometimes accused of taking their orthodoxy with a grain of salt.

I would dismiss the indictment and have done with this business of judicially examining other people's faiths.

C. FREE SPEECH FOR LABOR—AND MANAGEMENT

THOMAS V. COLLINS
323 U.S. 516 (January 8, 1945)

Jackson's faith in the individual's right to believe was put to a more severe test only a few months later, when the claimant was neither a leader nor a follower of crackpots, but, rather, a man with socioeconomic

and political influence over the lives of millions of ordinary Americans—
"workmen", as Jackson preferred to call them. It would have been easier
for Jackson to uphold this man's claim to freedom of speech had he been
an industrialist instead of a union leader. But, Jackson well knew that as
World War II drew to a close no direct claim on behalf of, say, Edsel
Ford, of the right to proselyte his auto workers with management's point
of view, stood much chance of support by four colleagues who would be
needed to form a majority sympathetic to free speech for management.
But Jackson was nothing if not a political realist; so it was that R. J.
Thomas, Walter Reuther's predecessor as head of the giant United Auto
Workers Union and Vice President of the Congress of Industrial Organizations, became Jackson's surrogate for the thousands of American
businessmen who were not in a position to speak for themselves on this
issue. For the other justices, the question was the less subtle one of
whether a state can make it a crime for a union, acting in accord with
federal statutory and administrative provisions, to attempt to organize
workers, unless the union's agents first register with state officials.

The litigation began on the Texas Gulf Coast, in a state and region
and in local and state courts none of which are now or were then notorious
for their pro-union sentiment. The C.I.O. had launched an organizational
campaign against the rich Texas oil industry, and R. J. Thomas went
carpetbagging from Detroit to Bay City ostensibly to address a mass meeting of workers of the Humble Oil and Refining Company. His particular
objective, however, was to foment a test case, that challenged the state
union registration requirement. The C.I.O.'s legal counsel could then
"appeal all the way to the Supreme Court, if necessary," as the stock
phrase goes, and as, of course, was necessary in this instance. Thomas
made his speech and took pains to include within it a public solicitation
of both an individual worker and the entire group assembled at the meeting to hear him. Of course, he had no permit, for his point in coming had
been to speak without one; and he had violated an ex parte injunction,
which a county judge[17] had supplied just a few hours before the meeting.
He was hauled off before a Justice of the Peace and the administrative-
judicial apparatus of the state law enforcement system was mobilized to
vindicate the rights of society. But these state proceedings did not take
long; Thomas quickly exhausted the relief which the Texas courts proffered to him and advanced to the United States Supreme Court where his
lawyer argued that the Texas statute and lower court order constituted a
prior restraint upon and an abridgement of his constitutional right to
freedom of speech.

---

[17] Cf. *Craig* v. *Harney,* 331 U.S. 367, 394 (1947), and Chap. 9C, *infra.*

The closeness of the Court's division was foreshadowed when the case, after having been argued initially in May 1944, was restored to the docket and when autumn came the Court participated in the second oral argument of Thomas' claim. The character of the division—Rutledge, Murphy, Douglas, and Black versus Roberts, Stone, Reed, and Frankfurter—suggests that Jackson's vote was the one most critical to the outcome of the decision; and he needed the extra time to work out a rationale that would justify his assuming the, for him, unusual stance of appearing to strike a blow in behalf of the interests of organized labor. For that is the way the decision came down, with Rutledge delivering the opinion of the Court, that is, for a four-man plurality of the five-man majority, in which the state statutory registration requirements were declared unconstitutional on the First Amendment ground that "peaceful assembly for lawful discussion cannot be made a crime." The Roberts group dissented, thinking it quite proper for a state, if it so chose, to require paid solicitors, including solicitors of labor, to identify themselves. Douglas, with Black and Murphy, concurred but for the sole purpose of rebutting Jackson's allegation that the libertarian four played favorites and were engaged, in this as in earlier decisions, in positing for union leaders constitutional liberties that were denied to employers. Jackson supplied the necessary fifth majority vote for Thomas to win his case; but his concurring opinion was for himself alone. It may be that Jackson had hoped to "get his big toe in" (as F.D.R. once described Hughes' tactics) and splinter the libertarians—after all, he *had* recently induced Murphy, Stone and Rutledge to support his opinion in the *Barnette* case—on the issue that he had formulated: that the Court itself should provide equal protection of its own laws, by recognizing equivalent rights of free speech for unions and employers in labor-management disputes. He needed only two supporters for such an opinion and, if the voting division held, *his* opinion might have become, as in *Barnette*, that of the Court; but if that was his ploy, this time it failed.

MR. JUSTICE JACKSON, *concurring.*

As frequently is the case, this controversy is determined as soon as it is decided which of two well-established, but at times overlapping, constitutional principles will be applied to it. The State of Texas stands on its well-settled right reasonably to regulate the pursuit of a vocation, including—we may assume— the occupation of labor organizer. Thomas, on the other hand, stands on the equally clear proposition that Texas may not interfere with the right of any person peaceably and freely to address a lawful assemblage of workmen intent on considering labor grievances.

Though the one may shade into the other, a rough distinction always exists,

I think, which is more shortly illustrated than explained. A state may forbid one without its license to practice law as a vocation, but I think it could not stop an unlicensed person from making a speech about the rights of man or the rights of labor, or any other kind of right, including recommending that his hearers organize to support his views. Likewise, the state may prohibit the pursuit of medicine as an occupation without its license, but I do not think it could make it a crime publicly or privately to speak urging persons to follow or reject any school of medical thought. So the state to an extent not necessary now to determine may regulate one who makes a business or a livelihood of soliciting funds or memberships for unions. But I do not think it can prohibit one, even if he is a salaried labor leader, from making an address to a public meeting of workmen, telling them their rights as he sees them and urging them to unite in general or to join a specified union.

This wider range of power over pursuit of a calling than over speech-making is due to the different effects which the two have on interests which the state is empowered to protect. The modern state owes and attempts to perform a duty to protect the public from those who seek for one purpose or another to obtain its money. When one does so through the practice of a calling, the state may have an interest in shielding the public against the untrustworthy, the incompetent, or the irresponsible, or against unauthorized representation of agency. A usual method of performance of this function is through a licensing system.

But it cannot be the duty, because it is not the right, of the state to protect the public against false doctrine. The very purpose of the First Amendment is to foreclose public authority from assuming a guardianship of the public mind through regulating the press, speech and religion. In this field every person must be his own watchman for truth, because the forefathers did not trust any government to separate the true from the false for us. *West Virginia State Board of Education* v. *Barnette,* 319 U.S. 624. Nor would I. Very many are the interests which the state may protect against the practice of an occupation, very few are those it may assume to protect against the practice of propagandizing by speech or press. These are thereby left great range of freedom.

This liberty was not protected because the forefathers expected its use would always be agreeable to those in authority or that its exercise always would be wise, temperate, or useful to society. As I read their intentions, this liberty was protected because they knew of no other way by which free men could conduct representative democracy.

The necessity for choosing collective bargaining representatives brings the same nature of problem to groups of organizing workmen that our representative democratic processes bring to the nation. Their smaller society, too, must choose between rival leaders and competing policies. This should not be an underground process. The union of which Thomas is the head was one of the choices offered to these workers, and to me it was in the best American tradition that they hired a hall and advertised a meeting, and that Thomas went there and publicly faced his labor constituents. How better could these men learn what they might be getting into? By his public appearance and speech he would disclose himself as a temperate man or a violent one, a reasonable leader that well-disposed workmen could follow or an irresponsible one from whom they might expect disappointment, an earnest and understanding leader or a self-seeker. If free speech anywhere serves a useful social purpose, to be jealously guarded, I should think it would be in such a relationship.

But it is said that Thomas urged and invited one and all to join his union, and so he did. This, it is said, makes the speech something else than a speech; it has been found by the Texas courts to be a "solicitation" and therefore its immunity from state regulation is held to be lost. It is not often in this country that we now meet with direct and candid efforts to stop speaking or publication as such. Modern inroads on these rights come from associating the speaking with some other factor which the state may regulate so as to bring the whole within official control. Here, speech admittedly otherwise beyond the reach of the states is attempted to be brought within its licensing system by associating it with "solicitation." Speech of employers otherwise beyond reach of the Federal Government is brought within the Labor Board's power to suppress by associating it with "coercion" or "domination." Speech of political malcontents is sought to be reached by associating it with some form or variety of "sedition." Whether in a particular case the association or characterization is a proven and valid one often is difficult to resolve. If this Court may not or does not in proper cases inquire whether speech or publication is properly condemned by association, its claim to guardianship of free speech and press is but a hollow one.

Free speech on both sides and for every faction on any side of the labor relation is to me a constitutional and useful right. Labor is free to turn its publicity on any labor oppression, substandard wages, employer unfairness, or objectionable working conditions. The employer, too, should be free to answer, and to turn publicity on the records of the leaders or the unions which seek the confidence of his men. And if the employees or organizers associate violence or other offense against the laws with labor's free speech, or if the employer's speech is associated with discriminatory discharges or intimidation, the constitutional remedy would be to stop the evil, but permit the speech, if the two are separable; and only rarely and when they are inseparable to stop or punish speech or publication.

But I must admit that in overriding the findings of the Texas court we are applying to Thomas a rule the benefit of which in all its breadth and vigor this Court denies to employers in National Labor Relations Board cases. . . . However, the remedy is not to allow Texas improperly to deny the right of free speech but to apply the same rule and spirit to free speech cases whoever the speaker.

D. TEST OATHS FOR UNION LEADERS

AMERICAN COMMUNICATIONS ASSOCIATION, C.I.O. V. DOUDS
339 U.S. 382 (May 8, 1950)

The *Douds* case found the Court announcing a decision under circumstances that approached maximal disintegration: only six justices, the
statutory minimum, participated; and of these, three joined in what was
for some purposes the opinion of the Court, Frankfurter and Jackson
each concurred in part and dissented in part, and Black dissented alone.
It must have taken some strong administrative ramrodding, from President Truman's Chief Justice Vinson, to have provoked any decision, let
alone such a decision, from a group so depleted and fragmented as was the
Supreme Court during the 1949 Term.[18] Murphy and Rutledge both had
died shortly before the term began; and their successors Clark and Minton, together with Douglas, disqualified themselves from participating in
the decision. Clark, as Attorney General, had been officially responsible
for the preparation of the government's case[19] in the appeal to the Supreme Court; Minton took his seat on October 12, 1949, the day after
oral argument of the case concluded; and Douglas also missed hearing
the argument: he had fallen from a horse on October 3rd, and remained
hospitalized two weeks later on the occasion of his fifty-first birthday.
Presumably, Clark's disability would not have changed, but a reargument
in the spring or fall of 1950 would have made it possible for both Minton
and Douglas to participate and, at least conceivably, to break the prevailing 3-3 deadlock on the question of the constitutionality of the test oath
provision of the statute under challenge. But this was not done; and the
unseemly haste in which the decision was announced doubtless reflects
that these were the days when Senator McCarthy's goose hung high;[20] so
the collective national security interest in purging American labor of
Commies and their fellow travelers overrode such lesser interests as constitutional rights to freedom of speech and of belief. Jackson was willing to
override freedom of speech for the suppression of union leaders who were
Communists,[21] but he drew the line at so doing when he believed the issue

---

[18] I have explained elsewhere how and why this term was a traumatic one. See my
The Judicial Mind (Evanston: Northwestern University Press, 1965), pp. 105, 210, 226-228.

[19] Douds was a regional director of the National Labor Relations Board.

[20] See Samuel A. Stouffer, *Communism, Conformity, and Civil Liberties: A Cross-section
of the Nation Speaks Its Mind* (New York: Doubleday & Company, Inc., 1955).

[21] *Dennis* v. *United States,* 341 U.S. 494, 561 (1951), and Chap. 3F, *infra.*

to be one involving a switch in the role of protagonist, from the claimant as proselyting speaker, to the government official as zealous inquisitor into values that an individual wished to keep internalized.

So a five-man majority, Vinson, Reed, Burton, Frankfurter, and Jackson, voted to uphold the statutory provision relating to disclosure of Communist Party membership; but the Court, for want of any majority, had no opinion on the revelation of belief requirement.[22] The first two parts of Jackson's opinion are a concurrence and have been largely deleted here; instead we shall focus upon Part III which constitutes Jackson's dissent from the Court's disposition of this case.

MR. JUSTICE JACKSON, *concurring and dissenting, each in part.*

If the statute before us required labor union officers to forswear membership in the Republican Party, the Democratic Party or the Socialist Party, I suppose all agree that it would be unconstitutional. But why, if it is valid as to the Communist Party?

The answer, for me, is in the decisive differences between the Communist Party and every other party of any importance in the long experience of the United States with party government....

I.

From information before its several Committees and from facts of general knowledge, Congress could rationally conclude that, behind its political party facade, the Communist Party is a conspiratorial and revolutionary junta, organized to reach ends and to use methods which are incompatible with our constitutional system....

II.

I cannot believe that Congress has less power to protect a labor union from Communist Party domination than it has from employer domination. This Court has uncompromisingly upheld power of Congress to disestablish labor unions where they are company-dominated and to eradicate employer influence, even when exerted only through spoken or written words which any person not the employer would be free to utter.

Congress has conferred upon labor unions important rights and powers in matters that affect industry, transport, communications, and commerce. And Congress has not now denied any union full self-government nor prohibited any union from choosing Communist officers. It seeks to protect the union from doing so unknowingly. And if members deliberately choose to put the union in

[22] The Court's decision, when an equal (that is, 3-3 or 4-4) division obtains, always is to leave the ruling below unchanged.

the hands of Communist officers, Congress withdraws the privileges it has conferred on the assumption that they will be devoted to the welfare of their members. It would be strange indeed if it were constitutionally powerless to protect these delegated functions from abuse and misappropriation to the service of the Communist Party and the Soviet Union. Our Constitution is not a covenant of nonresistance toward organized efforts at disruption and betrayal, either of labor or of the country. . . .

I conclude that we cannot deny Congress power to take these measures under the Commerce Clause to require labor union officers to disclose their membership in or affiliation with the Communist Party.

III.

Congress has, however, required an additional disclaimer, which in my view does encounter serious constitutional objections. A union officer must also swear that "he does not believe in . . . the overthrow of the United States Government by force or by any illegal or unconstitutional methods."

If Congress has power to condition any right or privilege of an American citizen upon disclosure and disavowal of belief on any subject, it is obviously this one. But the serious issue is whether Congress has power to proscribe any opinion or belief which has not manifested itself in any overt act. While the forepart of the oath requires disclosure and disavowal of relationships which depend on overt acts of membership or affiliation, the afterpart demands revelation and denial of mere beliefs or opinions, even though they may never have matured into any act whatever or even been given utterance. In fact, the oath requires one to form and express a conviction on an abstract proposition which many good citizens, if they have thought of it at all, have considered too academic and remote to bother about.

That this difference is decisive on the question of power becomes unmistakable when we consider measures of enforcement. The only sanction prescribed, and probably the only one possible in dealing with a false affidavit, is punishment for perjury. If one is accused of falsely stating that he was not a member of, or affiliated with, the Communist Party, his conviction would depend upon proof of visible and knowable overt acts or courses of conduct sufficient to establish that relationship. But if one is accused of falsely swearing that he did not believe something that he really did believe, the trial must revolve around the conjecture as to whether he candidly exposed his state of mind.

The law sometimes does inquire as to mental state, but only so far as I recall when it is incidental to, and determines the quality of, some overt act in question. From its circumstances, courts sometimes must decide whether an act was committed intentionally or whether its results were intended, or whether the action taken was in malice, or after deliberation, or with knowledge of certain facts. But in such cases the law pries into the mind only to determine the nature and culpability of an act, as a mitigating or aggravating circumstance, and I know of no situation in which a citizen may incur civil or criminal liability or disability because a court infers an evil mental state where no act at all has occurred. Our trial processes are clumsy and unsatisfying for inferring cogitations which are incidental to actions, but they do not even pretend to ascertain the thought that has had no outward manifestation. Attempts of the courts to fathom modern political meditations of an accused would be as futile and mischievous as the efforts in the infamous heresy trials of old to fathom religious beliefs.

Our Constitution explicitly precludes punishment of the malignant mental state alone as treason, most serious of all political crimes, of which the mental state of adherence to the enemy is an essential part. It requires a duly witnessed overt act of aid and comfort to the enemy. . . . It is true that in England of olden times men were tried for treason for mental indiscretions such as imagining the death of the king. But our Constitution was intended to end such prosecutions. Only in the darkest periods of human history has any Western government concerned itself with mere belief, however eccentric or mischievous, when it has not matured into overt action; and if that practice survives anywhere, it is in the Communist countries whose philosophies we loathe.

How far we must revert toward these discredited systems if we are to sustain this oath is made vivid by the Court's reasoning that the Act applies only to those "whose beliefs strongly indicate a will to engage in political strikes. . . ." Since Congress has never outlawed the political strike itself, the Court must be holding that Congress may root out mere ideas which, even if acted upon, would not result in crime. It is a strange paradox if one may be forbidden to have an idea in mind that he is free to put into execution. But apart from this, efforts to weed erroneous beliefs from the minds of men have always been supported by the argument which the Court invokes today, that beliefs are springs to action, that evil thoughts tend to become forbidden deeds. Probably so. But if power to forbid acts includes power to forbid contemplating them, then the power of government over beliefs is as unlimited as its power over conduct and the way is open to force disclosure of attitudes on all manner of social, economic, moral and political issues.

These suggestions may be discounted as fanciful and farfetched. But we must not forget that in our country are evangelists and zealots of many different political, economic and religious persuasions whose fanatical conviction is that all thought is divinely classified into two kinds—that which is their own and that which is false and dangerous. Communists are not the only faction which would put us all in mental strait jackets. Indeed all ideological struggles, religious or political, are primarily battles for dominance over the minds of people. It is not to be supposed that the age-old readiness to try to convert minds by pressure or suppression, instead of reason and persuasion, is extinct. Our protection against all kinds of fanatics and extremists, none of whom can be trusted with unlimited power over others, lies not in their forbearance but in the limitations of our Constitution.

It happens that the belief in overthrow of representative government by force and violence which Congress conditionally proscribes is one that I agree is erroneous. But "if there is any principle of the Constitution that more imperatively calls for attachment than any other it is the principle of free thought—not free thought for those who agree with us but freedom for the thought that we hate." Holmes, J., dissenting in *United States* v. *Schwimmer*, 279 U.S. 644, 654-55. Moreover, in judging the power to deny a privilege to think otherwise, we cannot ignore the fact that our own Government originated in revolution and is legitimate only if overthrow by force may sometimes be justified. That circumstances sometimes justify it is not Communist doctrine but an old American belief.

The men who led the struggle forcibly to overthrow lawfully constituted British authority found moral support by asserting a natural law under which their revolution was justified, and they broadly proclaimed these beliefs in the document basic to our freedom. Such sentiments have also been given ardent and rather extravagant expression by Americans of undoubted patriotism. Most of these utterances were directed against a tyranny which left no way to change by suffrage. It seems to me a perversion of their meaning to quote them, as the Communists often do, to sanction violent attacks upon a representative government which does afford such means. But while I think Congress may make it a crime to take one overt step to use or to incite violence or force against our Government, I do not see how in the light of our history a mere belief that one has a natural right under some circumstances to do so can subject an American citizen to prejudice any more than possession of any other erroneous belief. Can we say that men of our time must not even think about the propositions on which our own Revolution was justified? Or may they think, provided they reach only one conclusion—and that the opposite of Mr. Jefferson's?[23]

While the Governments, State and Federal, have expansive powers to curtail action, and some small powers to curtail speech or writing, I think neither has any power, on any pretext, directly or indirectly to attempt foreclosure of any line of thought. Our forefathers found the evils of free thinking more to be endured than the evils of inquest or suppression. They gave the status of almost absolute individual rights to the outward means of expressing belief. I cannot

[23] Not if they wish to become lawyers in Illinois; see the Warren Court's subsequent decision, *In re Anastaplo,* 366 U.S. 82 (1961). Jackson's successor, Harlan, provided the fifth and decisive vote to deny, over the dissents of Douglas, Black, Warren, and Brennan, that an honor graduate of the University of Chicago could have a legal right to believe in both the Constitution of the United States and the Declaration of Independence, and still be admitted to the Illinois bar. [Ed.]

believe that they left open a way for legislation to embarrass or impede the mere intellectual processes by which those expressions of belief are examined and formulated. This is not only because individual thinking presents no danger to society, but because thoughtful, bold and independent minds are essential to wise and considered self-government.

Progress generally begins in skepticism about accepted truths. Intellectual freedom means the right to re-examine much that has been long taken for granted. A free man must be a reasoning man, and he must dare to doubt what a legislative or electoral majority may most passionately assert. The danger that citizens will think wrongly is serious, but less dangerous than atrophy from not thinking at all. Our Constitution relies on our electorate's complete ideological freedom to nourish independent and responsible intelligence and preserve our democracy from that submissiveness, timidity and herd-mindedness of the masses which would foster a tyranny of mediocrity. The priceless heritage of our society is the unrestricted constitutional right of each member to think as he will. Thought control is a copyright of totalitarianism, and we have no claim to it. It is not the function of our Government to keep the citizen from falling into error; it is the function of the citizen to keep the Government from falling into error. We could justify any censorship only when the censors are better shielded against error than the censored.

The idea that a Constitution should protect individual nonconformity is essentially American and is the last thing in the world that Communists will tolerate. Nothing exceeds the bitterness of their demands for freedom for themselves in this country except the bitterness of their intolerance of freedom for others where they are in power. An exaction of some profession of belief or nonbelief is precisely what the Communists would enact—each individual must adopt the ideas that are common to the ruling group. Their whole philosophy is to minimize man as an individual and to increase the power of man acting in the mass. If any single characteristic distinguishes our democracy from Communism it is our recognition of the individual as a personality rather than as a soulless part in the jigsaw puzzle that is the collectivist state.

I adhere to views I have heretofore expressed, whether the Court agreed, *West Virginia Board of Education* v. *Barnette,* 319 U.S. 624, or disagreed, see dissenting opinion in *United States* v. *Ballard,* 322 U.S. 78, 92, that our Constitution excludes both general and local governments from the realm of opinions and ideas, beliefs and doubts, heresy and orthodoxy, political, religious or scientific. The right to speak out, or to publish, also is protected when it does not clearly and presently threaten some injury to society which the Government has a right to protect. Separate opinion, *Thomas* v. *Collins,* 323 U.S. 516. But I have protested the degradation of these constitutional liberties to immunize and approve mob movements, whether those mobs be religious or political, radical or conservative, liberal or illiberal, *Douglas* v. *City of Jeannette,* 319 U.S. 157; *Ter-*

miniello v. *Chicago,* 337 U.S. 1, 13, or to authorize pressure groups to use amplifying devices to drown out the natural voice and destroy the peace of other individuals. *Saia* v. *People of New York,* 334 U.S. 558; *Kovacs* v. *Cooper,* 336 U.S. 77. And I have pointed out that men cannot enjoy their right to personal freedom if fanatical masses, whatever their mission, can strangle individual thoughts and invade personal privacy. *Marvin* v. *Struthers,* 319 U.S. 141, dissent at 166. A catalogue of rights was placed in our Constitution, in my view, to protect the individual in his individuality, and neither statutes which put those rights at the mercy of officials nor judicial decisions which put them at the mercy of the mob are consistent with its text or its spirit.

I think that under our system, it is time enough for the law to lay hold of the citizen when he acts illegally, or in some rare circumstances when his thoughts are given illegal utterance. I think we must let his mind alone.

E. PUBLIC TRANSPORTATION TO PRIVATE SCHOOLS

EVERSON V. BOARD OF EDUCATION
330 U.S. 1, 18 (February 10, 1947)

Ewing Township (West Trenton), New Jersey, had a policy of reimbursing parents for the cost of transporting their children, by means of the local bus system, to and from either public or Catholic parochial schools. The reimbursement came from funds allocated out of township revenues derived from taxation. A state trial court upheld a taxpayer's claim that the diversion of public tax monies to subsidize the transportation of students to parochial schools violated the establishment clauses of both the New Jersey and the federal constitution; but the state Court of Errors and Appeals reversed, and an appeal from that decision constituted the case before the Supreme Court.

One might have supposed that a Court still dominated by "the libertarian four"[24] would have staunchly defended the separation of church and state, in this, the first opportunity that any group of Supreme Court justices accepted to explicate the establishment clause of the First Amendment. It is perhaps ironic that, after that clause had been in hibernation for over a century and a half, a few months might have made a crucial difference to the outcome of this decision: for Harlan Stone had died in the spring of the preceding year; and it seems quite likely that his

[24] C. Herman Pritchett, *Civil Liberties and the Vinson Court* (Chicago: The University of Chicago Press, 1954), Chapter X.

own vote, to say nothing of his leadership as the Chief Justice, and his power to assign the opinion of the Court, would have changed the 5-4 decision upholding the subsidization to a majority holding the opposite. But Fred Vinson was Chief Justice by the 1946 Term, and he let Black write the opinion for a majority that included also Douglas, Murphy, and Reed. Black produced a religiopolitical tract that would not have been inappropriate, in tone and style, to the pamphleteering of another day—two or three centuries earlier—in another land—Merrie Olde England. The issue, according to Black, was really one not of the establishment clause but rather of the free exercise clause of the First Amendment: by what right, he asked, could this taxpayer interfere with the free exercise of the religion of devout Roman Catholics? New Jersey, he thundered,

cannot exclude individual Catholics, Lutherans, Mohammedans, Baptists, Jews, Methodists, Non-believers, Presbyterians, or the members of any other faith *because of their faith, or lack of it,* from receiving the benefits of public welfare legislation.

Driving inexorably on to a reductio ad absurbum, he painted in the purple prose of obiter dicta a passionate picture of what might happen in some imaginary community if the Court were to deny to Ewing Catholics the right to practice their religion freely—that is, at public expense. Suppose, he argued, Ewing operated the bus system as a publicly owned utility; then "state-paid policemen, detailed to protect children going to and from church schools from the very real hazards of traffic, would serve much the same purpose." Might some future taxpayer object to detailing the police to subserve such parochial purposes? If so,

parents might refuse to risk their children to the serious danger of traffic accidents going to and from parochial schools, the approaches to which were not protected by policemen. Similarly, parents might be reluctant to permit their children to attend schools which the state had cut off from such general government services as ordinary police and fire protection, connections for sewage proposal, public highways and sidewalks.

After conjuring more such judicial bogies, Black concluded on what can only be viewed, in context, as an exceptionally disingenuous note. The First Amendment, he intoned,

has erected a wall between church and state. That wall must be kept high and impregnable. We could not approve the slightest breach. New Jersey has not breached it here.

Rutledge responded with a lengthy historical analysis of the intent of the Founding Fathers, which seemed to demonstrate the contrary of what the present Court majority had assumed. Jackson responded as follows.

MR. JUSTICE JACKSON, *dissenting.*

I find myself, contrary to first impressions, unable to join in this decision. I have a sympathy, though it is not ideological, with Catholic citizens who are compelled by law to pay taxes for public schools, and also feel constrained by conscience and discipline to support other schools for their own children. Such relief to them as this case involves is not in itself a serious burden to taxpayers and I had assumed it to be as little serious in principle. Study of this case convinces me otherwise. The Court's opinion marshals every argument in favor of state aid and puts the case in its most favorable light, but much of its reasoning confirms my conclusions that there are no good grounds upon which to support the present legislation. In fact, the undertones of the opinion, advocating complete and uncompromising separation of Church from State, seem utterly discordant with its conclusion yielding support to their commingling in educational matters. The case which irresistibly comes to mind as the most fitting precedent is that of Julia who, according to Byron's reports, "whispering 'I will ne'er consent,'—consented."

I.

The Court sustains this legislation by assuming two deviations from the facts of this particular case; first, it assumes a state of facts the record does not support, and secondly, it refuses to consider facts which are inescapable on the record.

The Court concludes that this "legislation, as applied, does no more than provide a general program to help parents get their children, regardless of their religion, safely and expeditiously to and from accredited schools," and it draws a comparison between "state provisions intended to guarantee free transportation" for school children with services such as police and fire protection, and implies that we are here dealing with "laws authorizing new types of public services. . . ." This hypothesis permeates the opinion. The facts will not bear that construction.

The Township of Ewing is not furnishing transportation to the children in any form; it is not operating school busses itself or contracting for their operation; and it is not performing any public service of any kind with this taxpayer's money. All school children are left to ride as ordinary paying passengers on the regular busses operated by the public transportation system. What the Township does, and what the taxpayer complains of, is at stated intervals to reimburse parents for the fares paid, provided the children attend either public schools or Catholic Church schools. This expenditure of tax funds has no possible effect on the child's safety or expedition in transit. As passengers on the public busses they travel as fast and no faster, and are as safe and no safer, since their parents are reimbursed as before.

In addition to thus assuming a type of service that does not exist, the Court also insists that we must close our eyes to a discrimination which does exist. The resolution which authorizes disbursement of this taxpayer's money limits reimbursement to those who attend public schools and Catholic schools. That is the way the Act is applied to this taxpayer.

The New Jersey Act in question makes the character of the school, not the needs of the children, determine the eligibility of parents to reimbursement. The Act permits payment for transportation to parochial schools or public schools but prohibits it to private schools operated in whole or in part for profit. Children often are sent to private schools because their parents feel that they require more individual instruction than public schools can provide, or because they are backward or defective and need special attention. If all children of the state were objects of impartial solicitude, no reason is obvious for denying transportation reimbursement to students of this class, for these often are as needy and as worthy as those who go to public or parochial schools. Refusal to reimburse those who attend such schools is understandable only in the light of a purpose to aid the schools, because the state might well abstain from aiding a profit-making private enterprise. Thus, under the Act and resolution brought to us by this case, children are classified according to the schools they attend and are to be aided if they attend the public schools or private Catholic schools, and they are not allowed to be aided if they attend private secular schools or private religious schools of other faiths.

Of course, this case is not one of a Baptist or a Jew or an Episcopalian or a pupil of a private school complaining of discrimination. It is one of a taxpayer urging that he is being taxed for an unconstitutional purpose. I think he is entitled to have us consider the Act just as it is written. . . .

If we are to decide this case on the facts before us, our question is simply this: Is it constitutional to tax this complainant to pay the cost of carrying pupils to Church schools of one specified denomination?

II.

Whether the taxpayer constitutionally can be made to contribute aid to parents of students because of their attendance at parochial schools depends upon the nature of those schools and their relation to the Church. The Constitution says nothing of education. It lays no obligation on the states to provide schools and does not undertake to regulate state systems of education if they see fit to maintain them. But they cannot, through school policy any more than through other means, invade rights secured to citizens by the Constitution of the United States. . . . One of our basic rights is to be free of taxation to support a transgression of the constitutional command that the authorities "shall make no law respecting an establishment of religion, or prohibiting the free exercise thereof. . . ." U.S. Const., Amend. I; . . .

The function of the Church school is a subject on which this record is meager. It shows only that the schools are under superintendence of a priest and that "religion is taught as part of the curriculum." But we know that such schools are parochial only in name—they, in fact, represent a world-wide and age-old policy of the Roman Catholic Church. . . .

It is no exaggeration to say that the whole historic conflict in temporal policy between the Catholic Church and non-Catholics comes to a focus in their respective school policies. The Roman Catholic Church, counseled by experience in many ages and many lands and with all sorts and conditions of men, takes what, from the viewpoint of its own progress and the success of its mission, is a wise estimate of the importance of education to religion. It does not leave the individual to pick up religion by chance. It relies on early and indelible indoctrination in the faith and order of the Church by the word and example of persons consecrated to the task.

Our public school, if not a product of Protestantism, at least is more consistent with it than with the Catholic culture and scheme of values. It is a relatively recent development dating from about 1840. It is organized on the premise that secular education can be isolated from all religious teaching so that the school can inculcate all needed temporal knowledge and also maintain a strict and lofty neutrality as to religion. The assumption is that after the individual has been instructed in worldly wisdom he will be better fitted to choose his religion. Whether such a disjunction is possible, and if possible whether it is wise, are questions that I need not try to answer.

I should be surprised if any Catholic would deny that the parochial school is a vital, if not the most vital, part of the Roman Catholic Church. If put to the choice, that venerable institution, I should expect, would forgo its whole services for mature persons before it would give up education of the young, and it would be a wise choice. Its growth and cohesion, discipline and loyalty, spring from its schools. Catholic education is the rock on which the whole structure rests, and to render tax aid to its Church school is indistinguishable to me from rendering the same aid to the Church itself.

III.

It is of no importance in this situation whether the beneficiary of this expenditure of tax-raised funds is primarily the parochial school and incidentally the pupil, of whether the aid is directly bestowed on the pupil with indirect benefits to the school. The state cannot maintain a Church and it can no more tax its citizens to furnish free carriage to those who attend a Church. The prohibition against establishment of religion cannot be circumvented by a subsidy, bonus or reimbursement of expense to individuals for receiving religious instruction and indoctrination.

The Court, however, compares this to other subsidies and loans to individuals and says, "Nor does it follow that a law has a private rather than a public purpose because it provides that tax-raised funds will be paid to reimburse individuals on account of money spent by them in a way which furthers a public program. See *Carmichael* v. *Southern Coal & Coke Co.*, 301 U.S. 495, 518." Of course, the state may pay out tax-raised funds to relieve pauperism, but it may not under our Constitution do so to induce or reward piety. It may spend funds to secure old age against want, but it may not spend funds to secure religion against skepticism. It may compensate individuals for loss of employment, but it cannot compensate them for adherence to a creed.

It seems to me that the basic fallacy in the Court's reasoning, which accounts for its failure to apply the principles it avows, is in ignoring the essentially religious test by which beneficiaries of this expenditure are selected. A policeman protects a Catholic, of course—but not because he is a Catholic; it is because he is a man and a member of our society. The fireman protects the Church school —but not because it is a Church school; it is because it is property, part of the assets of our society. Neither the fireman nor the policeman has to ask before he renders aid "Is this man or building identified with the Catholic Church?" But before these school authorities draw a check to reimburse for a student's fare they must ask just that question, and if the school is a Catholic one they may render aid because it is such, while if it is of any other faith or is run for profit, the help must be withheld. To consider the converse of the Court's reasoning will best disclose its fallacy. That there is no parallel between police and fire protection and this plan of reimbursement is apparent from the incongruity of the limitation of this Act if applied to police and fire service. Could we sustain an Act that said the police shall protect pupils on the way to or from public schools and Catholic schools but not while going to and coming from other schools, and firemen shall extinguish a blaze in public or Catholic school buildings but shall not put out a blaze in Protestant Church schools or private schools operated for profit? That is the true analogy to the case we have before us and I should think it pretty plain that such a scheme would not be valid.

The Court's holding is that this taxpayer has no grievance because the state has decided to make the reimbursement a public purpose and therefore we are bound to regard it as such. I agree that this Court has left, and always should leave to each state, great latitude in deciding for itself, in the light of its own conditions, what shall be public purposes in its scheme of things. It may socialize utilities and economic enterprises and make taxpayers' business out of what conventionally had been private business. It may make public business of individual welfare, health, education, entertainment or security. But it cannot make public business of religious worship or instruction, or of attendance at religious institutions of any character. There is no answer to the proposition, more fully expounded by MR. JUSTICE RUTLEDGE, that the effect of the religious freedom Amendment to our Constitution was to take every form of propagation of religion out of the realm of things which could directly or indirectly be made public business and thereby be supported in whole or in part at taxpayers' expense. That is a difference which the Constitution sets up between religion and almost every other subject matter of legislation, a difference which goes to the very root of religious freedom and which the Court is overlooking today. This freedom was first in the Bill of Rights because it was first in the forefathers' minds; it was set forth in absolute terms, and its strength is its rigidity. It was intended not only to keep the states' hands out of religion, but to keep religion's hands off the state, and, above all, to keep bitter religious controversy out of public life by denying to every denomination any advantage from getting control of public policy or the public purse. Those great ends I cannot but think are immeasurably compromised by today's decision.

This policy of our Federal Constitution has never been wholly pleasing to most religious groups. They all are quick to invoke its protections; they all are irked when they feel its restraints. This Court has gone a long way, if not an unreasonable way, to hold that public business of such paramount importance as maintenance of public order, protection of the privacy of the home, and taxation may not be pursued by a state in a way that even indirectly will interfere with religious proselyting. . . .

But we cannot have it both ways. Religious teaching cannot be a private affair when the state seeks to impose regulations which infringe on it indirectly, and a public affair to aid all. If these principles seem harsh in prohibiting aid to Catholic education, it must not be forgotten that it is the same Constitution that alone assures Catholics the right to maintain these schools at all when predominant local sentiment would forbid them. *Pierce* v. *Society of Sisters,* 268 U.S. 510. Nor should I think that those who have done so well without this aid would want to see this separation between Church and State broken down. If the state may aid these religious schools, it may therefore regulate them. Many groups have sought aid from tax funds only to find that it carried political controls with it. Indeed this Court has declared that "It is hardly lack of due process for the Government to regulate that which it subsidizes." *Wickard* v. *Filburn,* 317 U.S. 111, 131.

But in any event, the great purposes of the Constitution do not depend on the approval or convenience of those they restrain. I cannot read the history of the struggle to separate political from ecclesiastical affairs . . . without a conviction that the Court today is unconsciously giving the clock's hands a backward turn.

F. DENOMINATIONALISM IN THE PUBLIC SCHOOLS

MC COLLUM V. BOARD OF EDUCATION
333 U.S. 203, 232 (March 8, 1948)

Vashti McCollum was a resident taxpayer and the mother of a public school child in Champaign, Illinois. She was also an avowed atheist who objected to having her child either subjected to religious indoctrination or exposed to the sociopsychological deprivations that accompanied nonconformity. So she asked the local circuit court to rule that the public school program of the Champaign Council of Religious Education was prohibited by the First Amendment. The council was a federation of Jews, Protestants, and Roman Catholics who had persuaded the board of education to permit them to staff and conduct weekly classes in regular public school classrooms. Attendance was voluntary and conditioned upon prior written parental request; those not attending a religious class were confined in study halls until the religious exercises were concluded. Both the trial court and the Supreme Court of Illinois rejected Mrs. McCollum's claim that atheists have a right to be free *from* religion; but hardly a year after the *Everson* decision, eight of the same group of Supreme Court justices, with only Reed in dissent, agreed to reverse and brand as unconstitutional the Champaign program. Again Vinson assigned Black to write for the Court, although the four *Everson* dissenters, Frankfurter, Jackson, Rutledge, and Burton, did append a concurrence that was authored by Frankfurter, and Jackson wrote a separate concurrence alone.

Apart from its recitation of the facts of the case, Black's majority opinion was addressed primarily to the task of demonstrating that there was no conflict between the Court's recent ruling in *Everson,* and the (as Reed argued, seemingly contrary) decision in the present case. Frankfurter incongruously pointed out—he spoke for the dissenters who had *opposed* integration in *Everson*—that other forms of "released time" religious programs were not necessarily invalid, and that each would have to be judged on the basis of its own peculiar facts and merits. This statement seemed to invite a series of future decisions, in which interested parties and their attorneys could probe the attitudinal no-man's-land between the Maginot Line of *Everson* and the blitz pincer arm that *McCollum* seemed to represent—from the point of view, at least, of those who perceived the "wall of separation" to be a boundary which protected prevailing community practices against the threat of judicial interference in what Frankfurter otherwise often liked to call "the politics of the people." Even more peculiar, however, was Jackson's position. In *Everson,* Jackson had censured Black for his loose construction of establishment; now, in *McCollum,* Jackson censured Black for his rigid and intransigent construction of the same clause! But it had been less than two years since Jackson's cable from Nuremburg; and a comparison of Jackson's opinions in *McCollum* and in *Everson* raises the question of whether Jackson was dissenting in favor of his own views of the First Amendment, or against Black's position, whichever that might be. What Jackson says, particularly at the close of his opinion, is all very clever; but what it boils down to is little more than a conservative plea for caution, parsimony, and restraint. In effect, he gave his vote to McCollum, but his opinion was an affirmation of empathy, if not sympathy, for the religious transgressors of the wall throughout the country, and their acolyte boards of education.

MR. JUSTICE JACKSON, concurring.

I join the opinion of MR. JUSTICE FRANKFURTER, and concur in the result reached by the Court, but with these reservations: I think it is doubtful whether the facts of this case establish jurisdiction in this Court, but in any event that we should place some bounds in the demands for interference with local schools that we are empowered or willing to entertain. I make these reservations a matter of record in view of the number of litigations likely to be started as a result of this decision.

A Federal Court may interfere with local school authorities only when they invade either a personal liberty or a property right protected by the Federal Constitution. Ordinarily this will come about in either of two ways:

First. When a person is required to submit to some religious rite or instruction or is deprived or threatened with deprivation of his freedom for resisting such unconstitutional requirement. We may then set him free or enjoin his prosecution. Typical of such cases was *West Virginia State Board of Education* v. *Barnette,* 319 U.S. 624. There penalties were threatened against both parent and child for refusal of the latter to perform a compulsory ritual which offended his convictions. We intervened to shield them against the penalty. But here, complainant's son may join religious classes if he chooses and if his parents so request, or he may stay out of them. The complaint is that when others join and he does not, it sets him apart as a dissenter, which is humiliating. Even admitting this to be true, it may be doubted whether the Constitution which, of course, protects the right to dissent, can be construed also to protect one from the embarrassment that always attends non-conformity, whether in religion, politics, behavior or dress. Since no legal compulsion is applied to complainant's son himself and no penalty is imposed or threatened from which we may relieve him, we can hardly base jurisdiction on this ground.

Second. Where a complainant is deprived of property by being taxed for unconstitutional purposes, such as directly or indirectly to support a religious establishment, we can protect a taxpayer against such a levy. This was the *Everson Case,* 330 U.S. 1, as I saw it then and see it now. . . .

In this case, however, any cost of this plan to the taxpayers is incalculable and negligible. It can be argued, perhaps, that religious classes add some wear and tear on public buildings and that they should be charged with some expense for heat and light, even though the sessions devoted to religious instruction do not add to the length of the school day. But the cost is neither substantial nor measurable, and no one seriously can say that the complainant's tax bill has been proved to be increased because of this plan. I think it is doubtful whether the taxpayer in this case has shown any substantial property injury.

If, however, jurisdiction is found to exist, it is important that we circumscribe our decision with some care. What is asked is not a defensive use of judicial power to set aside a tax levy or reverse a conviction, or to enjoin threats of prosecution or taxation. The relief demanded in this case is the extraordinary writ of mandamus to tell the local Board of Education what it must do. The prayer for relief is that a writ issue against the Board of Education "ordering it to immediately adopt and enforce rules and regulations prohibiting all instruction in and teaching of religious education in all public schools . . . and in all public school houses and buildings in said district when occupied by public schools." The plaintiff, as she has every right to be, is an avowed atheist. What she has asked of the courts is that they not only end the "released time" plan but also ban every form of teaching which suggests or recognizes that there is a God. She would ban all teaching of the Scriptures. She especially mentions as an example of her rights "having pupils learn and recite such statements as 'The Lord is my Shepherd, I shall not want.' " And she objects to teaching that the King James version of the Bible "is called the Christian's Guide Book, the Holy Writ and the Word of God," and many other similar matters. This Court is directing the Illinois courts generally to sustain plaintiff's complaint without exception of any of these grounds of complaint, without discriminating between them and without laying down any standards to define the limits of the effect of our decision.

To me, the sweep and detail of these complaints is a danger signal which warns of the kind of local controversy we will be required to arbitrate if we do not place appropriate limitation on our decision and exact strict compliance with jurisdictional requirements. Authorities list 256 separate and substantial religious bodies to exist in the continental United States. Each of them, through the suit of some discontented but unpenalized and untaxed representative, has as good a right as this plaintiff to demand that the courts compel the schools to sift out of their teaching everything inconsistent with its doctrines. If we are to eliminate everything that is objectionable to any of these warring sects or inconsistent with any of their doctrines, we will leave public education in shreds. Nothing but educational confusion and a discrediting of the public school system can result from subjecting it to constant law suits.

While we may and should end such formal and explicit instruction as the Champaign plan and can at all times prohibit teaching of creed and catechism and ceremonial and can forbid forthright proselyting in the schools, I think it remains to be demonstrated whether it is possible, even if desirable, to comply with such demands as plaintiff's completely to isolate and cast out of secular education all that some people may reasonably regard as religious instruction. Perhaps subjects such as mathematics, physics, or chemistry are, or can be, completely secularized. But it would not seem practical to teach either practice or appreciation of the arts if we are to forbid exposure of youth to any religious influences. Music, without sacred music, architecture minus the cathedral, or painting without the scriptural themes would be eccentric and incomplete, even from a secular point of view. Yet the inspirational appeal of religion in these guises is often stronger than in forthright sermon. Even such a "science" as biology raises the issue between evolution and creation as an explanation of our presence on this planet. Certainly a course in English literature that omitted the Bible and other powerful uses of our mother tongue for religious ends would be pretty barren. And I should suppose it is a proper, if not an indispensable, part of preparation for a worldly life, to know the roles that religion and religions have played in the tragic story of mankind. The fact is that, for good or for ill, nearly everything in our culture worth transmitting, everything which gives meaning to life, is saturated with religious influences, derived from paganism, Judaism, Christianity— both Catholic and Protestant—and other faiths accepted by a large part of the world's peoples. One can hardly respect a system of education that would leave the student wholly ignorant of the currents of religious thought that move the world society for a part in which he is being prepared.

But how one can teach, with satisfaction or even with justice to all faiths, such subjects as the story of the Reformation, the Inquisition, or even the New England effort to found "a Church without a Bishop and a State without a King," is more than I know. It is too much to expect that mortals will teach subjects about which their contemporaries have passionate controversies with the detachment they may summon to teaching about remote subjects such as Confucius or Mohammed. When instruction turns to proselyting and imparting knowledge becomes evangelism is, except in the crudest cases, a subtle inquiry.

The opinions in this case show that public educational authorities have evolved a considerable variety of practices in dealing with the religious problem. Neighborhoods differ in racial, religious and cultural compositions. It must be expected that they will adopt different customs which will give emphasis to different values and will induce different experiments. And it must be expected that, no matter what practice prevails, there will be many discontented and possibly belligerent minorities. We must leave some flexibility to meet local conditions, some chance to progress by trial and error. While I agree that the religious classes involved here go beyond permissible limits, I also think the complaint demands more than plaintiff is entitled to have granted. So far as I can see this Court does not tell the State court where it may stop, nor does it set up any standards by which the State court may determine that question for itself.

The task of separating the secular from the religious in education is one of magnitude, intricacy and delicacy. To lay down a sweeping constitutional doctrine as demanded by complainant and apparently approved by the Court, applicable alike to all school boards of the nation, "to immediately adopt and enforce rules and regulations prohibiting all instruction in and teaching of religious education in all public schools," is to decree a uniform, rigid, and, if we are consistent, an unchanging standard for countless school boards representing and serving highly localized groups which not only differ from each other but which themselves from time to time change attitudes. It seems to me that to do so is to allow zeal for our own ideas of what is good in public instruction to induce us to accept the role of a super board of education for every school district in the nation.

It is idle to pretend that this task is one for which we can find in the Constitution one word to help us as judges to decide where the secular ends and the sectarian begins in education. Nor can we find guidance in any other legal source. It is a matter on which we can find no law but our own prepossessions. If with no surer legal guidance we are to take up and decide every variation of this controversy, raised by persons not subject to penalty or tax but who are dissatisfied with the way schools are dealing with the problem, we are likely to have much business of the sort. And, more importantly, we are likely to make the legal "wall of separation between church and state" as winding as the famous serpentine wall designed by Mr. Jefferson for the University he founded.

G. RELEASED TIME FOR RELIGIOUS SCHOOLS

ZORACH V. CLAUSON
343 U.S. 306, 323 (April 28, 1952)

The clear implication of Jackson's opinion in *McCollum* is that programs of religious instruction *in* the public schools ought to be deemed unconstitutional; but, those in which the instruction takes place *outside of* the physical facilities of the public schools might be viewed very differently. And so they were, by many of Jackson's colleagues, when such a case, *Zorach*, reached the Court for decision four years later. A majority of six justices approved such a program, while Frankfurter, consistent with his positions in the two previous decisions, dissented. Black and Jackson also dissented, although each wrote a separate opinion, of course. We can perhaps explain Black on the ground of personal *stare decisis,* because he now found himself defending his opinion in *McCollum* against a bearhug by Douglas (for the majority) which virtually distinguished it to death. What, however, of Jackson? One would think that, in the light of his previous behavior, both in voting and in his opinions, he would be happy to join in an opinion of the Court which would help to define the boundary which was missing in *McCollum*, especially because he could do this while remaining on the opposite side of the division from Black. But Jackson was a passionate man, and there is internal evidence in his opinion that suggests that he must have taken personal affront at certain remarks that were exchanged, apparently with Douglas, during the conference on this case. Having found a more proximate antagonist than Black, Jackson transferred his antipathy to the new spokesman for the majority, which left him no recourse but to dissent, strange bedfellow or not.

Contrary to his typically expansive attitude toward the desirability of having the Court view issues of public policy in all their socioeconomic and psychological fullness, Douglas, in this case, surpassed in parsimony the notorious remark by George Sutherland in the classic introduction of the Court to the "Brandeis Brief," that the majority had found it to be "interesting, but only mildly persuasive."[25] Indeed, Douglas indulged himself in the "slot-machine theory of jurisprudence" and in language reminiscent of that used in the A.A.A. case of New Deal fame, by Owen Roberts who had pontificated that,

> the judicial branch of the Government has only one duty,—to lay the article of the Constitution which is invoked beside the statute which is challenged and to decide whether the latter squares with the former. All the court does, or can do, is to announce its considered judgment upon the question. . . . This court neither approves nor condemns any legislative policy.[26]

In the even more pious and equally dogmatic language of Douglas in the present case:

> The briefs and arguments are replete with data bearing on the merits of this type of "released time" program. Views pro and con are expressed, based on practical experience with these programs and with their implications. We do not stop to summarize these materials nor to burden the opinion with an analysis of them. For they involve considerations not germane to the narrow constitutional issue presented. They largely concern the wisdom of the system, its efficiency from an educational point of view, and the political considerations which have motivated its adoption or rejection in some communities. Those matters are of no concern here, since our problem reduces itself to whether New York by this system has either prohibited the "free exercise" of religion or has made a law "respecting an establishment of religion" within the meaning of the First Amendment.

Rarely is such complete lack of candor encountered in a majority opinion of the Supreme Court during the past generation, and this in itself suggests a partial explanation of Jackson's being pushed, again, into the minority, for he himself was a forthright person who set a high regard upon candor.

The dissimulation of the Douglas opinion went considerably beyond the restatement of the Court's official theory of judicial review, however. The full and complete text of relevant language bearing upon the integration of religious and secular education is the first sixteen words of the First

---

[25] *Adkins* v. *Children's Hospital,* 261 U.S. 525, 560 (1923). The 1138 page brief in behalf of the National Consumers' League was filed by the then Professor Frankfurter.

[26] *United States* v. *Butler,* 297 U.S. 1, 62-63 (1936).

Amendment: "Congress shall make no law respecting an establishment of religion, or prohibiting the free exercise thereof." According to Douglas,

> The First Amendment, however, does not say that in every and all respects there shall be a separation of Church and State. Rather, it studiously defines the manner, the specific ways, in which there shall be no concert or union or dependency one on the other.

Where and how the First Amendment performs these wonders is by no means self-evident; and we have already examined the two most relevant precedents, if perchance the "it" that is the subject of his second sentence is meant to refer to the Supreme Court rather than the Constitution.

Invoking the same bogeymen who had served Black's purposes in *Everson*, Douglas warned that if the Court were to invalidate the New York released-time program, then "Municipalities would not be permitted to render police or fire protection to religious groups. Policemen who helped parishioners into their places of worship would violate the Constitution." There was more in like vein. The parade of horribles is one of the oldest—and cheapest—tricks in the lawyer's, and judge's, book.

In conclusion, Douglas stated three themes:

> We are a religious people whose institutions presuppose a Supreme Being.
> Our individual preferences . . . are not the constitutional standard.
> We follow the *McCollum* case.

It is largely in rebuttal of the latter two assertions that Jackson wrote his dissent.

MR. JUSTICE JACKSON, *dissenting.*

This released time program is founded upon a use of the State's power coercion, which, for me, determines its unconstitutionality. Stripped to its essentials, the plan has two stages: first, that the State compel each student to yield a large part of his time for public secular education; and, second, that some of it be "released" to him on condition that he devote it to sectarian religious purposes.

No one suggests that the Constitution would permit the State directly to require this "released" time to be spent "under the control of a duly constituted religious body." This program accomplishes that forbidden result by indirection. If public education were taking so much of the pupils' time as to injure the public or the students' welfare by encroaching upon their religious opportunity, simply shortening everyone's school day would facilitate voluntary and optional attendance at Church classes. But that suggestion is rejected upon the ground that if they are made free many students will not go to the Church. Hence, they must be deprived of freedom for this period, with Church attendance put to them as one of the two permissible ways of using it.

The greater effectiveness of this system over voluntary attendance after school hours is due to the truant officer who, if the youngster fails to go to the Church school, dogs him back to the public schoolroom. Here schooling is more or less suspended during the "released time" so the nonreligious attendants will not forge ahead of the churchgoing absentees. But it serves as a temporary jail for a pupil who will not go to Church. It takes more subtlety of mind than I possess to deny that this is governmental constraint in support of religion. It is as unconstitutional, in my view, when exerted by indirection as when exercised forthrightly.

As one whose children, as a matter of free choice, have been sent to privately supported Church schools, I may challenge the Court's suggestion that opposition to this plan can only be antireligious, atheistic, or agnostic. My evangelistic brethren confuse an objection to compulsion with an objection to religion. It is possible to hold a faith with enough confidence to believe that what should be rendered to God does not need to be decided and collected by Caesar.

The day that this country ceases to be free for irreligion it will cease to be free for religion—except for the sect that can win political power. The same epithetical jurisprudence used by the Court today to beat down those who oppose pressuring children into some religion can devise as good epithets tomorrow against those who object to pressuring them into a favored religion. And, after all, if we concede to the State power and wisdom to single out "duly constituted religious" bodies as exclusive alternatives for compulsory secular instruction, it would be logical to also uphold the power and wisdom to choose the true faith among those "duly constituted." We start down a rough road when we begin to mix compulsory public education with compulsory godliness.

A number of Justices just short of a majority of the majority that promulgates today's passionate dialectics joined in answering them in *Illinois ex rel. McCollum* v. *Board of Education,* 333 U.S. 203. The distinction attempted between that case and this is trivial, almost to the point of cynicism, magnifying its nonessential details and disparaging compulsion which was the underlying reason for invalidity. A reading of the Court's opinion in that case along with its opinion in this case will show such difference of overtones and undertones as to make clear that the *McCollum* case has passed like a storm in a teacup. The wall which the Court was professing to erect between Church and State has become even more warped and twisted than I expected. Today's judgment will be more interesting to students of psychology and of the judicial processes than to students of constitutional law.

3 DEMAGOGUERY

In the preceding chapter, attention was focused upon the kind of civil liberties claim for which Jackson was willing to write in support. We found that one of his principal concerns was the passive right to think and to believe free from the fear or the threat of compulsory disclosure and enforced expression. He argued for every individual's right to keep private ideas which he did not wish to expose to the public gaze. The depth of his conviction on this point is significantly revealed by his willingness, in order to advance this policy goal, to vote in support of charlatans, union leaders, and even communists, all of whom constituted classes of litigants whom he generally despised. For Jackson, freedom of belief was part of his expansive concept of the right to privacy, a theme to which we shall return often, and a goal in which he anticipated by at least a decade the institutional formation, by the Warren Court during the sixties, of such a new civil liberty.

The other major theme of Chapter 2 was the separation of Church and State. From the point of view of protesting parents and taxpayers, that issue was one of preventing community school systems from giving preferential support to the views of particular sects—at least, this was the way Jackson conceptualized it. But another way to look at this question was from the perspective typical of atheist claimants like Vashti McCollum and the much more notorious Madelyn Murray of a decade later, who resisted the persistent efforts of the Christian majority to use the public school apparatus as a mouthpiece for evangelistic efforts ranging from ceremony and ritual,[1] to direct dogmatic indoctrination as in the released-time cases. Thus seen, the problem was again one of the right to individual privacy, and the right of citizens to go about their own business without being forced to listen, and to respond to, the harangues of zealots grinding their own ideological axes—be it religious, political, racial, or whatever. It can hardly be argued, however, that such a right to privacy from exposure to controversial discussion obtains in public places; and so a central question is: what is a "public" and what is a "private" place, in the explicit set of fact circumstances associated with a particular claim to freedom from proselyting. It is the latter approach that characterizes Jackson's argument in the cases in the present chapter. He could not

---

[1] *Engel* v. *Vitale*, 370 U.S. 421 (1962); *School District of Abington* v. *Schempp* and *Murray* v. *Curlett*, 374 U.S. 203 (1963).

directly vote in support of individuals who claimed that their privacy had been invaded by zealous proselyters, because no such person was party to any of the cases in this chapter. So Jackson purported to defend instead a postulated interest that was represented constructively by "the public" in whose name the government officials (who were the plaintiffs in these cases) prosecuted the defendants for their various misdemeanors. In several of the cases, however, individual citizens did complain against the defendants, to appropriate governmental officials who in turn initiated the actions which resulted in the prosecutions. The interests of privacy which Jackson posited were involved in these proceedings, but in such a manner that the way for him to uphold them was to vote to affirm the convictions of the criminal defendants, as he did without exception.

Another aspect of these cases was apparently important for Jackson. In the Chapter 2 cases Jackson was willing to give his support to a number of litigants for whom he felt no empathy, but whose interests coincided with the policy position that he favored. None of those litigants had behaved in a manner such that he could fairly be characterized, on the records before Jackson, as a fanatic. Quite to the contrary, for Jackson to have upheld the claims of the defendants in the present chapter, invariably would have required him to vote *against* his policy goal; all of these defendants, with the possible exception of Kovacs, were extremist zealots whose behavior Jackson could and did, with considerable justification, describe as fanatical. The Court reversed the convictions of most of these defendants (extremist or not), but generally by one-vote margins, and in two instances without benefit of any opinion of the Court because the voting majority could agree on none.

In four of these six cases, Jackson supplies a lengthy recital of the facts which he charges the Court has either overlooked, ignored, or suppressed. He felt that full appreciation of the context in which the prosecution arose was indispensable, to comprehension of the issue before the Court for decision. Both the overtones and the undertones of his opinions in these four cases are replete with the semantic insignia of the pragmatic approach which Jackson so frequently professed. On the other hand, it is perhaps curious that this heavy emphasis upon the facts occurs only in cases in which Jackson dissents, and is attacking the decision of the majority. When, happily, he found himself in the majority, as in *Kovacs* and *Dennis*, his emphasis shifts sharply to questions of consistency in legal principles, the logic of rationales, and other matters of dogma.

Two of these cases, *Douglas* and *Kunz*, provided him with the kind of opportunity in which he delighted, to tweak his colleagues for their failure to practice what they preached to litigants.[2] This sort of irony was

2 See, for example, *United States* v. *Bryan*, 339 U.S. 323 (1950), and Chap. 7C, *infra*.

a recurring theme that marked his judicial style as idiosyncratic. There may have been such instances, but I cannot recall a single one during the past two decades in which any other justice has criticized his colleagues for a suggested discrepancy between the personal behavior of the justices, in either their institutional roles or their private lives, and the policy norms supported by the Court—for others—in its decisions. Indeed, it was this very quirk in Jackson, which both he and his friends considered to reflect an exceptional degree of candor, which found ultimate expression in Jackson's cable from Nuremburg with its unprecedented public attack upon his "judicial brother" Black.

A. JEHOVAH'S ENEMIES

DOUGLAS V. CITY OF JEANETTE
319 U.S. 157, 166 (May 3, 1943)

Although Jackson's opinion appears for purposes of publication as part of the report of the *Douglas* decision, it is mostly concerned with a discussion of the first of the two companion cases which precede *Douglas* in the reports. In the two latter cases, Mr. Justice Douglas wrote for a majority that included Black, Murphy, Rutledge, and Chief Justice Stone; dissents were filed by Frankfurter, by Reed (with whose opinion Roberts joined), and, of course, by Jackson. All three cases were concerned with the arrests and convictions of members of the Jehovah's Witnesses sect, whose so-called ministers carried out sweeping door-to-door campaigns in which they peddled tracts that advertised their views. When they refused to comply with the City of Jeanette's licensing ordinance, the Court majority said that they were within their constitutional rights, because the license fee, as applied to them, was a tax upon their religion. The crux of Jackson's argument was that a citizen's home is his castle, and not an involuntary camp meeting ground.

MR. JUSTICE JACKSON....

Unless we are to reach judgments as did Plato's men who were chained in a cave so that they saw nothing but shadows, we should consider the facts of [this] case at least as an hypothesis to test the validity of the conclusions.... This record shows us something of the strings as well as the marionettes. It reveals the problem of those in local authority when the right to proselyte comes in contact with what many people have an idea is their right to be let alone....

In 1939, a "Watch Tower Campaign" was instituted by Jehovah's Witnesses in Jeannette, Pennsylvania, an industrial city of some 16,000 inhabitants. Each home was visited, a bell was rung or the door knocked upon, and the householder advised that the Witness had important information. If the householder would listen, a record was played on the phonograph. Its subject was "Snare and Racket." . . .

When this campaign began, many complaints from offended householders were received, and three or four of the Witnesses were arrested. Thereafter, the "zone servant" in charge of the campaign conferred with the Mayor. He told the Mayor it was their right to carry on the campaign and showed him a decision of the United States Supreme Court, said to have that effect, as proof of it. The Mayor told him that they were at liberty to distribute their literature in the streets of the city and that he would have no objection if they distributed the literature free of charge at the houses, but that the people objected to their attempt to force these sales, and particularly on Sunday. The Mayor asked whether it would not be possible to come on some other day and to distribute the literature without selling it. The zone servant replied that that was contrary to their method of "doing business" and refused. He also told the Mayor that he would bring enough Witnesses into the City of Jeannette to get the job done whether the Mayor liked it or not. . . .

On Palm Sunday of 1939, the threat was made good. Over 100 of the Witnesses appeared. They were strangers to the city and arrived in upwards of twenty-five automobiles.[3] The automobiles were parked outside the city limits, and headquarters were set up in a gasoline station with telephone facilities through which the director of the campaign could be notified when trouble occurred. He furnished bonds for the Witnesses as they were arrested. As they began their work, around 9:00 o'clock in the morning, telephone calls began to come into the Police Headquarters, and complaints in large volume were made all during the day. They exceeded the number that the police could handle, and the Fire Department was called out to assist. The Witnesses called at homes singly and in groups, and some of the homes complained that they were called upon several times. Twenty-one Witnesses were arrested. Only those were arrested where definite proof was obtainable that the literature had been offered for sale or a sale had been made for a price. . . .

The national structure of the Jehovah's Witness movement is also somewhat revealed in this testimony. At the head of the movement in this country is the Watch Tower Bible & Tract Society, a corporation organized under the laws of Pennsylvania, but having its principal place of business in Brooklyn, N. Y. It prints all pamphlets, manufactures all books, supplies all phonographs and records, and provides other materials for the Witnesses. It "ordains" these Witnesses

---

[3] The actual direction of the campaign probably came from Bethel Home, the Society's Brooklyn headquarters: See William J. Whalen, *Armageddon Around the Corner* (New York: John Day Company, Inc., 1962), pp. 60-61. [Ed.]

by furnishing each, on a basis which does not clearly appear, a certificate that he is a minister of the Gospel. Its output is large and its revenues must be considerable. Little is revealed of its affairs. One of its "zone servants" testified that its correspondence is signed only with the name of the corporation and anonymity as to its personnel is its policy. The assumption that it is a "non-profit charitable" corporation may be true, but it is without support beyond mere assertion. In none of these cases has the assertion been supported by such usual evidence as a balance sheet or an income statement. What its manufacturing costs and revenues are, what salaries or bonuses it pays, what contracts it has for supplies or services we simply do not know. . . .[4]

The publishing output of the Watch Tower corporation is disposed of through converts, some of whom are full-time and some part-time ministers. These are organized into groups or companies under the direction of "zone servants." It is their purpose to carry on in a thorough manner so that every home in the communities in which they work may be regularly visited three or four times a year. The full-time Witnesses acquire their literature from the Watch Tower Bible & Tract Society at a figure which enables them to distribute it at the prices printed thereon with a substantial differential. Some of the books they acquire for 5¢ and dispose of for a contribution of 25¢. On others, the margin is less. . . .

The literature thus distributed is voluminous and repetitious. Characterization is risky, but a few quotations will indicate something of its temper.

Taking as representative the book "Enemies," of which J. F. Rutherford, the lawyer who long headed this group, is the author, we find the following: "The greatest racket ever invented and practiced is that of religion. The most cruel and seductive public enemy is that which employs religion to carry on the racket, and by which means the people are deceived and the name of Almighty God is reproached. There are numerous systems of religion, but the most subtle, fraudulent and injurious to humankind is that which is generally labeled the 'Christian religion,' because it has the appearance of a worshipful devotion to the Supreme Being, and thereby easily misleads many honest and sincere persons." *Id.* at 144-145. It analyzes the income of the Roman Catholic hierarchy and announces that it is "the great racket, a racket that is greater than all other rackets combined." *Id.* at 178. It also says under the chapter heading "Song of the Harlot," "Referring now to the foregoing Scriptural definition of *harlot*: What religious system exactly fits the prophecies recorded in God's Word? There is but one answer, and that is, The Roman Catholic Church organization." *Id.* at 204-205. "Those close or nearby and dependent upon the main organization, being of the same stripe, picture the Jewish and Protestant clergy and other allies of the Hier-

---

[4] For further details, See David R. Manwaring, *Render unto Caesar* (Chicago: University of Chicago Press, 1962), pp. 20-22. [Ed.]

archy who tag along behind the Hierarchy at the present time to do the bidding of the old 'whore'." *Id.* at 222. "Says the prophet of Jehovah: 'It shall come to pass in that day, that Tyre (modern Tyre, the Roman Catholic Hierarchy organization) shall be forgotten.' Forgotten by whom? By her former illicit paramours who have committed fornication with her." *Id.* at 264. Throughout the literature, statements of this kind appear amidst scriptural comment and prophecy, denunciation of demonology, which is used to characterize the Roman Catholic religion, criticism of government and those in authority, advocacy of obedience to the law of God instead of the law of man, and an interpretation of the law of God as they see it. . . .

The day of Armageddon, to which all of this is prelude, is to be a violent and bloody one, for then shall be slain all "demonologists," including most of those who reject the teachings of Jehovah's Witnesses. . . .

Such is the activity which it is claimed no public authority can either regulate or tax. This claim is substantially, if not quite, sustained today. I dissent—a disagreement induced in no small part by the facts recited.

As individuals many of us would not find this activity seriously objectionable. The subject of the disputes involved may be a matter of indifference to our personal creeds. Moreover, we work in offices affording ample shelter from such importunities and live in homes where we do not personally answer such calls and bear the burden of turning away the unwelcome. But these observations do not hold true for all. The stubborn persistence of the officials of smaller communities in their efforts to regulate this conduct indicates a strongly held conviction that the Court's many decisions in this field are at odds with the realities of life in those communities where the householder himself drops whatever he may be doing to answer the summons to the door and is apt to have positive religious convictions of his own.[5] . . .

Our difference of opinion cannot fairly be given the color of a disagreement as to whether the constitutional rights of Jehovah's Witnesses should be protected in so far as they are rights. These Witnesses, in common with all others, have extensive rights to proselyte and propagandize. These of course include the right to oppose and criticize the Roman Catholic Church or any other denomination. These rights are, and should be held to be, as extensive as any orderly society can tolerate in religious disputation. The real question is where their rights end and the rights of others begin. The real task of determining the extent of their rights on balance with the rights of others is not met by pronouncement of general propositions with which there is no disagreement.

If we should strip these cases to the underlying questions, I find them too

[5] Compare Chafee, *Freedom of Speech in the United States* (1941), p. 407: "I cannot help wondering whether the Justices of the Supreme Court are quite aware of the effect of organized front-door intrusions upon people who are not sheltered from zealots and imposters by a staff of servants or the locked entrance of an apartment house."

difficult as constitutional problems to be disposed of by a vague but fervent transcendentalism.

In my view, the First Amendment assures the broadest tolerable exercise of free speech, free press, and free assembly, not merely for religious purposes, but for political, economic, scientific, news, or informational ends as well. When limits are reached which such communications must observe, can one go farther under the cloak of religious evangelism? Does what is obscene, or commercial, or abusive, or inciting become less so if employed to promote a religious ideology? I had not supposed that the rights of secular and non-religious communications were more narrow or in any way inferior to those of avowed religious groups.

It may be asked why then does the First Amendment separately mention free exercise of religion? The history of religious persecution gives the answer. Religion needed specific protection because it was subject to attack from a separate quarter. It was often claimed that one was an heretic and guilty of blasphemy because he failed to conform in mere belief or in support of prevailing institutions and theology. It was to assure religious teaching as much freedom as secular discussion, rather than to assure it greater license, that led to its separate statement.

The First Amendment grew out of an experience which taught that society cannot trust the conscience of a majority to keep its religious zeal within the limits that a free society can tolerate. I do not think it any more intended to leave the conscience of a minority to fix its limits. Civil government can not let any group ride rough-shod over others simply because their "consciences" tell them to do so.

I cannot accept the holding . . . that the behavior revealed here "occupies the same high estate under the First Amendment as do worship in the churches and preaching from the pulpits." To put them on the same constitutional plane seems to me to have a dangerous tendency towards discrediting religious freedom.

Neither can I think it an essential part of freedom that religious differences be aired in language that is obscene, abusive, or inciting to retaliation. We have held that a Jehovah's Witness may not call a public officer a "God damned racketeer" and a "damned Fascist," because that is to use "fighting words," and such are not privileged. *Chaplinsky* v. *New Hampshire*, 315 U. S. 568. How then can the Court today hold it a "high constitutional privilege" to go to homes, including those of devout Catholics on Palm Sunday morning, and thrust upon them literature calling their church a "whore" and their faith a "racket"?

Nor am I convinced that we can have freedom of religion only by denying the American's deep-seated conviction that his home is a refuge from the pulling and hauling of the market place and the street. For a stranger to corner a man in his home, summon him to the door and put him in the position either of arguing his religion or of ordering one of unknown disposition to leave is a questionable use of religious freedom.

I find it impossible to believe that the . . . case can be solved by reference to the statement that "The authors of the First Amendment knew that novel and unconventional ideas might disturb the complacent, but they chose to encourage a freedom which they believed essential if vigorous enlightenment was ever to triumph over slothful ignorance." I doubt if only the slothfully ignorant wish repose in their homes, or that the forefathers intended to open the door to such forced "enlightenment" as we have here. . . .

This Court is forever adding new stories to the temples of constitutional law, and the temples have a way of collapsing when one story too many is added. So it was with liberty of contract, which was discredited by being overdone. The Court is adding a new privilege to override the rights of others to what has before been regarded as religious liberty. In so doing it needlessly creates a risk of discrediting a wise provision of our Constitution which protects all—those in homes as well as those out of them—in the peaceful, orderly practice of the religion of their choice but which gives no right to force it upon others.

Civil liberties had their origin and must find their ultimate guaranty in the faith of the people. If that faith should be lost, five or nine men in Washington could not long supply its want. Therefore we must do our utmost to make clear and easily understandable the reasons for deciding these cases as we do. Forthright observance of rights presupposes their forthright definition.

I think that the majority has failed in this duty. . . .

B. THE PREFERRED POSITION OF LOUDSPEAKERS

SAIA V. NEW YORK
334 U.S. 558, 566 (June 7, 1948)

Saia was an evangelist who used a sound truck to amplify the message he thrust upon Sunday picnickers in a public park. After repeated performances, he was arrested for using sound amplification equipment without a permit, this being against a municipal anti-noise ordinance. Although Stone was gone by the time this latter-day (for the Court) Jehovah's Witnesses case reached the Court, it was probably the religious overtones of the case which attracted what one otherwise would have expected to be the implausible vote of Chief Justice Vinson, and made it possible for the four libertarians to form a majority and reverse the defendant's conviction. This time, however, the reversal was based upon freedom of speech rather than on religious grounds. The majority viewed the local licensing authority, the chief of police, as a potential censor, although the Court did not rule that he had abused his discretion in this particular case. Nevertheless, the majority decided that a system under which a municipal official is able to make discriminatory decisions constitutes a prior restraint on speech, and is therefore unconstitutional in the light of the preferred position of First Amendment rights.

Reed, usually the most tender-minded member of the Vinson Court when claims of religious freedom were raised, joined with Burton in an opinion by Frankfurter which argued (as did Jackson) the implications for both individual privacy and mass recreation of a laissez-faire policy of free speech in the face of modern technological capabilities. In a small park such as the one in which Saia had broadcast, located in a suburban community at the fringe of a metropolitan area, unwilling listeners could walk away from a soap box orator, and find other parts of the park in which to seek repose; but there was no escape, in the Lockport Park, from Saia's sound truck—which explained, doubtless, why he chose to use that device.

MR. JUSTICE JACKSON, *dissenting.*

I dissent from this decision, which seems to me neither judicious nor sound and to endanger the great right of free speech by making it ridiculous and obnoxious, more than the ordinance in question menaces free speech by regulating use of loud speakers. Let us state some facts which the Court omits:

The City of Lockport, New York, owns and maintains a public park of some 28 acres dedicated by deed to "Park purposes exclusively." The scene of action in this case is an area therein set apart for the people's recreation. The City has provided it with tables, benches, and fireplaces for picnic parties, a playground and wading pool for children, and facilities for such games as horseshoe pitching, bowling and baseball.

The appellant, one of Jehovah's Witnesses, contends, and the Court holds, that without the permission required by city ordinance he may set up a sound truck so as to flood this area with amplified lectures on religious subjects. It must be remembered that he demands even more than the right to speak and hold a meeting in this area which is reserved for other and quite inconsistent purposes. He located his car, on which loud-speakers were mounted, either in the park itself, not open to vehicles, or in the street close by. The microphone for the speaker was located some little distance from the car and in the park, and electric wires were strung, in one or more instances apparently across the sidewalk from the one to the other. So that what the Court is holding, is that the Constitution of the United States forbids a city to require a permit for a private person to erect, in its streets, parks and public places, a temporary public address system, which certainly has potentialities of annoyance and even injury to park patrons if carelessly handled. It was for setting up this system of microphone, wires and sound truck without a permit, that this appellant was convicted—it was not for speaking. It

is astonishing news to me if the Constitution prohibits a municipality from policing, controlling or forbidding erection of such equipment by a private party in a
public park. . . .

The Court, however, . . . treats the issue only as one of free speech. To my
mind this is not a free speech issue. Lockport has in no way denied or restricted
the free use, even in its park, of all of the facilities for speech with which nature
has endowed the appellant. It has not even interfered with his inviting an assemblage in a park space not set aside for that purpose. But can it be that society has
no control of apparatus which, when put to unregulated proselyting, propaganda
and commercial uses, can render life unbearable? It is intimated that the City can
control the decibels; if so, why may it not prescribe zero decibels as appropriate
to some places? It seems to me that society has the right to control, as to place,
time and volume, the use of loud-speaking devices for any purpose, provided its
regulations are not unduly arbitrary, capricious or discriminatory.

But the Court points out that propagation of his religion is the avowed and
only purpose of appellant and holds that Lockport cannot stop the use of loud-
speaker systems on its public property for that purpose. If it is to be treated as
a case merely of religious teaching, I still could not agree with the decision. Only a
few weeks ago we held that the Constitution prohibits a state or municipality from
using tax-supported property to "aid religious groups to spread their faith."
McCollum v. *Board of Education,* 333 U.S. 203. Today we say it compels them
to let it be used for that purpose. In the one case the public property was appropriated to school uses; today it is public property appropriated and equipped
for recreational purposes. I think Lockport had the right to allocate its public
property to those purposes and to keep out of it installations of devices which
would flood the area with religious appeals obnoxious to many and thereby deprive the public of the enjoyment of the property for the purposes for which it
was properly set aside. And I cannot see how we can read the Constitution one
day to forbid and the next day to compel use of public tax-supported property to
help a religious sect spread its faith.

There is not the slightest evidence of discrimination or prejudice against the
appellant because of his religion or his ideas. This same appellant, not a resident
of Lockport but of Buffalo, by the way, was granted a permit by the Chief of
Police and used this park for four successive Sundays during the same summer in
question. What has been refused is his application for a second series of four more
uses of the park. Lockport is in a climate which has only about three months of
weather adaptable for park use. There are 256 recognized religious denominations
in the United States and, even if the Lockport populace supports only a few of
these, it is apparent that Jehovah's Witnesses were granted more than their share
of the Sunday time available on any fair allocation of it among denominations.

There is no evidence that any other denomination has ever been permitted to hold meetings or, for that matter, has ever sought to hold them in the recreation area. It appears that on one of the Sundays in question the Lutherans were using the ball park. This also appears to be public property. It is equipped with installed loud-speakers, a grandstand and bleachers, and surrounded by a fence six feet high. There is no indication that these facilities would not be granted to Jehovah's Witnesses on the same terms as to the Lutherans. It is evident, however, that Jehovah's Witnesses did not want an enclosed spot to which those who wanted to hear their message could resort. Appellant wanted to thrust their message upon people who were in the park for recreation, a type of conduct which invades other persons' privacy and, if it has no other control, may lead to riots and disorder.

The Court expresses great concern lest the loud-speakers of political candidates be controlled if Jehovah's Witnesses can be. That does not worry me. Even political candidates ought not to be allowed irresponsibly to set up sound equipment in all sorts of public places, and few of them would regard it as tactful campaigning to thrust themselves upon picnicking families who do not want to hear their message. I think the Court is over-concerned about danger to political candidacies and I would deal with that problem when, and if, it arises. . . .

I disagree entirely with the idea that "Courts must balance the various community interests in passing on the constitutionality of local regulations of the character involved here." It is for the local communities to balance their own interests—that is politics—and what courts should keep out of. . . .

The judgment of the Court of Appeals of New York should be affirmed.

C. THE RAUCOUS SOUND OF LABOR

KOVACS V. COOPER
336 U.S. 77, 97 (January 31, 1949)

In barely seven months, the "Court" had an opportunity to change its institutional mind on this issue. The result was an abrupt reversal of direction accomplished with the aid of some fancy brokenfield running by Reed, who wrote the opinion announcing the judgment of the Court. Reed's performance was notable because it involved a double contradiction of the normative parameters which, one learns from the law books, confine the discretion of the Court: his opinion upheld Kovacs' conviction on the basis of a different interpretation of the local ordinance in question, than had been given to it by the state courts of New Jersey; and a clear majority of the justices—the four libertarians plus Jackson—dis-

agreed with Reed's interpretation.[6] But Jackson continued to vote with
the Reed-Frankfurter-Burton group; and they were able to constitute the
majority in this decision because Vinson switched sides from what had
been his position in *Saia*. The critical difference between the two cases,
for Vinson, appeared to be the content of the messages broadcast by the
respective defendants.

Kovacs evidently was a union member who used his sound truck to
broadcast music and comment upon a labor dispute that was then in
progress. He broadcast what was indubitably a secular, if not a profane,
rather than a sacred, message; and he did so during ordinary working hours
on the public streets of the state capital city. Although there appeared to
be no explicit finding in the record before the Supreme Court of the volume of output in Kovacs' use of his equipment, Reed interpreted the
Trenton ordinance as prohibiting only "loud and raucous" noises; such a
standard was not unreasonable, so the prohibition did not violate the
Fourteenth Amendment on grounds of vagueness. Nor did this ordinance
violate any rights of freedom of speech, assembly, or communication
protected by the Fourteenth—as Reed was careful to put it, rather than
to invoke directly the First—Amendment. Here was no licensing procedure, subject to the possible caprice of a local official; instead, the city
forbade *any* use of mobile loudspeakers which would disturb the well-
being and tranquility of the community. This was, therefore, merely a
reasonable attempt to protect the privacy of citizens.

Of course, this was also precisely the policy for which the four dissenters in *Saia* had argued; and for Jackson and the four libertarians who
now found themselves in dissent, the proffered distinction between *Kovacs* and *Saia* was one without a difference.

At the end of his brief concurrence, Jackson indulges in a typical
"dissenter's lament" over the hopeless state of confusion in which the
law was now entangled, as a consequence of the devious machinations of
the Reed rationale for the majority outcome in this decision. But this
prediction, like most similar ones, proved to be overly pessimistic.[7] Local
communities, including the local police, got the Supreme Court's message: they could probably enforce most local anti-noise regulations,
without fear of frustration by the Supreme Court. And if *Kovacs* left
the Constitution in a state of confusion, it remains there still; for there

---

[6] Herman Pritchett, *Civil Liberties and the Vinson Court* (Chicago: University of
Chicago Press, 1954, p. 46.

[7] Cf. Jackson's needless concern (as it turned out) that the Court would be swamped
with released-time cases, and cast in the role of a "super board of education," as a consequence of the decision in *McCollum*, Chap. 2F, *supra*.

have been no subsequent decisions concerning the civil liberties of sound trucks.

MR. JUSTICE JACKSON, concurring.

I join the judgment sustaining the Trenton ordinance because I believe that operation of mechanical sound-amplifying devices conflicts with quiet enjoyment of home and park and with safe and legitimate use of street and market place, and that it is constitutionally subject to regulation or prohibition by the state or municipal authority. No violation of the Due Process Clause of the Fourteenth Amendment by reason of infringement of free speech arises unless such regulation or prohibition undertakes to censor the contents of the broadcasting. Freedom of speech for Kovacs does not, in my view, include freedom to use sound amplifiers to drown out the natural speech of others.

I do not agree that, if we sustain regulations or prohibitions of sound trucks, they must therefore be valid if applied to other methods of "communication of ideas." The moving picture screen, the radio, the newspaper, the handbill, the sound truck and the street corner orator have differing natures, values, abuses and dangers. Each, in my view, is a law unto itself, and all we are dealing with now is the sound truck.

But I agree with MR. JUSTICE BLACK that this decision is a repudiation of that in *Saia* v. *New York*, 334 U.S. 558. Like him, I am unable to find anything in this record to warrant a distinction because of "loud and raucous" tones of this machine. The *Saia* decision struck down a more moderate exercise of the state's police power than the one now sustained. Trenton, as the ordinance reads to me, unconditionally bans all sound trucks from the city streets. Lockport relaxed its prohibition with a proviso to allow their use, even in areas set aside for public recreation, when and where the Chief of Police saw no objection. Comparison of this our 1949 decision with our 1948 decision, I think, will pretty hopelessly confuse municipal authorities as to what they may or may not do.

I concur in the present result only for the reasons stated in dissent in *Saia* v. *New York*, 334 U.S. 558, 566.

D.   THE ANTI-CHRIST-KILLER

KUNZ V. NEW YORK
340 U.S. 290, 295 (January 15, 1951)

Jackson felt no great personal sympathy for union organizers, but he never questioned the legitimacy of their social role; and although he felt Jehovah's Witnesses clearly bordered upon the lunatic fringe of American political society, he also felt that they represented a form of corn-fed, home-grown, 100 percent native American religious fanaticism.[8] But, for him, Carl Jacob Kunz, the defendant in this case, was quite another matter, as evidenced by his sole dissent against an eight-man majority. This, in itself, was a somewhat unusual occurrence, because there were few civil liberties issues decided by the Supreme Court during Jackson's tenure in which it was possible for him to appear to be either the most liberal or the most conservative member of the participating justices.[9] The rest of the Court felt that Kunz presented less of a problem than did Saia or Kovacs, because he was a soap-box orator among the habitual speakers at Columbus Circle near Central Park; it is hard to imagine a more appropriate forum, in the American culture, in which he might claim to exercise his constitutional liberty of freedom of speech, unencumbered by any electronic paraphernalia or related problems of technology. However, Jackson objected, not to how Kunz spoke, but rather to what he said. Here we find Jackson assuming, both boldly and baldly, a posture which has not been common among Supreme Court justices since the Roosevelt revolution; that is, that speech which is evil in content can and ought to be suppressed, irrespective of the consequences ensuing from its utterance. Kunz evoked for Jackson a direct image of the Nazi pogroms against the German Jews.

In his argument, Jackson gives almost equal emphasis to the dangers of verbal attacks on race as to those on religion; and in this respect he anticipated the racial riots of Watts, Hough, and Newark and the long American summers of 1965, 1966, and 1967. There was one striking difference, however, and it is perhaps surprising that Jackson gave it so little weight, particularly when one considers the emphasis he placed upon the conspirational dimensions of Communist political activity—as a limit upon their right to file any claims of freedom of speech and of the press under the American constitution—in his opinions in *Douds*[10] and *Dennis*

[8] Herbert H. Stroup, *The Jehovah's Witnesses* (New York: Columbia University Press, 1945), p. 1; Edward A. Shils, "Authoritarianism: 'Right' and 'Left,'" *Studies in the Scope and Method of "The Authoritarian Personality,"* Richard Christie and Marie Jahoda, eds. (Glencoe, Illinois: The Free Press, 1954), pp. 24-49.

[9] Glendon Schubert, *The Judicial Mind*, (Evanston: Northwestern University Press, 1965), p. 125. During Jackson's last eight terms on the Court, after his return from Nuremburg, he participated in a total of 211 nonunanimous civil liberties decisions, and he dissented alone in only three of these cases (of which *Kunz* was, of course, one). *Ibid.*, pp. 104-107.

[10] In editing his opinion in that case for present purposes (Chap. 2D, *supra*), I have deleted almost all of Jackson's lengthy analysis of the facts and reasons that support his conclusion that the American Communist Party is a conspiracy, in the legal as well as the political sense of the word. See the first two parts of his opinion, which appear in pages 422-435 of *American Communications Association* v. *Douds*, 339 U.S. 382 (1950).

(*infra*). Although it is true that he was an ordained Baptist minister, there is no evidence in his case to suggest that he could call upon even the flimsy organizational resources available to the late George Lincoln Rockwell; Kunz was not a *national* facist leader like the perennial leader of the Silver Shirts, Gerald L. K. Smith. There was a vast difference between the opportunities for influence open to Kunz, and those available to contemporary headline hunters whose almost every word of public utterance will be reproduced for a worldwide audience by national wire services and TV networks: the self-styled comedian and Negro leader, Dick Gregory, is a case in point. For such a professed pragmatist as Jackson, one might have expected that the difference would be critical: society could tolerate soap-box orators, because the harm that they could do (that is, the change that could be expected to result from their oral efforts) would be minimal. Such was not the case, however; and soap-box orators like Kunz and that most callow of youths, college student Irving Feiner,[11] received just as short shrift at Jackson's hands as did the Secretary General of the Communist Party of the United States, Eugene Dennis. Nor did it really matter, as we shall observe presently in *Terminiello*, whether the local orator spoke in the streets, or in a hired hall to a self-selected audience who wanted to hear what he had to say. The real trouble with these zealots was that they were rabble rousers who appealed to the emotions rather than to the intellects of their auditors.

Near the end of his opinion, Jackson cites several of the Court's then recent decisions, which he finds to be something less than on all fours with each other, and utilizes that premise as the basis for coining the epigram, "It seems hypercritical to strike down local laws on their faces for want of standards when we have no standards." The manifest involution was, of course, intentional; but doubtless so also was the pun implicit in his carefully chosen adjective "hypercritical." He certainly meant it both ways.

MR. JUSTICE JACKSON, *dissenting.*

Essential freedoms are today threatened from without and within. It may become difficult to preserve here what a large part of the world has lost—the right to speak, even temperately, on matters vital to spirit and body. In such a setting, to blanket hateful and hate-stirring attacks on races and faiths under the protections for freedom of speech may be a noble innovation. On the other hand, it may be a quixotic tilt at windmills which belittles great principles of liberty.

---

[11] See *Feiner* v. *New York,* 340 U.S. 315 (1951); and Lucius J. Barker and Twiley W. Barker, Jr., *Freedoms, Courts, Politics: Studies in Civil Liberties* (Englewood Cliffs, New Jersey: Prentice-Hall, Inc., 1965), Chap. 2.

Only time can tell. But I incline to the latter view and cannot assent to the decision.

To know what we are doing, we must first locate the point at which rights asserted by Kunz conflict with powers asserted by the organized community. New York City has placed no limitation upon any speech Kunz may choose to make on private property, but it does require a permit to hold religious meetings in its streets. The ordinance, neither by its terms nor as it has been applied, prohibited Kunz, even in street meetings, from preaching his own religion or making any temperate criticism or refutation of other religions; indeed, for the year 1946, he was given a general permit to do so. His meetings, however, brought "a flood of complaints" to city authorities that he was engaging in scurrilous attacks on Catholics and Jews. On notice, he was given a hearing at which eighteen complainants appeared. The commissioner revoked his permit and applications for 1947 and 1948 were refused. For a time he went on holding meetings without a permit in Columbus Circle, where in September, 1948, he was arrested for violation of the ordinance. He was convicted and fined ten dollars.

At these meetings, Kunz preached, among many other things of like tenor, that "The Catholic Church makes merchandise out of souls," that Catholicism is "a religion of the devil," and that the Pope is "the anti-Christ." The Jews he denounced as "Christ-killers," and he said of them, "All the garbage that didn't believe in Christ should have been burnt in the incinerators. It's a shame they all weren't."

These utterances, as one might expect, stirred strife and threatened violence. Testifying in his own behalf, Kunz stated that he "become acquainted with" one of the complaining witnesses, whom he thought to be a Jew, "when he happened to sock one of my Christian boys in the puss." Kunz himself complained to the authorities, charging a woman interrupter with disorderly conduct. He also testified that when an officer is not present at his meetings "I have trouble then," but "with an officer, no trouble."

The contention which Kunz brings here and which this Court sustains is that such speeches on the streets are within his constitutional freedom and therefore New York City has no power to require a permit. He does not deny that this has been and will continue to be his line of talk.[12] He does not claim that he should have been granted a permit; he attacks the whole system of control of street meetings and says the Constitution gives him permission to speak and he needs none from the City. . . .

This Court today initiates the doctrine that language such as this, in the environment of the street meeting, is immune from prior municipal control. We would have a very different question if New York had presumed to say that Kunz

---

[12] . . . If there were otherwise any doubt that Kunz proposes to resume these attacks, it should be dispelled by the letters he has addressed to members of this Court asserting his right to do so and assailing, on religious grounds, judges who decided his case below.

could not speak his piece in his own pulpit or hall.[13] But it has undertaken to restrain him only if he chooses to speak at street meetings. There is a world of difference. The street preacher takes advantage of people's presence on the streets to impose his message upon what, in a sense, is a captive audience. A meeting on private property is made up of an audience that has volunteered to listen. The question, therefore, is not whether New York could, if it tried, silence Kunz, but whether it must place its streets at his service to hurl insults at the passer-by.

What Mr. Justice Holmes said for a unanimous Court in *Schenck* v. *United States*, 249 U. S. 47, 52, has become an axiom: "The most stringent protection of free speech would not protect a man in falsely shouting fire in a theatre and causing a panic." This concept was applied in one of its few unanimous decisions in recent years, when, through Mr. Justice Murphy, the Court said: "There are certain well-defined and narrowly limited classes of speech, *the prevention and punishment* of which *have never been thought to raise any Constitutional problem*. These include the lewd and obscene, the profane, the libelous, and *the insulting or 'fighting' words*—those which by their very utterance inflict injury or *tend to incite* an immediate breach of the peace. . . ." (Emphasis supplied.) *Chaplinsky* v. *New Hampshire,* 315 U. S. 568, 571-572.

There held to be "insulting or 'fighting' words" were calling one a "God damned racketeer" and a "damned Fascist." Equally inciting and more clearly "fighting words," when thrown at Catholics and Jews who are rightfully on the streets of New York, are statements that "The Pope is the anti-Christ" and the Jews are "Christ-killers." These terse epithets come down to our generation weighted with hatreds accumulated through centuries of bloodshed. They are recognized words of art in the profession of defamation. They are not the kind of insult that men bandy and laugh off when the spirits are high and the flagons are low. They are not in that class of epithets whose literal sting will be drawn if the speaker smiles when he uses them. They are always, and in every context, insults which do not spring from reason and can be answered by none. Their historical associations with violence are well understood, both by those who hurl and those who are struck by these missiles. Jews, many of whose families perished in extermination furnaces of Dachau and Auschwitz, are more than tolerant if they pass off lightly the suggestion that unbelievers in Christ should all have been burned. Of course, people might pass this speaker by as a mental case, and so they might file out of a theatre in good order at the cry of "fire." But in both cases there is genuine likelihood that someone will get hurt. . . .

And so the matter eventually comes down to the question whether the "words used are used in such circumstances and are of such a nature" that we can say a

---

[13] Cf. *Terminiello* v. *Chicago,* and footnote 20, both *infra.* this chapter. But perhaps (borrowing one of his own favorite quotations, from his opinion in the present case, at p. 312) we should recognize this assurance as "a promise to the ear to be broken to the hope." [Ed.]

reasonable man would anticipate the evil result. In this case the Court does not justify, excuse, or deny the inciting and provocative character of the language, and it does not, and on this record could not, deny that when Kunz speaks he poses a "clear and present" danger to peace and order. Why, then, does New York have to put up with it?

. . . Cities throughout the country have adopted permit requirements to control private activities on public streets and for other purposes. The universality of this type of regulation demonstrates a need and indicates widespread opinion in the profession that it is not necessarily incompatible with our constitutional freedoms. Is everybody out of step but this Court?

Until recently this custom of municipalities was regarded by this Court as consistent with the Constitution. It approved this identical ordinance in *Smith* v. *New York*, 292 U. S. 606. This decision is now overruled. . . .

The Court, as authority for stripping New York City of control of street meetings, resurrects *Saia* v. *New York*, [334 U. S. 558], which I, like some who now rely on it, had supposed was given decent burial by *Kovacs* v. *Cooper*, [336 U.S. 77]. Must New York, if it is to avoid chaos in its streets, resort to the sweeping prohibitions sanctioned in *Kovacs*, instead of the milder restraints of this permit system? Compelling a choice between allowing all meetings or no meetings is a dubious service to civil liberties.

Of course, as to the press, there are the best of reasons against any licensing or prior restraint. Decisions such as *Near* v. *Minnesota*, [283 U. S. 697, 708], hold any licensing or prior restraint of the press unconstitutional, and I heartily agree. But precedents from that field cannot reasonably be transposed to the street-meeting field. The impact of publishing on public order has no similarity with that of a street meeting. Publishing does not make private use of public property. It reaches only those who choose to read, and, in that way, is analogous to a meeting held in a hall where those who come do so by choice. Written words are less apt to incite or provoke to mass action than spoken words, speech being the primitive and direct communication with the emotions. Few are the riots caused by publication alone, few are the mobs that have not had their immediate origin in harangue. The vulnerability of various forms of communication to community control must be proportioned to their impact upon other community interests.

It is suggested that a permit for a street meeting could be required if the ordinance would prescribe precise standards for its grant or denial. This defect, if such it be, was just as apparent when, in the *Smith* case, this Court upheld the ordinance as it is today. The change must be found in the Court, not in the ordinance.

And what, in terms of its philosophy of decision, is this change? It is to require more severe and exacting standards of state and local statutes than of federal statutes.

. . . But I do not see how this Court can condemn municipal ordinances for not setting forth comprehensive First Amendment standards. This Court never has announced what those standards must be, it does not now say what they are, and it is not clear that any majority could agree on them. In no field are there more numerous individual opinions among the Justices. The Court as an institution not infrequently disagrees with its former self or relies on distinctions that are not very substantial. Compare *Jones* v. *Opelika* of 1942, 316 U. S. 584, with *Jones* v. *Opelika* of 1943, 319 U. S. 103; *Minersville School District* v. *Gobitis* of 1940, 310 U. S. 586, with *Board of Education* v. *Barnette* of 1943, 319 U. S. 624; *Saia* v. *New York* of 1948, *supra*, with *Kovacs* v. *Cooper* of 1949, *supra*. It seems hypercritical to strike down local laws on their faces for want of standards when we have no standards.[14] . . .

It is obvious that a permit is a source of security and protection for the civil liberties of the great number who are entitled to receive them. It informs the police of the time and place one intends to speak, which allows necessary steps to insure him a place to speak where overzealous police officers will not order everyone who stops to listen to move on, and to have officers present to insure an orderly meeting. Moreover, disorder is less likely, for the speaker knows that if he provokes disorder his permit may be revoked, and the objector may be told that he has a remedy by filing a complaint and does not need to take the law in his own hands. Kunz was not arrested in 1946, when his speeches caused serious objections, nor was he set upon by the crowd. Instead, they did the orderly thing and made complaints which resulted in the revocation of his permit. This is the method that the Court frustrates today. . . .

The law of New York does not segregate, according to their diverse nationalities, races, religions, or political associations, the vast hordes of people living in its narrow confines. Every individual in this frightening aggregation is legally free to live, to labor, to travel, when and where he chooses. In streets and

---

[14] It seems fair to contrast the precision which the Court imposes on municipalities with the standards set forth in the recent Act "Relating to the policing of the building and grounds of the Supreme Court of the United States." 63 Stat. 616. That makes it unlawful to "make any harangue or oration, or utter loud, threatening, or abusive language in the Supreme Court Building or grounds." . . . Moreover, it authorizes the Marshall to "prescribe such regulations, approved by the Chief Justice of the United States, as may be deemed necessary for the adequate protection of the Supreme Court Building and grounds and of persons and property therein, and for the maintenance of suitable order and decorum within the Supreme Court Building and grounds." § 7. Violation of these provisions or regulations is an offense punishable by fine and imprisonment. . . .

Here is exalted artistry in declaring crime without definition and authorizing permits without standards for use of public property for speaking. Of course, the statute would not be reported by the Judiciary Committees without at least informal approval of the Justices. The contrast between the standards set up for cities and those for ourselves suggests that our theorizing may be imposing burdens upon municipal authorities which are impossible or at least impractical to comply with.

public places, all races and nationalities and all sorts and conditions of men walk, linger and mingle. Is it not reasonable that the City protect the dignity of these persons against fanatics who take possession of its streets to hurl into its crowds defamatory epithets that hurt like rocks?

If any two subjects are intrinsically incendiary and divisive, they are race and religion. Racial fears and hatreds have been at the root of the most terrible riots that have disgraced American civilization. They are ugly possibilities that overhang every great American city. The "consecrated hatreds of sect" account for more than a few of the world's bloody disorders. These are the explosives which the Court says Kunz may play with in the public streets, and the community must not only tolerate but aid him. I find no such doctrine in the Constitution....

Addressing himself to the subject, "Authority and the Individual," one of the keenest philosophers of our time [Bertrand Russell] observes: "The problem, like all those with which we are concerned, is one of balance; too little liberty brings stagnation, and too much brings chaos." Perhaps it is the fever of our times that inclines the Court today to favor chaos. My hope is that few will take advantage of the license granted by today's decision. But life teaches one to distinguish between hope and faith.

E. FASCIST FORENSICS

TERMINIELLO V. CHICAGO
337 U.S. 1, 13 (May 16, 1949)

This is one of the last important civil liberties decisions dominated by the libertarian four, and it is certainly one of the most aborted deliveries of the Supreme Court. Terminiello was a cohort of American fascist leader Gerald L. K. Smith, and he was arrested for disorderly conduct for having incited a mob of his sympathizers to slug it out with a surrounding mob of persons hostile to Father Terminiello and his message. What was remarkable about the Supreme Court's disposition of this case was the avoidance of any decision on the issue of Terminiello's claim that his speech was protected by the First Amendment, notwithstanding the fact that eight of the nine participating justices would have preferred to rule on precisely that question. The difficulty was that these eight were equally divided in regard to the proper *direction* of such a decision on the freedom of speech claim. Douglas, Murphy, Rutledge, and Black favored a reversal of Terminiello's conviction, which had been previously upheld by three different Illinois courts. Vinson, Frankfurter, Burton, and Jackson were at least as favorable to an affirmance. Under these circumstances, the odd man, Reed, held the key to the outcome; and, although he was willing to vote to reverse the priest's conviction, he was *not* willing to lend his support to any opinion of the Court that would extend the libertarian dogma in behalf of free speech any further than the dangerous extremes to which it already had been pushed by the other members of the majority in previous decisions.[15] The solution to this dilemma, which according to the Chief Justice was "ferreted out" by Douglas' "independent research,"[16] was to base the decision on an exceptionally narrow ground of procedural due process: the oral charge of the jury, by the trial judge, was said (by the present Supreme Court majority) to have been ambiguous and imprecise in its explanation of the municipal ordinance defining disorderly conduct under which Terminiello had been tried and convicted. According to Frankfurter—in dissent, of course— this marked the first time in the history of the Court that a state supreme court was reversed on a point that had not been raised or argued before it (or before either of the two lower state courts). Indeed, the point was not objected to at the time of the trial, and had even been explicitly disclaimed by Terminiello's attorney as a ground upon which he relied in his appeal, in his argument before the Supreme Court.

None of the other opinions—that of Douglas for the Court, or of the Chief Justice and Frankfurter, in dissent—discussed the facts or the merits of the constitutional issues raised by Terminiello's claim, so Jackson did. And he had special reasons for protesting the Court's avoidance of what, to him, was a crucial question of democratic theory; that is, whether what many American political scientists term "the political struggle" among contending interest groups is going to be fought out through the structure of the political party system and the electoral processss—or with boots and brass knuckles in the streets. Jackson was much too close to the lesson of the downfall of the Weimar Republic—he was still at Nuremburg only three years prior to the announcement of this decision—not to interpret from the perspective of the German experience what was in reality (as we can observe with the benefit of hindsight) a relatively small-scale local disturbance that Chicago was quite competent to handle. In the light of

[15] Among the eighteen justices who served on the Supreme Court during the period from the end of World War II through June 1963, Reed ranked last in support of civil liberties. Moreover, his vote in behalf of Terminiello is denoted, in a scale of the civil liberties decisions of the 1948 Term, as a clear inconsistency; this was Reed's only inconsistent vote in those thirty decisions, which included only one other vote (besides his "error" in *Terminiello*) sympathetic to a civil liberties claim. Schubert, *The Judicial Mind*, pp. 123, 105.

[16] 337 U.S. 1, 7.

Jackson's unique socialization and consequent sensitization to this dimension of the issue raised by Terminiello, it is quite understandable that the record of Nazi internal aggression, which had been a necessary prelude to the external aggression that Jackson had worked so diligently to document,[17] was uppermost in his mind. It is also readily understandable, however, that his colleagues, lacking his special conditioning on the subject of riots as a political weapon, should have taken a more dispassionate view of the danger of the threat presented to the American polity by thunder on the right.

MR. JUSTICE JACKSON, dissenting.

The Court reverses this conviction by reiterating generalized approbations of freedom of speech with which, in the abstract, no one will disagree. Doubts as to their applicability are lulled by avoidance of more than passing reference to the circumstances of Terminiello's speech and judging it as if he had spoken to persons as dispassionate as empty benches, or like a modern Demosthenes practicing his Philippics on a lonely seashore.

But the local court that tried Terminiello was not indulging in theory. It was dealing with a riot and with a speech that provoked a hostile mob and incited a friendly one, and threatened violence between the two. When the trial judge instructed the jury that it might find Terminiello guilty of inducing a breach of the peace if his behavior stirred the public to anger, invited dispute, brought about unrest, created a disturbance or molested peace and quiet by arousing alarm, he was not speaking of these as harmless or abstract conditions. He was addressing his words to the concrete behavior and specific consequences disclosed by the evidence. He was saying to the jury, in effect, that if this particular speech added fuel to the situation already so inflamed as to threaten to get beyond police control, it could be punished as inducing a breach of peace. When the light of the evidence not recited by the Court is thrown upon the Court's opinion, it discloses that underneath a little issue of Terminiello and his hundred-dollar fine lurk some of the most far-reaching constitutional questions that can confront a people who value both liberty and order. This Court seems to regard these as enemies of each other and to be of the view that we must forego order to achieve liberty. So it fixes its eyes on a conception of freedom of speech so rigid as to tolerate no concession to society's need for public order.

An old proverb warns us to take heed lest we "walk into a well from looking at the stars." To show why I think the Court is in some danger of doing that, I must bring these deliberations down to earth by a long recital of facts.

Terminiello, advertised as a Catholic Priest, but revealed at the trial to be

---

[17] See Robert H. Jackson, *The Case Against the Nazi War Criminals: Opening Statement for the United States of America* (New York: Alfred A. Knopf, Inc., 1946).

under suspension by his Bishop, was brought to Chicago from Birmingham, Alabama, to address a gathering that assembled in response to a call signed by Gerald L. K. Smith, which, among other things, said:

"... The same people who hate Father Coughlin hate Father Terminiello. They have persecuted him, hounded him, threatened him, but he has remained unaffected by their anti-Christian campaign against him. You will hear all sorts of reports concerning Father Terminiello. But remember that he is a Priest in good standing and a fearless lover of Christ and America."

The jury may have considered that this call attempted to capitalize the hatreds this man had stirred and foreshadowed, if it did not intend to invite, the kind of demonstration that followed.

Terminiello's own testimony shows the conditions under which he spoke. So far as material it follows:

"... We got there [the meeting place] approximately fifteen or twenty minutes past eight. The car stopped at the front entrance. There was a crowd of three or four hundred congregated there shouting and cursing and picketing. . . .

"When we got there the pickets were not marching; they were body to body and covered the sidewalk completely, some on the steps so that we had to form a flying wedge to get through. Police escorted us to the building, and I noticed four or five others there.

"They called us 'God damned Fascists, Nazis, ought to hang the so and sos.' When I entered the building I heard the howls of the people outside. . . ."

The court below, in addition to this recital, heard other evidence, that the crowd reached an estimated number of 1,500. Picket lines obstructed and interfered with access to the building. The crowd constituted a "surging, howling mob hurling epithets" at those who would enter and "tried to tear their clothes off." One young woman's coat was torn off and she had to be assisted into the meeting by policemen. Those inside the hall could hear the loud noises and hear those on the outside yell, "Fascists," "Hitlers" and curse words like "damn Fascists." Bricks were thrown through the windowpanes before and during the speaking. About twenty-eight windows were broken. The street was black with people on both sides for at least a block either way; bottles, stink bombs and brickbats were thrown. Police were unable to control the mob, which kept breaking the windows at the meeting hall, drowning out the speaker's voice at times and breaking in through the back door of the auditorium. About 17 of the group outside were arrested by the police.

Knowing of this enviroment, Terminiello made a long speech, from the stenographic record of which I omit relatively innocuous passages and add emphasis to what seems especially provocative:

"Father Terminiello: Now, I am going to whisper my greetings to you, Fellow Christians. I will interpret it. I said, 'Fellow *Christians*,' and I suppose there are *some of the scum got in by mistake*, so I want to tell a story about *the scum:*

"... And nothing I could say tonight could begin to express the contempt I have for the *slimy scum* that got in by mistake.

"... The subject I want to talk to you tonight about is the attempt *that is going on right outside this hall tonight,* the attempt that is going on to *destroy America by revolution....*

"... I am not going to talk to you about the menace of Communism, which is already accomplished, in Russia, where from eight to fifteen million people were murdered in cold blood by their own countrymen, and millions more through Eastern Europe at the close of the war are being murdered by these murderous Russians, hurt, being raped and sent into slavery. *That is what they want for you, that howling mob outside....*

"*That is what they want for us, a blood-soaked reality but it was promised to us by the crystal gazers in Washington;* and you know what I mean by the 'crystal gazers,' I presume.

"First of all, we had Queen Eleanor. Mr. Smith said, 'Queen Eleanor is now one of the world's communists.['] She is one who said this—imagine, coming from the spouse of the former President of the United States for twelve long years—this is what she said: 'The war is but a step in the revolution. The war is but one step in the revolution, and we know who started the war.' ...

"*You will know who is behind it when I tell you the story* of a doctor in Akron, Ohio. He boasted to a friend of mine within the last few days, while he was in the service of this country as a doctor, he and others of his kind made it a practice—now, this was not only one man—made it a practice to amputate the limbs of every German they came in contact with whenever they could get away with it; so, that they could never carry a gun. Imagine men of that caliber, sworn to serve this beautiful country of ours, *why should we tolerate them?*

"My friends, this moment someone reminded me of the plan to sterilize them. The nurses, they tell me are going to inject diseases in them, syphilis and other diseases in *every one that came there all of one race, all non-Christians....*

"Now, let me say, I am going to talk about—I almost said, about the Jews. Of course, I would not want to say that. However, I am going to talk about some Jews. I hope that—I am a Christian minister. We must take a Christian attitude. I don't want you to go from this hall with hatred in your heart for any person, for no person....

"Now, this danger which we face—let us call them Zionist Jews if you will, let's call them atheistic, communistic Jewish or Zionist Jews, then let us not fear to condemn them. You remember the Apostles when they went into the upper room after the death of the Master, they went in there, after locking the doors; they closed the windows. (At this time there was a very loud noise as if something was being thrown into the building.)

"Don't be disturbed. That happened, by the way, while Mr. Gerald Smith was saying 'Our Father who art in heaven'; (just then a rock went through the window.) *Do you wonder they were persecuted in other countries in the world? ...*

"*You know I have always made a study of the psychology, sociology of mob reaction. It is exemplified out there.* Remember there has to be a leader to that mob. He is not out there. He is probably across the street, looking out the window. There must be certain things, money, other things in order to have successful mob action; there must be rhythm. There must be some to beat a cadence. Those mobs are chanting; that is the caveman's chant. They were trained to do it. They were trained this afternoon. They are being led; *there will be violence....*"

Such was the speech. Evidence showed that it stirred the audience not only to cheer and applaud but to expressions of immediate anger, unrest and alarm.

One called the speaker a "God damned liar" and was taken out by the police. Another said that "Jews, niggers and Catholics would have to be gotten rid of." One response was, "Yes, the Jews are all killers, murderers. If we don't kill them first, they will kill us." The anti-Jewish stories elicited exclamations of "Oh!" and "Isn't that terrible!" and shouts of "Yes, send the Jews back to Russia," "Kill the Jews," "Dirty kikes," and much more of ugly tenor. This is the specific and concrete kind of anger, unrest and alarm, coupled with that of the mob outside, that the trial court charged the jury might find to be a breach of peace induced by Terminiello. It is difficult to believe that this Court is speaking of the same occasion, but it is the only one involved in this litigation.

Terminiello, of course, disclaims being a fascist. Doubtless many of the indoor audience were not consciously such. His speech, however, followed, with fidelity that is more than coincidental, the pattern of European fascist leaders.

The street mob, on the other hand, included some who deny being communists, but Terminiello testified and offered to prove that the demonstration was communist-organized and communist-led. He offered literature of left-wing organizations calling members to meet and "mobilize" for instruction as pickets and exhorting followers: "All out to fight Fascist Smith."

As this case declares a nation-wide rule that disables local and state authorities from punishing conduct which produces conflicts of this kind, it is unrealistic not to take account of the nature, methods and objectives of the forces involved. This was not an isolated, spontaneous and unintended collision of political, racial or ideological adversaries. It was a local manifestation of a worldwide and standing conflict between two organized groups of revolutionary fanatics, each of which has imported to this country the strong-arm technique developed in the struggle by which their kind has devastated Europe. Increasingly, American cities have to cope with it. One faction organizes a mass meeting, the other organizes pickets to harass it; each organizes squads to counteract the other's pickets; parade is met with counterparade. Each of these mass demonstrations has the potentiality, and more than a few the purpose, of disorder and violence. This technique appeals not to reason but to fears and mob spirit; each is a show of force designed to bully adversaries and to overawe the indifferent. We need not resort to speculation as to the purposes for which these tactics are calculated nor as to their consequences. Recent European history demonstrates both.

Hitler summed up the strategy of the mass demonstration as used by both fascism and communism: "We should not work in secret conventicles, but in mighty mass demonstrations, and it is not by dagger and poison or pistol that the road can be cleared for the movement but *by the conquest of the streets*. We must teach the Marxists that the future *master of the streets* is National Socialism, just as it will some day be the master of the state." (Emphasis supplied.) 1 *Nazi Conspiracy and Aggression* (GPO, 1946) 204, 2 *id.* 140, Docs. 2760-PS, 404-PS, from *"Mein Kampf."* First laughed at as an extravagant figure of speech, the battle for the streets became a tragic reality when an organized *Sturmabteilung* began to give practical effect to its slogan that "possession of the streets is the key to power in the state." *Ibid.,* also Doc. 2168-PS.

The present obstacle to mastery of the streets by either radical or reactionary mob movements is not the opposing minority. It is the authority of local governments which represent the free choice of democratic and law-abiding elements of all shades of opinion, but who, whatever their differences, submit them to free elections which register the results of their free discussion. The fascist and communist groups, on the contrary, resort to these terror tactics to confuse, bully and discredit those freely chosen governments. Violent and noisy shows of strength discourage participation of moderates in discussions so fraught with violence and real discussion dries up and disappears. And people lose faith in the democratic process when they see public authority flouted and impotent and begin to think the time has come when they must choose sides in a false and terrible dilemma such as was posed as being at hand by the call for the Terminiello meeting: "Christian Nationalism or World Communism—Which?"

This drive by totalitarian groups to undermine the prestige and effectiveness of local democratic governments is advanced whenever either of them can win from this Court a ruling which paralyzes the power of these officials. This is such a case. The group of which Terminiello is a part claims that his behavior, because it involved a speech, is above the reach of local authorities. If the mild action those authorities have taken is forbidden, it is plain that hereafter there is nothing effective left that they can do. If they can do nothing as to him, they are equally powerless as to rival totalitarian groups. Terminiello's victory today certainly fulfills the most extravagant hopes of both right and left totalitarian groups, who want nothing so much as to paralyze and discredit the only democratic authority that can curb them in their battle for the streets.

I am unable to see that the local authorities have transgressed the Federal Constitution. Illinois imposed no prior censorship or suppression upon Terminiello. On the contrary, its sufferance and protection was all that enabled him to speak. . . .

Rioting is a substantive evil, which I take it no one will deny that the State and the City have the right and the duty to prevent and punish. Where an offense is induced by speech, the Court has laid down and often reiterated a test of the power of the authorities to deal with the speaking as also an offense. "The question in every case is whether the words *used are used in such circumstances* and are of *such a nature* as to create a *clear and present danger* that they will bring about the substantive evils that Congress [or the State or City] has a right to prevent." (Emphasis supplied.) Mr. Justice Holmes in *Schenck* v. *United States,* 249 U. S. 47, 52. No one ventures to contend that the State on the basis of this test, for whatever it may be worth, was not justified in punishing Terminiello. In this case the evidence proves beyond dispute that danger of rioting and violence in response to the speech was clear, present and immediate. . . . Quite apart from any other merits or defects, [however,] recent decisions have almost completely immunized this battle for the streets from any form of control. . . .

I do not think we should carry this handicap further, as we do today, but should adhere to the principles heretofore announced to safeguard our liberties against abuse as well as against invasion. It should not be necessary to recall these elementary principles, but it has been a long time since some of them were even mentioned in this Court's writing on the subject and results indicate they may have been overlooked.

I begin with the oft-forgotten principle which this case demonstrates, that freedom of speech exists only under law and not independently of it. What would Terminiello's theoretical freedom of speech have amounted to had he not been given active aid by the officers of the law? He could reach the hall only with their help, could talk only because they restrained the mob, and could make his get-away only under their protection. . . .

No one will disagree that the fundamental, permanent and overriding policy of police and courts should be to permit and encourage utmost freedom of utterance. . . .

But we must bear in mind also that no serious outbreak of mob violence, race rioting, lynching or public disorder is likely to get going without help of some speech-making to some mass of people. A street may be filled with men and women and the crowd still not be a mob. Unity of purpose, passion and hatred, which merges the many minds of a crowd into the mindlessness of a mob, almost invariably is supplied by speeches. It is naive, or worse, to teach that oratory with this object or effect is a service to liberty. No mob has ever protected any liberty, even its own, but if not put down it always winds up in an orgy of lawlessness which respects no liberties.

. . . [W]hile peaceful advocacy of communism or fascism is tolerated by the law, both of these doctrines arouse passionate reactions. A great number of people do not agree that introduction to America of communism or fascism is even debatable. Hence many speeches, such as that of Terminiello, may be legally permissible but may nevertheless in some surroundings be a menace to peace and order. When conditions show the speaker that this is the case, as it did here, there certainly comes a point beyond which he cannot indulge in provocations to violence without being answerable to society.

Determination of such an issue involves a heavy responsibility. Courts must beware lest they become mere organs of popular intolerance. Not every show of opposition can justify treating a speech as a breach of peace. Neither speakers nor courts are obliged always and in all circumstances to yield to prevailing opinion and feeling. As a people grow in capacity for civilization and liberty their tolerance will grow, and they will endure, if not welcome, discussion even on topics as to which they are committed. They regard convictions as tentative and know that time and events will make their own terms with theories, by whomever and by whatever majorities they are held, and many will be proved wrong. But on our way to this idealistic state of tolerance the police have to deal with men as they are. The crowd mind is never tolerant of any idea which does not conform to its herd opinion. It does not want a tolerant effort at meeting of minds. It does not know the futility of trying to mob an idea. Released from the sense of personal responsibility that would restrain even the worst individuals in it if alone and brave with the courage of numbers, both radical and reactionary mobs endanger liberty as well as order. The authorities must control them and they are entitled to place some checks upon those whose behavior or speech calls such mobs into being. When the right of society to freedom from probable violence should prevail over the right of an individual to defy opposing opinion, presents a problem that always tests wisdom and often calls for immediate and vigorous action to preserve public order and safety.

I do not think that the Constitution of the United States denies to the states and the municipalities power to solve that problem in the light of local conditions, at least so long as danger to public order is not invoked in bad faith, as a cover for censorship or suppression. The preamble declares domestic tranquility as well as liberty to be an object in founding a Federal government and I do not think the Forefathers were naive in believing both can be fostered by the law.

Certain practical reasons reinforce the legal view that cities and states should be sustained in the power to keep their streets from becoming the battleground for these hostile ideologies to the destruction and detriment of public order. There is no other power that can do it. Theirs are the only police that are on the spot. The Federal Government has no police force. The Federal Bureau of Investigation is, and should remain, not a police but an investigative service. To date, the only federal agency for preserving and restoring order when local authority fails has been the Army. And when the military steps in, the court takes a less liberal view of the rights of the individual and sustains most arbitrary exercises of military power. See *Korematsu* v. *United States,* 323 U.S. 214. Every failure of local authority to deal with riot problems results in a demand for the establishment of a federal police or intervention by federal authority. In my opinion, locally established and controlled police can never develop into the menace to general civil liberties that is inherent in a federal police.

The ways in which mob violence may be worked up are subtle and various. Rarely will a speaker directly urge a crowd to lay hands on a victim or class of victims. An effective and safer way is to incite mob action while pretending to deplore it, after the classic example of Antony, and this was not lost on Terminiello. . . .

Invocation of constitutional liberties as part of the strategy for overthrowing them presents a dilemma to a free people which may not be soluble by constitutional logic alone.

But I would not be understood as suggesting that the United States can or should meet this dilemma by suppression of free, open and public speaking on the part of any group or ideology. Suppression has never been a successful permanent policy; any surface serenity that it creates is a false security, while conspiratorial forces go underground. My confidence in American institutions and in the sound sense of the American people is such that if with a stroke of the pen I could silence every fascist and communist speaker, I would not do it. . . .

But if we maintain a general policy of free speaking, we must recognize that its inevitable consequence will be sporadic local outbreaks of violence, for it is the nature of men to be intolerant of attacks upon institutions, personalities and ideas for which they really care. In the long run, maintenance of free speech will be more endangered if the population can have no protection from the abuses which lead to violence. . . .

This Court has gone far toward accepting the doctrine that civil liberty means the removal of all restraints from these crowds and that all local attempts to maintain order are impairments of the liberty of the citizen. The choice is not between order and liberty.[18] It is between liberty with order and anarchy without either. There is danger that, if the Court does not temper its doctrinaire logic with a little practical wisdom, it will convert the constitutional Bill of Rights into a suicide pact.

I would affirm the conviction.

F. THE COMMUNIST CONSPIRACY

DENNIS V. UNITED STATES
341 U.S. 494, 561 (June 4, 1951)

When Eugene Dennis and his co-defendants, ten other top national leaders of the Communist Party, were tried and convicted in a celebrated trial before that paragon of judicial virtue, Harold Medina, they were

---

[18] "Liberty," he said a few years later in his farewell speech to the bar, "is not self-supporting, but is the child of a just and stable legal order. An immunity which too far undermines government would be self-destructive, while today's infringement of liberty may purpose its long-range preservation. One of the paradoxes of our history is that the administration of Mr. Lincoln, most prolific in invasion of individual rights, is most commemorated for its over-all service to human liberty. It is especially difficult to judge between immediate loss and ultimate gain to liberty when there is an organized movement to make the rights of some a weapon to destroy the rights of all. A balance suitable to one time or condition may not be valid for others. Not every defeat of authority is a gain for individual freedom, nor every judicial rescue of a convict a victory for liberty." Robert H. Jackson, "The Task of Maintaining Our Liberties: The Role of the Judiciary," *American Bar Association Journal*, XXXIX (1953), 964. [Ed.]

described by stalwart J. Edgar Hoover as "the most dangerous men in America." Their offense was that of conspiring to advocate the overthrow of the United States government by force and violence. This they did by sponsoring the distribution of, and instruction in, books such as *Capital* and *Little Lessons in Leninism*. Their guilt lay not in the use of such books for purposes of instruction—for hundreds of college and other classes in political science and related subjects do that, throughout the year, every year—but rather in believing what they preached, and in trying to convince students to believe also. The issue seemed to be homologous to that raised by Benjamin J. Gitlow, a national Communist Party leader of an earlier generation who was similarly tried and convicted, after World War I,[19] for teaching the Communist Manifesto which Marx and Engels had drafted and published long before the Civil War. Dennis and his crowd were tried under a federal statute but Gitlow was tried under a state statute; therefore, the Court deemed differences appropriate to the rationalization of the Constitution to fit the two situations. But that distinction is quite beside the point of the underlying issue: whether freedom of speech includes advocacy of the right of revolution? Only Holmes and Brandeis protested the affirmance of Gitlow's conviction in 1925; and a quarter of a century later, the interposition of the Court-packing episode of 1937 and Franklin Roosevelt's "reform" of the Court made no difference in the Supreme Court's processing of this kind of fundamental issue. Again the vote was 6-2 against the defendant; and only Black and Douglas voted to reverse the conviction of Dennis *et al.*

There was no opinion of the Court, because the six-man majority split behind a plurality opinion authored by Vinson, and independent concurrences written by Frankfurter and Jackson. Black and Douglas each wrote a separate dissenting opinion, so there were five opinions in all, no one of which really could make any higher claim to precedential authority than any of the others, under the strict legal concept of *stare decisis*, although the political tendency has been to treat Vinson's plurality opinion as the official rationale of the Court for the decision. The Chief Justice took advantage of the opportunity, presented by such well-known defendants and a well-publicized case, to attempt one of his few contributions to the constitutional law of civil liberties, by embracing the elderly Learned Hand (Chief Judge of the court immediately below, the United States Court of Appeals for the Second Circuit) as authority for a revitalized conception of the "clear and present danger" test. The Community Party itself, announced Vinson, was a menace to the peace and security of the United States for it constituted a clear and present danger of a

19 *Gitlow* v. *New York,* 268 U.S. 652 (1925).

substantive evil (revolution) which Congress has a right to prevent; therefore, the Smith Act was declared to be constitutional, and the Dennis
group properly adjudged guilty under it. Both Black and Douglas argued
that the statute was unconstitutional, and Frankfurter refused to join in
the Vinson opinion, because he felt that the Court should not decide
whether or not Communists were a clear and present danger to national
security; that issue already having been resolved, against the Communists, by the appropriate decision makers on such an issue—the President
and Congress. By Frankfurter's logic, the only relevant query was whether
Congress had the authority to enact a law to protect the national security
in war time—the Smith Act was adopted on the threshhold of World
War II—by outlawing groups of revolutionaries; if so, that was the end of
the matter. Jackson also refused to accept the Vinson rationale and
seemed to arrive at the same conclusion as Frankfurter, but he deemed the
circumstance appropriate for an independent expression of his own views.
He wished to demonstrate not only that the Congress should and the
Supreme Court should not make basic decisions defining political crimes
and criminals, but also that, in this particular instance, the notorious
political facts about the Communist Party showed that Congress had arrived at the correct conclusion. This argument is the more anomalous in
that Jackson emphasizes throughout the same opinion how incompetent
judges are to make the very appraisal that he so clearly proffers as the
right answer to the problem posed by the Communist conspiracy.

MR. JUSTICE JACKSON, *concurring.*

This prosecution is the latest of never-ending, because never successful,
quests for some legal formula that will secure an existing order against revolutionary radicalism. It requires us to reappraise, in the light of our own times and
conditions, constitutional doctrines devised under other circumstances to strike
a balance between authority and liberty.

Activity here charged to be criminal is conspiracy—that defendants conspired to teach and advocate, and to organize the Communist Party to teach and
advocate, overthrow and destruction of the Government by force and violence.
There is no charge of actual violence or attempt at overthrow.

The principal reliance of the defense in this Court is that the conviction
cannot stand under the Constitution because the conspiracy of these defendants
presents no "clear and present danger" of imminent or foreseeable overthrow.

The statute before us repeats a pattern, originally devised to combat the
wave of anarchistic terrorism that plagued this country about the turn of the
century, which lags at least two generations behind Communist Party techniques.

Anarchism taught a philosophy of extreme individualism and hostility to government and property. Its avowed aim was a more jus order, to be achieved by violent destruction of all government. Anarchism's sporadic and uncoordinated acts of terror were not integrated with an effective revolutionary machine, but the Chicago Haymarket riots of 1886, attempted murder of the industrialist Frick, attacks on state officials, and assassination of President McKinley in 1901, were fruits of its preaching.

However, extreme individualism was not conducive to cohesive and disciplined organization. Anarchism fell into disfavor among incendiary radicals, many of whom shifted their allegiance to the rising Communist Party. Meanwhile, in Europe anarchism had been displaced by Bolshevism as the doctrine and strategy of social and political upheaval. Led by intellectuals hardened by revolutionary experience, it was a more sophisticated, dynamic and realistic movement. Establishing a base in the Soviet Union, it founded an aggressive international Communist apparatus which has modeled and directed a revolutionary movement able only to harass our own country. But it has seized control of a dozen other countries.

Communism, the antithesis of anarchism, appears today as a closed system of thought representing Stalin's version of Lenin's version of Marxism. As an ideology, it is not one of spontaneous protest arising from American working-class experience. It is a complicated system of assumptions, based on European history and conditions, shrouded in an obscure and ambiguous vocabulary, which allures our ultrasophisticated intelligentsia more than our hard-headed working people.[20] From time to time it champions all manner of causes and grievances and makes alliances that may add to its foothold in government or embarrass the authorities.

The Communist Party, nevertheless, does not seek its strength primarily in numbers. Its aim is a relatively small party whose strength is in selected, dedicated, indoctrinated and rigidly disciplined members. From established policy it tolerates no deviation and no debate. It seeks members that are, or may be, secreted in strategic posts in transportation, communications, industry, government, and especially in labor unions where it can compel employers to accept and retain its members. It also seeks to infiltrate and control organizations of professional and other groups. Through these placements in positions of power it seeks a leverage over society that will make up in power of coercion what it lacks in power of persuasion.

The Communists have no scruples against sabotage, terrorism, assassination,

[20] For some empirical evidence bearing upon the beliefs and values of hard-headed workingmen, see Robert E. Lane, *Political Ideology* (New York: The Free Press of Glencoe, 1962); Herbert McClosky, "Consensus and Ideology in American Politics," *American Political Science Review*, LVIII (1964), 366-369; and Hans J. Eysenck's discussion of "tough-minded radicalism" in his *The Psychology of Politics* (London: Routledge and Kegan Paul, 1954), pp. 128-142. [Ed.]

or mob disorder; but violence is not with them, as with the anarchists, an end in itself. The Communist Party advocates force only when prudent and profitable. Their strategy of stealth precludes premature or uncoordinated outbursts of violence, except, of course, when the blame will be placed on shoulders other than their own. They resort to violence as to truth, not as a principle but as an expedient. Force or violence, as they would resort to it, may never be necessary, because infiltration and deception may be enough.

. . . [T]he Communist stratagem outwits the anti-anarchist pattern of statute aimed against "overthrow by force and violence" if qualified by the doctrine that only "clear and present danger" of accomplishing that result will sustain the prosecution.

The "clear and present danger" test was an innovation by Mr. Justice Holmes in the *Schenck* case, reiterated and refined by him and Mr. Justice Brandeis in later cases, all arising before the era of World War II revealed the subtlety and efficacy of modernized revolutionary techniques used by totalitarian parties. In those cases, they were faced with convictions under so-called criminal syndicalism statutes aimed at anarchists but which, loosely construed, had been applied to punish socialism, pacifism, and left-wing ideologies, the charges often resting on far-fetched inferences which, if true, would establish only technical or trivial violations. They proposed "clear and present danger" as a test for the sufficiency of evidence in particular cases.

I would save it, unmodified, for application as a "rule of reason" in the kind of case for which it was devised. When the issue is criminality of a hot-headed speech on a street corner,[21] or circulation of a few incendiary pamphlets, or parading by some zealots behind a red flag, or refusal of a handful of school children to salute our flag, it is not beyond the capacity of the judicial process to gather, comprehend, and weigh the necessary materials for decision whether it is a clear and present danger of substantive evil or a harmless letting off of steam. It is not a prophecy, for the danger in such cases has matured by the time of trial or it was never present. The test applies and has meaning where a conviction is sought to be based on a speech or writing which does not directly or explicitly advocate a crime but to which such tendency is sought to be attributed by construction or by implication from external circumstances. The formula in such cases favors freedoms that are vital to our society, and, even if sometimes applied too generously, the consequences cannot be grave. But its recent expansion has extended, in particular to Communists, unprecedented immunities. Unless we are to

21 Cf. *Feiner* v. *New York*, 340 U.S. 315 (January 15, 1951), a companion case which was decided on the same day as, and which is the next case in the *United States Reports* following, *Kunz* v. *New York*, *supra*. Feiner presented the Court with the classic case of the soap-box orator, but Jackson had *rejected* his claim of constitutional right less than six months prior to *Dennis*. It seems likely that the unwary reader of the statement in the text, above, might draw the opposite, and incorrect, inference. [Ed.]

hold our Government captive in a judge-made verbal trap, we must approach the problem of a well-organized, nation-wide conspiracy, such as I have described, as realistically as our predecessors faced the trivialities that were being prosecuted until they were checked with a rule of reason.

I think reason is lacking for applying that test to this case.

If we must decide that this Act and its application are constitutional only if we are convinced that petitioner's conduct creates a "clear and present danger" of violent overthrow, we must appraise imponderables, including international and national phenomena which baffle the best informed foreign offices and our most experienced politicians. We would have to foresee and predict the effectiveness of Communist propaganda, opportunities for infiltration, whether, and when, a time will come that they consider propitious for action, and whether and how fast our existing government will deteriorate. And we would have to speculate as to whether an approaching Communist *coup* would not be anticipated by a nationalistic fascist movement. No doctrine can be sound whose application requires us to make a prophecy of that sort in the guise of a legal decision. The judicial process simply is not adequate to a trial of such far-flung issues. The answers given would reflect our own political predilections and nothing more.

The authors of the clear and present danger test never applied it to a case like this, nor would I. If applied as it is proposed here, it means that the Communist plotting is protected during its period of incubation; its preliminary stages of organization and preparation are immune from the law; the Government can move only after imminent action is manifest, when it would, of course, be too late....

What really is under review here is a conviction of conspiracy, after a trial for conspiracy, on an indictment charging conspiracy, brought under a statute outlawing conspiracy. With due respect to my colleagues, they seem to me to discuss anything under the sun except the law of conspiracy. One of the dissenting opinions even appears to chide me for "invoking the law of conspiracy." As that is the case before us, it may be more amazing that its reversal can be proposed without even considering the law of conspiracy.

The Constitution does not make conspiracy a civil right. The Court has never before done so and I think it should not do so now. Conspiracies of labor unions, trade associations, and news agencies have been condemned, although accomplished, evidenced and carried out, like the conspiracy here, chiefly by letter-writing, meetings, speeches and organization. Indeed, this Court seems, particularly in cases where the conspiracy has economic ends, to be applying its doctrines with increasing severity. While I consider criminal conspiracy a dragnet device capable of perversion into an instrument of injustice in the hands of a partisan or complacent judiciary, it has an established place in our system of law, and no reason appears for applying it only to concerted action claimed to disturb interstate commerce and withholding it from those claimed to undermine our whole Government.

The basic rationale of the law of conspiracy is that a conspiracy may be an evil in itself, independently of any other evil it seeks to accomplish. . . .

There is lamentation in the dissents about the injustice of conviction in the absence of some overt act. Of course, there has been no general uprising against the Government, but the record is replete with acts to carry out the conspiracy alleged, acts such as always are held sufficient to consummate the crime where the state requires an overt act.

But the shorter answer is that no overt act is or need be required. The Court, in antitrust cases, early upheld the power of Congress to adopt the ancient common law that makes conspiracy itself a crime. . . .

Also, it is urged that since the conviction is for conspiracy to teach and advocate, and to organize the Communist Party to teach and advocate, the First Amendment is violated, because freedoms of speech and press protect teaching and advocacy regardless of what is taught or advocated. I have never thought that to be the law.

I do not suggest that Congress could punish conspiracy to advocate something, the doing of which it may not punish. Advocacy or exposition of the doctrine of communal property ownership, or any political philosophy unassociated with advocacy of its imposition by force or seizure of government by unlawful means could not be reached through conspiracy prosecution. But it is not forbidden to put down force or violence, it is not forbidden to punish its teaching or advocacy, and the end being punishable, there is no doubt of the power to punish conspiracy for the purpose.

The defense of freedom of speech or press has often been raised in conspiracy cases, because, whether committed by Communists, by businessmen, or by common criminals, it usually consists of words written or spoken, evidenced by letters, conversations, speeches or documents. Communication is the essence of every conspiracy, for only by it can common purpose and concert of action be brought about or be proved. . . .

When our constitutional provisions were written, the chief forces recognized as antagonists in the struggle between authority and liberty were the Government on the one hand and the individual citizen on the other. It was thought that if the state could be kept in its place the individual could take care of himself.

In more recent times these problems have been complicated by the intervention between the state and the citizen of permanently organized, well-financed, semisecret and highly disciplined political organizations. Totalitarian groups here and abroad perfected the technique of creating private paramilitary organizations to coerce both the public government and its citizens. These organizations assert as against our Government all of the constitutional rights and immunities of individuals and at the same time exercise over their followers much of the authority which they deny to the Government. The Communist Party realistically is a state within a state, an authoritarian dictatorship within a republic. It demands these freedoms, not for its members, but for the organized party. It denies to its own members at the same time the freedom to dissent, to debate, to deviate from the party line, and enforces its authoritarian rule by crude purges, if nothing more violent.

The law of conspiracy has been the chief means at the Government's disposal to deal with the growing problems created by such organizations. I happen to think it is an awkward and inept remedy, but I find no constitutional authority for taking this weapon from the Government. There is no constitutional right to "gang up" on the Government.

While I think there was power in Congress to enact this statute and that, as applied in this case, it cannot be held unconstitutional, I add that I have little faith in the long-range effectiveness of this conviction to stop the rise of the Communist movement. Communism will not go to jail with these Communists. No decision by this Court can forestall revolution whenever the existing government fails to command the respect and loyalty of the people and sufficient distress and discontent is allowed to grow up among the masses. Many failures by fallen governments attest that no government can long prevent revolution by outlawry. Corruption, ineptitude, inflation, oppressive taxation, militarization, injustice, and loss of leadership capable of intellectual initiative in domestic or foreign affairs are allies on which the Communists count to bring opportunity knocking to their door. Sometimes I think they may be mistaken. But the Communists are not building just for today—the rest of us might profit by their example.

4 LEGALITY

Political and religious freedom are flamboyant issues which tend to arouse widespread public interest and intense judicial feelings. Claims to freedom of speech and belief are conceptualized, by layman and lawman alike, as questions of "substance," that is, they understand such decisions to turn upon the propriety of *what* the claimant seeks to do—or to refrain from doing. But both the legal and the general public perceive quite differently the claims to constitutional rights of defendants accused or suspected of crime.

Usually there is no question about the merits of the substance of the behavior of which the defendant stands accused. At least in Jackson's day, crime was more or less consensually deemed to be evil by most Americans. So a man accused of murder, as distinguished from one accused of having committed disorderly conduct by use of a sound truck, does not ordinarily attempt to base his defense upon a plea of the right to commit murder. He may, it is true, claim that he didn't do it, but that question raises no *direct* issue for the Supreme Court to decide. If he gets to the Supreme Court, it will most likely be because the criminal defendant claims that persons responsible for the detection, prosecution, trial, and review of judgments concerning criminal offenses have *themselves* violated ancillary, *procedural* rights of his, in the process of determining his guilt. His claim, in short, is that a finding that he has been guilty of one offense ought to be quashed because others have committed offenses against him, and that their violations of his procedural rights have affected the validity of the judgment against him. The classic case is the victim of the third degree who confesses to a crime, irrespective of his guilt or innocence, in order to avoid further beating. The classic example of the classic case is that of the public confessors in the purge trials of 1936 in Moscow.[1]

The presumed policy base which justifies the reversal, on procedural grounds, of convictions, is really two-fold. These alternative arguments are quite independent of each other: that (1) the judgment may be untrustworthy, because the confessor may be innocent, and the scales of justice should be so weighted that some guilty persons escape punishment, rather than that any innocent persons receive it; and that (2) the

---

[1] See also *The Manipulation of Human Behavior*, Albert D. Biderman and Herbert Zimmer, eds. (New York: John Wiley & Sons, Inc., 1961).

only effective way to enforce the procedural rights of criminal defendants is to punish violations of such rights by reversing the convictions to which these violations have contributed. Whatever may be the substantive merits of either of these two justifications for the policy, these are the rationalizations upon which reliance has been widely placed, and which were prevalent among Supreme Court justices during Jackson's tenure.

Cases involving claims of criminal defendants differ on quantitative (as well as on the above qualitative) grounds, from those concerned primarily with political or religious freedom. The latter are relatively rare, and only a half dozen or so are decided by the Court on the merits, in any given term; and even the number that the Court is asked to consider constitutes a small proportion of the total workload. But the claims of criminal defendants (which I shall henceforth designate as the "fair procedure" and "right to privacy" cases) now preempt over half of the Court's calendar space, although less than 3 percent of these cases are accepted for oral argument and decision on the merits.[2]

In 1945, in the middle of Jackson's service, the Court established a new Miscellaneous Docket to segregate the swelling volume of petitions, mostly *in forma pauperis* and filed by persons who fell within the social group that Jackson once referred to as "our convict population," seeking release from prisons and penitentiaries on the basis of post hoc claims that their trials and convictions had been infected with procedural errors of constitutional significance. A contemporary legal commentator reported that even a decade earlier:

> It was then the rumor, and it probably was the fact, that there were prisoners in several of the big federal penitentiaries with enough legal training to be ranked by their associates as lawyers. For a carton of cigarettes, such "lawyers" would file any sort of paper for any prisoner in any court, completely without regard for the facts, the law, or any semblance of truth.[3]

The establishment of the new docket reflected the increasing willingness of a relatively more liberal Supreme Court to entertain such claims on the part of persons convicted of offenses against state and local law, as well as on the part of federal prisoners.

Together with cases raising questions of political or religious freedom,

---

[2] See "The Supreme Court, 1964 Term," *Harvard Law Review*, LXXIX (1965), 106 and insert. The anonymous student authors of this article point out that there was a noticeable *decline* in the volume (both relatively and absolutely) of *in forma pauperis* Miscellaneous Docket certiorari petitions during this and the preceding term. Throughout the preceding decade, and during Jackson's latter years on the Court, they constituted substantially more than half of the total jurisdictional workload.

[3] Edwin McElwain, "The Business of the Supreme Court as Conducted by Chief Justice Hughes," *Harvard Law Review*, LXIII (1949), 21-22, n. 21.

fair procedure claims constitute by far the bulk of decisions in that sector of the Court's policy-making which conventionally is denominated civil liberties. Jackson's position on both of these major subcomponent issues of civil liberties was, like that of Frankfurter, moderate compared with his associates during the forties and early fifties. It is quite clear how justices with relatively more extreme attitudes voted in these same decisions. There were several terms during this period in which, as one would have to infer from an examination of the outcomes on the merits of split decisions, it was almost impossible to get three other justices to vote with Frank Murphy to accept jurisdiction to consider a claim sufficiently frivolous that Murphy would reject it on the merits; and it was equally difficult to get four justices to bring before the Court a case sufficiently unfair in its procedural deprivations that Stanley Reed would support the claimant. So with liberals supporting practically all such claims, and conservatives rejecting them, Jackson and Frankfurter found themselves in the middle and voted about as often one way as the other.

Jackson showed a bias in favor of federal petitioners, however, which is reflected in the often interated rhetoric of his opinions. He frequently said that states and local communities ought to be permitted greater discretion in the administration of their criminal laws than the national government (because the letter of the Bill of Rights applies only to the national government, because of the potential menace of a national police, etc.). In practice both his votes and his opinions *upheld* the claims of federal petitioners in civil liberties cases three-fourths of the time, whereas he *rejected* a majority of the claims of state petitioners.[4] His general behavior on this issue is clearly mirrored in the cases we shall examine in this chapter. We shall consider first his opinions in the cases of the federal defendants.

A. EVERYMAN'S CASTLE

BRINEGAR V. UNITED STATES
338 U.S. 160, 180 (June 27, 1949)

All judges, like all people, have idiosyncratic variations in their constellations of values; for Jackson, one of the most conspicuous of these personal attitudinal biases seemed to be a relatively soft spot for defendants

---

[4] Glendon Schubert, "Jackson's Judicial Philosophy: An Exploration in Value Analysis," *American Political Science Review*, LIX (1965), 949.

who protested against allegedly illegal searches and seizures. Ironically, one factor which certainly accentuated the many other sources of friction between Jackson and Black was the opposite, and at least equally inconsistent, bias which Black manifested throughout his long tenure on the Court[5] *against* such claims. Indeed, Jackson's occasional eloquence, in pleading the cause of some bit of flotsam on the social sea, has misled some commentators into assuming that Jackson was the Court's staunchest supporter of search and seizure claimants, and that, therefore, if there was division on the Court, Jackson ought to be on the pro-defendant side. Judging on the basis of their joint participation and voting behavior, however, Frankfurter was more sympathetic to Fourth Amendment claims than was Jackson; and several of their colleagues, especially Murphy and Rutledge, voted more consistently than Jackson to uphold claims to what the Warren Court has come to describe as "the right to privacy." That Frankfurter and Jackson were somewhat more sympathetic to search-and-seizure claims than to other constitutional claims of criminal defendants[6] may be explained by the consideration that an illegal search and seizure almost invariably constitutes an abridgment of a man's property as well as of his person. For judges with as strong an individualist bent as Frankfurter and Jackson, the former was just as serious a violation of constitutional liberty as was the latter. As we shall observe in the next chapter, their faith was not shared by a majority of their colleagues, who tended to favor either personal over property rights, or vice versa.

Among the quirks with which Jackson rationalized his approach to the right to privacy was the parallel which he drew between eavesdropping, an old-fashioned means for invading personal privacy—which was, for that very reason, the more permissible?—and more up-to-date electronic techniques such as bugging and wiretapping. The Court's official position throughout Jackson's tenure was that evidence obtained by wiretapping was barred from admission in the federal courts because of a specific provision of the Federal Communications Act, not because of the Fourth Amendment. There were certain technical problems of rationalization, which the Court in Jackson's day had not quite resolved, associated with the reincarnation of this federal statutory right into a Fourteenth Amendment limitation upon state investigators. Nevertheless, two cases which

[5] Glendon Schubert, *Constitutional Politics* (New York: Holt, Rinehart and Winston, Inc., 1960), pp. 610-611; and also *Quantitative Analysis of Judicial Behavior* (Glencoe, Illinois: The Free Press, 1960), pp. 338-363.

[6] I have argued elsewhere that the right to privacy is better conceptualized as an independent attitudinal component, separate from other claims to fair procedure, precisely because so many Supreme Court justices, in addition to Frankfurter and Jackson, make such a distinction in their voting behavior. Glendon Schubert, *The Judicial Mind*, Chap. 6.

for Jackson involved mere eavesdropping entailed highly similar outcomes for the defendants and the Court as well as for Jackson himself.[7]

The first case was that of On Lee, an American laundryman of Chinese descent, who was suspected by federal agents of being an opium peddler. In order to get evidence against him, a friend of his, who was working as a "stool pigeon" for the Bureau of Narcotics, "was wired for sound," as Jackson put it, with a miniature walkie-talkie transmitter. The incriminating admissions that the defendant made in the conversation with his friend were heard by a federal agent equipped with a receiving set. The agent's testimony as to these admissions was subsequently admitted in evidence to convict On Lee. Jackson said that the situation was the same as if the federal agent had eavesdropped upon the conversation through an open window. "It would be a dubious service to the genuine liberties protected by the Fourth Amendment," he said, "to make them bedfellows with spurious liberties improvised by farfetched analogies."[8] There had been an invasion of On Lee's privacy, to be sure, but no "search," no "seizure," and consequently no violation of the Fourth Amendment. And because, technically, On Lee was not attempting to communicate with anyone by means of any "communications system within the Federal Communications Act," there was no violation of the anti-wiretapping provisions of that statute.

In the second case, Long Beach city police installed a microphone in a closet of the bedroom of a suspected small-time bookmaker who was the owner and bartender of the Red Onion Café. Wires were run through a hole which the police cut through his roof, and for the next few weeks officers listened, from their post in a neighboring garage, to the secrets of the barkeeper's boudoir. Eventually they overheard the defendant conducting business transactions over his bedroom telephone, and he was convicted on this evidence, of an offense against state law. "Few police measures have come to our attention," thundered Jackson, "that more flagrantly, deliberately, and persistently violated the fundamental principle declared by the Fourth Amendment as a restriction on the Federal Government."[9]

[7] The first was a federal and the second a state case; the first raised questions under the Fourth, and the second under the Fourteenth Amendment—and the latter was not yet (a decade ago) considered to incorporate (at least so far as concerns such evidentiary issues as were relevant in Irvine) the Fourth Amendment, as the majority was careful to point out. [This particular rationale was changed in 1961 in *Mapp* v. *Ohio*, 367 U.S. 643, with Tom Clark, who concurred in Irvine, leading the way.] Frankfurter, Douglas, Black, and Burton dissented in behalf of both On Lee and Irvine; and the majority was the same in both cases, except that Warren had replaced Vinson in the later decision.

[8] *On Lee* v. *United States*, 343 U.S. 747, 754 (1952).

[9] *Irvine* v. *California*, 347 U.S. 128, 131-132 (1954). See also Alan F. Westin, *The Uses of Power* (New York: Harcourt, Brace & World, Inc., 1962), pp. 117-171: "Bookies and 'Bugs' in California: Judicial Control of Police Practices."

But Irvine was a state criminal defendant; therefore, Jackson voted to uphold his conviction on the basis of evidence that clearly had been obtained as the result of an illegal and unreasonable search and seizure. What bothered Jackson was the actual physical breaking and entry of the police —which he characterized as "trespass, and probably a burglary" by the officers—and not that they were thereby enabled to eavesdrop by bugging the closet. "We do not suppose," he explained, "it is illegal to testify to what another person is heard to say merely because he is saying it into a telephone. We cannot sustain the contention that the conduct or reception of the evidence violated the Federal Communications Act." And so Jackson rejected the claims of both On Lee and Pat Irvine, writing the opinion of the Court in both cases, and providing in each the fifth vote critical to the outcome. The obvious inference is that Jackson did not consider listening in on the conversation of criminals, whether accomplished crudely or with sophistication, to be a serious enough invasion of the right to individual privacy to warrant the denial to society of the use of evidence needed to convict persons who patently were guilty of crimes.

When, however, the evidence was the fruit of direct physical coercion of the defendant's person (as well as of his property), and it stemmed from a sequence of arrest-search-and-seizure without benefit of a valid warrant, Jackson was less disposed to look for loopholes in the statute or the Constitution to justify a conviction. Such was the case of Brinegar, a common bootlegger, who evidently was a professional violator of the federal statute which prohibited the importation of intoxicating liquors into any state contrary to its laws. Brinegar was transporting booze in a private automobile from a wet state into a dry one when his car was stopped by a federal officer. The officer had no warrant for Brinegar's arrest, but he recognized and stopped him, provoked an oral admission of guilt, and then confirmed the presence of hooch in the heavily-laden car. Two decades earlier, when national prohibition coincided with the coming of age of the automobile, the Court had undertaken the modernization of the Constitution by a decision which approved the arrest and search of automobiles in transit, without a warrant, providing that there was "probable cause" for making the arrest and search.[10] The Constitution, however, stipulates that there must be "probable cause" for a *magistrate* to issue a search warrant; *not* that searches without warrants are reasonable if there is "probable cause" in the judgment of the investigating police officer.

The majority, which included three of the libertarians together with Vinson and Reed, with Burton concurring, agreed that this case was governed by the *Carroll* precedent; and because there was, in fact, probable

[10] *Carroll* v. *United States,* 267 U.S. 132 (1925).

cause to support the arrest, search, and seizure in this case, Brinegar's conviction was affirmed. There is, perhaps, some irony in the coincidence that, just as he chose to devote his most persuasive advocacy for the right of freedom of religious belief in the case of St. Germain, so here Jackson defended the sanctity of the Anglo-American's castle as symbolized by the old Ford coupe of this bootlegger, Everyman.

MR. JUSTICE JACKSON, dissenting.

When this Court recently has promulgated a philosophy that some rights derived from the Constitution are entitled to a "preferred position," *Murdock* v *Pennsylvania,* 319 U.S. 105, 115, dissent at p. 166; *Saia* v. *New York,* 334 U.S. 558, 562, I have not agreed. We cannot give some constitutional rights a preferred position without relegating others to a deferred position; we can establish no firsts without thereby establishing seconds. Indications are not wanting that Fourth Amendment freedoms are tacitly marked as secondary rights, to be relegated to a deferred position.

The Fourth Amendment states: "The right of the people to be secure in their persons, houses, papers, and effects, against unreasonable searches and seizures, shall not be violated, and no Warrants shall issue, but upon probable cause, supported by Oath or affirmation, and particularly describing the place to be searched, and the persons or things to be seized."

These, I protest, are not mere second-class rights but belong in the catalog of indispensable freedoms. Among deprivations of rights, none is so effective in cowing a population, crushing the spirit of the individual and putting terror in every heart. Uncontrolled search and seizure is one of the first and most effective weapons in the arsenal of every arbitrary government. And one need only briefly to have dwelt and worked among a people possessed of many admirable qualities but deprived of these rights to know that the human personality deteriorates and dignity and self-reliance disappear where homes, persons and possessions are subject at any hour to unheralded search and seizure by the police.

But the right to be secure against searches and seizures is one of the most difficult to protect. Since the officers are themselves the chief invaders, there is no enforcement outside of court.

Only occasional and more flagrant abuses come to the attention of the courts, and then only those where the search and seizure yields incriminating evidence and the defendant is at least sufficiently compromised to be indicted. If the officers raid a home, an office, or stop and search an automobile but find nothing incriminating, this invasion of the personal liberty of the innocent too often finds no practical redress. There may be, and I am convinced that there are, many unlawful searches of homes and automobiles of innocent people which turn up nothing incriminating, in which no arrest is made, about which courts do nothing, and about which we never hear.

Courts can protect the innocent against such invasions only indirectly and through the medium of excluding evidence obtained against those who frequently are guilty. Federal courts have used this method of enforcement of the Amendment, in spite of its unfortunate consequences on law enforcement, although many state courts do not. This inconsistency does not disturb me, for local excesses or invasions of liberty are more amenable to political correction, the Amendment was directed only against the new and centralized government, and any really dangerous threat to the general liberties of the people can come only from this source. We must therefore look upon the exclusion of evidence in federal prosecutions, if obtained in violation of the Amendment, as a means of extending protection against the central government's agencies. So a search against Brinegar's car must be regarded as a search of the car of Everyman.

We must remember that the extent of any privilege of search and seizure without warrant which we sustain, the officers interpret and apply themselves and will push to the limit. We must remember, too, that freedom from unreasonable search differs from some of the other rights of the Constitution in that there is no way in which the innocent citizen can invoke advance protection. For example, any effective interference with freedom of the press, or free speech, or religion, usually requires a course of suppressions against which the citizen can and often does go to the court and obtain an injunction. Other rights, such as that to an impartial jury or the aid of counsel, are within the supervisory power of the courts themselves. Such a right as just compensation for the taking of private property may be vindicated after the act in terms of money.

But an illegal search and seizure usually is a single incident, perpetrated by surprise, conducted in haste, kept purposely beyond the court's supervision and limited only by the judgment and moderation of officers whose own interests and records are often at stake in the search. There is no opportunity for injunction or appeal to disinterested intervention. The citizen's choice is quietly to submit to whatever the officers undertake or to resist at risk of arrest or immediate violence.

And we must remember that the authority which we concede to conduct searches and seizures without warrant may be exercised by the most unfit and ruthless officers as well as by the fit and responsible, and resorted to in case of petty misdemeanors as well as in the case of the gravest felonies.

With this prologue I come to the case of Brinegar. His automobile was one of his "effects" and hence within the express protection of the Fourth Amendment. Undoubtedly the automobile presents peculiar problems for enforcement agencies, is frequently a facility for the perpetration of crime and an aid in the escape of criminals. But if we are to make judicial exceptions to the Fourth Amendment for these reasons, it seems to me they should depend somewhat upon the gravity of the offense. If we assume, for example, that a child is kidnaped and the officers throw a roadblock about the neighborhood and search every outgoing car, it would be a drastic and undiscriminating use of the search.

The officers might be unable to show probable cause for searching any particular car. However, I should candidly strive hard to sustain such an action, executed fairly and in good faith, because it might be reasonable to subject travelers to that indignity if it was the only way to save a threatened life and detect a vicious crime. But I should not strain to sustain such a roadblock and universal search to salvage a few bottles of bourbon and catch a bootlegger.

The Court sustains this search as an application of *Carroll* v. *United States*, 267 U.S. 132. I dissent because I regard it as an extension of the *Carroll* case, which already has been too much taken by enforcement officers as blanket authority to stop and search cars on suspicion. . . .

While the Court sustained the search without warrant in the *Carroll* case, it emphatically declined to dispense with the necessity for evidence of probable cause for making such a search. . . .

In the *Carroll* case, the primary and the ultimate fact that the accused was engaged in liquor running was not surmise or hearsay, as it is here. . . .

Not only did the Court rely almost exclusively on information gained in personal negotiations of the officers to buy liquor from defendants to show probable cause, but the dissenting members asserted it to be the only circumstance which could have subjected the accused to any reasonable suspicion. And that is the sort of direct evidence on personal knowledge that is lacking here.

In contrast, the proof that Brinegar was trafficking in illegal liquor rests on inferences from two circumstances, neither one of which would be allowed to be proved at a trial: One, it appears that the same officers previously had arrested Brinegar on the same charge. But there had been no conviction and it does not appear whether the circumstances of the former arrest indicated any strong probability of it. In any event, this evidence of a prior arrest of the accused would not even be admissible in a trial to prove his guilt on this occasion.

As a second basis for inference, the officers also say that Brinegar had the reputation of being a liquor runner. The weakness of this hearsay evidence is revealed by contrasting it with the personal negotiations which proved that Carrol was one. The officers' testimony of reputation would not be admissible in a trial of defendant unless he was unwise enough to open the subject himself by offering character testimony. . . .

I do not say that no evidence which would be inadmissible to prove guilt at a trial may be considered in weighing probable cause, but I am surprised that the Court is ready to rule that inadmissible evidence alone, as to vital facts without which other facts give little indication of guilt, establish probable cause as matter of law. The only other fact is that Officer Malsed stated that twice, on September 23 and on September 30, about six months before this arrest, he saw Brinegar in a Missouri town, where liquor is lawful, loading liquor into a truck, not the car in this case. That is all. The Court from that draws the inference which the courts below, familiar we presume with the local conditions, refused to draw, *viz.*, that to be seen loading liquor into a truck where it is lawful is proof that defendant is unlawfully trafficking in liquor some distance away. There is not, as in the *Carroll* case, evidence that he was offering liquor for sale to anybody at any time. In the *Carroll* case, the offer to sell liquor to the officers would itself have been a law violation. It seems rather foggy reasoning to say that the courts are obliged to draw the same conclusion from legal conduct as from illegal conduct.

I think we cannot say the lower courts were wrong as matter of law in holding that there was no probable cause up to the time the car was put off the road and stopped, and that we cannot say it was proper to consider the deficiency supplied by what followed. When these officers engaged in a chase at speeds dangerous to those who participated, and to other lawful wayfarers, and ditched the defendant's car, they were either taking the initial steps in arrest, search and seizure, or they were committing a completely lawless and unjustifiable act. That they intended to set out on a search is unquestioned, and there seems no reason to doubt that in their own minds they thought there was cause and right to search. They have done exactly what they would have done, and done rightfully, if they had been executing a warrant. At all events, whatever it may have lacked technically of arrest, search and seizure, it was a form of coercion and duress under color of official authority—and a very formidable type of duress at that.

I do not, of course, contend that officials may never stop a car on the highway without the halting being considered an arrest or a search. Regulations of traffic, identifications where proper, traffic census, quarantine regulations, and many other causes give occasion to stop cars in circumstances which do not imply arrest or charge of crime. And to trail or pursue a suspected car to its destination, to observe it and keep it under surveillance, is not in itself an arrest nor a search. But when a car is forced off the road, summoned to stop by a siren, and brought to a halt under such circumstances as are here disclosed, we think the officers are then in the position of one who has entered a home: the search at its commencement must be valid and cannot be saved by what it turns up. . . .

The findings of the two courts below make it clear that this search began and proceeded through critical and coercive phases without the justification of probable cause. What it yielded cannot save it. I would reverse the judgment.

MR. JUSTICE FRANKFURTER and MR. JUSTICE MURPHY join in this opinion.

B.   PACKING THE JURY

FRAZIER V. UNITED STATES
335 U.S. 497, 514 (December 20, 1948)

Both the libertarians and Jackson's more conservative colleagues were split by the issue in this case, with Black and Rutledge joining Vinson, Reed, and Burton to form an unusual majority combination. The question was whether a federal criminal defendant could receive a fair trial at the hands of an all government-employee jury. Frazier was convicted by such a jury in the United States District Court of the District of Columbia, for a violation of the federal narcotics law. Narcotics regulation happens to fall within the ambit of the Treasury Department, the agency which employed one of the jurors and the wife of another. There were two independent bases on which the Supreme Court might have purported to justify the reversal of his conviction: (1) by ruling that the jury was not "impartial," within the meaning of the Sixth Amendment, or (2) by deciding that the Court should, as a matter of sound judicial policy, in the exercise of its supervisory power over the courts of the District of Columbia, forbid the use of such homogeneous juries.

All of the justices agreed that the constitutional claim was without merit; their division related to the wisdom of establishing such a policy, on their own authority and initiative. In his opinion for the Court, in which he rationalized the unwisdom of such a choice, Rutledge first distinguished the Court's precedents, explaining why they were either inapplicable or else supportive of the majority position. There was, he said, no proof of actual bias on the part of any juror individually, or of the jury collectively, in this case.[11] Moreover, the majority felt that counsel for the defendant had deliberately engaged in a form of self-entrapment, by using his peremptory challenges in such a way as to assure that his client would be tried by an all government-employee jury, presumably so that he could lay the ground for this very claim of reversible error upon appeal—because his case otherwise was so weak that he expected to lose.

Frankfurter, Douglas, and Murphy joined in Jackson's dissenting opinion.

MR. JUSTICE JACKSON, *dissenting.*

On one proposition I should expect trial lawyers to be nearly unanimous: that a jury, every member of which is in the hire of one of the litigants, lacks something of being an impartial jury. A system which has produced such an objectionable result and always tends to repeat it, should, in my opinion, be disapproved by this Court in exercise of its supervisory power over federal courts.

Were the employer an individual, a railroad, an industrial concern, or even a state, I think bias would more readily be implied; but its existence would be no more probable. This criminal trial was an adversary proceeding, with the Government both an actual and nominal litigant. It was the patron and benefactor of

11 Jackson's theory of the putative bias of bureaucrats, which permeates his opinion (below), may be more revealing of his own bias against civil servants, than convincing on the point of the likelihood of exceptional bias on the part of government employees, against narcotic peddlers. See Chap. 6, *infra.*

the whole jury, plus one juror's wife for good measure. At the same time that it made its plea to them to convict, it had the upper hand of every one of them in matters such as pay and promotion. Of late years, the Government is using its power as never before to pry into their lives and thoughts upon the slightest suspicion of less than complete trustworthiness. It demands not only probity but unquestioning ideological loyalty. A government employee cannot today be disinterested or unconcerned about his appearance of faithful and enthusiastic support for government departments whose prestige and record is, somewhat, if only a little, at stake in every such prosecution. And prosecutors seldom fail to stress, if not to exaggerate, the importance of the case before them to the whole social, if not the cosmic, order. Even if we have no reason to believe that an acquitting juror would be subjected to embarrassments or reprisals, we cannot expect every clerk and messenger in the great bureaucracy to feel so secure as to put his dependence on the Government wholly out of mind. I do not doubt that the government employees as a class possess a normal independence and fortitude. But we have grounds to assume also that the normal proportion of them are subject to that very human weakness, especially displayed in Washington, which leads men to ". . . crook the pregnant hinges of the knee where thrift may follow fawning." So I reject as spurious any view that government employment differs from all other employment in creating no psychological pressure of dependency or interest in gaining favor, which might tend to predetermine issues in the interest of the party which has complete mastery over the juror's ambition and position. But even if this suspicion can be dismissed by the Court as a mere phantasy, it cannot deny that such a jury has a one-sided outlook on problems before it and an appearance of government leverage which is itself a blemish on the name of justice in the District of Columbia.

Because this semblance of partiality reflects on the courts, even if it does not prejudice the defendant in a particular case, I am not disposed to labor the argument as to whether counsel for this defendant did all that he might or should have done by way of objection. He did protest as soon as it was apparent what was happening to him, and that seems to me sufficient in face of adverse rulings. But even if defendant's objection were belated or technically defective, I still think the court deserves and should require a more neutral jury for its own appearances, even if defendant does not deserve and cannot demand one.

The cause of overloading this jury with persons beholden to the Government is no mystery and no accident. It is due to a defect in a system which will continue to operate in the same direction so long as the same practice is followed. While counsel did not prove it under oath, he stated it for the record and neither the District Attorney nor the learned Trial Judge, both of whom must have known the facts, denied or questioned his statement or asked him for better evidence. That defect is this: when the panel of jurors was drawn, the court appears to have asked all those who did not wish to serve to step aside, and they were excused from serving.

This amiable concession in some jurisdictions might produce no distortion of the composition of the panel; but it is certain to do just that in the District of Columbia because of the dual standard and dubious method of jury compensation. The nongovernment juror receives $4 per day, which under present conditions is inadequate to be compensatory to nearly every gainfully employed juror. But the government employee is not paid specially; instead, he is given leave from his government work with full pay while serving on the jury. The latter class are thus induced to jury service by protection against any financial loss, while the former are subjected to considerable disadvantage.

This condition makes it obvious that, if jury service is put on virtually a voluntary basis and qualified persons are allowed to decline jury service at their own option, the panel will become loaded with government employees. If this undue concentration of such jurors were accomplished by any device which excluded nongovernment jurors, it unquestionably would be condemned not only by reason of but even without resort to the doctrine that prevailed in *Ballard* v. *United States,* 329 U.S. 187....

Is the result more lawful when it is accomplished by letting one class exclude themselves, stimulated to do so by the incentive of such a dual system of compensation?

Of course, the defendant and the prosecution each have peremptory challenges, ten in this case, which enable each without assigning any cause to excuse that number whom they do not wish to have sit. This defendant used many of his challenges to excuse talesmen not employed by the Government and it is hinted that he may have packed this jury against himself. The learned Trial Judge made no such suggestion, however, and he would be better able than we to detect such tactics. He blamed the situation on "chance." But the fickle goddess is hardly to be blamed for the result when it can be seen that the cards were stacked from the beginning. This was plainly the case when we contrast unequal advantages which the two parties could get from their equal numbers of challenges.

The Government was confronted by no occasion to use any of its peremptory challenges to get rid of its adversary's employees. The defendant was. But if the defendant should try to use his challenges to excuse employees of the Government, he would dismiss one only to incur a probability of getting another. If he exhausted his challenges in this effort, it would still be futile, for no one claims he had enough to displace them all. It might not be wise tactics to show suspicion or disapproval of a class some of whom will have to sit anyway. Moreover, if he used his challenges as far as they would go to dislodge government servants, it would leave him helpless to challenge any of the nongovernment jurors, for which challenge he might have good reason.

The disadvantage of defendant as to talesmen from government ranks is more apparent but not more prejudicial than with talesmen from other walks of life. Whatever reason he may have had for excusing such a one, the price he would probably have had to pay for using his challenge was to have one government employee take another's place. The Government could vacate the seat of a non-government talesman with no such unwelcome results. The short of the thing is: in no case where the court has intervened to use its supervisory power to revise federal jury systems has there been any result so consistently and inevitably prejudicial to one of the litigants as here, under our noses. . . . And in cases where a strong minority of the Court has wanted to go so far as to upset a state jury system, as offensive to fundamental considerations of justice spelled out from the due process clause of the Fourteenth Amendment, there has been no such brazen unfairness in actual practice. . . .

The precedent of *United States* v. *Wood*, 299 U.S. 123, on which the Court leans heavily, is a weak crutch. That decision held only that the absolute disqualification of any federal employee, which had been declared in *Crawford* v. *United States*, 212 U.S. 183, could constitutionally be removed by the Congress. In the case the Court was considering only three out of the twelve were by chance government beneficiaries and the Court was not confronted with such a systematic distortion of the jury as was at work here. It held that, individually, they were not subject to challenge for cause; that is, they were not excusable by the court merely because they were government employees. But to hold that one or a few government employees may sit by chance is no precedent for holding that they may fill all of the chairs by a system of retiring everyone else. Furthermore, that opinion emphasized that the prosecution in that case was for larceny from a private corporation. That was not an offense against the Federal Government as such, except as it has responsibility for prosecuting crimes in the District that in the state would be a matter of no federal concern or even jurisdiction. But the prosecution before us is not for an offense of a private aspect; it is an offense against no one except federal government policy; and the Secretary of the Treasury, in whose own office one of these jurors was employed, has exclusive and nationwide responsibility for enforcement of the law involved.

If we admit every fact, premise, argument and conclusion stated in the Court's opinion, it still leaves this one situation unexplained and unjustified. In federal courts, over which we have supervisory power, sitting almost within a stone's throw of where we sit, a system is in operation which has produced and is likely again and again to produce what disinterested persons are likely to regard as a packed jury. Approval of it, after all that has been written of late on the subject of juries, makes these lofty pronouncements sound a little hollow.

I would reverse this rather insignificant conviction and end this system before it builds up into a scandalous necessity for reversal of some really significant conviction.

C.   SAUCE FOR THE GANDER

DENNIS V. UNITED STATES
339 U.S. 162 (March 27, 1950)

The brave words with which Jackson ended his opinion may possibly have stirred some false hopes in the breast of Eugene Dennis, the Secretary General of the Communist Party (3F, *supra*). Indeed, his was the very case that Jackson had in mind, and the government, at least, considered the *Dennis* conviction to be really significant, both from the point of view of world public opinion and from the perspective of Senator McCarthy. The moment of "scandalous necessity" might seem to have arrived when Dennis appealed his conviction—in the present case, for contempt of Congress—to the Supreme Court. After the Frazier case, we would anticipate that the Court would turn Dennis down, but surely not with Jackson's help! Yet so it was; and Jackson's concluding plea in *Frazier* was thus made to appear (in the words of one of Jackson's own favorite quotations) to have been no more than a "promise to the ear to be broken to the hope, a teasing illusion like a munificent bequest in a pauper's will."

Dennis originally had appeared voluntarily before the House Committee on Un-American Activities, to lobby against a bill to outlaw the Communist Party. Newsreels of the day carried an implicitly hilarious sequence,[12] in the fashion of Shakespeare's *A Comedy of Errors*, in which the committee chairman was pointing his finger at Dennis and demanding, "What is your name?" Had Dennis done his research as well as the committee, Dennis doubtless would have replied by demanding of the chairman, "What is *your* real name?" J. Parnell Thomas, *né* Feeney,[13] was soon to be convicted in a federal court for an action more contumacious of the Congress than that of Dennis—the illegal padding of his office payroll. As it was, Dennis refused to state his name, standing on what he apparently assumed to be his right as an American citizen to remain anonymous. This led to the issuance of a subpoena to bring Dennis, under compulsion, before the committee again; Dennis' refusal to appear resulted in his indictment for contempt of Congress and his subsequent trial and conviction.

Even before the trial, Dennis' attorney had moved for a change of

12 See *The New York Times*, August 1, 1948, Sec. VI, pp. 11, 30.
13 *Ibid.*, p. 31; *Who's Who in America, 1946-1947* (Chicago: A. N. Marquis, 1946), XXIV, p. 2352.

venue, on the ground that he could not receive a fair trial by a jury stacked with government employees, who were themselves subject to the duress of the President's Loyalty Executive Order. When this motion was denied, counsel for petitioner attempted to challenge the selection of all government employees as jurors; and two of his three peremptory challenges were used to eliminate government workers. The final jury panel included seven federal civil servants. The question before the Supreme Court was whether the petitioner's conviction should be reversed and a new trial granted on the grounds that Dennis could not have received a fair trial by such a jury.

A majority of four of the participating justices joined in Minton's opinion for the Court; and after a review of the statutes and precedents, they concluded that government employees could be challenged for cause only on grounds of "actual," not constructive, bias. In this case they felt the evidence did not support a finding of actual bias. Only Black and Frankfurter dissented, arguing that the *Frazier* precedent should not be followed in the case of Dennis, because of the much greater possibility that the not improbable bias of government jurors against this notorious Communist leader constituted a potential denial of his constitutional rights. Black, who had voted with the majority in *Frazier*, switched sides in this case, arguing that:

> . . . under the circumstances here it seems . . . "far-fetched and chimerical" to suggest that government employees, however convinced of innocence, would feel completely free to acquit a defendant charged with disobeying a command of the Committee on Un-American Activities. My belief is that no defendant charged with such an offense, whatever his political affiliation, should be forced to accept a government employee as a juror. Nor should the Government want such an unfair advantage.

Frankfurter, who had dissented in *Frazier*, took specific issue with the cynical antilitigant argument in Jackson's concurrence, stating:

> Let there be no misunderstanding. To recognize the existence of a group whose views are feared and despised by the community at large does not even remotely imply any support of that group. To take appropriate measures in order to avert injustice even towards a member of the despised group is to enforce justice. It is not to play favorites. The boast of our criminal procedure is that it protects an accused, so far as legal procedure can, from a bias operating against such a group to which he belongs. This principle should be enforced whatever the tenets of the group—whether the old Locofocos or the Know-Nothings, the Ku Klux Klan or the Communists. This is not to coddle Communists but to respect our profession of equal justice to all. It was a wise man who said that there is no greater inequality than the equal treatment of unequals.

Douglas and Clark did not participate in the 5-2 decision; but presumably they were in effect "paired" (as we would describe legislative voting), so their absence did not affect the outcome.[14] In fact, the *Frazier* opposition had lost support when Rutledge and Murphy, who had split in that decision, were replaced by Minton and Clark, who represented one actual and another potential vote for the pro-*Frazier* policy. So Black's switch in sides was counterbalanced by Clark's appointment; the effect of Clark's nonparticipation was cancelled by that of Douglas; and there was no net gain. But this does perhaps explain Jackson's dialectics. Black (as Jackson doubtless thought) was willing to forget his libertarian scruples in order to railroad a common crook, and then to *volte-face* as the Court's John Donne at the behest of the first lousy Communist to come along! Jackson was outraged; and he took the same way out that he had before in the face of what he considered to be Black's political shenanigans,[15] claiming that he now considered himself bound, under the rule of *stare decisis,* by the *Frazier* precedent, notwithstanding that he had opposed and that he remained opposed to the policy established in that case. The strong tone of his opinion tends to create an equally strong suspicion, however, that for Jackson the guarantee of an impartial jury was a function of the virtue of the defendant. "The case which irresistibly comes to mind as the most fitting precedent"[16] is that of the Star Chamber, which, as a court of criminal equity, could let the penalty suit the criminal.

MR. JUSTICE JACKSON, *concurring in the result.*

In but two ways could the Court avoid affirming the conviction of Dennis. One is to rescind the general rule established in *Frazier* v. *United States,* 335 U. S. 497, that a jury is, in contemplation of law "impartial," even when entirely composed of government employees. The other is to retain, and thereby strengthen, that general rule but create a special exemption for Communists.

I adhere with increasing conviction to my dissent in *Frazier* v. *United States supra* at 514. The Court there dug a pit dangerous for civil liberties. The right to fair trial is the right that stands guardian over all other rights. Reference to the reports will show what otherwise one would not believe: that the Court, by a bare majority, held it to be entirely fair to try a person before a jury consisting solely of government employees, plus the fact that one juror and the wife of another worked in the office of the department head responsible for enforcement of the law charged to be violated. The common instinct of men for fair dealing

---

[14] Even if Douglas had been able to participate, and Clark had not; and even if Jackson had then been willing to join forces with Black, Douglas, and Frankfurter, Dennis' conviction would still have been affirmed by an equal division of the Court.

[15] *Magnolia Petroleum* v. *Hunt,* 320 U.S. 430, 446 (1943), and Chap. 7A, *infra.*

[16] Citing a poem by George Gordon, Lord Byron, so quoth Jackson in his opinion in *Everson* v. *Board of Education,* 330 U.S. 1, 19 (1947), and Chap. 2E, *supra.*

and the experience of trial lawyers alike reject this holding. Whenever any majority can be mustered to over-rule that weird and misguided decision, I shall be one of it.

But the way for the Court to get out of the hole it fell into with *Frazier* is not to dig another and worse one. We are actually urged to hold that the kind of jury a defendant may have depends upon his political opinions or affiliations. The offense for which Dennis was tried was contempt of a Committee of Congress. That is not an offense that touches the immediate security of the Nation. Nor does guilt or innocence depend upon defendant's political views or party membership. Of course, he is, and the jury was bound to learn that he is, a prominent figure in the Communist Party. But the same acts would be the same offense if he were an orthodox Democrat. The sole ground for creating an exemption from the *Frazier* rule is that the defendant is a Communist, and Communists are now exceedingly unpopular in Washington, I agree that this highlights the unfairness of the *Frazier* rule and provides reason for overruling it; but I do not agree that it justifies the proposed exception to that decision.

The *Frazier* doctrine was promulgated by a majority of the Court which well knew that its rule would apply to this type of case and in these times. That decision was handed down on December 20, 1948, with this present case just around the corner. Dennis had already been convicted and his conviction had been affirmed in highly publicized proceedings occurring only a few city blocks from us; and his petition for certiorari had been filed in this Court. The four of us dissenting in *Frazier* warned specifically that the Government in these times is using its power as never before to pry into lives and thoughts of government employees. All that is urged now is more of the same and there is nothing in this situation that should not have been within the contemplation of the Court when the *Frazier* case was decided the way it was. The proposal now is a partial repeal— for Communists only.

Courts should give to a Communist every right and advantage that they give to any defendant. But it is inconceivable that being a Communist can entitle a defendant to more. Let us picture the proposal in operation. Two defendants are brought to trial for contempt of Congress. One, a Communist, had defied the Un-American Activities Committee. The other, a Republican, had defied the Committee investigating the State Department. Both make well-founded claims that the Executive branch of the Government is hostile to them; both ask to exclude its employees from the jury so they may be tried by persons under no obligation to their adversaries. The proposal is that the trial judge should grant the motion of the Communist and deny that of the Republican! What then becomes of equal justice under law?

It is true that Communists are the current phobia in Washington. But always, since I can remember, some group or other is being investigated and castigated here. At various times it has been Bundists and Germans, Japanese, lobbyists,

tax evaders, oil men, utility men, bankers, brokers, labor leaders, Silver Shirts
and Fascists. At times, usually after dramatic and publicized exposures, members
of these groups have been brought to trial for some offense. I think that none
of them at such times ever should be forced to defend themselves against the
Government's accusations before the Government's employees. But so long as
accused persons who are Republicans, Dixiecrats, Socialists, or Democrats must
put up with such a jury, it will have to do for Communists.

D. CRIMINAL INTENT

MORISSETTE V. UNITED STATES
342 U.S. 246 (January 7, 1952)

The United States Supreme Court notes the fall of few sparrows, but
this was one such instance. It was also one of the very few cases in which
Jackson wrote, in support of a fair procedure (or any other kind of civil
liberties) claim, for a unanimous Court.[17] The two cases which Jackson
distinguished as precedents were decided seriatim on the same day in
1922. Both involved prosecutions under the, then, relatively new federal narcotics statute: one for selling drugs without a prescription, and the
other for a doctor's abusive use of prescriptions to make available to a
known addict massive doses of heroine, morphine, and cocaine. Chief Justice Taft massed a unanimous Court in support of his opinion reversing
the court below and upholding the indictment in the first case, but
Holmes and Brandeis and McReynolds dissented from the similar decision
against the physician. Taft's opinion does make the distinction, upon
which Jackson relies below, between traditional criminal defenses defined
by common law, that is, by judges, and modern offenses against public
policy defined by legislatures. To the extent that following dicta rather
than the holding of a precedent decision can be described as *stare decisis,*
Jackson follows precedent in the opinion below. But the point in Taft's
opinion had been to justify the *upholding* of a conviction for a statutory
offense for which no criminal intent was required by Congress; Jackson,
in the present case, justifies the *reversal* of a conviction for a statutory offense for which no criminal intent was required by Congress. By so doing,
the Court championed the virtues of individualism in which Jackson believed so staunchly; but the decision also entailed the inescapable consequence of weakening much socioeconomic legislation intended, to employ

[17] Minton did not participate, and Douglas concurred in the result only.

Jackson's own characterization of such laws, to protect the public health and welfare.

MR. JUSTICE JACKSON delivered the opinion of the Court.

This would have remained a profoundly insignificant case to all except its immediate parties had it not been so tried and submitted to the jury as to raise questions both fundamental and far-reaching in federal criminal law. . . .

On a large tract of uninhabited and untilled land in a wooded and sparsely populated area of Michigan, the Government established a practice bombing range over which the Air Force dropped simulated bombs at ground targets. These bombs consisted of a metal cylinder about forty inches long and eight inches across, filled with sand and enough black powder to cause a smoke puff by which the strike could be located. At various places about the range signs read "Danger— Keep Out—Bombing Range." Nevertheless, the range was known as good deer country and was extensively hunted.

Spent bomb casings were cleared from the targets and thrown into piles "so that they will be out of the way." They were not stacked or piled in any order but were dumped in heaps, some of which had been accumulating for four years or upwards, were exposed to the weather and rusting away.

Morissette, in December of 1948, went hunting in this area but did not get a deer. He thought to meet expenses of the trip by salvaging some of these casings. He loaded three tons of them on his truck and took them to a nearby farm, where they were flattened by driving a tractor over them. After expending this labor and trucking them to market in Flint, he realized $84.

Morissette, by occupation, is a fruit stand operator in summer and a trucker and scrap iron collector in winter. An honorably discharged veteran of World War II, he enjoys a good name among his neighbors and has had no blemish on his record more disreputable than a conviction for reckless driving.

The loading, crushing and transporting of these casings were all in broad daylight, in full view of passers-by, without the slightest effort at concealment. When an investigation was started, Morissette voluntarily, promptly and candidly told the whole story to the authorities, saying that he had no intention of stealing but thought the property was abandoned, unwanted and considered of no value to the Government. He was indicted, however, on the charge that he "did unlawfully, wilfully and knowingly steal and convert" property of the United States of the value of $84, in violation of 18 U. S. C. §641, which provides that "whoever embezzles, steals, purloins, or knowingly converts" government property is punishable by fine and imprisonment. Morissette was convicted and sentenced to imprisonment for two months or to pay a fine of $200. The Court of Appeals affirmed, one judge dissenting.

On his trial, Morrissette, as he had at all times told investigating officers, testified that from appearances he believed the casings were cast-off and abandoned, that he did not intend to steal the property, and took it with no wrongful or criminal intent. The trial court, however, was unimpressed, and ruled: . . . "That is presumed by his own act."

The Court of Appeals . . . affirmed the conviction because, "As we have interpreted the statute, appellant was guilty of its violation beyond a shadow of doubt, as evidenced even by his own admissions." Its construction of the statute is that it creates several separate and distinct offenses, one being knowing conversion of government property. The court ruled that this particular offense requires no element of criminal intent. This conclusion was thought to be required by the failure of Congress to express such a requisite and this Court's decisions in *United States* v. *Behrman*, 258 U. S. 280, and *United States* v. *Balint*, 258 U. S. 250.

I.

In those cases this Court did construe mere omission from a criminal enactment of any mention of criminal intent as dispensing with it. If they be deemed precedents for principles of construction generally applicable to federal penal statutes, they authorize this conviction. Indeed, such adoption of the literal reasoning announced in those cases would do this and more—it would sweep out of all federal crimes, except when expressly preserved, the ancient requirement of a culpable state of mind. We think a résumé of their historical background is convincing that an effect has been ascribed to them more comprehensive than was contemplated and one inconsistent with our philosophy of criminal law.

The contention that an injury can amount to a crime only when inflicted by intention is no provincial or transient notion. It is as universal and persistent in mature systems of law as belief in freedom of the human will and a consequent ability and duty of the normal individual to choose between good and evil. A relation between some mental element and punishment for a harmful act is almost as instinctive as the child's familiar exculpatory "But I didn't mean to," and has afforded the rational basis for a tardy and unfinished substitution of deterrence and reformation in place of retaliation and vengeance as the motivation for public prosecution. Unqualified acceptance of this doctrine by English common law in the Eighteenth Century was indicated by Blackstone's sweeping statement that to constitute any crime there must first be a "vicious will." . . .

Crime, as a compound concept, generally constituted only from concurrence of an evil-meaning mind with an evil-doing hand, was congenial to an intense individualism and took deep and early root in American soil. As the states codified the common law of crimes, even if their enactments were silent on the subject, their courts assumed that the omission did not signify disapproval of the principle but merely recognized that intent was so inherent in the idea of the offense that it required no statutory affirmation. Courts, with little hesitation or division, found an implication of the requirement as to offenses that were taken over from the common law. The unanimity with which they have adhered to the central thought that wrongdoing must be conscious to be criminal is emphasized by the variety, disparity and confusion of their definitions of the requisite but elusive mental element. However, courts of various jurisdictions, and for the purposes of different offenses, have devised working formulae, if not scientific ones, for the instruction of juries around such terms as "felonious intent," "criminal intent," "malice aforethought," "guilty knowledge," "fraudulent intent," "wilfulness," "*scienter*," to denote guilty knowledge, or "*mens rea*," to signify an evil purpose or mental culpabilit*y*. By use or combination of these various tokens, they have sought to protect those who were not blameworthy in mind from conviction of infamous common-law crimes.

However, the *Balint* and *Behrman* offenses belong to a category of another character, with very different antecedents and origins. The crimes there involved depend on no mental element but consist only of forbidden acts or omissions. This, while not expressed by the Court, is made clear from examination of a century-old but accelerating tendency, discernible both here and in England, to call into existence new duties and crimes which disregard any ingredient of intent. The industrial revolution multiplied the number of workmen exposed to injury from increasingly powerful and complex mechanisms, driven by freshly discovered sources of energy, requiring higher precautions by employers. Traffic of velocities, volumes and varieties unheard of came to subject the wayfarer to intolerable casualty risks if owners and drivers were not to observe new cares and uniformities of conduct. Congestion of cities and crowding of quarters called for health and welfare regulations undreamed of in simpler times. Wide distribution of goods became an instrument of wide distribution of harm when those who dispersed food, drink, drugs, and even securities, did not comply with reasonable standards of quality, integrity, disclosure and care. Such dangers have engendered increasingly numerous and detailed regulations which heighten the duties of those in control of particular industries, trades, properties or activities that affect public health, safety or welfare.

While many of these duties are sanctioned by a more strict civil liability, lawmakers, whether wisely or not, have sought to make such regulations more effective by invoking criminal sanctions to be applied by the familiar technique of criminal prosecutions and convictions. This has confronted the courts with a multitude of prosecutions, based on statutes or administrative regulations, for what have been aptly called "public welfare offenses." These cases do not fit neatly into any of such accepted classifications of common-law offenses, such as those against the state, the person, property, or public morals. Many of these offenses are not in the nature of positive aggressions or invasions, with which the common law so often dealt, but are in the nature of neglect where the law requires care, or inaction where it imposes a duty. Many violations of such regulations result in no direct or immediate injury to person or property but merely create the danger or probability of it which the law seeks to minimize. While such offenses do not threaten the security of the state in the manner of treason, they may be regarded as offenses against its authority, for their occurrence impairs the efficiency of controls deemed essential to the social order as presently constituted. In this respect, whatever the intent of the violator, the injury is the same, and the consequences are injurious or not according to fortuity. Hence legislation applicable to such offenses, as a matter of policy, does not specify intent as a necessary element. The accused, if he does not will the violation, usually is in a position to prevent it with no more care than society might reasonably expect and no more exertion than it might reasonably exact from one who assumed his responsibilities. Also, penalties commonly are relatively small, and conviction does no grave damage to an offender's reputation. Under such considerations, courts have turned to construing statutes and regulations which make no mention of intent as dispensing with it and holding that the guilty act alone makes out the crime. . . .

Neither this Court nor, so far as we are aware, any other has undertaken to delineate a precise line or set forth comprehensive criteria for distinguishing between crimes that require a mental element and crimes that do not. We attempt no closed definition, for the law on the subject is neither settled nor static. The conclusion reached in the *Balint* and *Behrman* cases has our approval and adherence for the circumstances to which it was there applied. A quite different question here is whether we will expand the doctrine of crimes without intent to include those charged here.

Stealing, larceny, and its variants and equivalents, were among the earliest offenses known to the law that existed before legislation; they are invasions of rights or property which stir a sense of insecurity in the whole community and arouse public demand for retribution, the penalty is high and, when a sufficient amount is involved, the infamy is that of a felony, which, says Maitland, is ". . . as bad a word as you can give to man or thing." State courts of last resort, on whom fall the heaviest burden of interpreting criminal law in this country, have consistently retained the requirement of intent in larceny-type offenses. If any state has deviated, the exception has neither been called to our attention nor disclosed by our research.

Congress, therefore, omitted any express prescription of criminal intent from the enactment before us in the light of an unbroken course of judicial decision in all constituent states of the Union holding intent inherent in this class of offense, even when not expressed in a statute. Congressional silence as to mental elements in an Act merely adopting into federal statutory law a concept of crime already so well defined in common law and statutory interpretation by the states may warrant quite contrary inferences than the same silence in creating an offense new to general law, for whose definition the courts have no guidance except the Act. Because the offenses before this Court in the *Balint* and *Behrman* cases were of this latter class, we cannot accept them as authority for eliminating intent from offenses incorporated from the common law. Nor do exhaustive studies of state court cases disclose any well-considered decisions applying the doctrine of crime without intent to such enacted common-law offenses, although a few deviations are notable as illustrative of the danger inherent in the Government's contentions here.

The Government asks us by a feat of construction radically to change the weights and balances in the scales of justice. The purpose and obvious effect of doing away with the requirement of a guilty intent is to ease the prosecution's path to conviction, to strip the defendant of such benefit as he derived at common law from innocence of evil purpose, and to circumscribe the freedom heretofore allowed juries. Such a manifest impairment of the immunities of the individual should not be extended to common-law crimes on judicial invitiative.

The spirit of the doctrine which denies to the federal judiciary power to create crimes forthrightly admonishes that we should not enlarge the reach of enacted crimes by constituting them from anything less than the incriminating components contemplated by the words used in the statute. And where Congress borrows terms of art in which are accumulated the legal tradition and meaning of centuries of practice, it presumably knows and adopts the cluster of ideas that were attached to each borrowed word in the body of learning from which it was taken and the meaning its use will convey to the judicial mind unless otherwise instructed. In such case, absence of contrary direction may be taken as satisfaction with widely accepted definitions, not as a departure from them.

We hold that mere omission from §641 of any mention of intent will not be construed as eliminating that element from the crimes denounced.

II

...[T]reason—the one crime deemed grave enough for definition in our Constitution itself—requires not only the duly witnessed overt act of aid and comfort to the enemy but also the mental element of disloyalty or adherence to the enemy. In view of the care that has been bestowed upon the subject, it is significant that we have not found, nor has our attention been directed to, any instance in which Congress has expressly eliminated the mental element from a crime taken over from the common law. . . .

Had the statute applied to conversions without qualification, it would have made crimes of all unwitting, inadvertent and unintended conversions. Knowledge, of course, is not identical with intent and may not have been the most apt words of limitation. But knowing conversion requires more than knowledge that defendant was taking the property into his possession. He must have had knowledge of the facts, though not necessarily the law, that made the taking a conversion. In the case before us, whether the mental element that Congress required be spoken of as knowledge or as intent, would not seem to alter its bearing on guilt. For it is not apparent how Morissette could have knowingly or intentionally converted property that he did not know could be converted, as would be the case if it was in fact abandoned or if he truly believed it to be abandoned and unwanted property. . . .

III

As we read the record, this case was tried on the theory that even if criminal intent were essential its presence (a) should be decided by the court (b) as a presumption of law, apparently conclusive, (c) predicated upon the isolated act of taking rather than upon all of the circumstances. In each of these respects we believe the trial court was in error.

Where intent of the accused is an ingredient of the crime charged, its existence is a question of fact which must be submitted to the jury. State court authorities cited to the effect that intent is relevant in larcenous crimes are equally emphatic and uniform that it is a jury issue. . . .

It follows that the trial court may not withdraw or prejudge the issue by instruction that the law raises a presumption of intent from an act. It often is tempting to cast in terms of a "presumption" a conclusion which a court thinks probable from given facts. . . .

We think presumptive intent has no place in this case. A conclusive presumption which testimony could not overthrow would effectively eliminate intent as an ingredient of the offense. A presumption which would permit but not require the jury to assume intent from an isolated fact would prejudge a conclusion which the jury should reach of its own volition. A presumption which would permit the jury to make an assumption which all the evidence considered together does not logically establish would give to a proven fact an artificial and fictional effect. In either case, this presumption would conflict with the overriding presumption of innocence with which the law endows the accused and which extends to every element of the crime. Such incriminating presumptions are not to be improvised by the judiciary. . . .

Of course, the jury, considering Morissette's awareness that these casings were on government property, his failure to seek any permission for their removal and his self-interest as a witness, might have disbelieved his profession of innocent intent and concluded that his assertion of a belief that the casings were abandoned was an afterthought. Had the jury convicted on proper instructions it would be the end of the matter. But juries are not bound by what seems inescapable logic to judges. They might have concluded that the heaps of spent casings left in the hinterland to rust away presented an appearance of unwanted and abandoned junk, and that lack of any conscious deprivation of property or intentional injury was indicated by Morissette's good character, the openness of the taking, crushing and transporting of the casings, and the candor with which it was all admitted. They might have refused to brand Morissette as a thief. Had they done so, that too would have been the end of the matter.

E. THE THIRD DEGREE

WATTS V. INDIANA
338 U.S. 49, 57 (June 27, 1949)

Like *Brinegar*, *Watts* was announced on the final day of the 1948 Term, and they were both among the last decisions in which Murphy and Rutledge were to participate. *Watts* was the first of three companion cases. Jackson's colleagues were divided in the same manner in all three decisions, with the four libertarians plus Frankfurter forming a voting majority from which Burton, Reed, and Chief Justice Vinson dissented (and without opinion in each case). Jackson wrote a single opinion to justify his concurrence in *Watts* and his dissent in the other two cases.[18]

The cases variously reversed the supreme courts of Indiana, Pennsylvania, and South Carolina, in their affirmance of convictions of defendants for sundry murders. The problem in all three cases related to the admissibility of confessions obtained from the defendants after arrest, extended interrogation without benefit of counsel, and consequent arraignment only after confessions had been obtained. In each case, a majority of the Court declared that such procedures were unconstitutional. Douglas, who concurred alone in each case, argued that *any* confession secured under such circumstances was inadmissible. Frankfurter, Murphy, and Rutledge said that the critical question was whether the confession was obtained only as the result of coercion, irrespective of whether the pressure was physical or "mental." This meant that "constitutionality" hinged upon the judgment of individual Supreme Court justices of the "fact" question whether the confession was "voluntary," based upon each justice's appraisal of the evidence as it appeared in the record of the case. Black concurred without opinion in each case.

Jackson saw no abridgment of the Fourteenth Amendment in practices whereby the police subjected suspects to the third degree, with varying degrees of sophistication short of direct physical torture and literally beating a confession out of a suspect—and not necessarily even then.[19] Evidently he decided that here, in the light of the peculiar fact circumstances of each of these cases, coercion had been "undue" in the *Watts* case but not in the other two.[20] His opinion argued against the wisdom of

[18] *Turner* v. *Pennsylvania,* 338 U.S. 62; *Harris* v. *South Carolina,* 338 U.S. 68.

[19] See his opinion (with Frankfurter and Roberts) in the case of a Georgia sheriff (whose name, appropriately enough, was Screws) who quite literally kicked to death, in the public square in front of the county jail, a manacled young Negro prisoner. *Screws* v. *United States,* 325 U.S. 91 (1945).

[20] For a theoretical explanation of such weighing of degrees of deprivation, in a study of over two dozen of the Court's involuntary confession decisions over a period of a quarter

Supreme Court justices substituting their own appraisal of the evidence for that of state and local judges, however, so it would seem that Jackson was whipped by his own lash, and he was guilty of the very conduct against which he was protesting.

MR. JUSTICE JACKSON *concurring in the result in* Watts v. Indiana *and dissenting in* [Harris v. *South Carolina and* Turner v. *Pennsylvania*].

These three cases, from widely separated states, present essentially the same problem. Its recurrence suggests that it has roots in some condition fundamental and general to our criminal system.

In each case police were confronted with one or more brutal murders which the authorities were under the highest duty to solve. Each of these murders was unwitnessed, and the only positive knowledge on which a solution could be based was possessed by the killer. In each there was reasonable ground to *suspect* an individual but not enough legal evidence to *charge* him with guilt. In each the police attempted to meet the situation by taking the suspect into custody and interrogating him. This extended over varying periods. In each, confessions were made and received in evidence at the trial. Checked with external evidence, they are inherently believable, and were not shaken as to truth by anything that occurred at the trial. Each confessor was convicted by a jury and state courts affirmed. This Court sets all three convictions aside.

The seriousness of the Court's judgment is that no one suggests that any course held promise of solution of these murders other than to take the suspect into custody for questioning. The alternative was to close the books on the crime and forget it, with the suspect at large. This is a grave choice for a society in which two-thirds of the murders already are closed out as insoluble.

A concurring opinion, however, goes to the very limit and seems to declare for outlawing any confession, however freely given, if obtained during a period of custody between arrest and arraignment—which, in practice, means all of them.

Others would strike down these confessions because of conditions which they say make them "involuntary." In this, on only a printed record, they pit their judgment against that of the trial judge and the jury. Both, with the great advantage of hearing and seeing the confessor and also the officers whose conduct and bearing toward him is in question, have found that the confessions were voluntary. In addition, the majority overrule in each case one or more state appellate courts, which have the same limited opportunity to know the truth that we do.

Amid much that is irrelevant or trivial, one serious situation seems to me to

---

of a century (enveloping Jackson's tenure and including the *Watts, Turner,* and *Harris* cases), see Fred Kort, "Content Analysis of Judicial Opinions and Rules of Law" in my *Judicial Decision-Making* (New York: The Free Press of Glencoe, 1963), Chap. VI, and especially p. 137.

stand out in these cases. The suspect neither had nor was advised of his right to get counsel. This presents a real dilemma in a free society. To subject one without counsel to questioning which may and is intended to convict him, is a real peril to individual freedom. To bring in a lawyer means a real peril to solution of the crime, because, under our adversary system, he deems that his sole duty is to protect his client—guilty or innocent—and that in such a capacity he owes no duty whatever to help society solve its crime problem. Under this conception of criminal procedure, any lawyer worth his salt will tell the suspect in no uncertain terms to make no statement to police under any circumstances.

If the state may arrest on suspicion and interrogate without counsel, there is no denying the fact that it largely negates the benefits of the constitutional guaranty of the right to assistance of counsel. Any lawyer who has ever been called into a case after his client has "told all" and turned any evidence he has over to the Government, knows how helpless he is to protect his client against the facts thus disclosed.

I suppose the view one takes will turn on what one thinks should be the right of an accused person against the State. Is it his right to have the judgment on the facts? Or is it his right to have a judgment based on only such evidence as he cannot conceal from the authorities, who cannot compel him to testify in court and also cannot question him before? Our system comes close to the latter by any interpretation, for the defendant is shielded by such safeguards as no system of law except the Anglo-American concedes to him.

Of course, no confession that has been obtained by any form of physical violence to the person is reliable and hence no conviction should rest upon one obtained in that manner. Such treatment not only breaks the will to conceal or lie, but may even break the will to stand by the truth. Nor is it questioned that the result can sometimes be achieved by threats, promises, or inducements, which torture the mind but put no scar on the body. . . . But if ultimate quest in a criminal trial is the truth and if the circumstances indicate no violence or threats of it, should society be deprived of the suspect's help in solving a crime merely because he was confined and questioned when uncounseled?

We must not overlook that, in these as in some previous cases, once a confession is obtained it supplies ways of verifying its trustworthiness. In these cases before us the verification is sufficient to leave me in no doubt that the admissions of guilt were genuine and truthful. Such corroboration consists in one case of finding a weapon where the accused has said he hid it, and in others that conditions which could only have been known to one who was implicated correspond with his story. It is possible, but it is rare, that a confession if repudiated on the trial, standing alone will convict unless there is external proof of its verity.

In all such cases, along with other conditions criticized, the continuity and duration of the questioning is invoked and it is called an "inquiry," "inquest" or "inquisition," depending mainly on the emotional state of the writer. But as in some cases here, if interrogation is permissible at all, there are sound reasons for prolonging it—which the opinions here ignore. The suspect at first perhaps makes an effort to exculpate himself by alibis or other statements. These are verified, found false, and he is then confronted with his falsehood. Sometimes (though such cases do not reach us) verification proves them true or credible and the suspect is released. Sometimes, as here, more than one crime is involved. The duration of an interrogation may well depend on the temperament, shrewdness and cunning of the accused and the competence of the examiner. But, assuming a right to examine at all, the right must include what is made reasonably necessary by the facts of the particular case.

If the right of interrogation be admitted, then it seems to me that we must leave it to trial judges and juries and state appellate courts to decide individual cases, unless they show some want of proper standards of decision. I find nothing to indicate that any of the courts below in these cases did not have a correct understanding of the Fourteenth Amendment, unless this Court thinks it means absolute prohibition of interrogation while in custody before arraignment.

I suppose no one would doubt that our Constitution and Bill of Rights, grounded in revolt against the arbitrary measures of George III and in the philosophy of the French Revolution, represent the maximum restrictions upon the power of organized society over the individual that are compatible with the maintenance of organized society itself. They were so intended and should be so interpreted. It cannot be denied that, even if construed as these provisions traditionally have been, they contain an aggregate of restrictions which seriously limit the power of society to solve such crimes as confront us in these cases. Those restrictions we should not for that reason cast aside, but that is good reason for indulging in no unnecessary expansion of them.

I doubt very much if they require us to hold that the State may not take into custody and question one suspected reasonably of an unwitnessed murder. If it does, the people of this country must discipline themselves to seeing their police stand by helplessly while those suspected of murder prowl about unmolested. Is it a necessary price to pay for the fairness which we know as "due process of law"? And if not a necessary one, should it be demanded by this Court? I do not know the ultimate answer to these questions; but, for the present, I should not increase the handicap on society.

F.   VOX POPULI

SHEPHERD V. FLORIDA
341 U.S. 50 (April 9, 1951)

The unanimous decision in this case was *per curiam,* and in its entirety the opinion of the Court reads:

The judgment is reversed. *Cassell* v. *Texas,* 339 U.S. 282.

Cassell itself had been decided not quite a year earlier, on April 24, 1950, when it had provoked considerable disagreement in regard to the appropriate rationalization of a decision in which there was very little disagreement as to *outcome*. *Cassell* produced no opinion of the Court, because the majority was divided between a plurality subset of four and a minority group of three. The larger subgroup (Reed, Vinson, Black, and Clark) took a position in support of what they called the federal rule: that it is a denial of equal protection to convict a Negro of murder if there was discrimination against Negro participation in the grand jury which indicted the defendant. The Texas Court of Criminal Appeals had invoked this same policy for its guidance, but had reached the conclusion that in fact there had been no discrimination in the grand jury that indicted Cassell; so the only difference between the Supreme Court plurality and the state court lay in their respective and differing inferences about the facts of record. Frankfurter, with whom Burton and Minton joined, thought that the state court had misunderstood the rule, and that the Texas judges labored under the misapprehension that token representation of a single Negro on each grand jury list sufficed. Douglas did not participate; and Jackson dissented, arguing that there was no showing that Cassell had been prejudiced by the absence of Negroes on the jury that brought him to trial, because no question was raised about the jury that convicted him or the fairness of his trial in any other respect. Jackson also disagreed that the only practical method for enforcing the right of qualified Negroes to serve on grand juries was for appellate courts to reverse the convictions of killers:

> The case before us is that of a Negro convicted of murder by crushing the skull of a sleeping watchman with a piece of iron pipe to carry out a burglary. No question is here as to his guilt. . . . [and] it is frivolous to contend that any grand jury, however constituted, could have done its duty in any way other than to indict.

> . . . I doubt if any good purpose will be served in the long run by identifying the right of the most worthy Negroes to serve on grand juries with the efforts of the least worthy to defer or escape punishment for crime.[21]

As the sole dissenter in *Cassell*, it is understandable that Jackson preferred to avoid (as his silent acquiescence in the *per curiam* order would have implied) lending support to *Cassell* as a precedent; and whatever the present citation might be construed to mean, Frankfurter was opposed to having the Reed opinion in that decision reinterpreted post hoc as anything other than the views of four justices (rather of the Court). So Jackson and Frankfurter joined forces in Shepherd's case, to suggest what might be termed a Gestalt concept of a fair trial, as an independent and

[21] *Cassell* v. *Texas*, 339 U.S. 298, 302, 304.

much broader alternative justification for the reversal of his conviction.

MR. JUSTICE JACKSON, whom MR. JUSTICE FRANKFURTER joins, concurring in the result.

On the 16th of July, 1949, a seventeen-year-old white girl in Lake County, Florida, reported that she had been raped, at the point of a pistol, by four Negroes. Six days later petitioners were indicted and, beginning September 1, were tried for the offense, convicted without recommendation of mercy, and sentenced to death. The Supreme Court of Florida, in reviewing evidence of guilt, said, "As we study the testimony, the only question presented here is which set of witnesses would the jury believe, that is, the State's witnesses or the testimony as given by the defendant-appellants."

But prejudicial influences outside the courtroom, becoming all too typical of a highly publicized trial, were brought to bear on this jury with such force that the conclusion is inescapable that these defendants were prejudged as guilty and the trial was but a legal gesture to register a verdict already dictated by the press and the public opinion which it generated.

Newspapers published as a fact, and attributed the information to the sheriff, that these defendants had confessed. No one, including the sheriff, repudiated the story. Witnesses and persons called as jurors said they had read or heard of this statement. However, no confession was offered at the trial. The only rational explanations for its nonproduction in court are that the story was false or that the confession was obtained under circumstances which made it inadmissible or its use inexpedient.

If the prosecutor in the courtroom had told the jury that the accused had confessed but did not offer to prove the confession, the court would undoubtedly have declared a mistrial and cited the attorney for contempt. If a confession had been offered in court, the defendant would have had the right to be confronted by the persons who claimed to have witnessed it, to cross-examine them, and to contradict their testimony. If the court had allowed an involuntary confession to be placed before the jury, we would not hesitate to consider it a denial of due process of law and reverse. When such events take place in the courtroom, defendant's counsel can meet them with evidence, arguments, and requests for instructions, and can at least preserve his objections on the record.

But neither counsel nor court can control the admission of evidence if unproven, and probably unprovable, "confessions" are put before the jury by newspapers and radio. Rights of the defendant to be confronted by the witnesses against him and to cross-examine them are thereby circumvented. It is hard to imagine a more prejudicial influence than a press release by the officer of the court charged with defendants' custody stating that they had confessed and here just such a statement, unsworn to, unseen, uncross-examined and uncontradicted, was conveyed by the press to the jury.

This Court has recently gone a long way to disable a trial judge from dealing with press interference with the trial process, . . . though it is to be noted that none of these cases involved a trial by jury. And the Court, by strict construction of an Act of Congress, has held not to be contemptuous any kind of interference unless it takes place in the immediate presence of the court, . . . the last place where a well-calculated obstruction of justice would be attempted. No doubt this trial judge felt helpless to give the accused any real protection against this out-of-court campaign to convict. But if freedoms of press are so abused as to make fair trial in the locality impossible, the judicial process must be protected by removing the trial to a forum beyond its probable influence. Newspapers, in the enjoyment of their constitutional rights, may not deprive accused persons of their right to fair trial. These convictions, accompanied by such events, do not meet any civilized conception of due process of law. That alone is sufficient, to my mind, to warrant reversal.

But that is not all. Of course, such a crime stirred deep feeling and was exploited to the limit by the press. These defendants were first taken to the county jail of Lake County. A mob gathered and demanded that defendants be turned over to it. By order of court, they were quickly transferred for safekeeping to the state prison, where they remained until about two weeks before the trial. Meanwhile, a mob burned the home of defendant Shepherd's father and mother and two other Negro houses. Negroes were removed from the community to prevent their being lynched. The National Guard was called out on July 17 and 18 and, on July 19, the 116th Field Artillery was summoned from Tampa. The Negroes of the community abandoned their homes and fled.

Every detail of these passion-arousing events was reported by the press under such headlines as, "Night Riders Burn Lake Negro Homes" and "Flames from Negro Homes Light Night Sky in Lake County." These and many other articles were highly prejudicial, including a cartoon published at the time of the grand jury, picturing four electric chairs and headed, "No Compromise—Supreme Penalty."

Counsel for defendants made two motions, one to defer the trial until the passion had died out and the other for a change of venue. These were denied. The Supreme Court of Florida, in affirming the conviction, observed that "The inflamed public sentiment was against the crime with which the appellants were charged rather than defendants' race." Such an estimate seems more charitable than realistic, and I cannot agree that the prejudice had subsided at the time of trial.

The trial judge, anxious to assure as fair a trial as possible under the circumstances, was evidently concerned about violence at the trial. He promulgated special rules which limited the number of visitors to those that could be seated, allowed no one to stand or loiter in hallways, stairways, and parts of the courthouse for thirty minutes before court convened and after it recessed, closed the elevators except to officers of the court or individuals to whom the sheriff gave special permit, required each person entering the courtroom to submit to search, prohibited any person from taking a "valise, satchel, bag, basket, bottle, jar, jug, bucket, package, bundle, or other such item" to the courtroom floor of the courthouse, allowed crutches, canes, and walking sticks only after inspection by the sheriff showed them to be necessary aids, prohibited demonstrations of any nature and made various other regulations, all of which the sheriff was charged to enforce and to that end was authorized to employ such number of deputies as might be necessary. Such precautions, however commendable, show the reaction that the atmosphere which permeated the trial created in the mind of the trial judge.

The situation presented by this record is not different, in essentials, from that which was found a denial of due process in *Moore* v. *Dempsey*, 261 U. S. 86 [1923]. Under these circumstances, for the Court to reverse these convictions upon the sole ground that the method of jury selection discriminated against the Negro race, is to stress the trivial and ignore the important. While this record discloses discrimination which under normal circumstances might be prejudicial, this trial took place under conditions and was accompanied by events which would deny defendants a fair trial before any kind of jury. I do not see, as a practical matter, how any Negro on the jury would have dared to cause a disagreement or acquittal. The only chance these Negroes had of acquittal would have been in the courage and decency of some sturdy and forthright white person of sufficient standing to face and live down the odium among his white neighbors that such a vote, if required, would have brought. To me, the technical question of discrimination in the jury selection has only theoretical importance. The case presents one of the best examples of one of the worst menaces to American justice. It is on that ground that I would reverse.

5 PROPERTY

Thus far we have been concerned with Jackson's opinions in regard to claims of personal liberty or right. In this chapter, we shall focus instead upon claims which Jackson conceptualized as those of property rights. The distinction between "personal" and "property" rights is, of course, itself an example of legal conceptualism. Although the dichotomy is a fundamental component of the politicolegal thinking that underlies the United States Constitution and American polity today, it is quite possible (as anthropologists remind us) to have a social system without either category of "right," as such. Indeed, the first case to which we shall turn raised difficult problems, in Jackson's view, precisely because of the absence of any concept of real property among members of one of the two societies involved in the transactions underlying the litigation.

It bears repeating at this point that, in this sample of the decisions in which he wrote opinions, substantially more of Jackson's opinions and votes are concerned primarily with questions of property rather than with personal rights. His more interesting and best written opinions, however, tend to focus upon discussions of personal rather than property rights. Hence, almost two-thirds of the fifty opinions included in this anthology deal with personal rights; whereas in the universe of the more than three hundred opinions from which our sample was drawn, almost precisely the opposite ratio obtains. We might well infer that Jackson found it easier to dramatize issues of civil liberties than the more mundane cases of income taxation which frequently were assigned to him. Apparently he was deemed something of an expert on taxation in view of his two years as General Counsel of the Bureau of Internal Revenue of the Treasury Department and one year as Assistant Attorney General in charge of the Tax Division of the Department of Justice during the first term of the New Deal. Nevertheless, at least the first two of his opinions in this chapter are remarkable for the poetic quality of the language with which Jackson describes the rhythms of nature and of people who live and work close to her. This is a characteristic feature of his writing: he was born and raised in a family that had farmed in Appalachian country for several generations, and this is reflected in the depth of feeling with which he spoke and imbued life into what, for his colleagues, seemed to be hackneyed claims raising technical questions of breach of contract, property tort, *respondeat superior*, patent infringement, and bankruptcy administration.

The general trend in Jackson's decision making was for him to write dissenting opinions upholding claims of property rights much more frequently after his year's leave of absence from the Court than before.[1] This change in his behavior as a judge was significant, even in a statistical sense, and cannot be attributed to the changing character either of the substantive issues or his colleagues. From the point of view of an individualist such as Jackson, the economic issues before the Court for decision represented less extreme claims after than during World War II; and the trend among his associates was similarly toward a group who were less liberal in their attitudes toward economic policy. Vinson and Burton constituted no net gain in economic liberalism over Stone and Roberts; and Clark and Minton clearly were a move in the conservative direction, in relation to Murphy and Rutledge. The change was in Jackson himself, and primarily reflected changes in his career aspirations, for reasons we already have discussed in the introductory chapter. (There was, incidentally, no corresponding change in his decision-making behavior in cases raising civil liberties issues.)

Given this trend both toward dissenting, and toward economic conservatism, in Jackson's opinions, one might possibly expect to find in the cases included in this chapter a more clearcut replication of that trend than in fact is evident. Of course, our present sample of only eight opinions is too small to support any meaningful generalizations of this sort, no matter what their direction, because many considerations beyond those relevant to statistical stratification affected our selection of which ones were to be included in this chapter. There are four opinions from the World War II period and four from after this period. A majority of the opinions are dissents; and Jackson argues, in a majority of the opinions, in defense of the conservative economic position. The reason that this chapter does not include relatively more of Jackson's wartime opinions, written for the majority of the Court and from an economically liberal point of view, is not their scarcity—for some of these, such as *Wickard* v. *Filburn*[2] are among the best known of his utterances as a judge—but rather because they make for less interesting reading.

The first three cases (A-C) all reached the Supreme Court from a relatively less-traveled route, the Court of Claims, and are concerned with demands for monetary compensation from the government, for damages and injuries, by various groups of persons. More broadly, each presents the problem, as Jackson states it, of accommodating a particular socioecono-

---

[1] Glendon Schubert, "Jackson's Judicial Philosophy: An Exploration in Value Analysis," *American Political Science Review,* LIX (1965), 961-963.

[2] 317 U.S. 111, 113 (1942).

mic interest in relation to a complex of other partially overlapping and
partially conflicting or competing social and economic interests. The next
two cases (D-E) provide a study in contrasts with efforts by Jackson and
his colleagues to define the appropriate role for the Supreme Court to play
in relation to the disestablishment of the legal monopolies created by administrative sufferance under the patent system. F presents a bankrupt
small-time entrepreneur, whose free-wheeling proclivities touched a re-
sponsive chord in the man who had spent the first half of his professional
life—over a score of years—as legal advisor, confidant, and country club
confrère of small town merchants who were "trying to make a buck," as
their idiom puts it, without having to go to jail for it. The final two cases
(G and H) deal with labor-management relations, which for Jackson represented another facet of the troubles of entrepreneurs (that is, their labor
costs). Jackson clearly identified with employers, and his deep-seated hostility toward unions often found expression in the affective words which
he chose to describe the problems that owners often had with organized
(or organizing) labor.[3] Frequently, however, Jackson's antilabor bias
found expression in the form not so much of direct criticism of union behavior, as in his tender solicitude for the economic rights of the "forgotten" third party to the relationship:[4] the simple but honest, hard-working,
once (alas!) independent, individual employee (or "workingman," as
Jackson preferred to call him) who constantly was caught in a cross-fire
between hard-bitten corporate management, on the one hand, and ruthless, driving, union professionals, on the other hand. In practice, of course,
such a posture had the effect of advancing the coinciding interests of employers, and of opposing the conflicting interests of noncompany unions.

The position toward which he was moving, in his latter years on the
Court, is perhaps better indicated in his last speech to the organized bar,
than in any one of his opinions. His remarks here contrast sharply, in both
content and tone, with his speeches a decade and a half earlier, when he
was still very much on the political make and happily identified himself
as "the New Dealer" on the program.[5] But now he sounded like an Old

3 For a contrary conclusion, se Robert J. Steamer, *The Constitutional Doctrines of Mr.
Justice Robert H. Jackson* (Ph.D. dissertation, Cornell University, 1954; University Microfilms No. 9802, Ann Arbor, Michigan), p. 185: "The evidence seems preponderant from a
reading of Justice Jackson's opinions that he bows to no inherent bias either toward labor
or toward management. His approach to the problem is one of fairness to both sides within
the framework of his usual disciplined restraint of judicial law-making."

4 See, for example, his dissenting opinion in *National Labor Relations Board* v. *A.J.
Tower Co.,* 329 U.S. 324, 335 (1946).

5 See Chap 1, footnote 3, *supra;* and cf. Eugene C. Gerhart, *America's Advocate: Robert
H. Jackson* (Indianapolis: The Bobbs-Merrill Company, Inc.), pp. 97-98. In those days, he
was laying down the gauntlet to the economic royalists, taunting them for their hypocrisy

Dealer, with views that hardly can be distinguished from those of the *right* wing of the Nine Old Men—McReynolds, Butler, VanDevanter, and Sutherland—whom he himself had so roundly berated for standing in the path of economic and social progress, such a relatively short time earlier.

It seems to me that . . . traditional freedoms are less in danger of any sudden overthrow than of being gradually bartered or traded for something else on which the people place a higher current value. In this anxiety-ridden time, many are ready to exchange some of their liberties for a real or fancied increase in security against external foes, internal betrayers or criminals. Others are eager to bargain away local controls for a federal subsidy. Many will give up individual rights for promise of collective advantages. The real question posed by the Fascist and Communist movements, which together have captivated a large part of the world's population, is whether, today, liberty is regarded by the masses of men as their most precious possession. Certainly in the minds of many foreign peoples our type of individual liberty has been outvalued by promises of social welfare and economic security, which they want too passionately to be critical of the price. If this indifference to traditional values should spread to us, it would be the greatest threat to our own liberties.

Measures of public welfare or security are apt to be demanded without considering that execution of each added function requires an incalculable number of detailed official decisions important to the property, welfare or perhaps the liberty of those affected. However, most are of small consequence to the general public and constitute routine, tiresome duties for often anonymous officials secure in their tenure and beyond the reach of aggrieved citizens. That among their multitude of acts are many careless or arbitrary ones we may be sure. Many of them are immune from judicial review, but the very mass of these decisions and their particularized character make review, even if allowed, sporadic, costly, superficial and largely futile. Thus, unless new safeguards are devised, an administration that is all-embracing will of necessity tend to become all-powerful. It will take considerable ingenuity and diligence to find techniques to extend the protection of individual rights to keep pace with the expansion of power. The Federal Tort Claims Act, to give remedies for injury from official negligence, and the Administrative Procedure Act, to assure more impartial administrative decisions,

as well as for their avarice. "Those who talk rugged individualism," he wrote in a typical tract for the time, "seem always to be those who live softly themselves. These same persons who advocate life in the raw, to make people sturdy, take none of the rugged individualism to themselves. They are terrified at the suggestion of inheritance taxes, the effect of which at the worst would be to give their own sons a chance to be rugged individualists." Robert H. Jackson, "The People's Business: The Truth About Taxes," *Forum*, XCV (January, 1936), 25.

are examples of measures that may help to prevent government from becoming arbitrary and oppressive as it grows big.

It is said, by advocates of the expanding socialization, that it chiefly affects "property rights", as to which it is safe to let the legislators and administrators have their way so long as courts uncompromisingly protect "human rights". For purposes of that argument, it is assumed that our forefathers were absentminded when the citizen's property, as well as his person, was assured due process of law. The longer I work with these problems the less certain I am that what they joined we can put asunder. My equal right to drive an automobile may be only a claim to use of property, but it concerns my personal freedom as well. Prohibition may be looked upon as no more than a regulation of a particular kind of property, but many took it as rather personal. If officers search my house and seize my papers, with no threat to my person, only property may be directly touched; but I can think of no greater affront to my person. But, even if we think property sometimes has had undue protection against regulation, the question remains, how far so-called rights of property can be swept away without encroaching upon rights of the person as well. Every foreign state that has deprived persons of fundamental "property rights" has eventually also taken away the rights of the person. Those who operate intensive state controls of property have found it necessary soon to take equally intensive state control of labor also.[6]

A.   THE NOBLE RED MAN

NORTHWESTERN BANDS OF SHOSHONE INDIANS V.
UNITED STATES
324 U.S. 335, 354 (March 12, 1945)

Among the more recondite specialties of the legal profession in America is the trade plied by the Indian lawyer. Not usually himself a noble savage, nor an inmate of a reservation, this kind of lawyer makes his living by unearthing and pressing through a variety of adjudicative tribunals—including an occasional but rare appearance before the Supreme Court itself—stale claims on behalf of dead people. The legal fees from this business make it worthwhile for him, because the proceedings invariably are complicated, extended, and largely irrelevant to the needs and interests of the present generation of Indian-American citizens. The days of the large, direct windfall monetary settlement are gone, as Jackson ex-

---

[6] Robert H. Jackson, "The Task of Maintaining Our Liberties: The Role of the Judiciary," *American Bar Association Journal*, XXXIX (1953), 963.

plains in his opinion. But the habit persists of suing the government to atone for Minuit's successful low bid in the acquisition of Manhattan, thus substituting the shyster for the sharper, in the continuing exploitation of the descendants of the earliest Americans.

There is, of course, another and more usual point of view: that the task of the Supreme Court is not to concern itself with what would be wise social policy. Rather, it is to see that the Court of Claims carries out the legislative intent of the Congress, as expressed in various public and private acts. Most of the justices participating in the decision of this case thought it best to cast the issue in the latter rhetoric.

The Shoshones had sued Uncle Sam for fifteen million dollars, at the rate of approximately a dollar an acre, for lands formerly claimed by the Indians but preempted by American military might and conquest. The basis of the present Indian claim was the Box Elder (Utah Territory) Treaty of July 30, 1863; various subsequent statutes, treaties, and executive orders; and a special jurisdictional act of February 28, 1929, authorizing the Court of Claims to try the issue, which can be stated for present purposes as whether the Box Elder Treaty had intended to recognize a valid prior Indian title in the realty in question. Douglas, Murphy, Frankfurter, and (apparently) Roberts said that it did; Reed, with Stone and Rutledge, said that it didn't; and Jackson, in one of the very rare instances in which only he and Hugo Black shared an opinion about property rights, said that it didn't matter, because neither of the alternative possibilities for legal disposition could make any meaningful contribution to the resolution of the underlying socioeconomic problem. Jackson and Black did vote with the Reed group to reject the claim, in a five to four division which split libertarians and conservatives alike right down the middle. In effect, Jackson's opinion gives the lyrics to the Indians, and the music to the Treasury.

MR. JUSTICE JACKSON, *concurring.*

MR. JUSTICE BLACK and I think it may be desirable to state some of the difficulties which underlie efforts to leave such an Indian grievance as this to settlement by a lawsuit.

It is hard to see how any judicial decision under such a jurisdictional act can much advance solution of the problem of the Shoshones. Any judgment that we may render gives to these Indians neither their lands nor money. The jurisdictional act provides that the proceeds above attorneys' fees shall "be deposited in the Treasury of the United States to the credit of the Indians" at 4 per cent interest and "shall be subject to appropriation by Congress only for the health, education, and industrial advancement of said Indians." The only cash payment is attorneys' fees. Section 7 provides that the Court of Claims shall determine a reasonable fee, not to exceed 10 per cent of the recovery, together with expenses, to be paid to the attorneys for the Northwestern Bands out of the sums found due. After counsel are thus paid, not a cent is put into the reach of the Indians; all that is done for them by a judgment is to earmark some funds in the Treasury from which Congress may as it sees fit from time to time make appropriations "for the health, education, and industrial advancement of said Indians." Congress could do this, of course, without any judgment or earmarking of funds, as it often has done. Congress, even after judgment, still must decide the amount and times of payment to the Indians according to their needs.

We would not be second to any other in recognizing that—judgment or no judgment—a moral obligation of a high order rests upon this country to provide for decent shelter, clothing, education, and industrial advancement of the Indian. Nothing is gained by dwelling upon the unhappy conflicts that have prevailed between the Shoshones and the whites—conflicts which sometimes leaves one in doubt which side could make the better claim to be civilized. The generation of Indians who suffered the privations, indignities, and brutalities of the westward march of the whites have gone to the Happy Hunting Ground, and nothing that we can do can square the account with them. Whatever survives is a moral obligation resting on the descendants of the whites to do for the descendants of the Indians what in the conditions of this twentieth century is the decent thing.

It is most unfortunate to try to measure this moral duty in terms of legal obligations and ask the Court to spell out Indian legal rights from written instruments made and probably broken long ago and to put our moral duty in figures as legal damages. The Indian problem is essentially a sociological problem, not a legal one. We can make only a pretense of adjudication of such claims, and that only by indulging the most unrealistic and fictional assumptions.

Here we are asked to go back over three quarters of a century to spell out the meaning of a most ambiguous writing made in 1863. One of the parties did not keep, or know how to keep, written records of negotiations. Written evidence bearing on intention is only that which the whites chose to make. It does not take a particularly discerning eye to see that these records, written usually by Indian agents, are quite apt to speak well of the writer's virtue and good intention. Evidence from the memory of man is no longer available. Even if both parties to these agreements were of our own stock, we being a record-keeping people, a court would still have the gravest difficulty determining what their motives and intentions and meanings were. Statutes of limitations cut off most such inquiries, not because a claim becomes less just the longer it is denied, but because another policy intervenes—the policy to leave in repose matters which can no longer be the subject of intelligent adjudication.

Even if the handicap of time could be overcome, we could not satisfactorily apply legal techniques to interpretation of this treaty. The Indian parties to the treaty were a band of simple, relatively peaceful, and extremely primitive men.

The population of the band was only about 1,500, and the territories claimed to have been occupied as their home consisted of over 15,000,000 acres of land in Idaho, Utah, and Nevada—about 10,000 acres for every individual in the band. Of course so few could not patrol and defend so vast a territory against inroads by the more aggressive and efficient whites. The white was a better killer. The game disappeared, the lands were not productive, and in peace the Indians became destitute. Desperation stimulated or perhaps produced predatory tendencies and they began to fall upon the overland caravans and to steal and rob. The whites brought forth their armies and reduced the Indians to submission. Then the whites "negotiated" a treaty.

We realize that for over a century it has been a judicial practice to construe these "agreements" with Indians, as if they were contracts between white men. In some cases, where the provisions are simple and definite and deal with concrete lands or matters, this may be practicable. But despite antiquity of the custom, to apply the litigation process to such a problem as we have here seems far-fetched. The most elemental condition of a bargain was not present, for there was nothing like equality of bargaining power. On one side were dominant, powerful, shrewd, and educated whites, who knew exactly what they wanted. On the other side were destitute, illiterate Indians who primarily wanted to be let alone and who wanted by some means to continue to live their own accustomed lives. Here we are asked to decide whether their intent was to relinquish titles or make reservations of titles or recognition of titles. The Indian parties did not know what titles were, had no such concept as that of individual land title, and had no sense of property in land. Here we are asked to attribute legal meanings to subscribers of a written instrument who had no written language of their own in which to express any meaning. We doubt if any interpreter could intelligently translate the contents of a writing that deals with the property concept, for the Indians did not have a word for it. People do not have words to fit ideas that have never occurred to them. Ownership meant no more to them than to roam the land as a great common, and to possess and enjoy it in the same way that they possessed and enjoyed sunlight and the west wind and the feel of spring in the air. Acquisitiveness, which develops a law of real property, is an accomplishment only of the "civilized."

Of course the Indians may have had some vague idea that thereafter they were to stay off certain lands and the white men in return were to stay off certain other land. But we do not think it is possible now to reduce such a nebulous accord to terms of common-law contract and conveyancing. The treaty was a political document. It was intended to pacify the Indians and to let the whites travel in peace a route they somehow were going to travel anyway.

How should we turn into money's worth the rights, if any, of which the Indians have been deprived? Should we measure it in terms of what was lost to a people who needed 10,000 acres apiece to sustain themselves through hunting and nomadic living, who had no system or standard of exchange, and whose representatives in making the treaty appear to have been softened for the job by gifts of blankets and trinkets? Should we measure it in terms of what was gained to our people, who sustain themselves in large numbers on few acres by greater efficiency and utilization? Of course amends can be made only to progeny in terms of their present needs as the jurisdictional Act recognizes will ultimately be done. The Indians' grievance calls for sympathetic, intelligent, and generous help in developing the latent talents and aspirations of the living generation, and there is little enlightenment for that task from endless and pointless lawsuits over the negotiation of generations long gone to their rest.

We agree with MR. JUSTICE REED that no legal rights are today to be recognized in the Shoshones by reason of this treaty. We agree with MR. JUSTICE DOUGLAS and MR. JUSTICE MURPHY as to their moral deserts. We do not mean to leave the impression that the two have any relation to each other. The finding that the treaty creates no legal obligations does not restrict Congress from such appropriations as its judgment dictates "for the health, education, and industrial advancement of said Indians," which is the position in which Congress would find itself if we found that it did create legal obligations and tried to put a value on them.

B. PASTORAL

UNITED STATES V. GERLACH LIVE STOCK COMPANY
339 U.S. 725 (June 5, 1950)

This is a decision that might very well have been adequately supported by a brief *per curiam* opinion if Vinson had not assigned the opinion to Jackson, who saw in it an opportunity to write an extended essay on the natural and social bases of legal change. The principal question for the Supreme Court was one which it ordinarily does not even purport to decide—whether the claimant had a legal right under state law—and the Court was unanimously agreed that in this case the answer was affirmative. (Douglas and Black did dissent in part, but only from the ancillary ruling that, the claim being valid, the United States was liable for interest under federal law.)

MR. JUSTICE JACKSON delivered the opinion of the Court.

We are asked to relieve the United States from six awards by the Court of Claims as just compensation for deprivation of riparian rights along the San Joaquin River in California caused by construction of Friant Dam, and its dependent irrigation system, as part of the Central Valley Project.

This is a gigantic undertaking to redistribute the principal fresh-water resources of California. Central Valley is a vast basin, stretching over 400 miles on its polar axis and a hundred in width, in the heart of California. Bounded by the Sierra Nevada on the east and by coastal ranges on the west, it consists actually of two separate river valleys which merge in a single pass to the sea at the Golden Gate. Its rich acres, counted in the millions, are deficient in rainfall and must remain generally arid and unfruitful unless artificially watered.

Water resources there are, if they can be captured and distributed over the land. From the highland barricade at the north the Sacramento River flows southerly, while from the Yosemite region at the southeast the San Joaquin River winds northeasterly until the two meet and consort in outlet to the sea through estuaries that connect with San Francisco Bay. These dominating rivers collect tribute from many mountain currents, carry their hoardings past parched plains and thriftlessly dissipate them in the Pacific tides. When it is sought to make these streams yield their wasting treasures to the lands they traverse, men are confronted with a paradox of nature; for the Sacramento, with almost twice the water, is accessible to the least land, whereas about three-fifths of the valley lies in the domain of the less affluent San Joaquin.

To harness these wasting waters, overcome this perversity of nature and make water available where it would be of greatest service, the State of California proposed to re-engineer its natural water distribution. This project was taken over by the United States in 1935 and has since been a federal enterprise. The plan, in broad outline, is to capture and store waters of both rivers and many of their tributaries in their highland basins, in some cases taking advantage of the resulting head for generation of electric energy. Shasta Dam in the north will produce power for use throughout much of the State and will provide a great reservoir to equalize seasonal flows of the Sacramento. A more dramatic feature of the plan is the water storage and irrigation system at the other end of the valley. There the waters of the San Joaquin will be arrested at Friant, where they would take leave of the mountains, and will be diverted north and south through a system of canals and sold to irrigate more than a million acres of land, some as far as 160 miles away. A cost of refreshing this great expanse of semiarid land is that, except for occasional spills, only a dry river bed will cross the plain below the dam. Here, however, surplus waters from the north are utilized, for through a 150-mile canal Sacramento water is to be pumped to the cultivated lands formerly dependent on the San Joaquin.

Both rivers afford navigation—the Sacramento for a considerable distance inland, the San Joaquin practically only at tidewater levels. The plan will have navigation consequences, principally on the Sacramento; but the effects on navigation are economically insignificant as compared with the values realized from redistribution of water benefits.

Such a project inevitably unsettles many advantages long enjoyed in reliance upon the natural order, and it is with deprivation of such benefits that we are here concerned.

Claimants own land parcels riparian to the San Joaquin. These are called "uncontrolled grass lands," to distinguish them from either crop lands or "controlled grass lands," both of which have long been irrigated through controlled systems supplied from the stream. Neither of these latter will be injured by the diversion, for they are to be provided with the replacement water from the Sacramento.

Uncontrolled grass lands involved in the claims are parts of a large riparian area which benefits from the natural seasonal overflow of the stream. Each year, with predictable regularity, the stream swells and submerges and saturates these low-lying lands. They are moistened and enriched by these inundations so that forage and pasturage thrive, as otherwise they can not. The high stage of the river, while fluctuating in height and variable in arrival, is not a flood in the sense of an abnormal and sudden deluge. The river rises and falls in rhythm with the cycle of seasons, expansion being normal for its time as curtailment is for others, and both are repeated with considerable constancy over the years. It should be noted, however, that claimants' benefit comes only from the very crest of this seasonal stage, which crest must be elevated and borne to their lands on the base of a full river, none of which can be utilized for irrigation above and little of it below them. Their claim of right is, in other words, to enjoy natural, seasonal fluctuation unhindered, which presupposes a peak flow largely unutilized.

The project puts an end to all this. Except at rare intervals, there will be no spill over Friant Dam, the bed of the San Joaquin along claimants' lands will be parched, and their grass lands will be barren. Unlike the supply utilized for nearby crop and "controlled" lands, the vanishing San Joaquin inundation cannot be replaced with Sacramento water. Claimants have been severally awarded compensation for this taking of their annual inundations, on the theory that, as part of the natural flow, its continuance is a right annexed to their riparian property....

As long ago as the Institutes of Justinian, running waters, like the air and the sea, were *res communes*—things common to all and property of none. Such was the doctrine spread by civil-law commentators and embodied in the Napoleonic Code and in Spanish law. This conception passed into the common law. From these sources, but largely from civil-law sources, the inquisitive and powerful minds of Chancellor Kent and Mr. Justice Story[7] drew in generating the basic doctrines of American water law.

---

[7] James Kent and Joseph Story, the authors, respectively, of *Commentaries on American Law* (New York: O. Halsted, 1826-1830), 4 vols., and of *Commentaries of the Constitution of the United States* (Boston Hilliard, Gray and Co., 1833), 3 vols., were eminent conservative thinkers and leading jurisprudes of their day. Kent was from Jackson's native state of New York, and Story was a Bostonian who—surpassing Frankfurter, at least in this respect—taught on the Harvard Law faculty while retaining his seat on the Supreme Court. Both men were staunch believers in, and supporters of, the rights of property. [Ed.]

Riparian rights developed where lands were amply watered by rainfall. The primary natural asset was land, and the run-off in streams or rivers was incidental. Since access to flowing waters was possible only over private lands, access became a right annexed to the shore. The law followed the principle of equality which requires that the corpus of flowing water becomes no one's property and that, aside from rather limited use for domestic and agricultural purposes by those above, each riparian owner has the right to have the water flow down to him in its natural volume and channels unimpaired in quality. The riparian system does not permit water to be reduced to possession so as to become property which may be carried away from the stream for commercial or nonriparian purposes. . . .

Then in the mountains of California there developed a combination of circumstances unprecedented in the long and litigious history of running water. Its effects on water laws were also unprecedented. Almost at the time when Mexico ceded California, with other territories, to the United States, gold was discovered there and a rush of hardy, aggressive and venturesome pioneers began. If the high lands were to yield their treasure to prospectors, water was essential to separate the precious from the dross. The miner's need was more than a convenience—it was a necessity; and necessity knows no law. But conditions were favorable for necessity to make law, and it did—law unlike any that had been known in any part of the Western world.

The adventurers were in a little-inhabited, unsurveyed, unowned and almost ungoverned country, theretofore thought to have little value. It had become public domain of the United States and miners regarded waters as well as lands subject to preemption. To be first in possession was to be best in title. Priority—of discovery, location and appropriation—was the primary source of rights. Fortuitously, along lower reaches of the streams there were no riparian owners to be injured and none to challenge customs of the miners. . . .

The Twentieth Century inducted new parties into the old struggle. Gigantic electric power and irrigation projects succeeded smaller operations, and municipalities sought to by-pass intervening agricultural lands and go into the mountains to appropriate the streams for city supply. Increasing dependence of all branches of the State's economy, both rural and urban, upon water centered attention upon its conservation and maximum utilization. . . .

But the public welfare, which requires claimants to sacrifice their benefits to broader ones from a higher utilization, does not necessarily require that their loss be uncompensated any more than in other takings where private rights are surrendered in the public interest. The waters of which claimants are deprived are taken for resale largely to other private land owners not riparian to the river and to some located in a different water shed. Thereby private lands will be made more fruitful, more valuable, and their operation more profitable. The reclamation laws contemplate that those who share these advantages shall, through water charges, reimburse the Government for its outlay. This project anticipates recoupment of its cost over a forty-year period. No reason appears why those who get the waters should be spared from making whole those from whom they are taken. Public interest requires appropriation; it does not require expropriation. We must conclude that by the Amendment California unintentionally destroyed and confiscated a recognized and adjudicated private property right, or that it remains compensable ... [and so] we conclude that claimants' right to compensation has a sound basis in California law. ...

We think the awards of the Court of Claims correctly applied the law of California as made applicable to these claims by Congress.

Affirmed.

C.   RESPONDEAT SUPERIOR

DALEHITE V. UNITED STATES
346 U.S. 15, 47 (June 8, 1953)

If the setting in *Gehrlach* was pastoral, that of *Dalehite* was explosive. A substantial portion of the port area of an American city was blown up when fire broke out in the hold of a ship where commercial fertilizer, produced under the auspices of the United States government and intended for shipment overseas under a federal foreign aid program, was being stored. Several hundred lawsuits emerged out of the disastrous losses in life, limb, and property that resulted from the holocaust; and the question before the Supreme Court was whether the United States was financially liable. No individual acts of negligence had been, or apparently could be, proved. As the opinion of the Court put it, "The negligence charged was that the United States, without definite investigation of FGAN [the fertilizer's] properties, shipped, or permitted shipment to a congested area without warning of the possibility of explosion under certain conditions."

The Dalehite claim was selected for trial as the test case, and the federal district court found the United States guilty of causal negligence, for carelessness in the general planning and administration of the fertilizer export program, for specific negligence in various phases of the manufacturing process, and for official dereliction of duty in failing adequately to police the loading on shipboard. The Court of Appeals for the Fifth Circuit, in an unusual *en banc* decision (of the entire group of six judges assigned to the court), unanimously reversed in favor of the government; and the Supreme Court affirmed, but by the slimmest of margins: 4-3 with less than a majority of the full Court uniting in the opinion of the Court. The ruling plurality consisted of three Truman appointees (Vinson, Burton, and Minton) plus Reed; neither Douglas nor Clark participated in the decision. Evidently, Clark disqualified himself because of his earlier official responsibility for the defense of the case in the lower courts, while he was Attorney General. There seems little doubt that both he and Douglas would have voted in support of Dalehite's claim, if they had participated; so the decision presents the anomaly of a minority establishing a policy contrary to that which was favored by a majority of the full Court. But if Clark could not take part in the decision, then it would not have changed the outcome even if Douglas had done so, because a 4-4 division also would have resulted in affirmance. There was only one dissent, with Frankfurter and Black joining in Jackson's opinion.[8]

MR. JUSTICE JACKSON, joined by MR. JUSTICE BLACK and MR. JUSTICE FRANKFURTER, dissenting.

All day, April 15, 1947, longshoremen loaded bags of ammonium nitrate fertilizer aboard the S. S. *Grandcamp,* docked at Texas City, Texas. Shortly after 8 a.m. next morning, when work resumed, smoke was seen coming from the No. 4 hold and it was discovered that fire had broken out in the fertilizer. The ship's master ordered the hatch covered and battened down, and steam was introduced into the hold. Local fire-fighting apparatus soon arrived, but the combined efforts to extinguish the fire were unavailing. Less than an hour after smoke was first seen, 880 tons of fertilizer in the No. 4 hold exploded and, in turn, detonated the fertilizer stored in the No. 2 hold. Fire spread to the dock area of Texas City and to the S. S. *High Flyer,* berthed at an adjoining pier and carrying a cargo of sulphur and ammonium nitrate fertilizer. Further efforts to extinguish or even contain the fire failed and, about 11 p.m., tugs unsuccessfully attempted to tow the *High Flyer* out to sea. Shortly after one o'clock on the morning of April 17, the sulphur and fertilizer aboard the *High Flyer* exploded, demolishing both that ship and the S. S. *Wilson B. Keene,* lying alongside. More than 560 persons perished in this holocaust, and some 3,000 were injured. The entire dock area of a thriving port was leveled and property damage ran into millions of dollars.

This was a man-made disaster; it was in no sense an "act of God." The fertilizer had been manufactured in government-owned plants at the Government's

[8] Although this decision and the one in the case of the Shoshone Indians appear contiguously in this chapter, that does not contradict our earlier remark: it *was* very unusual for Jackson and Black to dissent together in a decision relating to economic issues. In a sample of over two hundred such decisions in which they both participated and there was division on the Court, there was only one case in which Black and Jackson both dissented, together or otherwise, either for or against the claim of property right, and irrespective of whether or not others joined them in dissent: *Nathanson* v. *National Labor Relations Board,* 344 U.S. 25, 31 (1952). See my *The Judicial Mind,* pp. 130-133. *Dalehite* was not included in that particular sample of decisions, for the reason explained in *ibid.,* p. 154.

order and to its specifications. It was being shipped at its direction as part of its program of foreign aid. The disaster was caused by forces set in motion by the Government, completely controlled or controllable by it. Its causative factors were far beyond the knowledge or control of the victims; they were not only incapable of contributing to it, but could not even take shelter or flight from it.

Over 300 suits were brought against the United States under the Federal Tort Claims Act, alleging that its negligence was responsible for the disaster. After consolidating the suits, the District Court ordered the case of the present petitioners to be tried. The parties to all of the suits, in effect, agreed that the common issue of the Government's negligence should abide the outcome of this test litigation. The Court of Appeals for the Fifth Circuit reversed the trial court's judgment in favor of petitioners. Supporting that reversal, the Government here urges that (1) a private person would not be liable in these circumstances, and (2) even if a private person were liable, the Government is saved from liability by the statute's exception of discretionary acts.

This is one of those cases that a judge is likely to leave by the same door through which he enters. As we have been told by a master of our craft, "*Some* theory of liability, some philosophy of the end to be served by tightening or enlarging the circle of rights and remedies, is at the root of any decision in novel situations when analogies are equivocal and precedents are silent."[9] So, we begin by avowing a conception of the function of legal liability in cases such as this quite obviously at variance with the approach of the Court.

Congress has defined the tort liability of the Government as analogous to that of a private person. Traditionally, one function of civil liability for negligence is to supply a sanction to enforce the degree of care suitable to the conditions of contemporary society and appropriate to the circumstances of the case. The civil damage action, prosecuted and adjusted by private initiative, neither burdening our overworked criminal processes nor confined by the limits of criminal liability, is one of the law's most effective inducements to the watchfulness and prudence necessary to avoid calamity from hazardous operations in the midst of an unshielded populace.

Until recently, the influence of the Federal Government has been exerted in the field of tort law to tighten liability and liberalize remedies. Congress has even imposed criminal liability without regard to knowledge of danger or intent where potentially dangerous articles are introduced into interstate commerce. But, when the Government is brought into court as a tort defendant, the very proper zeal of its lawyers to win their case and the less commendable zeal of officials involved to conceal or minimize their carelessness militate against this trend. The Government, as a defendant, can exert an unctuous persuasiveness because it can

---

9 Cardozo, *The Growth of the Law*, p. 102. (Emphasis his own.)

clothe official carelessness with a public interest. Hence, one of the unanticipated consequences of the Tort Claims Act has been to throw the weight of government influence on the side of lax standards of care in the negligence cases which it defends.

It is our fear that the Court's adoption of the Government's view in this case may inaugurate an unfortunate trend toward relaxation of private as well as official responsibility in making, vending or transporting inherently dangerous products. For we are not considering here everyday commodities of commerce or products of nature but a complex compound not only proven by the event to be highly dangerous, but known from the beginning to lie somewhere within the range of the dangerous. Ammonium nitrate, as the Court points out, had been "long used as a component in explosives." This grade of it was manufactured under an explosives patent, in plants formerly used for the manufacture of ordnance, under general supervision of the Army's Chief of Ordnance, and under the local direction of the Army's Field Director of Ammunition Plants. Advice on detailed operations was sought from such experienced commercial producers of high explosives as the du Ponts and the Atlas and the Hercules powder concerns. There is not the slightest basis for any official belief that this was an innocuous product.

Because of reliance on the reservation of governmental immunity for acts of discretion, the Court avoids direct pronouncement on the duty owing by the Government under these circumstances but does sound overtones and undertones with which we disagree. We who would hold the Government liable here cannot avoid consideration of the basic criteria by which courts determine liability in the conditions of modern life. This is a day of synthetic living, when to an ever-increasing extent our population is dependent upon mass producers for its food and drink, its cures and complexions, its apparel and gadgets. These no longer are natural or simple products but complex ones whose composition and qualities are often secret. Such a dependent society must exact greater care than in more simple days and must require from manufacturers or producers increased integrity and caution as the only protection of its safety and well-being. Purchasers cannot try out drugs to determine whether they kill or cure. Consumers cannot test the youngster's cowboy suit or the wife's sweater to see if they are apt to burst into fatal flames. Carriers, by land or by sea, cannot experiment with the combustibility of goods in transit. Where experiment or research is necessary to determine the presence or the degree of danger, the product must not be tried out on the public, nor must the public be expected to possess the facilities or the technical knowledge to learn for itself of inherent but latent dangers. The claim that a hazard was not foreseen is not available to one who did not use foresight appropriate to his enterprise.

Forward-looking courts, slowly but steadily, have been adapting the law of negligence to these conditions. The law which by statute determines the Government's liability is that of the place where the negligent act or omission occurred.

This fertilizer was manufactured in Iowa and Nebraska, thence shipped to Texas. Speculation as to where the negligence occurred is unnecessary, since each of these jurisdictions recognizes the general proposition that a manufacturer is liable for defects in his product which could have been avoided by the exercise of due care. Where there are no specific state decisions on the point, federal judges may turn to the general doctrines of accepted tort law, whence state judges derive their governing principles in novel cases. We believe that whatever the source to which we look for the law of this case, if the source is as modern as the case itself, it supports the exaction of a higher degree of care than possibly can be found to have been exercised here.

We believe it is the better view that whoever puts into circulation in commerce a product that is known or even suspected of being potentially inflammable or explosive is under an obligation to know his own product and to ascertain what forces he is turning loose. If, as often will be the case, a dangerous product is also a useful one, he is under a strict duty to follow each step of its distribution with warning of its dangers and with information and directions to keep those dangers at a minimum.

It is obvious that the Court's only choice is to hold the Government's liability to be nothing or to be very heavy, indeed. But the magnitude of the potential liability is due to the enormity of the disaster and the multitude of its victims. The size of the catastrophe does not excuse liability but, on its face, eloquently pleads that it could not have resulted from any prudently operated government project, and that injury so sudden and sweeping should not lie where it has fallen. It should at least raise immediate doubts whether this is one of those "discretionary" operations Congress sought to immunize from liability. With this statement of our general approach to the liability issue, we turn to its application to this case. . . .

The Government's attack on the purely factual determination by the trial judge seems to us utterly unconvincing. Reputable experts testified to their opinion that the fire could have been caused by spontaneous combustion. The Government's contention that it was probably caused by someone smoking about the hold brought forth sharp conflict in the testimony. There was no error in adopting one of two permissible inferences as to the fire's origin. And, in view of the absence of any warning that FGAN was inflammable or explosive, we would think smoking by longshoremen about the job would not be an abnormal phenomenon.

The evidence showed that this type of fertilizer had been manufactured for about four years at the time of the explosion in Texas City. Petitioners' experts testified to their belief that at least a segment of informed scientific opinion at the time regarded ammonium nitrate as potentially dangerous, especially when combined with carbonaceous material as it was in this fertilizer. One witness had been hired by the War Production Board to conduct tests into explosion and fire hazards of this product. The Board terminated these tests at an intermediate stage, against the recommendation of the laboratory and in the face of the suggestion that further research might point up suspected but unverified dangers. In addition, there was a considerable history over a period of years of unexplained fires and explosions involving such ammonium nitrate. The zeal and skill of government counsel to distinguish each of these fires on its facts appears to exceed that of some of the experts on whose testimony they rely. . . .

In this situation, even the simplest government official could anticipate likelihood of close packing in large masses during sea shipment, with aggravation of any attendant dangers. Where the risk involved is an explosion of a cargo-carrying train or ship, perhaps in a congested rail yard or at a dock, the producer is not entitled as a matter of law to treat industry practice as a conclusive guide to due care. Otherwise, one free disaster would be permitted as to each new product before the sanction of civil liability was thrown on the side of high standards of safety. . . . This Court certainly would hold a private corporation liable in this situation, and the statute imposes the same liability upon the Government unless it can bring itself within the Act's exception, to which we now turn.

The Government insists that each act or omission upon which the charge of negligence is predicated—the decisions as to discontinuing the investigation of hazards, bagging at high temperature, use of paper-bagging material, absence of labeling and warning—involved a conscious weighing of expediency against caution and was therefore within the immunity for discretionary acts provided by the Tort Claims Act. It further argues, by way of showing that by such a construction the reservation would not completely swallow the waiver of immunity, that such discretionary decisions are to be distinguished from those made by a truck driver as to the speed at which he will travel so as to keep the latter within the realm of liability.

We do not predicate liability on any decision taken at "Cabinet level" or on any other high-altitude thinking. Of course, it is not a tort for government to govern, and the decision to aid foreign agriculture by making and delivering fertilizer is no actionable wrong. Nor do we find any indication that in these deliberations any decision was made to take a calculated risk of doing what was done, in the way it was done, on the chance that what did happen might not happen. Therefore, we are not deterred by fear that governmental liability in this case would make the discretion of executives and administrators timid and restrained. However, if decisions are being made at Cabinet levels as to the temperature of bagging explosive fertilizers, whether paper is suitable for bagging hot fertilizer, and how the bags should be labeled, perhaps an increased sense of caution and responsibility even at that height would be wholesome. The common sense of this matter is that a policy adopted in the exercise of an immune discretion was carried out carelessly by those in charge of detail. We cannot agree that all the way down the line there is immunity for every balancing of care against cost, of safety against production, of warning against silence. . . .

The Government's negligence here was not in policy decisions of a regulatory or governmental nature, but involved actions akin to those of a private manufacturer, contractor, or shipper. Reading the discretionary exception as we do, in a way both workable and faithful to legislative intent, we would hold that the Government was liable under these circumstances. Surely a statute so long debated was meant to embrace more than traffic accidents. If not, the ancient and discredited doctrine that "The King can do no wrong" has not been uprooted; it has merely been amended to read, "The King can do only little wrongs."

D. PATENT MONOPOLY

MERCOID CORPORATION V. MID-CONTINENT
INVESTMENT COMPANY
320 U.S. 661, 678 (January 3, 1944)

"To promote the Progress of Science and useful Arts, by securing for limited Times to Authors and Inventors the exclusive Right to their respective Writings and Discoveries," the Founding Fathers ordained, in their wisdom, that the Congress might enact all laws necessary and proper. Therefore, from the very beginning of our national polity, patent monopolies have constituted an exception to the general bias in favor of free enterprise and laissez faire that many judges—and certainly not least Jackson, his earlier partisan advocacy[10] to the seeming contrary notwithstanding—faithfully have perceived. That bias finds perhaps its ultimate expression in the Clayton and the Sherman Anti-Trust Acts of approximately half and three-quarters of a century ago, respectively.[11] This is not an appropriate forum in which to debate the consistency of the liberal ideology,[12] so we shall simply note in passing that, although in general the

[10] Robert Jackson, *The Struggle for Judicial Supremacy,* (New York: Alfred A. Knopf, Inc., 1941).

[11] And for the enforcement of which, it should be recalled, Jackson was directly responsible during his year in charge of the Anti-Trust Division of the Department of Justice. He was then an outspoken antagonist of big business, and proponent of vigorous enforcement of the anti-trust laws (notwithstanding that many of the New Deal's specific programs—which he defended also—encouraged monopolistic combination and practices and constituted in effect exceptions to both the letter and the spirit of federal anti-trust policy, as this related to Jackson's responsibilities at the time.) See, for example, his speech on December 29, 1937, to the American Political Science Association, "The Menace to Free Enterprise," *Congressional Record,* LXXXIII (1938; 75th Congress, 3rd Session), Appendix pp. 19-21; and his article with Edward Dumbauld, "Monopolies and the Courts," *University of Pennsylvania Law Review,* LXXXVI (1938), 231-257; and Gerhart, *America's Advocate,* pp. 88-95, 123-132.

[12] See Kenneth R. Minogue, *The Liberal Mind* (New York: Random House, Inc., 1964).

liberal position favors the collectivization and regulation of the economy whereas conservatives favor individual initiative and economic freedom from governmental controls, in the case of business monopolies the liberal favors competition and an open market whereas the conservative upholds the industrial integration, collectivization, and regulation that are inherent in monopolistic or ologopolistic control and domination. It is well understood by students of the Supreme Court that in regard to its relatively limited patent monopoly function of occasionally auditing an adjudication of patent infringement claims, the liberal position finds its characteristic expression in narrowing, and the conservative in widening, the scope of the monopolies established under the patent laws.

The voting of the justices in the *Mercoid* case was in perfect accord with this generalization. The same is true of *Jungersen* (which follows below) which was decided precisely five years to the day later. The decision in *Mercoid* was 5-4, with the four libertarians plus Stone forming a majority which used the opinion of the Court as an instrument for narrowing the scope of the doctrine of contributory infringement. The explicit question was whether the holder of a system patent could extend the domain of his monopoly to include the right of exclusive manufacture of component parts which, though themselves unpatented, were essential parts of the system that was. The case began as a suit by the respondent, Mid-Continent Investment Company, against the petitioner, Mercoid Corporation, for infringement of its system by making and competing with Mid-Continent in the sale of one of the component parts. The trial court dismissed the complaint, only to be reversed by the Court of Appeals for the Seventh Circuit, which in turn now was reversed by the Supreme Court. The case was complicated by a prior litigation, in the lower courts, in which Mercoid had lost and this same patent was adjudged valid.

What had happened was that Mercoid understandably had failed to anticipate certain intervening decisions of the Supreme Court, which in turn had encouraged its counsel to put up a more enlightened (to say nothing of more effective) defense in the present proceeding. Under these circumstances, it is not surprising that the opinion of the Court now ruled that although the principle of *res adjudicata* applied to the points affirmatively decided in an earlier litigation, it did not extend to bar the raising, at the later time, of a possible defense that might have been, but in fact was not, relied upon in the earlier decision. All four dissenters—Roberts, Reed, Jackson, and Frankfurter—opposed the majority's ruling on the issue of *res adjudicata;* but only Frankfurter protested the disposition of the substantive ruling which not only eliminated the kind of competition involved in this case as a form of contributory infringement of a system patent, but went further and in Frankfurter's words, cast "animadversions upon" the doctrine itself, which to him was "an expression both of law and morals."

> MR. JUSTICE JACKSON, *in dissent*:

"A patent," said Mr. Justice Holmes, "is property carried to the highest degree of abstraction—a right *in rem* to exclude, without a physical object or content." Here the patent covers a combination—a system—a sequence—which is said to be new, although every element and factor in it is old and unpatentable. Thus we have an abstract right in an abstruse relationship between things in which individually there is no right—a legal concept which either is very profound or almost unintelligible, I cannot be quite sure which.

Undoubtedly the man who first devised a thermostat to control the flow of electric energy gave something to the world. But one who merely carried it to a new location, or used two instead of one, or three instead of two, or used it to control current for a stoker motor rather than for a damper, did not do much that I would not expect of a good mechanic familiar with the instrument. But that question of validity is not here. I assume that this patent confers some rights and ask what they are.

Of course the abstract right to the "sequence" has little economic importance unless its monopoly comprehends not only the arrangement but some, at least, of its components. If the patentee may not exclude competitors from making and vending strategic unpatented elements such as the thermostat, adapted to use in the combination, the patented system is so vulnerable to competition as to be almost worthless. On the other hand, if he may prohibit such competition, his system patent gathers up into its monopoly devices long known to the art and hence not themselves subject to any patent.

It is suggested that such a patent should protect the patentee at least against one who knowingly and intentionally builds a device for use in the combination and vends it for that purpose. That is what appears to have been done here. As to ethics, the parties seem to me as much on a parity as the pot and the kettle. But want of knowledge or innocent intent is not ordinarily available to diminish patent protection. I do not see how intent can make infringement of what otherwise is not. The less legal rights depend on someone's state of mind, the better.

The practical issue is whether we will leave such a combination patent with little value indeed or whether we will give it value by projecting its economic effects to elements not by themselves a part of its legal monopoly. In these circumstances I think we should protect the patent owner in the enjoyment of just what he has been granted—an abstract right in an abstruse combination—worth whatever such a totality may be worth. I see no constitutional or statutory authority for giving it additional value by bringing into its monopoly all or any of the unpatentable parts.

For these reasons I agree with the Court that no case of infringement could have been made out had the issue been raised when it was timely. But I agree with the views of the doctrine of *res adjudicata* expressed by Mr. Justice Roberts and for that reason join the dissent.

E.   THE SPARK OF INVENTIVE GENIUS

JUNGERSEN V. OSTBY AND BARTON COMPANY
335 U.S. 560, 571 (January 3, 1949)

Stone and Roberts had been replaced by Vinson and Burton by the time this case was decided, but Vinson joined the majority which declared invalid the relevant patent and Burton dissented, just as their predecessors probably would have done. Six other justices took positions consistent with their stands in *Mercoid*, and Reed alone took a different stance, joining the majority here so that the division became 6-3.

Jungersen had been granted a patent, over a decade earlier, for the rapid reproduction of intricate designs, in the jewelry industry. The lower courts had ruled that the patent was partially valid and partially invalid, but that there had been no infringement of the valid parts by Ostby and Barton. The Supreme Court now decided that none of the patent could be upheld, because an examination of Jungersen's method indicated that almost everything he included was previously known in the art and his own contribution consisted simply of refinements of these earlier processes (patented and otherwise). Such innovations as Jungersen had introduced, such as the use of centrifugal force at a particular point in the process, were not "an exemplification of inventive genius such as is necessary to render the patent valid." The circumstance that Jungersen's method had met with commercial success was deemed of little relevance. Like Frankfurter and Burton, Jackson disagreed. In doing so he voted as he had in *Mercoid*; but one who disregarded his voting behavior and paid primary attention to his rhetoric in these two opinions might well come to the conclusion that Robert Jackson was of more than one mind on the issue of property rights in patents.

MR. JUSTICE JACKSON, dissenting:

I think this patent meets the patent statute's every requirement. And confronted by this record an industry heretofore galled by futility and frustration may well be amazed at the Court's dismissal of Jungersen's ingenious and successful efforts.

Of course, commercial success will not fill any void in an invalid patent. But it may fill the void in our understanding of what the invention has meant to those whose livelihood, unlike our own, depends upon their knowledge of the art. Concededly, in this high-pressure age sales volume may reflect only powerful promotion or marketing magic, and its significance as an index of novelty or utility may rightly be suspected. But Jungersen's success was grounded not in the gullibility of the public but in the hard-headed judgment of a highly competitive and critical if not hostile industry. Knowing well its need for and its failure to achieve improvements on available processes, that industry discarded them, adopted this outsider's invention, and made it a commercial success.

It would take a singular self-assurance on the part of one who knows as little of this art as I do, or as I can learn in the few hours that can be given to consideration of this case, to ignore the judgment of these competitors who grew up in the industry and say that they did not know something new and useful when they saw it. And if Benvenuto Cellini's age-old writings are so revealing to us laymen of the appellate Bench, it is hard to see why this practical-minded industry which the Court says was following Cellini failed through all the years to get his message.

It would not be difficult to cite many instances of patents that have been granted, improperly I think, and without adequate tests of invention by the Patent Office. But I doubt that the remedy for such Patent Office passion for granting patents is an equally strong passion in this Court for striking them down so that the only patent that is valid is one which this Court has not been able to get its hands on.

F. THE ENTREPRENEUR

MAGGIO V. ZEITZ
333 U.S. 56 (February 9, 1948)

On one level of analysis, this case questioned whether trial courts should be permitted, let alone encouraged, to adapt the civil processes of bankruptcy administration to subserve punitive goals, thereby avoiding such encumbrances to efficient judicial management of bankrupt estates as trial by jury and other constitutional rights associated with criminal proceedings. Jackson's opinion for the Court made it clear that this was the substantive issue with which most of the justices were concerned, and upon which the Court purported to rule. Indeed, Black and Rutledge wrote a separate opinion because they agreed so fully with the policy outcome stated above that they disagreed with the majority's disposition of petitioner Maggio: Jackson remitted him to the hands of the federal district judge with supervisory authority over the bankruptcy proceeding, whereas Black and Rutledge wanted to go further and quash any possibility that the district court might prolong the punishment, for contempt of court, for Maggio's continuing failure to deliver the goods which that court had sought to make him turn over to the trustee in bankruptcy. For all except Jackson and Frankfurter, who saw other dimensions in it, this was the case.

For Jackson, there was the additional circumstance that Maggio had been dealt with unjustly,[13] as well as illegally, by the trial court. He apparently felt that Maggio, a "fast-living adventurer" rather than a stolid banker or insurance broker, ought to be judged by different (and looser) standards than the more stable members of a business community. Like the soapbox orator, the political speaker, and the soundtruck, bankers and entrepreneurs each should be a law unto himself; and here all the Court was dealing with was an entrepreneur.

The other dimension, for both Jackson and Frankfurter, was that this petitioner had come from the Second Circuit; and although their reasons were different, each had a special interest in how this case related to a more general question of judicial policy and administration in the lower courts of this circuit. Jackson's reason was that this was his circuit, the one to which he was assigned and had a particular responsibility for the Court.[14] Frankfurter's frequently stated reason for a special interest in this circuit was that it was a sort of judicial Valhalla, including (to speak —borrowing one of his favorite phrases—only of the recently dead) such demigods of the law as Learned Hand, his cousin Augustus, Charles Clark, and Jerome Frank. Frank, who had done as much as anyone to bring the Freudian metaphor to the attention of the legal profession,[15] appears to have put some of his psychological lore to practical use in the drafting of the Court of Appeals' opinion in this case, speaking for Learned Hand and himself (with Swan concurring in the result). Indulging in what Frankfurter referred to as "almost imprecating language," Frank invited the Supreme Court to accept (in due course) jurisdiction in this case, for the ostensible, and certainly not unreasonable, purpose of straightening out a problem of judicial policy making in the Second Circuit.

At that time there were only six circuit judges assigned to this court

---

[13] In sharp contrast stands Jackson's subsequent approval of the use of summary judicial contempt power—also in a case from the Second Circuit, by the way—as a substitute for trial by jury, in another and better publicized trial, when he felt less empathy for the Communist-lawyer defendants. *Sacher* v. *United States,* 343 U.S. 1 (1952).

[14] See his paternal advice to the bar of the Second Circuit, in *Williamson* v. *United States,* 184 F.2nd 280 (1950), and in his very last judicial opinion, which was filed in his role as circuit justice (rather than in a decision of the Supreme Court): *Knickerbocker Printing Co.* v. *United States,* 73 S.Ct. 212 (September 2, 1954).

[15] Jerome Frank, *Law and the Modern Mind* (New York: Coward-McCann, Inc., 1930).

of appeals and they acted in groups of three, never *en banc*. Consequently, another panel of three circuit judges had previously decided, in a different case, the same policy question at issue in Maggio's case, and Frank and Learned Hand now considered themselves bound to follow the precedent established by their colleagues, even though they disagreed with it. What alternatives were open to them? They could, of course, have gone ahead and followed the policy that they believed right in Maggio's case. If they had done this, the outcome for any particular defalcating bankrupt would depend upon the luck of the draw: which panel reviewed a civil contempt order against him by the district judge. (And no doubt, this is precisely the posture in which many parties find themselves when they take appeals to any of the larger courts of appeals, today as in Maggio's day.) [16] But if they were too rigid to accept such a pragmatic and realistic solution to their problem, and if they and their colleagues were also unwilling to utilize the historic device for inducing intrabench consensus (the *en banc* procedure), the only alternative left was to ask the Supreme Court to back up one or the other of the two conflicting points of view in the court of appeals. The latter also is seemingly consonant with the usual function of judicial appeals; but the Supreme Court had refused to permit such review in the past—indeed, in this very case. Therefore, Frankfurter objected to the willingness of Jackson and the rest of the Supreme Court to disregard the orderly way of doing things, and to use the present disposition to solve indirectly a problem which the Court previously had consistently refused to meet head-on. The desultory result was that Jackson's opinion constituted, as Frankfurter characterized it, "an effort to whip the devil round the stump."

MR. JUSTICE JACKSON delivered the opinion of the Court.

Joseph Maggio, the petitioner, was president and manager of Luma Camera Service, Inc., which was adjudged bankrupt on April 23, 1942. In January of 1943 the trustee asked the court to direct Maggio to turn over a considerable amount of merchandise alleged to have been taken from the bankrupt concern in 1941, and still in Maggio's possession or control. After hearing, the referee found that "the Trustee established by clear and convincing evidence that the merchandise hereinafter described, belonging to the estate of the bankrupt, was knowingly and fraudulently concealed by the respondent [Maggio] from the Trustee herein and that said merchandise is now in the possession or under the control of the respondent." A turnover order issued and was affirmed by the District Court and then unanimously affirmed by the Circuit Court of Appeals, Second Circuit, without opinion other than citation of its own prior cases. . . .

[16] Cf. Sheldon Goldman, "Voting Behavior on the United States Court of Appeals, 1961–1964," *American Political Science Review*, LX (1966), 374-383.

As Maggio failed to turn over the property or its proceeds, the Referee found him in contempt. After hearing, the District Court affirmed and ordered Maggio to be jailed until he complied or until further order of the court. Again the Circuit Court of Appeals affirmed. 157 F. 2d 951.

But in affirming the Court [Judge Jerome Frank] said: "Although we know that Maggio cannot comply with the order, we must keep a straight face and pretend that he can, and must thus affirm orders which first direct Maggio 'to do an impossibility, and then punish him for refusal to perform it.' " Whether this is to be read literally as its deliberate judgment of the law of the case or is something of a decoy intended to attract our attention to the problem, the declaration is one which this Court, in view of its supervisory power over courts of bankruptcy, cannot ignore. Fraudulent bankruptcies probably present more difficulties to the courts in the Second Circuit than they do elsewhere. These conditions are reflected in conflicting views within the Court of Appeals. . . .

The proceeding which leads to commitment consists of two separate stages which easily become out-of-joint because the defense to the second often in substance is an effort to relitigate, perhaps before another judge, the issue supposed to have been settled in the first, and because while the burden of proof rests on the trustee, frequently evidence of the facts is entirely in possession of his adversary, the bankrupt, who is advantaged by nondisclosure. . . .

The turnover procedure is one not expressly created or regulated by the Bankruptcy Act. It is a judicial innovation by which the court seeks efficiently and expeditiously to accomplish ends prescribed by the statute, which, however, left the means largely to judicial ingenuity. . . .

To compel [trustees and bankrupts] to discharge their duty, the statute imposes criminal sanctions. It denounces a comprehensive list of frauds, concealments, falsifications, mutilation of records and other acts that would defeat or obstruct collection of the assets of the estate, and prescribes heavy penalties of fine or imprisonment or both. . . . It also confers on the courts power to arraign, try and punish persons for violations, but "in accordance with the laws of procedure" regulating trials of crimes. . . . And it specifically provides for jury trial of offenses against the Bankruptcy Act. . . .

Courts of bankruptcy have no authority to compensate for any neglect or lack of zeal in applying these prescribed criminal sanctions by perversion of civil remedies to ends of punishment, as some judges of the Court of Appeals suggest is being done. . . . Conduct which has put property beyond the limited reach of the turnover proceeding may be a crime, or, if it violates an order of the referee, a criminal contempt, but no such acts, however reprehensible, warrant issuance of an order which creates a duty impossible of performance, so that punishment can follow. It should not be necessary to say that it would be a flagrant abuse of process to issue such an order to exert pressure on friends and relatives to ransom the accused party from being jailed. . . .

The trustee usually can show that the missing assets were in the possession or under the control of the bankrupt at the time of bankruptcy. To bring this past possession down to the date involved in the turnover proceedings, the trustee has been allowed the benefit of what is called a presumption that the possession continues until the possessor explains when and how it ceased. This inference, which might be entirely permissible in some cases, seems to have settled into a rigid presumption which it is said the lower courts apply without regard to its reasonableness in the particular case.

However, no such presumption, and no such fiction, is created by the bankruptcy statute. None can be found in any decision of this Court dealing with this procedure. Language can, of course, be gleaned from judicial pronouncements and texts that conditions once existing may be presumed to continue until they are shown to have changed. But such generalizations, useful enough, perhaps, in solving some problem of a particular case, are not rules of law to be applied to all cases, with or without reason.

Since no authority imposes upon either the Court of Appeals or the Bankruptcy Court any presumption of law, either conclusive or disputable, which would forbid or dispense with further inquiry or consideration of other evidence and testimony, turnover orders should not be issued, or approved on appeal, merely on proof that at some past time property was in possession or control of the accused party, unless the time element and other factors make that a fair and reasonable inference. . . .

Of course, the fact that a man at one time had a given item of property is a circumstance to be weighed in determining whether he may properly be found to have it at a later date. But the inference from yesterday's possession is one thing, that permissible from possession twenty months ago quite another. With what kind of property do we deal? Was it salable or consumable? The inference of continued possession might be warranted when applied to books of account which are not consumable or marketable, but quite inappropriate under the same circumstances if applied to perishable merchandise or salable goods in considerable demand. Such an inference is one thing when applied to a thrifty person who withdraws his savings account after being involved in an accident, for no apparent purpose except to get it beyond the reach of a tort creditor . . .; it is very different when applied to a stock of wares being sold by a fast-living adventurer using the proceeds to make up the difference between income and outgo. . . .

We are well aware that . . . generalities do little to solve concrete issues. The latter can be resolved only by the sound sense and good judgment of trial courts, mindful that the order should issue only as a responsible and final adjudication of possession and ability to deliver, not as a questionable experiment in coercion which will recoil to the discredit of the judicial process if time proves the adjudication to have been improvident and requires the courts to abandon its enforcement. . . .

When . . . a misapprehension of the law has led both courts below to adjudicate rights without considering essential facts in the light of the controlling law, this Court will vacate the judgments and remand the case to the District Court for further proceedings consistent with the principles laid down in this Court's opinion. . . .

G. THE OBLIGATION OF THE LABOR CONTRACT

JEWELL RIDGE COAL CORPORATION v. LOCAL #6167,
UNITED MINE WORKERS OF AMERICA
325 U.S. 161, 170 (May 7, 1945)

Probably no other case was as intimately involved in the unfolding of Jackson's judicial career as this one. He could hardly have realized the implications at the time, but at least one result of the case was the cable from Nuremberg, protesting Truman's failure to carry out F.D.R.'s commitments, full of sound and fury and signifying the knell of Jackson's political aspirations. But it was a long way from the working face of the Jewell Ridge mine in Virginia, five miles of underground tunnels away from the main portal, to the office of the Chief Counsel of the United States at the International Military Tribunal in Nuremberg, Germany, although the time interval between the Jewell Ridge decision and the Nuremberg cable was only thirteen months.

The Supreme Court divided 5-4 in this decision, with Murphy writing the majority opinion for the four libertarians and Reed. Jackson wrote a dissenting opinion in which Stone, Roberts, and Frankfurter joined. The majority ruled that their affirmance of the decision below was a necessary consequence of the Supreme Court's recent 7-2 precedent decision in *Tennessee Coal, Iron & R.R. Co.* v. *Muscoda Local #123,* 321 U.S. 590 (1944), which had upheld portal-to-portal pay for iron miners over the protests of Roberts and the Chief Justice. Murphy now explained, under the familiar principle of *stare decisis,* that the same policy must apply to soft-coal miners.

Although he and Frankfurter had concurred in the case of the iron miners, Jackson was deeply disturbed by the present outcome. The decision initially had gone in the opposite direction, and Chief Justice Stone had assigned to Jackson the task of writing what eventually turned out to be the dissent, but which then was presumed to be the opinion of the Court.[17] Subsequently, under what Jackson believed to be strong and un-

17 Eugene C. Gerhart, *America's Advocate: Robert H. Jackson* (Indianapolis: The Bobbs-Merrill Company, Inc., 1958), p. 250.

ethical pressure from Black, one justice—probably Reed[18]—switched his vote, so that the Supreme Court's decision was in support of, rather than against, the present claims of John L. Lewis and his United Mine Workers. Black, as the senior associate justice voting with the majority, reassigned the opinion of the Court to Murphy, and then proceeded, so Jackson believed, to pressure him to get the opinion out in a rush in order to influence then-pending contract negotiations. Lewis' union remained on a "holiday" (strike) at the time the Supreme Court's decision was announced.[19]

As the United States Senator in charge of the bill which became the Fair Labor Standards Act, Black had given assurances, concerning the proposed statute's application to collective bargaining agreements, that Jackson felt were contradicted by Black's vote in this decision as a Supreme Court Justice.[20] Even worse, thought Jackson, was Black's breach of judicial ethics by participating in the case at all, because the attorney for the United Mine workers was Crampton Harris, Black's former law partner and close associate until Black's appointment to the Court in 1937. In view of what he considered to be Black's long-standing and intimate personal relationship with Harris, Jackson believed that Black should disqualify himself from taking any part in the Jewell Ridge decision.[21] Of course, the same argument could have been raised against Black's participation in *Tennessee Coal & Iron*, because Harris had presented the miner's union in that case also. But in *Tennessee Coal & Iron*, Black's vote may not have

[18] A scale of similar decisions, but for the 1946 Term, shows that Reed was the Court's middleman, with the four libertarians to his left and Burton, Vinson, Frankfurter, and Jackson to his right. One would infer from this circumstance that Reed would be the justice most likely to provide the fifth vote needed for a majority, for either the four-man left group, or the four-man right group; and that certainly if any single justice were so marginal in his decision that he could be persuaded to change his position, it would most likely, at that time, have been Reed. See my *The Judicial Mind,* p. 130; and cf. Anon., "Mr. Justice Reed: Swing Man or Not?" *Stanford Law Review,* I (1949), 714-729.

[19] Gerhart, *America's Advocate,* p. 251.

[20] Cf. Jackson's sometime views when the shoe was on the other foot: *McGrath* v. *Kristensen,* 340 U.S. 162, 176 (1950), and Chap. 9E, *infra.*

[21] Gerhart, *America's Advocate,* p. 250. The problem of disqualification was one that especially plagued Stone's Court, because its members included three former Attorneys General (Stone, Murphy, Jackson) and one former Solicitor General (Reed). Rigid adherence to a custom of attributing constructive bias because of a justice's earlier official relationship to cases in which the government was a party could, and did on occasion, deprive the Court of the quorum necessary for it to act. Indeed, Roberts had attacked the propriety of Stone's participation in a group of such cases early in 1944, and although Stone ultimately decided that he was qualified to sit, consideration of the cases was stalled so that the matter still hung in abeyance when the challenge to Black was raised as an open question for decision by the Court. Jackson and other members of the Court were privy to the Roberts-Stone dispute, of course, but there had been no public discussion of the issue. See Alpheus T. Mason, *Harlan Fiske Stone* (New York: The Viking Press, Inc., 1956), pp. 640-642.

seemed so critical to the outcome, and, therefore, the question of ethics seemed less urgent than in *Jewell Ridge.*

In any event, Jackson's views either were communicated to, or at least subsequent to the announcement of the Court's decision on May 7, 1945, they became shared by, counsel for the coal company, who proceeded to file with the Court a highly unusual motion that the Court grant a rehearing and, in effect, expunge its decision of May 7 and decide the case anew, but after first having barred Black from participating because of his putative personal bias in favor of the party represented by his own ex-partner. Harris, arguing in opposition to the motion, scored the technical point that Black's participation could not have had an effect on the outcome, because without him the Court would (presumably) have divided 4-4, which still would have resulted in an affirmance of the judgment below. Such a legal argument, of course, overlooks completely the political as well as the sociopsychological consequences of Black's participation. If it was true that Black was the most zealous member of the pro-miners group of five justices, then everything we know about small group behavior[22] indicates that qualitative implications would be at least as important as quantitative ones, if the leader of a five-man group were removed and action were taken instead by the remaining four non-leader members of the original group. Even from a strictly legal point of view there were important differences: Black, as a senior associate justice, had assigned the opinion of the Court in both *Tennessee Coal & Iron* and in *Jewell Ridge;* and with a 4-4 division, there could have been no opinion of the Court, and the decision would have been considerably less valuable as a precedent to be manipulated in the shaping of future policy by both lower courts and the Supreme Court.

Of course, no one really expected that a majority of the Supreme Court would agree to take the quite literally unprecedented step of excluding any justice from participation in decision making. In the past, the Court had suffered in silence the continuing participation of colleagues who had become variously blind, dumb, and insane, to say nothing of the not infrequent cases of senility.[23] Black was then none of these, he had violated no law or regulation, and it is most doubtful that he had violated anything even approaching a consensual custom of the Court. But the motion did provide Jackson with the opportunity, of which he took full advantage, to file an opinion for Frankfurter and himself, in which he

[22] E.g., Barry E. Collins and Harold E. Guetzkow, *A Social Psychology of Group Processes for Decision-Making* (New York: John Wiley & Sons, Inc., 1964); and Bernard Berelson and Gary A. Steiner, *Human Behavior: An Inventory of Scientific Findings* (New York: Harcourt, Brace & World, Inc., 1964), Chap. 8.

[23] Charles Fairman, "The Retirement of Federal Judges," *Harvard Law Review,* LI (1938), 397-443.

pointed out that the Court had no authority to grant the motion; and that, in any event, motions for rehearing were not passed upon by the full Court, but only by those justices who comprised the majority, because nothing could come of reargument unless one of them was willing to at least consider the possibility of changing his mind.[24] "Hence, being in dissent," he concluded, "I have no voice as to rehearing, except that I continue to adhere to the dissent." Nonetheless, his opinion is labeled as "concurring" and he explicitly states in it that he concurs in "denial of the petition."

However ambiguous his action may seem his inuendo was clear enough: somebody in the majority, presumably Black himself, ought to have done the decent thing and voted to grant this motion; but, alas, there was just nothing more that Jackson could do about it. The date of this opinion was June 18, 1945. This was the same day that the decision in *Hunt* v. *Crumboch* (H, below) was announced; and it was also the day that Jackson left Washington for Europe and the International Conference on War Crimes Trials, and his triumphant role at Nuremberg. According to the biographer, in whom he confided several years after the event, Jackson was so outraged by Black's behavior in the Jewell Ridge case that "There was a question in my mind of whether I would resign from the Court. I was glad to get away from here."[25] This was the mood in which he took leave of his colleagues; and thus it is that the portal-to-portal issue anticipates his cabled charges against Black a year later. In that cable Jackson discusses the Jewell Ridge case at length, and states that at the final conference of the term on June 16, 1945, Black was very much opposed to having Jackson file his concurrence on the motion for rehearing:

> Mr. Justice Black became very angry and said that any opinion which discussed the subject at all would mean a declaration of war. I told Justice Black in language that was sharp but no different than I would use again that I would not stand for any more of his bullying and that, whatever I would otherwise do, I would now have to write my opinion to keep self-respect in the face of his threats. . . . However innocent the coincidence of these two victories at successive terms by Justice Black's former law partner, I wanted that practice stopped. If it is ever repeated while I am on the bench I will make my *Jewell Ridge* opinion look like a letter of recommendation by comparison.[26]

MR. JUSTICE JACKSON, dissenting.

THE CHIEF JUSTICE, MR. JUSTICE ROBERTS, MR. JUSTICE FRANKFURTER, and I are constrained respectfully to dissent from this decision. . . .

[24] *Jewell Ridge Coal Corporation* v. *Local No. 6167, United Mine Workers of America,* 325 U.S. 897 (June 18, 1945).

[25] Gerhart, *America's Advocate,* p. 251.

[26] *New York Times,* June 11, 1946, p. 2.

1. *The Court's decision either invalidates or ignores the explicit terms of collectively bargained agreements between these parties based on a half century of custom in the industry....*

But the Court does not honor these agreements. We have repeatedly and consistently held that collectively bargained agreements must be honored, even to the extent that employers may not, while they exist, negotiate with an individual employee or a minority . . . and must pay heavy penalties for violating them. . . .[27] And now at the first demand of employees the Court throws these agreements overboard, even intimating that to observe agreements, bargained long before enactment of the Fair Labor Standards Act, would be "legalizing" a frustration of the statutory scheme. . . .

2. *Neither invalidation nor disregard of collectively bargained agreements is authorized by the Fair Labor Standards Act. Both its legislative history and contemporaneous legislation are convincing that Congress did not itself intend to nullify them or to provide any legislative basis for this Court to do so.* It is admitted that the Act contains no express authority for this decision. . . .

Likewise, the Court is unable to cite any item of legislative history which hints that Congress expected these words to be given this meaning. On the other hand, we find that pains were taken to assure Congress that there was no such intent. . . .

The debates on the bill appear to us to make this intention more explicit. For example, the Congressional Record, Vol. 81, p. 7650, shows that the following took place in debate in the Senate July 27, 1937:

"MR. WALSH. Next, does the bill affect collective-bargaining agreements already made or hereafter to be made between employer and employee?

"MR. BLACK. It does not."

Of course it was agreed on all hands that no agreement could be validly bargained which provided for less than the minimum wages to be fixed by the proposed Board or for more than the specified hours of labor. But beyond observance of these limitations, we read the legislative history to indicate that the control of wages, hours and working conditions by collective contract was left undisturbed. . . .

3. *Congress refrained from enacting authority for this result at the request of the United Mine Workers, expressed in the testimony of their responsible representatives, whose plan for regulating the coal industry was enacted in the Guffey Coal Act....*

In the light of the sustained attention Congress had given to the delicate economy of the coal industry and its plan to stabilize it by collective bargaining and

[27] The deleted cases which Jackson cited here are: *J. I. Case Co.,* v. *Labor Board,* 321 U.S. 322 (1944), and *Order of Railroad Telegraphers* v. *Railway Express Agency,* 321 U.S. 342 (1944), companion cases decided on the same day a year earlier. He wrote for the Court in these two cases, and these were the only opinions that he ever wrote to support a prounion vote. [Ed.]

price-fixing, it is unbelievable that it would undo a substantial part of that plan by the casual and ambiguous implication which the Court now attributes to the Fair Labor Standards Act.

4. *The decision of the Court is contrary to the interpretations of the Act made by its Administrator on the recommendation of the United Mine Workers, and it denies to the Administrator's rulings the respect we have been compelling lower courts to render to such administrative rulings in the cases of others.* It was not until 1940 that anyone appears to have thought the Act affected the coal miners' agreements. In the year 1940, an investigator of the Wage and Hour administration, investigating operations of a coal mining company in Pennsylvania, raised the question whether underground travel time must be included in the workweek under the terms of the Act. He stated his opinion that the "face to face" basis, excluding travel time, was the proper one to be applied in the coal-mining industry, but indicated that if a rule theretofore applied in the case of a gold mining company were required the coal company would owe some $70,000 to underground workers. This was brought to the attention of the President of the Central Pennsylvania Coal Producers Association, and he in turn brought it to the attention of other operators and of Mr. Lewis, President of the International Union, United Mine Workers of America. Thereafter representatives of both the operators and the United Mine Workers conferred from time to time with the representatives of the Wage and Hour Administration. Both the operators and the Union officials opposed any construction of the Act which would require payment for travel time....

5. *This decision necessarily invalidates the basis on which the Government in operating the mines contracted with the miners and brings into question the validity of all the existing mine agreements.* It appears to have been wartime restrictions on flat wage increases which finally led the United Mine Workers to reverse their former and to take their present position. . . . [T]he Government [took] over the mines and on November 3, 1943, the Ickes-Lewis agreement was made. The method of wage calculation under the Ickes-Lewis agreement was to treat each employee as having forty-five minutes of travel time, irrespective of his actual travel time. The War Labor Board on November 5, 1943 approved the Ickes-Lewis agreement, and thus in effect granted a flat wage increase, uniform for all miners irrespective of their individual actual travel time. . . . If the Fair Labor Standards Act entitles each individual miner to travel time, not according to the terms of his collectively bargained agreements, but according to the time actually spent, as the Court now holds, these Government agreements violated that law, the present agreements do also, and heavy liabilities both for overtime and penalties are daily being incurred by the entire industry.

6. *This decision proceeds on a principle denied to unorganized workmen for whose benefit the Act was passed.* The ink is hardly dry on this Court's pronouncement, in which all of the majority in this case joined, that: "The legislative debates

indicate that the prime purpose of the legislation was to aid the unprotected, unorganized and lowest paid of the nation's working population; that is, those employees who lacked sufficient bargaining power to secure for themselves a minimum subsistence wage." *Brooklyn Savings Bank* v. *O'Neil,* 324 U.S. 697, 707, n. 18. That coat ill fits the United Mine Workers. But let us contrast the advantage which this decision extends to a powerful group so plainly outside of the policy of the Act with the treatment of groups that, being unprotected and unorganized, were clearly within it.

Little more than six months ago this Court unanimously remanded to the lower courts for trial and findings on the facts a case involving night waiting time of seven unorganized firemen. It said that "We have not attempted to, and we cannot, lay down a legal formula to resolve cases so varied in their facts as are the many situations in which employment involves waiting time. Whether in a concrete case such time falls within or without the Act is a question of fact to be resolved by appropriate findings of the trial court. . . . This involves scrutiny and construction of the agreements between the particular parties, appraisal of their practical construction of the working agreement by conduct, consideration of the nature of the service, and its relation to the waiting time, and all of the surrounding circumstances. . . . The law does not impose an arrangement upon the parties. It imposes upon the courts the task of finding what the arrangement was." *Skidmore* v. *Swift & Co.,* 323 U.S. 134, 136-37. That was in keeping with other holdings. . . .

Now comes this case involving the organized miners, and the Court holds that ". . . we are not concerned here with the use of bona fide contracts or customs to settle difficult and doubtful questions as to whether certain activity or nonactivity constitutes work." It is held in this case that the time must be counted "regardless of any custom or contract to the contrary at the time in question." Can it be that this sudden refusal to weigh the facts is because as found by the District Court on almost undisputed evidence they are so decisively against the conclusion the Court is reaching? . . . We ought not to play fast and loose with the basic implications of this Act.

The "face to face" method, whatever its other defects, is a method by which both operators and miners have tried to bring about uniformity of labor costs in the different unionized mines and to remove the operators resistance to improved wage scales based on fear of competition. Under this decision there can be no uniform wage in this industry except by disregarding the very duty which this decision creates to pay each miner for his actual travel time. Thus, two men working shoulder to shoulder, but entering the mine at different portals must receive either different amounts of pay in their envelopes or must stay at their productive work a different length of time. Thus, too, old mines which have burrowed far from their portals must shoulder greatly increased labor cost per ton. The differential may be sufficient to make successful operation of some of the older mines impossible. Mining labor has tended to locate its dwellings near its work, and the closing of mines results in corresponding dislocations of mining labor. . . .

We can not shut our eyes to the consequence of this decision which is to impair for all organized labor the credit of collective bargaining, the only means left by which there could be a reliable settlement of marginal questions concerning hours of work or compensation. We have just held that the individual workman is deprived of power to settle such question. . . . Now we hold collective bargaining incompetent to do so. It is hard to see how the long-range interests of labor itself are advanced by a holding that there is no mode by which it may bind itself to any specified future conduct, however fairly bargained. A genuinely collectively bargained agreement as to wages, hours or working conditions is not invalidated or superseded by this Act and both employer and employee should be able to make and rely upon them, and the courts in deciding such cases should honor them.

We doubt if one can find in the long line of criticized cases one in which the Court has made a more extreme exertion of power or one so little supported or explained by either the statute or the record in the case. Power should answer to reason none the less because its fiat is beyond appeal.

H. THE BOYCOTT

HUNT V. CRUMBOCH
325 U.S. 821, 828 (June 18, 1945)

His personal problems with Hugo Black aside, Jackson's disagreement with the majority, on the merits of the policy issue in *Jewell Ridge*, is well expressed by a legal metaphor that was so overworked during the early decades of this century that it had become quite unfashionable by the time Jackson reached the Court. In the older parlance, Jackson disapproved the impairment, by fiat of a majority of his colleagues, of the obligation of labor contracts. In *Hunt* v. *Crumboch*, decided just six weeks later and in the same term, the issue, as Jackson saw it, was whether a union could from motives of pure revenge use its monopoly power over labor to force an employer out of business.

The 5-4 division of the Court was identical with that of *Jewell Ridge*. Black wrote for the Court, and there were two dissenting opinions this time, one by Roberts and another by Jackson. In a companion case the Court had ruled by an 8-1 margin, with Murphy dissenting alone, that a joint conspiracy between certain employers and a union was enjoinable under the antitrust laws.[28]

---

[28] *Allen Bradley Co.,* v. *Local Union No. 3, I.B.E.W.,* 325 U.S. 797 (June 18, 1945),

The problem in *Hunt* v. *Crumboch*, which involved a civil suit for damages and to enjoin a union boycott, was whether a conspiracy by a union alone violated the Sherman and Clayton acts. The union had established an ironclad secondary boycott against a trucking firm, in retaliation for the slaying of a union man, allegedly by a partner in the firm, during a bitter and violent strike that occurred earlier. The majority ruled that the general statutory exemption of organized labor, for conspiracies to restrain interstate commerce by collective action against employers, applied to the circumstances of this case. "It is not a violation of the Sherman Act," said Black, "for laborers in combination to refuse to work. They can sell or not sell their labor as they please, and upon such terms and conditions as they choose, without infringing the Anti-trust laws. . . . A worker is privileged under congressional enactments, acting either alone or in concert with his fellow workers, to associate, or to decline to associate with other workers, to accept, refuse to accept, or to terminate a relationship of employment, and his labor is not to be treated as 'a commodity or article of commerce.' "

To Roberts, however, it was "hardly an accurate description of their attitude to say that the union men decided not to sell their labor to the petitioners. They intended to drive petitioners out of business as interstate motor carriers, and they suceeded in so doing." (The events of the case had transpired in his home town, Philadelphia.) But the record did not show that there had been any actual restraint of interstate commerce; and the question whether the union's admitted and deliberate destruction of the employer's business subjected the union to liability for damages under state law was not before the Supreme Court, nor was it even a federal question. Jackson, nevertheless, was convinced that a zealously prolabor majority was riding roughshod over the legitimate rights of the employer in this case.

MR. JUSTICE JACKSON, *dissenting.*

The Court concedes that if business competitors alone or in combination with labor had conspired to drive petitioners out of business by refusing goods or services, competitors and labor organization would have violated the Sherman Act. The only question then is whether respondent is exempted from the prohibition of the Act. It is hard to see how this union is excused from the terms of the Act when in the Allen Bradley case [decided earlier this same day] we hold that labor unions even though furthering their members' interests as wage earners violate the Act when they combine with business to do the things prohibited by the Act. There, too, labor performed its part of the conspiracy by denying or threatening to deny labor to employers. But in that case we hold that no absolute immunity is granted by the statute, and that because of its purpose and its association, the labor union violated the Act. Here too, the purpose of the respondent union is such as to remove the union's activities from the protection of the Clayton and Norris-LaGuardia Acts.

We say in the *Allen Bradley* case that, since a labor dispute existed, the refusal of the union to work would not have violated the Sherman Act if it had acted alone. In that case, the Court reviews fully the *conflicting* policies expressed in those Acts intended to preserve competition and in those which permit labor organizations to pursue their objectives. Those statutes which restricted the application of the Sherman Act against unions were intended only to shield the legitimate objectives of such organizations, not to give them a sword to use with unlimited immunity. The social interest in allowing workers to better their condition by their combined bargaining power was thought to outweigh the otherwise undesirable restriction on competition which all successful union activity necessarily entails. But there is no social interest served by union activities which are directed not to the advantage of union members but merely to capricious and retaliatory misuse of the power which unions have simply to impose their will on the employer. . . .

With this decision, the labor movement has come full circle. The working man has struggled long, the fight has been filled with hatred, and conflict has been dangerous, but now workers may not be deprived of their livelihood merely because their employers oppose and they favor unions. Labor has won other rights as well, unemployment compensation, old-age benefits and, what is most important and the basis of all its gains, the recognition that the opportunity to earn his support is not alone the concern of the individual but is the problem which all organized societies must contend with and conquer if they are to survive. This Court now sustains the claim of a union to the right to deny participation in the economic world to an employer simply because the union disagrees with him. This Court permits to employees the same arbitrary dominance over the economic sphere which they control that labor so long, so bitterly and so rightly asserted should belong to no man.

Strikes aimed at compelling the employer to yield to union demands are not within the Sherman Act. Here the employer has yielded and the union has achieved the end to which all legitimate union pressure is directed and limited. The union cannot consistently with the Sherman Act refuse to enjoy the fruits of its victory and deny peace terms to an employer who has unconditionally surrendered.

Mr. Justice Brandeis, for a unanimous Court, held that a union cannot lawfully strike for an unlawful purpose. "The right to carry on business—be it called liberty or property—has value. To interfere with this right without just cause is unlawful. The fact that the injury was inflicted by a strike is sometimes a justification. But a strike may be illegal because of its purpose, however orderly the manner in which it is conducted. To collect a stale claim due to a fellow member of the

union who was formerly employed in the business is not a permissible purpose."
. . . No more permissible is an exaction of privately-determined punishment for
alleged murder. And being unlawful, union activities of this kind are not protected
by the Clayton and Norris-LaGuardia Acts.

THE CHIEF JUSTICE [STONE] and MR. JUSTICE FRANKFURTER join in this
opinion.

6 BUREAUCRACY

In perfect accord with his strong individualistic bias in behalf of the rights of private property, Robert Jackson was a stalwart antagonist of governmental bureaucracy, in general, and of the sprawling federal behemoth with its thousands of zealous clerks and officials, in particular. Not only did he bring to Washington the anti-government suspicions characteristic of the small-town merchant; it appears that his own administrative experience reinforced and confirmed his Main Street outlook. Jackson was General Counsel of the Bureau of Internal Revenue for two years; for one year in charge of the tax division, and for another year in charge of the anti-trust division, both of the Department of Justice; Solicitor General for two years; and Attorney General for a year and a half. These seven and a half years spanned the period from the first year of the New Deal through the Third Term campaign and the declaration of the unlimited national emergency which foreshadowed active American military participation in World War II. All of these positions were what Karl Llewellyn would call "law-jobs," and during all except the final year and a half Jackson was concerned primarily with the prosecution, defense, or compromise of litigation, particularly in regard to the collection of debts owed to the national government.[1]

Possibly experience in alternative roles of public service, such as in Agriculture, or in State, or in the then newly established Social Security Board, might have helped to sow the seeds for subsequent doubts, rather than certitude, concerning the stereotyped personality of governmental employees; but he did not gain such experience. As an attorney in private practice in Jamestown, as a government lawyer, as a Supreme Court justice, and as the American prosecutor at Nuremberg, he remained within the framework and confines of professional legal roles of one kind or another. In those legal roles that he occupied before joining the Court, non-legal bureaucrats were either his adversaries, his competitors, or else his clerical subordinates. Even as Attorney General he considered his role to be that of counsel to the President rather than as the administrator of a diversified program of specialized technical services. So as a judge, he frequently

---

[1] "[W]hen Bob came to Washington as general counsel for the Bureau of Internal Revenue," according to the authentic voice of the business community, "he won a reputation as 'the most zealous tax collector Uncle Sam ever had!' " "Jack the Giant Killer—Heir Apparent?" *Business Week,* No. 545 (February 10, 1940), 24.

adopted the mantle and pose of the insider, who knows the ropes of official chicanery and can be neither fooled nor intimidated by the insolence of office.

The first three of the opinions included in this chapter discuss administrative transgressions of property rights, and the other three opinions deal with bureaucratic invasions of personal liberty. The first case concerns one of the two most celebrated issues of constitutional politics in the decision of which Jackson participated as a Supreme Court justice, the other decision being the School Segregation Case of 1954. In his opinion in the Steel Seizure Case, Jackson cast the President in the role of Chief Bureaucrat of the Nation, and dealt with him accordingly. The next two opinions discuss the so-called independent federal regulatory commissions, which Jackson didn't think of as part of the executive branch in the constitutional sense, although some of them, because of their functions, might remain subject to at least partial presidential power of supervision and policy direction.[2] The *Knauff* and *Mezei* opinions, which follow, both involve decision making by a subdivision of the Department of Justice, over which Jackson in the then not too remote past had presided as Attorney General and in the name of the President. The pair of regulatory commission cases and the pair concerning the admission of aliens deal with fairly routine questions of the management of the civilian economy and polity by agencies presumed, at least by Jackson, to be subject to routine patterns of legislative and judicial direction and audit, in addition to whatever bureaucratic authority might be exercised by the President in his civilian status. The last opinion in this chapter, however, discusses direct military rule over American civilians in wartime and a consequent benediction by the civilian courts that justified drastic policy decisions by military bureaucrats that invaded the personal freedom and property rights of thousands of civilians. In all of these instances, Jackson voted in support of the individual claimants and in opposition to sundry commissioners, inspectors, generals, and, indeed, the President himself. He felt that all such officials, no matter how high or how low, must submit to the Rule of Law—that is, the rule of judges in general, and of Supreme Court justices in particular—if the American democratic way of life is to survive.

Jackson's antipathy for officialdom probably was sincere enough, although he once quoted Holmes as the source of the insight that seeming candor often is the most effective form of deception. In levying his advocacy against the bureaucracy, he could at the same time typically uphold positions of either economic conservatism or political liberalism; so

[2] See, for example, his opinion for the Court in *Chicago and Southern Air Lines* v. *Waterman Steamship Corp.*, 333 U.S. 103 (1948).

his bureaucratic bias coincided with, and tended to reinforce, the dominant trends in his ideological synthesis. No doubt this helps to explain in part the typically passionate tone in which he exposed the unbridled zeal that characterizes the behavior of employees of the federal government. But there is a latent, as well as a manifest, explanation for his wrath toward the minions of the President.

Jackson's constitutional theory was pristine in its orthodoxy and simplicity.[3] He believed in a Newtonian political structure, with a governmental machine which functioned best when all of its interacting forces were confined within appropriate critical range values.[4] A democratic machine is one in which citizens exert their energies to produce political pressures that motivate legislators to enact laws that are the vectorial products of the dominant combinations of civic forces. The job of executive and administrative bureaucrats alike is to see that legislative norms are translated into empirical behaviors which constitute the results that the legislature intended to bring about: administration is a transmission belt[5] which transforms legislative policy directives into a structure of governmental services and controls that conform to the legislative blueprint. The task of judges is to see that bureaucrats do what legislators want them to do; and the particular task of the Supreme Court is to assure that the nuts and bolts of the governmental machine, namely, these other legislative, administrative, and inferior judicial decision makers, work within the range of their appropriate critical values, or are replaced by substitute nuts and bolts that will function properly. But the Supreme Court can carry out such a monitoring function only when there are relatively minor breakdowns in the system; its role is akin to that of the "mechanic on duty" at the neighborhood gasoline station. Any really serious breakdown can only be repaired by a major overhaul, which will necessitate widespread civic participation and involvement, presumably through constituent activity.

The mechanical metaphor is by no means a minority point of view;[6] Jackson's conception of the American constitutional system is shared by

[3] Robert Jackson, *The Supreme Court in the American System of Government* (Cambridge: Harvard University Press, 1955), *passim*.

[4] See my "The Rhetoric of Constitutional Change," *Journal of Public Law*, XVI (1967), 16-50. "The vice of judicial supremacy, as exerted for ninety years in the field of policy," Jackson once remarked, "has been its progressive closing of the avenues to peaceful and democratic conciliation of our social and economic conflicts." *The Struggle for Judicial Supremacy*, p. 321.

[5] Cf. Norton E. Long, "Power and Administration," *Public Administration Review*, IX (1949), 257-264.

[6] Martin Landau, "On the Use of Metaphor in Political Science," *Social Research*, XXVIII (1961), 331-357.

some law professors,[7] probably by a majority of American lawyers, and, if one is to judge by survey research evidence, by a majority of adult lay Americans. It is no longer the modal view among political scientists, nor among at least the younger generation of law professors. But Jackson, in this chapter, mirrors the predominant attitudes of his profession toward the specific institutional subjects of his opinions: the federal regulatory commissions are a headless fourth branch of the government which ought to be brought under closer judicial surveillance,[8] and forced to make decisions more like courts; citizens ought, with the aid of their counsel, to be able to challenge the excesses of bureaucrats in the regular courts. Shades of A. V. Dicey! But it is precisely because his concept of the constitutional structure of the American polity—and of the political structure of the American constitution—is so unmitigatedly orthodox, that his euarticulation of this point of view constitutes a classic rendition of a major American ideological perspective. His intense vocal opposition to officialdom was, however, both a caricature and an anachronism. Here he was still carrying a torch for a cause that had been lost to the indigenous forces of American political progressivism during his own youth. Indeed, his own migration to Washington to join the New Deal contributed to, and certainly helped to symbolize, the very triumph of the federal bureaucracy as a permanent feature of the American polity that Jackson, the judge, came to lament so loudly, as in his valedictory address to the organized bar:

[W]e must consider the momentum and potency of two distinguishable but closely related movements that hold some threat to our traditions.

One now is called authoritarianism, a new name for the old practice by which official authority, unconfined by law, rides roughshod over individual rights. Our forefathers sought to forestall this kind of oppression by providing that official actions affecting life, liberty and property be confined to those legislatively authorized and executed by procedures which conform to due process of law. Out of these texts have grown our many decisions that support the principle of individual freedom as opposed to the principle of authority.

But a more subtle form of aggression against individual freedom comes, not from the usurping officeholder, but from the state itself, under the philosophy that all else must give way to the interests of the state. This movement is likely to progress strictly within the terms

[7] Bernard Schwartz, *A Commentary on the Constitution of the United States; Part I: The Powers of Government* (New York: The Macmillan Company, 1963), 2 Vols.

[8] As Attorney General, Jackson himself had been the recipient of the *Final Report* (Washington: Government Printing Office, 1941) of the Committee on Administrative Procedure, whom Murphy had appointed. This report was laid on the table by the imminence of World War II, but it did contribute to the subsequent Administrative Procedure Act of 1946. At the time of his death, Jackson was serving as a special consultant to the "Task Force" of attorneys and judges who made the recommendations that became the basis for: the (Hoover) Commission on the Organization of the Executive Branch of the Government of the United States, *Legal Services and Procedure* (Washington: Government Printing Office, 1955).

of legislation and forms of law. Government gradually takes over direction of the total life of the citizen—economic, educational, social, artistic and religious. It regulates each step of one's daily affairs and tolerates no conflicting loyalties or duties. In moderation, many may welcome this as a "planned economy" or "welfare state"; in excess, it becomes the totalitarian state. Our forefathers knew, too, the dangers of excessive government and sought to forestall it by confining the reach of the Federal Government to a small segment of the daily life of the individual or of the local community.[9]

Perhaps "the man who ha[d] always been a New Dealer" and who F.D.R. (as widely reported at the time the ploy for the Third Term was unfolded) thought "would some day make a great liberal President"[10] suffered from the pangs of despised love now that he had settled for the law's delay. Maybe he protested too much.

A. THE SECOND BRANCH

YOUNGSTOWN SHEET & TUBE V. SAWYER
343 U.S. 579, 634 (June 2, 1952)

The Bureaucrat in Chief who, in Jackson's view, was the protagonist in the Steel Seizure Case was none other than President Harry S ("for nothing") Truman, the man who, Jackson believed, had welched on F.D.R.'s commitment to make Jackson Chief Justice when Stone stepped down. There were excellent, sufficient, and independent reasons for Jackson to have voted in favor of "Big Steel," and against the government, as he did in this decision; but he would have been less than human—and Bob Jackson was an intensely human being—had he not been aware, and reinforced in his judgment by the circumstance, that one effect of the outcome was to brand Boss Pendergast's protege as a lawless usurper of the constitutional rights and powers of the Congress. Jackson's sensitivity to such matters is suggested by his comment[11] only nine days after the decision was announced, that "It must have taken great courage for Tom Clark to vote against the man who appointed him."

The issue before the Court had come to focus on Truman's executive

---

[9] Robert H. Jackson, "The Task of Maintaining our Liberties: The Role of the Judiciary," *American Bar Association Journal*, XXXIX (1953), 962-963.

[10] "Young Hickory," *Time*, XXXV (January 15, 1940), 11; Marquis W. Childs, "The Man Who Has Always Been a New Dealer," *Forum*, CIII (March, 1940), 148-154; "Roosevelt's Man," *Senior Scholastic*, XXXVI (March 25, 1940), 10; "Jack the Giant Killer—Heir Apparent?" *Business Week*, No. 545 (February 10, 1940), 24; Karl Shriftgeisser, "Career Man of the New Deal: Robert H. Jackson," *North American Review*, CCXLVIII (1939), 334-344; "F.D.R.'s Successor?" *Senior Scholastic*, XXXI (January 15, 1938), 14s.

[11] Oral statement in an interview with the author on June 11, 1952.

order directing Secretary of Commerce Sawyer to "seize"—namely, to assume temporary control over the management of—the country's major steel mills, for the ostensible purpose of avoiding a major strike and of assuring continuing defense production in support of American troops in the then undeclared, but quite "hot," Korean War. (This "seizure order" came just a year after Truman had removed Douglas MacArthur from his command, and only a few months before Dwight Eisenhower made his pilgrimage to Korea to bring peace to that troubled land.) The case reached the Court surcharged with political dimensions of the first magnitude, and the Court reacted accordingly. Literally unprecedented was the Court's decision that Truman's seizure order was unconstitutional, in that the Court was defying an incumbent President during a national crisis and making a decision which had an immediate and disastrous impact upon the nation's steel production. In the past, it had been the practice of the Court to wait until the war was over and the President cold in his grave before delivery of an inspirational sermon on the subject of the constitutional separation of powers and the judicial obligation to uphold the Constitution against executive pretensions and usurpations of power.[12]

Black wrote the opinion of the Court, although every other member of the six-man majority also wrote a separate opinion, and Clark concurred in the judgment only. The majority concluded that neither the Constitution nor any statute authorized the President to interfere in a dispute between labor and management, in time of peace (sic!), by "seizing" the private property of mill owners. Without such power, the President could not authorize any of his minions to take such action; and, therefore, Secretary Sawyer—a man who, like most American secretaries of commerce, was hardly an ideological Marxist—was portrayed as a buccaneer who wandered about the countryside collectivizing steel mills. Black's opinion for the Court was the most rigid of all those written, positing the problem as a simple, straightforward question of the constitutional principle of separation of powers: only Congress could authorize seizure, because the condemnation of private property for public purposes is a legislative power which, by its very nature, could not belong to the President.[13]

In fact, the Presidency was goaded into bumbling action, which it finally resolved to take only after all other efforts to avert the steel strike had failed.[14] The strike began as soon as the Supreme Court's decision was

12 See Clinton Rossiter, *The Supreme Court and the Commander in Chief* (Ithaca: Cornell University Press, 1951); and Glendon Schubert, *The Presidency in the Courts* (Minneapolis: University of Minnesota Press, 1957), Chap. 6.

13 Cf. Edward S. Corwin, "The Steel Seizure Case: A Judicial Brick without Straw," *Columbia Law Review*, LIII (1953), 53-66.

14 Grant McConnell, *The Steel Seizure of 1952* (University Ala.: University of Alabama Press, 1960; Inter-University Case Program, #52), Part V and pp. 47-53.

announced, and it lasted for 55 days throughout most of the following summer. Truman's decision was "A plague o' both your houses," since management feared that the result would be an involuntary increase in wages and other labor costs without the corresponding increase in steel prices favored by the industry; whereas the steelworkers were confident that they could get a higher raise out of the owners, after a strike, than out of the government, without one. So both labor and management preferred the strike; it was the men in and around the White House, the civilian and military bureaucrats who were concerned with defense production and the prosecution of the war, who wished to avoid it. Whether the Presidency offered a better approximation of "the public interest" in this dispute than the opposing hierarchies of union bureaucrats, corporate bureaucrats, or even of judicial bureaucrats, is a question which depends upon the theory with which one approaches the problem.[15] But Truman clearly lost this case in the nation's press even before he lost it in the Supreme Court; and the underlying explanation for both decisions doubtless was the lack of an articulate, organized political interest to support the Administration in its unpopular cause. And so it was that economic liberals, like Black, Douglas,[16] and Clark, found themselves ad hoc compatriots of economic conservatives like Burton, Jackson, and Frankfurter. Only the three middle-of-the-roaders on the economic issue. Vinson, Minton, and Reed,[17] supported the steel seizure. Presumably, their relative lack of attachment to the fortunes of either of the two contenders made it possible for them to adopt and to voice a more neutral and dispassionate view of the issue.

MR. JUSTICE JACKSON, concurring in the judgment and opinion of the Court.

That comprehensive and undefined presidential powers hold both practical advantages and grave dangers for the country will impress anyone who has served as legal adviser to a President in time of transition and public anxiety. While an interval of detached reflection may temper teachings of that experience, they probably are a more realistic influence on my views than the conventional materials of judicial decision which seem unduly to accentuate doctrine and legal fic-

15 See my *The Public Interest* (Glencoe, Illinois: The Free Press, 1960), and "The Steel Case: Presidential Responsibility and Judicial Irresponsibility," *Western Political Quarterly*, VI (1953), 61-77.

16 Douglas concluded his opinion with the observation that "tomorrow another President might use the same power to prevent a wage increase, to curb trade-unionists, to regiment labor as oppressively as industry thinks it has been regimented by this seizure."

17 Glendon Schubert, *The Judicial Mind*, (Evanston: Northwestern University Press, 1945), pp. 132, 145.

tion. But as we approach the question of presidential power, we half overcome mental hazards by recognizing them. The opinions of judges, no less than executives and publicists, often suffer the infirmity of confusing the issue of a power's validity with the cause it is invoked to promote, of confounding the permanent executive office with its temporary occupant. The tendency is strong to emphasize transient results upon policies—such as wages or stabilization—and lose sight of enduring consequences upon the balanced power structure of our Republic.

A judge, like an executive adviser, may be surprised at the poverty of really useful and unambiguous authority applicable to concrete problems of executive power as they actually present themselves. Just what our forefathers did envision, or would have envisioned had they foreseen modern conditions, must be divined from materials almost as enigmatic as the dreams Joseph was called upon to interpret for Pharaoh. A century and a half of partisan debate and scholarly speculation yields no net result but only supplies more or less apt quotations from respected sources on each side of any question. They largely cancel each other. And court decisions are indecisive because of the judicial practice of dealing with the largest questions in the most narrow way.

The actual art of governing under our Constitution does not and cannot conform to judicial definitions of the power of any of its branches based on isolated clauses or even single Articles torn from context. While the Constitution diffuses power the better to secure liberty, it also contemplates that practice will integrate the dispersed powers into a workable government. It enjoins upon its branches separateness but interdependence, autonomy but reciprocity. Presidential powers are not fixed but fluctuate, depending upon their disjunction or conjunction with those of Congress. We may well begin by a somewhat over-simplified grouping of practical situations in which a President may doubt, or others may challenge, his powers, and by distinguishing roughly the legal consequences of this factor of relativity.

1. When the President acts pursuant to an express or implied authorization of Congress, his authority is at its maximum, for it includes all that he possesses in his own right plus all that Congress can delegate. In these circumstances, and in these only, may he be said (for what it may be worth) to personify the federal sovereignty. If his act is held unconstitutional under these circumstances, it usually means that Federal Government as an undivided whole lacks power. A seizure executed by the President pursuant to an Act of Congress would be supported by the strongest of presumptions and the widest latitude of judicial interpretation, and the burden of persuasion would rest heavily upon any who might attack it.

2. When the President acts in absence of either a congressional grant or denial of authority, he can only rely upon his own independent powers, but there is a zone of twilight in which he and Congress may have concurrent authority, or in which its distribution is uncertain. Therefore, congressional inertia, indiffer-

ence or quiescence may sometimes, at least as a practical matter, enable, if not invite, measures on independent presidential responsibility. In this area, any actual test of power is likely to depend on the imperatives of events and contemporary imponderables rather than on abstract theories of law.

3. When the President takes measures incompatible with the expressed or implied will of Congress, his power is at its lowest ebb, for then he can rely only upon his own constitutional powers minus any constitutional powers of Congress over the matter. Courts can sustain exclusive presidential control in such a case only by disabling the Congress from acting upon the subject. Presidential claim to a power at once so conclusive and preclusive must be scrutinized with caution, for what is at stake is the equilibrium established by our constitutional system.

Into which of these classifications does this executive seizure of the steel industry fit? It is eliminated from the first by admission, for it is conceded that no congressional authorization exists for this seizure. That takes away also the support of the many precedents and declarations which were made in relation, and must be confined, to this category.

Can it then be defended under flexible tests available to the second category? It seems clearly eliminated from that class because Congress has not left seizure of private property an open field but has covered it by three statutory policies inconsistent with this seizure. In cases where the purpose is to supply needs of the Government itself, two courses are provided: one, seizure of a plant which fails to comply with obligatory orders placed by the Government; another, condemnation of facilities, including temporary use under the power of eminent domain. The third is applicable where it is the general economy of the country that is to be protected rather than exclusive governmental interests. None of these were invoked. In choosing a different and inconsistent way of his own, the President cannot claim that it is necessitated or invited by failure of Congress to legislate upon the occasions, grounds and methods for seizure of industrial properties.

This leaves the current seizure to be justified only by the severe tests under the third grouping, where it can be supported only by any remainder of executive power after subtraction of such powers as Congress may have over the subject. In short, we can sustain the President only by holding that seizure of such strike-bound industries is within his domain and beyond control by Congress. Thus, this Court's first review of such seizures occurs under circumstances which leave presidential power most vulnerable to attack and in the least favorable of possible constitutional postures. . . .

The Solicitor General seeks the power of seizure in three clauses of the Executive Article, the first reading, "The executive Power shall be vested in a President of the United States of America." Lest I be thought to exaggerate, I quote the interpretation which his brief puts upon it: "In our view, this clause constitutes a grant of all the executive powers of which the Government is capable." If that be true, it is difficult to see why the forefathers bothered to add several specific items, including some trifling ones.

The example of such unlimited executive power that must have most impressed the forefathers was the prerogative exercised by George III, and the description of its evils in the Declaration of Independence leads me to doubt that they were creating their new Executive in his image. Continental European examples were no more appealing. And if we seek instruction from our own times, we can match it only from the executive powers in those governments we disparagingly describe as totalitarian. I cannot accept the view that this clause is a grant in bulk of all conceivable executive power but regard it as an allocation to the presidential office of the generic powers thereafter stated.

The clause on which the Government next relies is that "The President shall be Commander in Chief of the Army and Navy of the United States. . . ." These cryptic words have given rise to some of the most persistent controversies in our constitutional history. Of course, they imply something more than an empty title. But just what authority goes with the name has plagued presidential advisers who would not waive or narrow it by nonassertion yet cannot say where it begins or ends. It undoubtedly puts the Nation's armed forces under presidential command. Hence, this loose appellation is sometimes advanced as support for any presidential action, internal or external, involving use of force, the idea being that it vests power to do anything, anywhere, that can be done with an army or navy.

That seems to be the logic of an argument tendered at our bar—that the President having, on his own responsibility, sent American troops abroad derives from that act "affirmative power" to seize the means of producing a supply of steel for them. To quote, "Perhaps the most forceful illustration of the scope of Presidential power in this connection is the fact that American troops in Korea, whose safety and effectiveness are so directly involved here, were sent to the field by an exercise of the President's constitutional powers." Thus, it is said, he has invested himself with "war powers."

I cannot foresee all that it might entail if the Court should indorse this argument. Nothing in our Constitution is plainer than that declaration of a war is entrusted only to Congress. Of course, a state of war may in fact exist without a formal declaration. But no doctrine that the Court could promulgate would seem to me more sinister and alarming than that a President whose conduct of foreign affairs is so largely uncontrolled, and often even is unknown, can vastly enlarge his mastery over the internal affairs of the country by his own commitment of the Nation's armed forces to some foreign venture. I do not, however, find it necessary or appropriate to consider the legal status of the Korean enterprise to discountenance argument based on it.

Assuming that we are in a war *de facto*, whether it is or is not a war *de jure*, does that empower the Commander in Chief to seize industries he thinks necessary to supply our army? The Constitution expressly places in Congress power "to raise and *support* Armies" and "to *provide* and *maintain* a Navy." (Emphasis supplied.) This certainly lays upon Congress primary responsibility for supplying the armed forces. Congress alone controls the raising of revenues and their appropriation and may determine in what manner and by what means they shall be spent for military and naval procurement. I suppose no one would doubt that Congress can take over war supply as a Government enterprise. On the other hand, if Congress sees fit to rely on *free private enterprise collectively bargaining with free labor*[18] for support and maintenance of our armed forces, can the Executive, because of lawful disagreements incidental to that process, seize the facility for operation upon Government-imposed terms?

There are indications that the Constitution did not contemplate that the title Commander in Chief *of the Army and Navy* will constitute him also Commander in Chief of the country, its industries and its inhabitants. He has no monopoly of "war powers," whatever they are. While Congress cannot deprive the President of the command of the army and navy, only Congress can provide him an army or navy to command. It is also empowered to make rules for the "Government and Regulation of land and naval Forces," by which it may to some unknown extent impinge upon even command functions. . . .

[But we] should not use this occasion to circumscribe, much less to contract, the lawful role of the President as Commander in Chief. I should indulge the widest latitude of interpretation to sustain his exclusive function to command the instruments of national force, at least when turned against the outside world for the security of our society. But, when it is turned inward, not because of rebellion but because of a lawful economic struggle between industry and labor, it should have no such indulgence. His command power is not such an absolute as might be implied from that office in a militaristic system but is subject to limitations consistent with a constitutional Republic whose law and policy-making branch is a representative Congress. The purpose of lodging dual titles in one man was to insure that the civilian would control the military, not to enable the military to subordinate the presidential office. No penance would ever expiate the sin against free government of holding that a President can escape control of executive powers by law through assuming his military role. What the power of command may include I do not try to envision, but I think it is not a military prerogative, without support of law, to seize persons or property because they are important or even essential for the military and naval establishment.

The third clause in which the Solicitor General finds seizure powers is that "he shall take Care that the Laws be faithfully executed. . . ." That authority must be matched against words of the Fifth Amendment that "No person shall be . . . deprived of life, liberty or property, without due process of law. . . ." One gives a government authority that reaches so far as there is law, the other gives a private right that authority shall go no farther. These signify about all there is of the

---

[18] Emphasis added. [Ed.]

principle that ours is a government of laws, not of men, and that we submit our-selves to rulers only if under rules.

The Solicitor General lastly grounds support of the seizure upon nebulous, inherent powers never expressly granted but said to have accrued to the office from the customs and claims of preceding administrations. The plea is for a resulting power to deal with a crisis or an emergency according to the necessities of the case, the unarticulated assumption being that necessity knows no law.

Loose and irresponsible use of adjectives colors all non-legal and much legal discussion of presidential powers. "Inherent" powers, "implied" powers, "inciden-tal" powers, "plenary" powers, "war" powers and "emergency" powers are used, often interchangeably and without fixed or ascertainable meanings.

The vagueness and generality of the clauses that set forth presidential pow-ers afford a plausible basis for pressures within and without an administration for presidential action beyond that supported by those whose responsibility it is to defend his actions in court. The claim of inherent and unrestricted presiden-tial powers has long been a persuasive dialectical weapon in political controversy. While it is not surprising that counsel should grasp support from such unadjudi-cated claims of power, a judge cannot accept self-serving press statements of the attorney for one of the interested parties as authority in answering a constitutional question, *even if the advocate was himself*.[19] But prudence has counseled that actual reliance on such nebulous claims stop short of provoking a judicial test....

In the practical working of our Government we already have evolved a technique within the framework of the Constitution by which normal executive powers may be considerably expanded to meet an emergency. Congress may and has granted extraordinary authorities which lie dormant in normal times but may be called into play by the Executive in war or upon proclamation of a national emergency. In 1939, upon congressional request, the Attorney General listed ninety-nine such separate statutory grants by Congress of emergency or wartime executive powers. They were invoked from time to time as need appeared. Under this procedure we retain Government by law—special, temporary law, perhaps, but law nonetheless. The public may know the extent and limitations of the pow-ers that can be asserted, and persons affected may be informed from the statute of their rights and duties.

In view of the ease, expedition and safety with which Congress can grant and has granted large emergency powers, certainly ample to embrace this crisis, I am quite unimpressed with the argument that we should affirm possession of them without statute. Such power either has no beginning or it has no end. If it exists, it need submit to no legal restraint. I am not alarmed that it would plunge

---

[19] Emphasis added. Cf. *McGrath* v. *Kristensen*, 340 U.S. 162, 176 (1950), and Chap. 9E, *infra;* and Robert H. Jackson, "A Presidential Legal Opinion," *Harvard Law Review*, LXVI (1953), 1353-1361. [Ed.]

us straightway into dictatorship, but it is at least a step in that wrong direction.

As to whether there is imperative necessity for such powers, it is relevant to note the gap that exists between the President's paper powers and his real powers. The Constitution does not disclose the measure of the actual controls wielded by the modern presidential office. That instrument must be understood as an Eighteenth-Century sketch of a government hoped for, not as a blueprint of the Government that is. Vast accretions of federal power, eroded from that reserved by the States, have magnified the scope of presidential activity. Subtle shifts take place in the centers of real power that do not show on the face of the Constitution.

Executive power has the advantage of concentration in a single head in whose choice the whole Nation has a part, making him the focus of public hopes and expectations. In drama, magnitude and finality his decisions so far overshadow any others that almost alone he fills the public eye and ear. No other personality in public life can begin to compete with him in access to the public mind through modern methods of communications. By his prestige as head of state and his influence upon public opinion he exerts a leverage upon those who are supposed to check and balance his power which often cancels their effectiveness.

Moreover, rise of the party system has made a significant extraconstitutional supplement to real executive power. No appraisal of his necessities is realistic which overlooks that he heads a political system as well as a legal system. Party loyalties and interests, sometimes more binding than law, extend his effective control into branches of government other than his own and he often may win, as a political leader, what he cannot command under the Constitution. . . . I cannot be brought to believe that this country will suffer if the Court refuses further to aggrandize the presidential office, already so potent and so relatively immune from judicial review, at the expense of Congress.

But I have no illusion that any decision by this Court can keep power in the hands of Congress if it is not wise and timely in meeting its problems. A crisis that challenges the President equally, or perhaps primarily, challenges Congress. If not good law, there was worldly wisdom in the maxim attributed to Napoleon that "The tools belong to the man who can use them." We may say that power to legislate for emergencies belongs in the hands of Congress, but only Congress itself can prevent power from slipping through its fingers.

The essence of our free Government is "leave to live by no man's leave, underneath the law"—to be governed by those impersonal forces which we call law. Our Government is fashioned to fulfill this concept so far as humanly possible. The Executive, except for recommendation and veto, has no legislative power. The executive action we have here originates in the individual will of the President[20] and represents an exercise of authority without law. No one, perhaps not even the President, knows the limits of the power he may seek to exert in this

---

[20] But cf. McConnell, *The Steel Seizure of 1952*, pp. 1-2, 53, *passim.* [Ed.]

instance and the parties affected cannot learn the limit of their rights. We do not know today what powers over labor or property would be claimed to flow from Government possession if we should legalize it, what rights to compensation would be claimed or recognized, or on what contingency it would end. With all its defects, delays and inconveniences, men have discovered no technique for long preserving free government except that the Executive be under the law, and that the law be made by parliamentary deliberations.

Such institutions may be destined to pass away. But it is the duty of the Court to be last, not first, to give them up.

B. THE FOURTH BRANCH[21]

FEDERAL TRADE COMMISSION V. RUBEROID COMPANY
343 U.S. 470, 480 (May 26, 1952)

In sharp contrast to the Steel Seizure Case, this was a relatively obscure and routine case of price discrimination that Jackson seized as an opportunity for writing an essay on the proper role of independent regulatory commissions. The corporation, a major manufacturer of asphalt and asbestos roofing materials, had committed repeated and admitted violations of the anti-trust laws over an extended period of time. This proceeding before the Supreme Court was but another phase in Ruberoid's strategy of delay. Almost a decade had slipped by; and Ruberoid now turned to litigation which interposed the lower federal courts as a shield to forestall enforcement of an order by the Federal Trade Commission which would have directed the corporation explicitly to comply with the requirements of the Clayton Act of 1914. In formulating its order, the Commission had refused to include a restatement of certain types of price discrimination which were explicitly permitted by the statute as exceptions to the general policy. The ostensible ground for the Commission's refusal was that it had no authority to revise acts of Congress, and, therefore, that any order which it made was necessarily subject to any and all relevant statutory provisions, including these statutory exemptions. Ruberoid complained that the order was invalid because it was thus in conflict with the statute, and argued that past violations were now all water over the dam. The corporation's counsel also argued that the lower federal court could not direct the

21 "So far as administrative decisions are concerned," wrote Jackson, it would seem that if this headless fourth branch has a head, it must be the Supreme Court." Jackson, *The Supreme Court in the American System*, p. 48.

corporation to obey the Commission's order until *after* the Commission had proved (in interminable administrative-judicial proceedings, which predictably would stretch on for several more years) that the corporation had violated an order of the Commission—certainly not this invalid one—which the lower court, with the Supreme Court's affirmance or denial of review, could uphold as legal. Such an argument may seem farfetched to those who have not previously been exposed to the intricacies of "administrative law," as lawyers define (and practice) the subject; but it is the very warp and woof of the process of accommodation (as the followers of group-interest theorist Arthur F. Bentley would put it) whereby public policies mandating socioeconomic change become dissipated in their effect upon interests of private property.

The Court of Appeals for the Second Circuit affirmed, in a 2-1 decision, the validity of the Commission's order, but refused to enforce it pending proof of its violation *in futuro*. This was only half a loaf apiece; so both parties carried cross-petitions in certiorari to the Supreme Court, the Commission arguing for enforcement now, and the corporation for the invalidation of the order which the court below had upheld. A fiveman majority of the Court, dominated by Truman's appointees, (Vinson, Burton, Minton, and Reed, with Clark writing the opinion), affirmed the compromise decision of the court below. Black concurred, without opinion, in the result only; Frankfurter did not participate because of illness; and Douglas dissented, without opinion but presumably because he thought that the Court should have required immediate enforcement of the order. Jackson, of course, had no quarrel with that aspect of the majority decision; he dissented instead (and, therefore, alone) from the Court's refusal to go whole hog with the corporation, invalidate this lawless order, and direct the Federal Trade Commission to start in all over again from scratch.

MR. JUSTICE JACKSON, dissenting. . . .

The Federal Trade Commission, in July of 1943, instituted before itself a proceeding against petitioner on a charge of discriminating in price between customers in violation of subsection (a) of § 2 of the Clayton Act. . . .

Several violations were proved and admitted to have occurred in 1941. No serious opposition was offered to an order to cease and desist from such discriminations, but petitioner did object to being ordered to cease types of violations it never had begun and asked that any order include a clause to the effect that it did not forbid the price differentials between customers which are expressly allowed by statute.

However, the Commission refused to include such a provision as "unnecessary to assure respondent its full legal rights." It also rejected the specific and limited order recommended by its Examiner and substituted a sweeping general order to "cease and desist from discriminating in price: By selling such products of like grade and quality to any purchaser at prices lower than those granted other purchasers who in fact compete with the favored purchaser in the resale or distribution of such products." It wrote no opinion and gave only the most cryptic reasons in its findings.

On proceedings for review, petitioner attacked this order for its indeterminateness and its prohibition of differentials allowed by statute. The Court of Appeals, however, affirmed, saying:

We sympathize with the petitioner's position and can realize the difficulties of conducting business under such general prohibitions. Nevertheless we are convinced that the cause of the trouble is the Act itself, which is vague and general in its wording and which cannot be translated with assurance into any detailed set of guiding yardsticks.

This appraisal of the result of almost ten years of litigation exposes a grave deficiency either in the Act itself or in the administrative process by which it has been applied. Admitting that the statute is "vague and general in its wording," it does not follow that a cease and desist order implementing it should be. I think such an outcome of administrative proceedings is not acceptable. We would rectify and advance the administrative process, which has become an indispensable adjunct to modern government, by returning this case to the Commission to perform its most useful function in administering an admittedly complicated Act. . . .

If the unsound result here were an isolated example of malaise in the administrative scheme, its tolerance by the Court would be less troubling, though no less wrong. But I think its decision may encourage a deterioration of the administrative process of which this case is symptomatic and which invites invasion of the independent agency administrative field by executive agencies. Other symptoms, betokening the same basic confusion, are the numerous occasions when administrative findings are inadequate for purposes of review and recent instances in which part of the government appears before us fighting another part—usually a wholly executive-controlled agency attacking one of the independent administrative agencies—the Departments of Agriculture (*Secretary of Agriculture* v. *United States et al.*, No. 710, now pending in this Court) and Justice (*United States* v. *Interstate Commerce Commission*, 337 U.S. 426) against the Interstate Commerce Commission, the Department of Justice against the Maritime Commission (*Far East Conference* v. *United States*, 342 U.S. 570), the Secretary of the Interior against the Federal Power Commission (*United States ex rel. Chapman* v. *Federal Power Commission*, No. 658, now pending in this Court, certiorari granted 343 U.S. 941). Abstract propositions may not solve concrete cases, but, when basic confusion is responsible for a particular result, resort to the fundamental principles which determine the position of the administrative process in our system may help to illuminate the shortcomings of that result.

I.

The Act, like many regulatory measures, sketches a general outline which contemplates its completion and clarification by the administrative process before court review or enforcement.

This section of the Act admittedly is complicated and vague in itself and even more so in its context. Indeed, the Court of Appeals seems to have thought it almost beyond understanding. . . .

This Act exemplifies the complexity of the modern lawmaking task and a common technique for regulatory legislation. It is typical of instances where the Congress cannot itself make every choice between possible lines of policy. It must legislate in generalities and delegate the final detailed choices to some authority with considerable latitude to conform its orders to administrative as well as legislative policies. . . .

A seller may violate this section of the Act without guilty knowledge or intent and may unwittingly subject himself to a cease and desist order. But neither violation of the Act nor of the order will call for criminal sanctions; neither is even enforceable on behalf of the United States by injunction until after an administrative proceeding has resulted in a cease and desist order and it has been reviewed and affirmed, if review be sought, by the Court of Appeals. Only an enforcement order issued from the court carries public sanctions, and its violation is punishable as a contempt. . . .

II.

The constitutional independence of the administrative tribunal presupposes that it will perform the function of completing unfinished law.

The rise of administrative bodies probably has been the most significant legal trend of the last century and perhaps more values today are affected by their decisions than by those of all the courts, review of administrative decisions apart. They also have begun to have important consequences on personal rights. . . .They have become a veritable fourth branch of the Government, which has deranged our three-branch legal theories much as the concept of a fourth dimension unsettles our three-dimensional thinking.

Courts have differed in assigning a place to these seemingly necessary bodies in our constitutional system. Administrative agencies have been called quasi-legislative, quasi-executive or quasi-judicial, as the occasion required, in order to validate their functions within the separation-of-powers scheme of the Constitution. The mere retreat to the qualifying "quasi" is implicit with confession that all recognized classifications have broken down and "quasi" is a smooth cover which we draw over our confusion as we might use a counterpane to conceal a disordered bed. . . .

When Congress enacts a statute that is complete in policy aspects and ready

to be executed as law, Congress has recognized that enforcement is only an executive function and has yielded that duty to wholly executive agencies, even though
determination of fact questions was necessary. Examples of the creation of such
rights and obligations are patent, revenue and customs laws. Only where the law
is not yet clear of policy elements and therefore not ready for mere executive
enforcement is it withdrawn from the executive department and confined to independent tribunals. If the tribunal to which such discretion is delegated does
nothing but promulgate as its own decision the generalities of its statutory charter, the rationale for placing it beyond executive control is gone.

III.

The quasi-legislative function of filling in blank spaces in regulatory legis-
lation and reconciling conflicting policy standards must neither be passed on to the
courts nor assumed by them.

.... [A] determination by an independent agency, with "quasi-legislative"
discretion in its armory, has a much larger immunity from judicial review than
does a determination by a purely executive agency. The court, in review of a case
under the tax law or the patent law, where the legislative function has been exhausted and policy considerations are settled in the Acts themselves, follows the
same mental operation as the executive officer. On the facts, there results an obligation to pay tax, or there is a right to a patent. The court can deduce these legal
rights or obligations from the statute in the same manner as the executive officer.
Hence, review of such executive decisions proceeds with no more deference to the
administrative judgment than to a decision of a lower court.

Very different, however, is the review of the "quasi-legislative" decision.
There the right or liability of the parties is not determined by mere application of
statute to the facts. The right or obligation results not merely from the abstract
expression of the will of Congress in the statute, but from the Commission's completion and concretization of that will in its order. . . .

On review, the Court does not decide whether *the* correct determination has
been reached. So far as the Court is concerned, a wide range of results may be
equally correct. In review of such a decision, the Court does not at all follow the
same mental processes as the Commission did in making it, for the judicial function excludes (in theory, at least) the policy-making or legislative element,
which rightfully influences the Commission's judgment but over which judicial
power does not extend. Since it is difficult for a court to determine from the record
where quasi-legislative policy making has stopped and quasi-judicial application
of policy has begun, the entire process escapes very penetrating scrutiny. . . .

Courts are no better equipped to handle policy questions and no more empowered to exercise legislative discretion on contempt proceedings than on review
proceedings. It is plain that, if the scheme of regulating complicated enterprises
through unfinished legislation is to be just and effective, we must insist that the

legislative function be performed and exhausted by the administrative body before the case is passed on to the courts.

IV.

This proceeding should be remanded for a more definitive and circumscribed order.

Returning to this case, I cannot find that ten years of litigation have served any useful purpose whatever. No doubt it is administratively convenient to blanket an industry under a comprehensive prohibition in bulk—an undiscriminating prohibition of discrimination. But this not only fails to give the precision and concreteness of legal duties to the abstract policies of the Act, it really promulgates an inaccurate partial paraphrase of its indeterminate generalities. Instead of completing the legislation by an order which will clarify the petitioner's duty, it confounds confusion by literally ordering it to cease what the statute permits it to do.

This Court and the court below defer solution of the problems inherent in such an order, on the theory that if petitioner offends again there may be an enforcement order, and if it then offends again there may be a contempt proceeding and that will be time enough for the court to decide what the order against the background of the Act really means. While I think this less than justice, I am not greatly concerned about what the Court's decision does to this individual petitioner, for whom I foresee no danger more serious than endless litigation. But I am concerned about what it does to administrative law.

To leave definition of the duties created by an order to a contempt proceeding is for the courts to end where they should begin. Injunctions are issued to be obeyed, even when justification to issue them may be debatable. . . . But in this case issues that seem far from frivolous as to what is forbidden are reserved for determination when punishment for disobedience is sought. The Court holds that some modifications are "implicit" in this order. Why should they not be made explicit? Why approve an order whose literal terms we know go beyond the authorization, on the theory that its excesses may be retracted if ever it needs enforcement? Why invite judicial indulgence toward violation by failure to be specific, positive and concrete?

It does not impress me as lawyerly practice to leave to a contempt proceeding the clarification of the reciprocal effects of this Act and order, and determination of the effect of statutory provisos which are then to be read into the order. The courts cannot and should not assume that function. It is, by our own doctrine, a legislative or "quasi-legislative" function, and the courts cannot take over the discretionary functions of the Commission which should enter into its determinations. Plainly this order is not in shape to enforce and does not become so by the Court's affirmance.

This proceeding should be remanded to the Commission with directions to make its order specific and concrete, to specify the types of discount which are forbidden and reserve to petitioner the rights which the statute allows it, unless they are deemed lost, forfeited or impaired by the violations, in which case any limitation should be set forth. The Commission should, in short, in the light of its own policy and the record, translate this Act into a "set of guiding yardsticks," admittedly now lacking. If that cannot be done, there should be no judicial approval for an order to cease and desist from we don't know what.

If that were done, I should be inclined to accept the Government's argument that, along with affirmance, enforcement may be ordered. I see no real sense, when the case is already before the Court and is approved, in requiring one more violation before its obedience will be made mandatory on pain of contempt. But, as this order stands, I am not surprised that enforcement should be left to some later generation of judges.

C. THE ADMINISTRATIVE HYDRA

SECURITIES AND EXCHANGE COMMISSION
V. CHENERY CORPORATION
332 U.S. 194, 209 (June 23, 1947)

William O. Douglas had been Chairman of the Securities and Exchange Commission immediately prior to his appointment to the Supreme Court, just as Jackson had been Attorney General. It was during the Douglas regime that many of the S.E.C.'s basic policies were formulated. Litigation challenging these policies continued to reach the Supreme Court throughout the following decade, and Douglas disqualified himself from participating in such decisions of the Court. Jackson, however, appeared to enjoy the opportunity to project, stylistically by means of vicarious combat with the federal agency that undoubtedly was most disliked by the financial segment of the business community, the frustration that he must have experienced after his return from Nuremberg, when the Court continued to move slowly but steadily in the direction of more liberal economic policies in its decisions, while Jackson himself moved in the opposite direction.[22] Such a case was *Chenery*.

The Supreme Court's initial decision in this case had come during World War II, in 1943.[23] The S.E.C. had decided, as an incident to its

---

[22] See Glendon Schubert, "Jackson's Judicial Philosophy: An Exploration in Value Analysis," *American Political Science Review,* LIX (1965), 960-963. For a statement of his earlier, pre-judicial (and much more tolerant) attitude toward administrative decision makers, see his "Problem of the Administrative Process," *Wisconsin State Bar Association Proceedings,* XXIX (1939), 155-165.

[23] *Securities and Exchange Commission* v. *Chenery Corporation,* 318 U.S. 80.

responsibility for bringing about corporate reorganization under the Public Utility Holding Company Act of 1935, that officers of a corporation under reorganization should not be permitted to enjoy a personal financial advantage through trading on the open market, on the basis of "inside information," in the stock of the corporation that employed them. The corporate managers undeniably had preferential access to such information, for it was they who prepared, subject to S.E.C. approval, proposed plans for the fiscal structure of the reorganized corporation. Analogizing the relationship of the managers to the stockholders as being like that of a fiduciary or trustee under traditional equitable principles, the S.E.C. cited in its opinion, and appeared to rely upon for legal support, precedents in equity, of the federal courts. A majority of the Court which included Jackson, and over the dissent of Black, Reed, and Murphy, remanded the case to the commission.

The basis of the Court's decision was that the S.E.C. had no authority to solve the problem (as a court most certainly could and probably would have done) by analogizing this fact situation to other similar ones which were, without question, covered by the law of equity. The S.E.C., said the Court (through Frankfurter, a former Professor of Administrative Law), should exercise the broad discretion vested in it by the statute and, on the basis of its expertise and experience in dealing with technical problems in the field of corporate fiscal reorganization, make a decision which would be supported by findings of facts. These should, in turn, be supported by evidence which would become part of the administrative record of the case. Black's dissent suggested that all the Commission would have to do to get the approval of the Court would be to reconsider the case, recast its rationale emphasizing its administrative expertise in this area, and on that basis, come to the same decision that the Court now refused to uphold.

This is precisely what the Commission did, although it emphasized, upon reconsideration, the point that the corporate managers' stock purchases resulted in "an unfair and inequitable distribution of voting power" contrary to the statute. Nor did this appear to be inconsistent with anything in the majority opinion of the Court in the first *Chenery* decision, because the Court's disapproval had not been of the merits of the S.E.C. decision, but of the manner in which it was reached. Under these circumstances, one might have expected that the Supreme Court would uphold the S.E.C. order in the second *Chenery* decision; and this is exactly what happened. But the Court was an instrument of a quite different group of justices in the second case, with the dissenters (plus two new converts) forming the new majority, and with the surviving members of the old majority of *Chenery I* now in dissent.

The first decision had been 4-3, which meant that there was a quorum and an adequate majority to dispose of the case, although this was not a majority of the full Court. Douglas had, of course, disqualified himself; and there had been one vacancy on the Court at the time, with Rutledge taking his seat two weeks after the decision was announced. In the second *Chenery* decision, Douglas remained disqualified; Vinson, who had replaced Stone since the first decision, also did not participate; Rutledge joined the three dissenters of the first case in support of the opinion of the new majority in this case; and Burton, who had replaced Roberts, concurred in the decision, but not in the opinion, of the majority. This left only Jackson and Frankfurter of the original four-man majority in the first case, and these two dissented in an opinion written by Jackson. There was, nevertheless, substantial consistency in these proceedings: the three justices who had favored the S.E.C. in the first case continued to vote to uphold the administrative order; and the two remaining of the group in opposition to the administrative decision continued in opposition.

The latter circumstance suggests that the Frankfurter opinion, in the first case, may have been only a smokescreen, and that at least these two of the justices who joined in it were really out of sympathy with the *merits* of the administrative policy and not merely with the process by which it was made and justified. If this was so, the anguished tone of Jackson's dissent, in which he flayed the administrative agency and the new Court majority alike for their "lawless" and politically motivated behavior, was the less warranted; it would have been more justified had he turned his lash on himself and his brother Frankfurter. Both factions switched their voting position because of changes in their relative numbers (and, therefore, power); but Jackson and Frankfurter appear to be the only ones who changed their position on the question of *how* the S.E.C. should make its policy decisions,[24] as well as upon the underlying question of *what* that policy should be. In any event, the opinion below can be assumed to represent Jackson's considered judgment and views, rather than something dashed off under emotional strain during the heat of the conflict, because the decision and opinion of the majority in the second *Chenery* case both were announced on June 23, 1947. Jackson then took the summer vacation period to think it over and waited until the opening of the new term, on October 6, 1947, to file his opinion.

---

[24] In the earlier decision, Frankfurter had said that the S.E.C. might, but did not have to, establish its proposed policy in the form of a regulation. But now Frankfurter and Jackson appear, according to Murphy's opinion, to have argued that the S.E.C. could not establish its policy on a case-to-case basis; if permissible at all, it should be accomplished by a regulation having prospective effect only.

MR. JUSTICE JACKSON, dissenting.

The Court by this present decision sustains the identical administrative order which only recently it held invalid. *S.E.C.* v. *Chenery Corp.*, 318 U. S. 80. As the Court correctly notes, the Commission has only "recast its rationale and reached the same result." . . . There being no change in the order, no additional evidence in the record and no amendment of relevant legislation, it is clear that there has been a shift in attitude between that of the controlling membership of the Court when the case was first here and that of those who have the power of decision on this second review.

I feel constrained to disagree with the reasoning offered to rationalize this shift. It makes judicial review of administrative orders a hopeless formality for the litigant, even where granted to him by Congress. It reduces the judicial process in such cases to a mere feint. While the opinion does not have the adherence of a majority of the full Court, if its pronouncements should become governing principles they would, in practice, put most administrative orders over and above the law.

I.

The essential facts are few and are not in dispute. This corporation filed with the Securities and Exchange Commission a voluntary plan of reorganization. While the reorganization proceedings were pending sixteen officers and directors bought on the open market about $7\frac{1}{2}\%$ of the corporation's preferred stock. Both the Commission and the Court admit that these purchases were not forbidden by any law, judicial precedent, regulation or rule of the Commission. Nevertheless, the Commission has ordered these individuals to surrender their shares to the corporation at cost, plus 4% interest, and the Court now approves that order.

It is helpful, before considering whether this order is authorized by law, to reflect on what it is and what it is not. It is not conceivably a discharge of the Commission's duty to determine whether a proposed plan of reorganization would be "fair and equitable." It has nothing to do with the corporate structure, or the classes and amounts of stock, or voting rights or dividend preferences. It does not remotely affect the impersonal financial or legal factors of the plan. It is a personal deprivation denying particular persons the right to continue to own their stock and to exercise its privileges. Other persons who bought at the same time and price in the open market would be allowed to keep and convert their stock. Thus, the order is in no sense an exercise of the function of control over the terms and relations of the corporate securities.

Neither is the order one merely to regulate the future use of property. It literally takes valuable property away from its lawful owners for the benefit of other private parties without full compensation and the Court expressly approves the taking. . . . Admittedly, the value above cost, and interest on it, simply is taken from the owners, without compensation. No such power has ever been confirmed in any administrative body.

It should also be noted that neither the Court nor the Commission purports to adjudge a forfeiture of this property as a consequence of sharp dealing or breach of trust. The Court says, "The Commission admitted that the good faith and personal integrity of this management were not in question". . . .

II.

The reversal of the position of this Court is due to a fundamental change in prevailing philosophy. The basic assumption of the earlier opinion as therein stated was, *"But before transactions otherwise legal can be outlawed or denied their usual business consequences, they must fall under the ban of some standards of conduct prescribed by an agency of government authorized to prescribe such standards. . . ."* S.E.C. v. *Chenery Corp.*, 318 U.S. 80, 92-93. The basic assumption of the present opinion is stated thus: *"The absence of a general rule or regulation governing management trading during reorganization did not affect the Commission's duties in relation to the particular proposal before it."* . . . This puts in juxtaposition the two conflicting philosophies which produce opposite results in the same case and on the same facts. The difference between the first and the latest decision of the Court is thus simply the difference between holding that administrative orders must have a basis in law and a holding that absence of a legal basis is no ground on which courts may annul them.

As there admittedly is no law or regulation to support this order, we peruse the Court's opinion diligently to find on what grounds it is now held that the Court of Appeals, on pain of being reversed for error, was required to stamp this order with its approval. We find but one. That is the principle of judicial deference to administrative experience. That argument is five times stressed in as many different contexts. . . .

What are we to make of this reiterated deference to "administrative experience" when in another context the Court says, "Hence, we refuse to say that the Commission, *which had not previously been confronted with the problem of management trading during reorganization,* was forbidden from utilizing this particular proceeding for announcing and applying *a new standard of conduct."*? . . .

The Court's reasoning adds up to this: The Commission must be sustained because of its accumulated experience in solving a problem with which it had never before been confronted!

Of course, thus to uphold the Commission by professing to find that it has enunciated a "new standard of conduct" brings the Court squarely against the invalidity of retroactive law-making. But the Court does not falter. "That such action might have a retroactive effect was not necessarily fatal to its validity." . . .

"But such retroactivity must be balanced against the mischief of producing a result which is contrary to a statutory design or to legal and equitable principles." ... Of course, if what these parties did really was condemned by "statutory design" or "legal and equitable principles," it could be stopped without resort to a new rule and there would be no retroactivity to condone. But if it had been the Court's view that some law already prohibited the purchases, it would hardly have been necessary three sentences earlier to hold that the Commission was not prohibited "from utilizing this particular proceeding for announcing and applying a *new standard of conduct.*" ...

I give up. Now I realize fully what Mark Twain meant when he said, "The more you explain it, the more I don't understand it."

III.

But one does not need to comprehend the processes by which other minds reach a given result in order to estimate the practical consequences of their pronouncement upon judicial review of administrative orders.

If it is of no consequence that no rule of law be existent to support an administrative order, and the Court of Appeals is obliged to defer to administrative experience and to sustain a Commission's power merely because it has been asserted and exercised, of what use is it to print a record or briefs in the case, or to hear argument? Administrative experience always is present, at least to the degree that it is here, and would always dictate a like deference by this Court to an assertion of administrative power. Must the reviewing court, as this Court does in this opinion, support the order on a presumptive or imputed experience even though the Court is obliged to discredit such experience in the very same opinion? Is fictitious experience to be conclusive in matters of law and particularly in the interpretation of statutes, as the Court's opinion now intimates, or just in fact finding which has been the function which the Court has heretofore sustained upon the argument of administrative experience?

I suggest that administrative experience is of weight in judicial review only to this point— it is a persuasive reason for deference to the Commission in the exercise of its discretionary powers under and within the law. It cannot be invoked to support action outside of the law. And what action is, and what is not, within the law must be determined by courts, when authorized to review, no matter how much deference is due to the agency's fact finding. Surely an administrative agency is not a law unto itself, but the Court does not really face up to the fact that this is the justification it is offering for sustaining the Commission action.

Even if the Commission had, as the Court says, utilized this case to announce a new legal standard of conduct, there would be hurdles to be cleared, but we need not dwell on them now. Because to promulgate a general rule of law, either by regulation or by case law, is something the Commission expressly declined to do. It did not previously promulgate, and it does not by this order profess to promulgate, any rule or regulation to prohibit such purchases absolutely or under stated conditions. On the other hand, its position is that no such rule or standard would be fair and equitable in all cases.

IV.

Whether, as matter of policy, corporate managers during reorganization should be prohibited from buying or selling its stock, is not a question for us to decide. But it is for us to decide whether, so long as no law or regulation prohibits them from buying, their purchases may be forfeited, or not, in the discretion of the Commission. If such a power exists in words of the statute or in their implication, it would be possible to point it out and thus end the case. Instead, the Court admits that there was no law prohibiting these purchases when they were made, or at any time thereafter. And, except for this decision, there is none now.

The truth is that in this decision the Court approves the Commission's assertion of power to govern the matter *without* law, power to force surrender of stock so purchased whenever it will, and power also to overlook such acquisitions if it so chooses. The reasons which will lead it to take one course as against the other remain locked in its own breast, and it has not and apparently does not intend to commit them to any rule or regulation. This administrative authoritarianism, this power to decide without law, is what the Court seems to approve in so many words. . . . This seems to me to undervalue and to belittle the place of law, even in the system of administrative justice. It calls to mind Mr. Justice Cardozo's statement that "Law as a guide to conduct is reduced to the level of mere futility if it is unknown and unknowable."

V.

The Court's averment concerning this order, that "It is the type of judgment which administrative agencies are best equipped to make and which justifies the use of the administrative process," . . . is the first instance in which the administrative process is sustained by reliance on that disregard of law which enemies of the process have always alleged to be its principal evil. It is the first encouragement this Court has given to conscious lawlessness as a permissible rule of administrative action. This decision is an ominous one to those who believe that men should be governed by laws that they may ascertain and abide by, and which will guide the action of those in authority as well as of those who are subject to authority.

I have long urged, and still believe, that the administrative process deserves fostering in our system as an expeditious and nontechnical method of *applying law* in specialized fields. I can not agree that it be used, and I think its continued effectiveness is endangered when it is used, as a method of *dispensing with law* in those fields.

D. THE WAR BRIDE

UNITED STATES EX REL KNAUFF V. SHAUGHNESSY
338 U.S. 537, 550 (January 16, 1950)

Although for different reasons than Frankfurter, Jackson also took a
special interest in cases involving aliens. As Attorney General, he had been
responsible for the administration of the Immigration and Naturalization
Service, which at that time had been recently transferred from the Department of Labor to the Department of Justice. It is certain that he felt he
understood the administrative process involved in cases of alien exclusion
or deportation better than that of other agencies with which he had had
no direct personal experience. Moreover, both his bias against bureaucratic
zeal and that in favor of lawyerlike ways of doing business and reaching
decisions could coalesce in behalf of the notion that due process implied
that there ought to be a meaningful administrative hearing, especially in
the absence of any provision for direct judicial review, before an alien
could be banished from the country.

Such was the case of Ellen Knauff, the wife of an American citizen,
who sought admission under the special immigration provisions of the
War Brides Act. She not only was denied admission and a hearing but was
detained for what turned out to be several years on Ellis Island.[25] The Attorney General based his refusal to grant her a hearing, at which she could
be informed of the reasons the government denied her entry and present
evidence in her own behalf, on a presidential proclamation and administrative regulations which authorized him to deny a hearing in cases involving security risks "on the basis of information of a confidential nature, the
disclosure of which would be prejudicial to the public interest." The presidential proclamation authorized the Attorney General and the Secretary
of State jointly to make the administrative regulations, and specified that
the Secretary of State should make the final determination that an alien
security risk should be excluded without a hearing.

Because Attorney General Tom C. Clark had, in fact, made that determination in the case of Mrs. Knauff, in accordance with both the administrative regulations and established departmental practice of the past
several years, her counsel challenged the legality of the administrative
regulations and the decision in his argument to the Supreme Court. The
government met this challenge by simply mooting the issue. The President,

---

[25] The story, from her point of view, has been related in Ellen Raphael Knauff, *The
Ellen Knauff Story* (New York: W. W. Norton & Company, Inc., 1952).

after decisions had been rendered in the lower federal courts and the Supreme Court had accepted jurisdiction over the case, issued an amendatory proclamation, retroactively delegating authority to the Attorney General and the Secretary of State to continue doing what they had been doing, apparently illegally, in the past. The only apparent reason for the issuance of this amendatory proclamation was to frustrate Supreme Court review of the procedural irregularities. However, this did raise a new issue: that the second proclamation was *ex post facto*, as applied to Mrs. Knauff.

While the case was being argued before the Supreme Court, Jackson remarked to counsel for the government that he had had some personal experience as Attorney General in this kind of proceeding, and that that official could give only limited attention to any one of the thousands of cases handled by the Immigration and Naturalization Service each year. Moreover, in the absence of any administrative hearing, the only information available to the Attorney General was that which the immigration officials sent forward with the file, which necessarily was structured in a self-serving way to support their decision. It was also notable that, although the information derogatory to Mrs. Knauff was too confidential to be disclosed at an official hearing conducted by the department, it was not too confidential for the Attorney General to reveal in a private letter to a personal friend of his, an attorney in New York City who had made inquiries about Mrs. Knauff's case.

Neither Clark, who by this time was on the Court, nor Douglas participated; and the remaining members of the Court divided 4-3 in favor of the government. The *ex post facto* claim was brushed aside as hardly worthy of mention by Minton, who wrote for a majority of the sitting Court that also included Vinson, Reed, and Burton. The exclusion of aliens was "a fundamental act of sovereignty"; and sovereignty in this respect was a constitutional power of the President as well as of the Congress. Courts had no power to exercise judicial review over such decisions, unless specifically authorized by statute to do so; and Congress had made no specific provisions for judicial review of administrative decisions excluding aliens. Moreover, "Whatever the procedure authorized by Congress is, it is due process as far as an alien denied entry is concerned." In short, the admission of aliens raised only questions of *privilege*, not questions of constitutional right, and any questions of procedural irregularity were moot, in view of the amendatory presidential proclamation.

Frankfurter, Black, and Jackson dissented. Frankfurter thought that the majority misconstrued the intent of Congress to create special rights for the citizen-spouses of aliens (whatever might be the alien's own rights); and he reminded his brethren that "It is true also of Acts of Congress that 'The letter killeth.'" Jackson argued that the majority failed to distinguish between substantive and procedural due process. There was no question, he said, of the substantive power of Congress to exclude aliens whose admission would be dangerous to national security. The real questions were: (1) whether this was what Congress had done, in view of the clear purpose of the War Brides Act; and (2) whether Congress had authorized, or the Supreme Court should approve, administrative flaunting of the right to procedural due process, when basic questions of personal liberty were at issue.

MR. JUSTICE JACKSON, whom MR. JUSTICE BLACK and MR. JUSTICE FRANKFURTER join, dissenting.

I do not question the constitutional power of Congress to authorize immigration authorities to turn back from our gates any alien or class of aliens. But I do not find that Congress has authorized an abrupt and brutal exclusion of the wife of an American citizen without a hearing.

Congress held out a promise of liberalized admission to alien brides, taken unto themselves by men serving in or honorably discharged from our armed services abroad, as the Act, set forth in the Court's opinion, indicates. The petitioning husband is honorably discharged and remained in Germany as a civilian employee. Our military authorities abroad required their permission before marriage. The Army in Germany is not without a vigilant and security-conscious intelligence service.[26] This woman was employed by our European Command and her record is not only without blemish, but is highly praised by her superiors. The marriage of this alien woman to this veteran was approved by the Commanding General at Frankfurt-on-Main.

Now this American citizen is told he cannot bring his wife to the United States, but he will not be told why. He must abandon his bride to live in his own country or forsake his country to live with his bride.

So he went to court and sought a writ of *habeas corpus*, which we never tire of citing to Europe as the unanswerable evidence that our free country permits no arbitrary official detention. And the Government tells the Court that not even a court can find out why the girl is excluded. But it says we must find that Congress authorized this treatment of war brides and, even if we cannot get any reasons for it, we must say it is legal; security requires it.

Security is like liberty in that many are the crimes committed in its name. The menace to the security of this country, be it great as it may, from this girl's admission is as nothing compared to the menace to free institutions inherent in

26 This was another subject on which Jackson undoubtedly considered himself to be something of an expert, at least in relation to his colleagues and to the domestic bureaucrats who were prosecuting the case against Mrs. Knauff. Jackson had resided in Western Germany during most of the first year of American military occupation, and throughout that time was intimately involved with American intelligence activities there. [Ed.]

procedures of this pattern. In the name of security the police state justifies its arbitrary oppressions on evidence that is secret, because security might be prejudiced if it were brought to light in hearings. The plea that evidence of guilt must be secret is abhorrent to free men, because it provides a cloak for the malevolent, the misinformed, the meddlesome, and the corrupt to play the role of informer undetected and uncorrected. . . .

I am sure the officials here have acted from a sense of duty, with full belief in their lawful power, and no doubt upon information which, if it stood the test of trial, would justify the order of exclusion. But not even they know whether it would stand this test. And anyway, as I have said before, personal confidence in the officials involved does not excuse a judge for sanctioning a procedure that is dangerously wrong in principle. . . .

Congress will have to use more explicit language than any yet cited before I will agree that it has authorized an administrative officer to break up the family of an American citizen or force him to keep his wife by becoming an exile. Likewise, it will have to be much more explicit before I can agree that it authorized a finding of serious misconduct against the wife of an American citizen without notice of charges, evidence of guilt and a chance to meet it.

I should direct the Attorney General either to produce his evidence justifying exclusion or to admit Mrs. Knauff to the country.

As is usually the case, the decision of the Supreme Court was an interlude in the controversy, not the end of the matter. First came an unsuccessful attempt to induce the Congress to adopt a private bill specially admitting Mrs. Knauff to the country, including one cops-and-robbers episode in which immigration officials were in the process of bundling Mrs. Knauff onto a Europe-bound plane at Idlewild airport, with the apparent purpose of physically deporting her before Congress could act, and before the Supreme Court could act on an appeal from a lower court decision denying her a stay of deportation. Jackson signed an order that prohibited her forcible ejection, notification of which reached immigration officials only minutes before the airplane was scheduled to depart.[27]

Some newspapers and various civil rights organizations became interested in her case, and sufficient political pressure was put on the incumbent Attorney General that he granted Mrs. Knauff a hearing. The evidence against her, developed at the administrative hearing, was most unpersuasive: her chief accuser, an army counterintelligence corps captain, said that Mrs. Knauff was part of an "indigenous operation" and then, under cross-examination, revealed that he had no idea what "indigenous"

[27] Jackson's opinion is reported in Walter Gellhorn and Clark L. Byse, *Administrative Law* (Brooklyn: Foundation Press, 1954), p. 822. Cf. *The Ellen Knauff Story*, pp. 147-149, 152-154.

meant. The charge that she had revealed cryptographic secrets to foreign spies turned out to relate to the Signal Corps M-209 field code converter, an unclassified device of which thousands had been turned over to the West German government by the army itself. And so it went. Upon the advice of the Board of Immigration Appeals, the Attorney General ultimately approved her admission, on the basis the evidence developed at the administrative hearing.[28] This was precisely what Jackson had argued: that it was in the interests of the government, as well as of the Knauffs, to base any decision with such momentous impact upon personal liberty upon something more than the unverified confidential reports of its own secret agents, to say nothing of the accusations of anonymous informers, which would also be a part of the official dossier.

The Immigration and Naturalization Service provided further evidence, by way of a postscript to the case, that Jackson's suspicions of the excesses of bureaucratic zeal may not have been completely without foundation. After being admitted, Mrs. Knauff applied for naturalization, only to have the same old charges raised once again, this time as a bar to her naturalization. Weary of the notoriety and the prospect of interminable and expensive litigation, Mrs. Knauff gave up her struggle against the bureaucracy.[29]

E.   THE MAN WITHOUT A COUNTRY

SHAUGHNESSY V. UNITED STATES EX REL MEZEI
345 U.S. 206, 218 (March 16, 1953)

Ellen Knauff had always had the alternative of going back to Germany, presumably in the company of her husband. But in the case of Ignatz Mezei, which reached the Court three years later, the possibility of leaving Ellis Island to go to some other country had become just as foreclosed as the possibility of admission to the United States. In effect, the Court was asked whether the Immigration and Naturalization Service could detain the petitioner in what appeared to be custody for life, or whether such a result was forbidden by the due process clause of the Fifth Amendment. Mezei was under sentence of no court, he was accused of no crime, and he had been denied an administrative hearing for the purpose

---

[28] *In re Knauff*, 1 *Pike and Fisher Ad. Law 2nd* 639 (November 2, 1951).

[29] Personal letter to me, from Mrs. Knauff's attorney, Alfred Feingold of New York City, dated March 5, 1954. See also the *New York Times*, July 3, 1953, p. 6, col. 2.

of examining the charges against him and any evidence he might wish to present in his own behalf. But the Immigration and Naturalization Service considered him to be a security risk.

It appeared that Mezei was born in Gibraltar of Hungarian or Rumanian parents, and that he had been a resident alien living in Buffalo, New York, for twenty-five years. In 1948 he applied for and was granted a visa to go to Rumania, for the ostensible purpose of visiting his dying mother. He never got beyond Budapest, however, and after being denied entrance to Rumania, he waited some nineteen months for an exit visa to return to the United States. Eventually he received a quota immigration visa which was issued by the American consul in Budapest, and he returned to the United States only to be held in custody for the next three years on Ellis Island. He was denied admission to the United States under the same regulations that had been invoked in Ellen Knauff's case. He then tried to leave Ellis Island for some other country. But neither he nor the State Department could find a country that would accept him as an immigrant. Since there was no place for him to go, he remained on Ellis Island. After four unsuccessful attempts to secure his release on *habeas corpus* on the grounds that his indefinite detention was unlawful, a federal district court granted the writ, taking the position that his further detention could be justified only by an affirmative demonstration of the danger to national security that would result from his admission and return to his home and family in Buffalo. This ruling implied that the Department of Justice would have to grant him a hearing, and defend his continued confinement on the basis of evidence against Mezei, in the light of any evidence he might introduce in his own behalf. The federal court of appeals affirmed.

The Supreme Court reversed in a 5-4 decision. The alignment was identical with that of the *Knauff* decision, except that Clark and Douglas, who had been "paired" in the earlier case, now participated. Clark, of course, voted to uphold the government and Douglas joined the dissenters. In fact, Clark wrote for the majority, relying upon the traditionally recognized sovereign power to exclude aliens, and the finality of executive decisions in such matters. The courts, he said, had no power to force the Attorney General to disclose the confidential information on which he relied, nor to involve themselves in a re-evaluation of his decision. The majority thought that the factual situation in this particular case was irrelevant to the legal and constitutional issues; and because Mezei's voluntary departure abroad removed him from the category of resident aliens, he no longer had any right to invoke the constitutional guarantees of the Fifth Amendment. (The Court for decades had indulged in the constitutional fiction that aliens on Ellis Island seeking admission to the United States were not *in* the United States; they were rather "at the threshold," knocking at the gate.) The will of Congress, concluded the majority, must be respected by the courts. Black and Jackson wrote separate dissenting opinions, but they agreed that Mezei had been denied his liberty without due process of law.

MR. JUSTICE JACKSON, whom MR. JUSTICE FRANKFURTER joins, dissenting.

Fortunately it still is startling, in this country, to find a person held indefinitely in executive custody without accusation of crime or judicial trial. Executive imprisonment has been considered oppressive and lawless since John, at Runnymede, pledged that no free man should be imprisoned, dispossessed, outlawed, or exiled save by the judgment of his peers or by the law of the land. The judges of England developed the writ of habeas corpus largely to preserve these immunities from executive restraint. Under the best tradition of Anglo-American law, courts will not deny hearing to an unconvicted prisoner just because he is an alien whose keep, in legal theory, is just outside our gates. Lord Mansfield, in the celebrated case holding that slavery was unknown to the common law of England, ran his writ of habeas corpus in favor of an alien, an African Negro slave, and against the master of a ship at anchor in the Thames.

I.

What is our case? In contemplation of law, I agree, it is that of an alien who asks admission to the country. Concretely, however, it is that of a lawful and law-abiding inhabitant of our country for a quarter of a century, long ago admitted for permanent residence, who seeks to return home. After a foreign visit to his aged and ailing mother that was prolonged by disturbed conditions of Eastern Europe, he obtained a visa for admission issued by our consul and returned to New York. There the Attorney General refused to honor his documents and turned him back as a menace to this Nation's security. This man, who seems to have led a life of unrelieved insignificance, must have been astonished to find himself suddenly putting the Government of the United States in such fear that it was afraid to tell him why it was afraid of him. He was shipped and reshipped to France, which twice refused him landing. Great Britain declined, and no other European country has been found willing to open its doors to him. Twelve countries of the American Hemisphere refused his applications. Since we proclaimed him a Samson who might pull down the pillars of our temple, we should not be surprised if peoples less prosperous, less strongly established and less stable feared to take him off our timorous hands. With something of a record as an unwanted man, neither his efforts nor those of the United States Government any longer promise to find him an abiding place. For nearly two years he has held in custody of the immigration authorities of the United States at Ellis Island, and if the Government has its way he seems likely to be detained indefinitely, perhaps for life, for a cause known only to the Attorney General. . . . We must regard this alien as deprived of liberty, and the question is whether the deprivation is a denial of due process of law. . . .

The interpretations of the Fifth Amendment's command that no person shall be deprived of life, liberty or property without due process of law, come about to this: reasonable general legislation reasonably applied to the individual. The question is whether the Government's detention of respondent is compatible with these tests of substance and procedure.

II. Substantive Due Process

Substantively, due process of law renders what is due to a strong state as well as to a free individual. It tolerates all reasonable measures to insure the national safety, and it leaves a large, at times a potentially dangerous, latitude for executive judgment as to policies and means.

After all, the pillars which support our liberties are the three branches of government, and the burden could not be carried by our own power alone. Substantive due process will always pay a high degree of deference to congressional and executive judgment, especially when they concur, as to what is reasonable policy under conditions of particular times and circumstances. Close to the maximum of respect is due from the judiciary to the political departments in policies affecting security and alien exclusion. . . .

Due process does not invest any alien with a right to enter the United States, nor confer on those admitted the right to remain against the national will. Nothing in the Constitution requires admission or sufferance of aliens hostile to our scheme of government.

Nor do I doubt that due process of law will tolerate some impounding of an alien where it is deemed essential to the safety of the state. Even the resident, friendly alien may be subject to executive detention without bail, for a reasonable period, pending consummation of deportation arrangements. . . . The alien enemy may be confined or his property seized and administered because hostility is assumed from his continued allegiance to a hostile state. . . .

If due process will permit confinement of resident aliens friendly in fact because of imputed hostility, I should suppose one personally at war with our institutions might be confined, even though his state is not at war with us. In both cases, the underlying consideration is the power of our system of government to defend itself, and changing strategy of attack by infiltration may be met with changed tactics of defense.

Nor do I think the concept of due process so paralyzing that it forbids all detention of an alien as a preventive measure against threatened dangers and makes confinement lawful only after the injuries have been suffered. In some circumstances, even the citizen in default of bail has long been subject to federal imprisonment for security of the peace and good behavior. While it is usually applied for express verbal threats, no reason is known to me why the power is not the same in the case of threats inferred by proper procedures from circumstances. The British, with whom due process is a habit, if not a written constitutional dictum, permit a court in a limited class of cases to pass a "sentence of preventive detention" if satisfied that it is expedient for the protection of the public.

I conclude that detention of an alien would not be inconsistent with substantive due process, provided—and this is where my dissent begins—he is accorded procedural due process.

III. PROCEDURAL DUE PROCESS

Procedural fairness, if not all that originally was meant by due process of law, is at least what it most uncompromisingly requires. Procedural due process is more elemental and less flexible than substantive due process. It yields less to the times, varies less with conditions, and defers much less to legislative judgment. Insofar as it is technical law, it must be a specialized responsibility within the compliance of the judiciary on which they do not bend before political branches of the Government, as they should on matters of policy which comprise substantive law.

If it be conceded that in some way this alien could be confined, does it matter what the procedure is? Only the untaught layman or the charlatan lawyer can answer that procedures matter not. Procedural fairness and regularity are of the indispensable essence of liberty. Severe substantive laws can be endured if they are fairly and impartially applied. Indeed, if put to the choice, one might well prefer to live under Soviet substantive law applied in good faith by our common-law procedures than under our substantive law enforced by Soviet procedural practices. Let it not be overlooked that due process of law is not for the sole benefit of an accused. It is the best insurance for the Government itself against those blunders which leave lasting stains on a system of justice but which are bound to occur on *ex parte* consideration. Cf. *Knauff* v. *Shaughnessy,* 338 U.S. 537, which was a near miss, saved by further administrative and congressional hearings from perpetrating an injustice. See Knauff, *The Ellen Knauff Story* (New York, 1952).

Our law may, and rightly does, place more restrictions on the alien than on the citizen. But basic fairness in hearing procedures does not vary with the status of the accused. If the procedures used to judge this alien are fair and just, no good reason can be given why they should not be extended to simplify the condemnation of citizens. If they would be unfair to citizens, we cannot defend the fairness of them when applied to the more helpless and handicapped alien. This is at the root of our holdings that the resident alien must be given a fair hearing to test an official claim that he is one of a deportable class. . . .

The most scrupulous observance of due process, including the right to know a charge, to be confronted with the accuser, to cross-examine informers and to produce evidence in one's behalf, is especially necessary where the occasion of detention is fear of future misconduct, rather than crimes committed. Both the old proceeding by which one may be bound to keep the peace and the newer British "preventive detention" are safeguarded with full rights to judicial hearings for the accused. On the contrary, the Nazi regime in Germany installed a system of "protective custody" by which the arrested could claim no judicial or other hearing process, and as a result the concentration camps were populated with victims of summary executive detention for secret reasons. That is what renders Communist justice such a travesty. There are other differences, to be sure, between authoritarian procedure and common law, but differences in the process of administration make all the difference between a reign of terror and one of law. Quite unconsciously, I am sure, the Government's theory of custody for "safekeeping" without disclosure to the victim of charges, evidence, informers or reasons, even in an administrative proceeding, has unmistakable overtones of the "protective custody" of the Nazis more than of any detaining procedure known to the common law. Such a practice, once established with the best of intentions, will drift into oppression of the disadvantaged in this country as surely as it has elsewhere. That these apprehensive surmises are not "such stuff as dreams are made on" appears from testimony of a top immigration official concerning an applicant that "He has no rights."

Because the respondent has no right of entry, does it follow that he has no rights at all? Does the power to exclude mean that exclusion may be continued or effectuated by any means which happen to seem appropriate to the authorities? It would effectuate his exclusion to eject him bodily into the sea or to set him adrift in a rowboat. Would not such measures be condemned judicially as a deprivation of life without due process of law? Suppose the authorities decide to disable an alien from entry by confiscating his valuables and money. Would we not hold this a taking of property without due process of law? Here we have a case that lies between the taking of life and the taking of property; it is the taking of liberty. It seems to me that this, occurring within the United States or its territorial waters, may be done only by proceedings which meet the test of due process of law.

Exclusion of an alien without judicial hearing, of course, does not deny due process when it can be accomplished merely by turning him back on land or returning him by sea. But when indefinite confinement becomes the means of enforcing exclusion, it seems to me that due process requires that the alien be informed of its grounds and have a fair chance to overcome them. This is the more due him when he is entrapped into leaving the other shore by reliance on a visa which the Attorney General refuses to honor.

It is evident that confinement of respondent no longer can be justified as a step in the process of turning him back to the country whence he came. Confinement is no longer ancillary to exclusion; it can now be justified only as the alternative to normal exclusion. It is an end in itself.

The Communist conspiratorial technique of infiltration poses a problem

which sorely tempts the Government to resort to confinement of suspects on secret information secretly judged. I have not been one to discount the Communist
evil. But my apprehensions about the security of our form of government are
about equally aroused by those who refuse to recognize the dangers of Communism
and those who will not see danger in anything else.

Congress has ample power to determine whom we will admit to our shores
and by what means it will effectuate its exclusion policy. The only limitation is
that it may not do so by authorizing United States officers to take without due
process of law the life, the liberty or the property of an alien who has come within our jurisdiction; and that means he must meet a fair hearing with fair notice of
the charges.

It is inconceivable to me that this measure of simple justice and fair dealing
would menace the security of this country. No one can make me believe that we
are that far gone.

But here was another sparrow whose fall attracted sufficient national
publicity that the political process corrected the injustice which, so far as
Harry S Truman's Supreme Court majority was concerned, could have
left Ignatz Mezei as a permanent political prisoner of the federal government. (He could not have remained much longer on Ellis Island, however,
because that outmoded facility was closed, as a screening and detention
center for immigrants, during the year following the Supreme Court's decision.) The Immigration and Naturalization Service relented, having
successfully established the legal principle of the unassailability of its decisions in the exclusion of alien security risks. After an administrative
hearing exposed the weakness of the government's case against him, Mezei
finally was admitted, but by grace of the Attorney General rather than the
Supreme Court.[30]

F. AMERICANS BETRAYED

KOREMATSU V. UNITED STATES
323 U.S. 214, 242 (December 18, 1944)

Among the domestic by-products of World War II had been a "relocation" program for Japanese aliens resident in the United States and their
American citizen children. Fred Korematsu, a citizen of the United States

[30] Kenneth Culp Davis, "The Requirement of a Trial-Type Hearing," *Harvard Law Review*, LXX (1956), 279.

whose loyalty to his country was unquestioned, asked the Supreme Court to review his conviction in a federal district court for the crime of having violated a military order which forbade him to continue to live in his home. All persons of the Japanese "race" who resided in the far western states at the outbreak of World War II were "resettled" during the spring and summer of 1942 in concentration camps.[31] Although Jackson's opinion sublimates this point, the legal basis for the relocation program consisted of an executive order of the President and a joint resolution of Congress which authorized military administration of the evacuation and civilian administration of the custodial function. Jackson did not argue that the military orders which Korematsu violated were beyond the scope of the commanding general's authority under the executive order and joint resolution. Therefore, the basic issue—which Jackson sought to avoid—was whether the Supreme Court was prepared to declare unconstitutional a military order of the Commander in Chief and an act of Congress based on the "war power." Moreover, the penalty for Korematsu's crime was defined by Congress by statute, and the jurisdiction of the federal courts (including the Supreme Court) which considered his case was determined by act of Congress, not by military order. Seemingly, if the Court was going to free Korematsu, it would have to find either that the military bureaucrats who were his custodians had exceeded the authority delegated to them by the President and the Congress, or else that the political branches of the government (as Jackson liked to refer to them)[32] had exceeded *their* joint authority under the Constitution, in time of active and declared warfare.

It is difficult to imagine any Supreme Court majority taking such a position. It had never happened in the past; nor did it happen in this decision. Black himself wrote the opinion of the Court for a five-man "libertarian activist" majority that included Douglas, Rutledge, Stone, and Reed. Black bestowed the imprimatur of the Court on the military, offering Korematsu the consolation that "hardships are part of war, and war is an aggregation of hardships." In a separate concurrence, Frankfurter added that as long as the military order under review "does not transcend the means appropriate for conducting war" it should be deemed constitutional.

Owen Roberts, the last of the "Nine Old Men" of the New Deal Court, with his resignation upon reaching the age of seventy only a few

[31] See Morton Grodzins, *Americans Betrayed* (Chicago: The University of Chicago Press, 1949); Alexander Leighton, *The Governing of Men* (Princeton: Princeton University Press, 1959); and Eugene V. Rostow, "Our Worst Wartime Mistake," *Harper's Magazine,* CXCI (1945), 193-201.

[32] Jackson, *The Supreme Court in the American System of Government,* pp. 10-11.

months away, dissented. So did Frank Murphy and Jackson; but true it is that politics makes for strange bedfellows. Like the majority, Roberts and Murphy wanted to decide the issue of the constitutional authority of the military, but in a direction opposite to that which the Court had decided upon. Roberts stated bluntly that the action taken against Korematsu was no longer simply a curfew or a temporary exclusion from a restricted area for purposes of protecting the public safety.[33] Rather, it was a conviction that punished him for not submitting to imprisonment in a concentration camp for reasons of racial ancestry rather than for any suspicion (even) of disloyalty; and Roberts thought it evident that for the military to present American citizens with Hobson's choice of going to a concentration camp, no matter which of two contradictory orders they obeyed, was a clear violation of constitutional rights.

Murphy said that the discriminatory action of the military had plunged the country into the "ugly abyss of racism"—the very crime with which, in barely six months, Robert Jackson would be charging the likes of Hitler, Goebbels, and Goering. It is the more ironic, therefore, that the man who was to indict the Nazi military leaders for their transgressions against an inchoate, unwritten, and ex post facto "international law of war" should be the one and only justice of the United States Supreme Court who argued that the herding of citizens into concentration camps, by American military officers who, at least nominally, were bound by the norms of a Constitution with an explicit Bill of Rights, presented only a political, not a legal, question.[34] Jackson voted to reverse the conviction of Korematsu only because the military bureaucrats had made the mistake of attempting to use the civil courts to wash their dirty linen. What they should have done, apparently, would have been to convict the Nisei by judgment of courts martial, in which event the military could go their own way, and the civil courts could ignore whatever depredations of civilian life, liberty and property might result from the unbridled excesses of military zealots determined to win the war at any and all costs. All the justices of the Supreme Court would have to do, to follow Jackson's advice, would be to harness themselves with constitutional blinders.

---

[33] As, presumably, had been the Court's decision of a year and a half earlier, in *Hirabayashi* v. *United States*, 320 U.S. 81 (1943), which was now relied upon by the majority as a direct precedent which the court "had" to follow in Korematsu's case.

[34] In some afterthoughts about the decision Jackson, although still of the same mind about his position, admitted that "my view, if followed, would come close to a suspension of the writ of habeas corpus or recognition of a state of martial law at the time and place found proper for military control." Robert H. Jackson, "Wartime Security and Liberty Under Law," *Buffalo Law Review*, I (1951), 116.

MR. JUSTICE JACKSON, *dissenting.*

Korematsu was born on our soil, of parents born in Japan. The Constitution makes him a citizen of the United States by nativity and a citizen of California by residence. No claim is made that he is not loyal to this country. There is no suggestion that apart from the matter involved here he is not law-abiding and well disposed. Korematsu, however, has been convicted of an act not commonly a crime. It consists merely of being present in the state whereof he is a citizen, near the place where he was born, and where all his life he has lived.

Even more unusual is the series of military orders which made this conduct a crime. They forbid such a one to remain, and they also forbid him to leave. They were so drawn that the only way Korematsu could avoid violation was to give himself up to the military authority. This meant submission to custody, examination, and transportation out of the territory, to be followed by indeterminate confinement in detention camps.

A citizen's presence in the locality, however, was made a crime only if his parents were of Japanese birth. Had Korematsu been one of four—the others being, say, a German alien enemy, an Italian alien enemy, and a citizen of American-born ancestors, convicted of treason but out on parole—only Korematsu's presence would have violated the order. The difference between their innocence and his crime would result, not from anything he did, said, or thought, different than they, but only in that he was born of different racial stock.

Now, if any fundamental assumption underlies our system, it is that guilt is personal and not inheritable. Even if all of one's antecedents had been convicted of treason, the Constitution forbids its penalties to be visited upon him, for it provides that "no attainder of treason shall work corruption of blood, or foreiture except during the life of the person attainted." But here is an attempt to make an otherwise innocent act a crime merely because this prisoner is the son of parents as to whom he had no choice, and belongs to a race from which there is no way to resign. If Congress in peace-time legislation should enact such a criminal law, I should suppose this Court would refuse to enforce it.

But the "law" which this prisoner is convicted of disregarding is not found in an act of Congress, but in a military order. Neither the Act of Congress nor the Executive Order of the President, nor both together, would afford a basis for this conviction. It rests on the orders of General DeWitt. And it is said that if the military commander had reasonable military grounds for promulgating the orders, they are constitutional and become law, and the Court is required to enforce them. There are several reasons why I cannot subscribe to this doctrine.

It would be impracticable and dangerous idealism to expect or insist that each specific military command in an area of probable operations will conform to conventional tests of constitutionality. When an area is so beset that it must be put under military control at all, the paramount consideration is that its measures be successful, rather than legal. The armed services must protect a society, not merely its Constitution. The very essence of the military job is to marshal physical force, to remove every obstacle to its effectiveness, to give it every strategic advantage. Defense measures will not, and often should not, be held within the limits that bind civil authority in peace. No court can require such a commander in such circumstances to act as a reasonable man; he may be unreasonably cautious and exacting. Perhaps he should be. But a commander in temporarily focusing the life of a community on defense is carrying out a military program; he is not making law in the sense the courts know the term. He issues orders, and they may have a certain authority as military commands, although they may be very bad as constitutional law.

But if we cannot confine military expedients by the Constitution, neither would I distort the Constitution to approve all that the military may deem expedient. That is what the Court appears to be doing, whether consciously or not. I cannot say, from any evidence before me, that the orders of General DeWitt were not reasonably expedient military precautions, nor could I say that they were. But even if they were permissible military procedures, I deny that it follows that they are constitutional. If, as the Court holds, it does follow, then we may as well say that any military order will be constitutional and have done with it.

The limitation under which courts always will labor in examining the necessity for a military order are illustrated by this case. How does the Court know that these orders have a reasonable basis in necessity? No evidence whatever on that subject has been taken by this or any other court. There is sharp controversy as to the credibility of the DeWitt report. So the Court, having no real evidence before it, has no choice but to accept General DeWitt's own unsworn, self-serving statement, untested by any cross-examination, that what he did was reasonable. And thus it will always be when courts try to look into the reasonableness of a military order.

In the very nature of things, military decisions are not susceptible of intelligent judicial appraisal. They do not pretend to rest on evidence, but are made on information that often would not be admissible and on assumptions that could not be proved. Information in support of an order could not be disclosed to courts without danger that it would reach the enemy. Neither can courts act on communications made in confidence. Hence courts can never have any real alternative to accepting the mere declaration of the authority that issued the order that it was reasonably necessary from a military viewpoint.

Much is said of the danger to liberty from the Army program for deporting and detaining these citizens of Japanese extraction. But a judicial construction of the due process clause that will sustain this order is a far more subtle blow to liberty than the promulgation of the order itself. A military order, however unconstitutional, is not apt to last longer than the military emergency. Even during

that period a succeeding commander may revoke it all. But once a judicial opinion rationalizes such an order to show that it conforms to the Constitution, or
rather rationalizes the Constitution to show that the Constitution sanctions such
an order, the Court for all time has validated the principle of racial discrimination
in criminal procedure and of transplanting American citizens. The principle then
lies about like a loaded weapon ready for the hand of any authority that can bring
forward a plausible claim of an urgent need. Every repetition imbeds that principle more deeply in our law and thinking and expands it to new purposes. All who
observe the work of courts are familiar with what Judge Cardozo described as
"the tendency of a principle to expand itself to the limit of its logic." A military
commander may overstep the bounds of constitutionality, and it is an incident.
But if we review and approve, that passing incident becomes the doctrine of the
Constitution. There it has a generative power of its own, and all that it creates
will be in its own image. Nothing better illustrates this danger than does the
Court's opinion in this case.

It argues that we are bound to uphold the conviction of Korematsu because
we upheld one in *Hirabayashi* v. *United States*, 320 U.S. 81, when we sustained
these orders insofar as they applied a curfew requirement to a citizen of Japanese
ancestry. I think we should learn something from that experience.

In that case we were urged to consider only the curfew feature, that being all
that technically was involved, because it was the only count necessary to sustain
Hirabayashi's conviction and sentence. We yielded, and the Chief Justice guarded
the opinion as carefully as language will do. . . . However, in spite of our limiting
words we did validate a discrimination on the basis of ancestry for mild and temporary deprivation of liberty. Now the principle of racial discrimination is pushed
from support of mild measures to very harsh ones, and from temporary deprivations to indeterminate ones. And the precedent which it is said requires us to
do so is *Hirabayashi*. The Court is now saying that in *Hirabayashi* we did decide
the very things we there said we were not deciding. Because we said that these
citizens could be made to stay in their homes during the hours of dark, it is said
we must require them to leave home entirely; and if that, we are told they may
also be taken into custody for deportation; and if that, it is argued they may also
be held for some undetermined time in detention camps. How far the principle
of this case would be extended before plausible reasons would play out, I do not
know.

I should hold that a civil court cannot be made to enforce an order which
violates constitutional limitations even if it is a reasonable exercise of military
authority. The courts can exercise only the judicial power, can apply only law, and
must abide by the Constitution, or they cease to be civil courts and become instruments of military policy.

Of course the existence of a military power resting on force, so vagrant, so
centralized, so necessarily heedless of the individual, is an inherent threat to lib-

erty. But I would not lead people to rely on this Court for a review that seems to me wholly delusive. The military reasonableness of these orders can only be determined by military superiors. If the people ever let command of the war power fall into irresponsible and unscrupulous hands, the courts wield no power equal to its restraint. The chief restraint upon those who command the physical forces of the country, in the future as in the past, must be their responsibility to the political judgments of their contemporaries and to the moral judgments of history.

My duties as a justice as I see them do not require me to make a military judgment as to whether General DeWitt's evacuation and detention program was a reasonable military necessity. I do not suggest that the courts should have attempted to interfere with the Army in carrying out its task. But I do not think they may be asked to execute a military expedient that has no place in law under the Constitution. I would reverse the judgment and discharge the prisoner.

7 POLICY

From the days of THE FEDERALIST *papers,* attention has focused intermittently upon the policy-making role of the Supreme Court in constitutional adjudication.[1] The conspicuous involvement of the justices in constitutional politics has waxed and waned with a regularity that is certainly neither solar nor lunar but which does suggest a movement that ranges (in the words of Holmes) from the molar to the molecular.[2] But the Court's involvement in the great issues of each new political generation—contemporaneously, in racial integration during the fifties, and legislative reapportionment during the early sixties—tends to focus public attention upon only the very pinnacle of the visible facet of the volcanic cone. Public spectators tend to observe the smoke and fire that occasionally belches forth, and the molten lava which spills over the rim and flows down the precipitous walls of the old cinder cone; it is this latter effluent which traces the movement, through the political system, of the so-called landmark decisions of the Court's constitutional policy making. But, at least in quantitative terms, and, from more than one perspective in qualitative terms as well, what attracts public attention to the volcano is less important than the continuing seething of the tides that flow through the turb-

---

[1] Just before he joined the Court, Jackson remarked that: "These constitutional lawsuits are the stuff of power politics in America. Such proceedings may for a generation or more deprive an elected Congress of power, or may restore a lost power, or confirm a questioned one. Such proceedings may enlarge or restrict the authority of an elected President. They settle what power belongs to the Court itself and what it concedes to its 'coordinate' departments. Decrees in litigation write the final word as to distribution of powers as between the Federal Government and the state governments and mark out and apply the limitations and denials of power constitutionally applicable to each. To recognize or to deny the power of governmental agencies in a changing world is to sit as a continuous allocator of power in our governmental system. The Court may be, and usually is, above party politics and personal politics, but the politics of power is a most important and delicate function, and adjudication of litigation is its technique." Robert Jackson, *The Struggle for Judicial Supremacy,* (New York: Alfred A. Knopf, 1941), pp. 287-288. And after a dozen years of experience on the other side of the bench, he could still say that "all constitutional interpretations have political consequences." Robert Jackson, *The Supreme Court in the American System of Government,* (Cambridge: Harvard University Press, 1955), p. 56.

[2] Dissenting in *Southern Pacific Co.* v. *Jensen,* 244 U.S. 205, 221 (1917): "I recognize without hesitation that judges do and must legislate, but they can do so only interstitially; they are confined from molar to molecular motions." It was in the very next page of this same opinion that Holmes remarked that "The common law is not a brooding omnipresence in the sky. . . ."

ulent mass that remains contained by the caldron within. The latter policy content, concerned as it is with issues that do not rise to the level of constitutional rationalization, constitutes the staff of judicial life for Supreme Court justices.

Nonconstitutional policy adjudication by the Court is concerned in part with the supervision of administrative policy making (see Chap. 6). We have just examined Jackson's views in that regard. But it is to an even greater extent concerned with the "interpretation" of statutes, that is, with the reshaping of congressional policy by attributing meaning to statutory language.[3] There is an evident analogy here to constitutional interpretation, and the analogy is well taken. From a quantitative point of view, the content of statutory language is vastly greater than that of the constitutional document; but the very diffuseness of the continuing outputs of the Congress serves to reinforce other factors which together make for more judicial discretion in pronouncing the legitimate meaning of acts of Congress, than in explicating the Constitution. Of course there are differences in the associated rhetorics, and much attention of scholars has been diverted to an explanation of these rhetorical differentials. In each instance, however, the fiction usually is posited that what the Court seeks is, on the one hand, the intent of the Founding Fathers, and on the other, of the Congress which enacted the statute; and although the justices often voice their obligation to defer to the will of the Congress, they are at least equally prone to genuflect—for whatever such ritualistic gestures may be worth—before the will of "the People" who are said to have made the Constitution. *Vox juris, vox populī.*

Two ancillary questions arise for the Court in its work of statutory interpretation. Once the meaning of a particular statute, or fragment of statutory language, has been pronounced, are future Courts stuck with these policy decisions of their judicial predecessors? Or should the meaning attributed to statutes change (like that of the Constitution) to reflect such variables as socioeconomic circumstances and associated technologies, the balance of interests among parties directly and indirectly affected by the policy, and the composition of the Court itself? The traditional view has been that it is proper for the Supreme Court to redefine the meaning of the

---

[3] On more than one occasion Jackson saw fit to quote a remark which he attributed to his mentor, Cardozo: "It [the New York Court of Appeals] is a great common law court; its chief problems are lawyers' problems. But the Supreme Court is occupied chiefly with statutory construction—which no man can make interesting—and with politics." *Full Faith and Credit: The Lawyer's Clause of the Constitution* (New York: Columbia University Press, 1945), p. 2; *The Supreme Court in the American System,* p. 54. At least in a small way, the accuracy of that prediction can be checked against Jackson's opinions in this chapter.

Constitution, because constitutions are difficult (and dangerous?) to amend formally; but it is improper for the Court to remold statutory interpretations, because the Congress is in continuing session, must be presumed to be aware of the Court's decisions, can make any further changes in a judicially-interpreted statute that it sees fit, and must be presumed to agree with Court interpretations which are "acquiesced in" by congressional inaction. A political scientist may doubt the empirical validity of many of these lawyerlike presumptions concerning the legislative process; but our present interest lies not in what the facts are but rather in what kinds of arguments Jackson and his colleagues characteristically employed either in support of, or in opposition to, the application of the principle of *stare decisis* when policy issues were formulated as questions of the reinterpretation of statutes.

The other question is a function of the mystique of the quest for congressional intent. Should judges stick to the letter of the statute, thereby confining themselves to grammatical exegesis in their task of rationalizing a preferred meaning? Or should they roam through the backup materials of the legislative process (committee reports, hearings, the pages of the journals of the respective houses, or even the pages of the *Congressional Record*—including the Appendix?) to search for evidence "of record" which will "build a case" in one policy direction or another? The empirical answer is that most justices (including Jackson) sometimes take one and sometimes the other tack, depending upon which lends itself better to the justification of the outcome decided upon in a given decision. But this involves the Courts in continuing (and highly *un*-systematized) reliance, for purposes of rationale construction, upon data that are not readily available to either the public at large or the ordinary attorney.

The problem, to which Jackson directs attention in the concluding cases of this chapter, is one that today we would term one of information retrieval: with their unique role status, with their location on Capitol Hill across a small park from the Congress, and with the Library of Congress literally a next door neighbor, Supreme Court justices have direct and ready access to a supply of supporting legislative materials which no other judges, or lawyers, could possibly replicate. Jackson's argument is that, as a consequence of the Supreme Court's privileged access to the legislative record, no one could know what statutes "mean" until *after* the Court has spoken and interpreted them. His point is true, but trite. Many other components of Supreme Court decision making are also inaccessible to outsiders; and the relevant question is whether exclusive reliance upon the manipulation of grammar, as the basis for justification of statutory interpretation, would make outcomes any more predictable for country lawyers than prevailing practices for the divination of legislative intent.

The first three of Jackson's opinions here argue, seriatim, the varying possible standpoints relevant to the *stare decisis* issue: that precedents ought to be followed, that they should be ignored when they do not support the desired outcome, and that they should be repudiated openly—the better to symbolize that a change in policy is taking place.[4] The next pair of opinions argue, alternatively, the merits of the two principal approaches to statutory interpretation: that the Court should stick to the letter of the law, and that the Court should keep law in touch with life by examining the record of what went on in the smithy when the statute was forged.[5] The remaining opinions discuss the problem of information retrieval, as Jackson saw the matter.

A. FOLLOWING PRECEDENTS
MAGNOLIA PETROLEUM CO. V. HUNT
320 U.S. 430, 446 (December 20, 1943)

Prior to his appointment to the Court, Jackson was sharply critical of precedential policy making by judges:

Legal learning is largely built around the principle known as *stare decisis*. It means that on the same point of law yesterday's decision shall govern today's decision. Like a coral reef, the common law thus becomes a structure of fossils. Preparation for admission to the bar is largely a study of old authorities. At the bar, cases are won by finding in the maze of legal literature a controlling case or by distinguishing or discrediting the case found by an adversary. Precedents largely govern the conclusions and surround the reasoning of lawyers and judges. In the field of common law they are a force for stability and predictabilty, but in constitutional law they are the most powerful influence in forming and supporting reactionary opinions. The judge who can take refuge in a precedent does not need to justify his decision to the reason. He may "reluctantly feel himself bound" by a doctrine, supported by a respected historical name, that he would not be able to justify to contemporary opinion or under modern conditions.[6]

[4] Cf. Robert Jackson, "Decisional Law and Stare Decisis," *American Bar Association Journal*, XXX (1944), 334-335.

[5] Cf. Robert Jackson, "The Meaning of Statutes: What Congress Says or What the Court Says," *American Bar Association Journal*, XXXIV (1948), 535-538.

[6] Jackson, *The Struggle for Judicial Supremacy*, p. 295. "Normally," he added, "judicial decision is law-making after the event. The function of judges is to decide controversies, and their decisions must necessarily be made to relate back to govern the transaction which provoked the controversy. This led Bentham to assert that judges make the common law 'just as a man makes laws for his dog. When your dog does anything you want to break him of, you wait till he does it, and then beat him for it.' " *Ibid.*, pp. 306-307.

But only two years later, after the experience of a term on the Court, Jackson appears to have changed his mind:

> This Court may follow precedents, irrespective of their merits, as a matter of obedience to the rule of *stare decisis*. Consistency and stability may be so served. They are ends desirable in themselves, for only thereby can the law be predictable to those who must shape their conduct by it and to lower courts which must apply it. But we can break with established law, overrule precedents, and start a new cluster of leading cases to define what we mean, only as a matter of deliberate policy.[7]

Typically, in arguing the latter position in behalf of *stare decisis*, Jackson would say that a justice should follow a precedent with which he disagrees until a majority of the Court forthrightly agrees to overrule it— although it is not without interest to observe that his own anti-*stare decisis* arguments appear almost invariably in concurrences or dissents where he was still waging a battle for a previously lost cause. He also argued that the Court should follow precedent, even when it leads to a wrong result, if Congress has "acquiesced" in the earlier decision of the Court; and that the Court generally should follow its precedents—except, of course, when a proposed new policy *clearly* is preferable to the old one; and that the Court should not make a new law unless the old law is unsound and "works badly in our present day and society." On the other hand, the Court should not follow precedents that are clearly "blunders," nor precedents that are unacceptable to a majority of the incumbent justices; nor when to do so would lead to a wrong decision.[8] Throughout its history the Court had been required from time to time to reconsider a precedent decision, and (as Jackson once remarked) it should do so in the case then under consideration because it was far better to create temporary confusion by overruling a precedent, than for the Court to continue to pay lip service to a rule that it could not and would not respect in application. So Jackson walked both sides of the street on this issue. In so doing, he was no different from his colleagues, although at times he seemed to think—or, at least, to want to persuade others to think—that he alone stood fast in the true faith of the democratic judge.

Magnolia Petroleum illustrates the equanimity with which Jackson could argue both for and against *stare decisis* within the confines of the

---

[7] *Williams* v. *North Carolina,* 317 U.S. 287, 323 (1942), and Chap. 8C *infra.* "[T]he mere fact that a path is a beaten one," wrote Jackson, "is a persuasive reason for following it." Jackson, *Full Faith and Credit,* p. 45.

[8] For example, "if I have agreed," he said, "to any prior decision which forecloses what now seems to be a sensible construction of this Act, I must frankly admit that I was unaware of it. . . . Under these circumstances, except for any personal humiliation involved in admitting that I do not always understand the opinions of this Court, I see no reason why I should be consciously wrong today because I was unconsciously wrong yesterday." Dissenting in *Massachusetts* v. *United States,* 333 U.S. 611, 639-640 (1948).

same brief opinion. The economically conservative majority, including Jackson, decided that an injured workman must accept the less generous of two different awards of compensation which had been made to him. The employee, a resident of Louisiana employed under a contract made in Louisiana, had suffered a personal injury while on the job in Texas. Initially he filed for and obtained a Texas compensation award, and then subsequently he applied for and was granted a larger award in Louisiana. His present argument was, of course, that he should be permitted to retain not both awards, but rather the larger one.

The four libertarians, no doubt motivated primarily by a sympathy for generous workmen's compensation awards,[9] distinguished the Court's inconvenient precedents and urged that Louisiana should be free to apply her own social policies to her own residents. Only a year earlier, three of these libertarians had insisted, over Jackson's protest, that North Carolina was bound by Nevada's ex parte divorce decrees, in the Court's initial decision in the case of *Williams* v. *North Carolina,* which we shall discuss in the following chapter. The outcome of the first *Williams* decision had reflected the libertarian point of view, in that it encouraged a social policy of easier divorce. The fourth liberal, and the only other justice to agree with Jackson in this decision, was Frank Murphy, a Roman Catholic. (Jackson was an Episcopalian.) So Jackson now took full advantage of the tactical opportunity of accusing his adversaries of wanting to have their cake and eat it, too: they talked, he said, about *full* faith and credit when this led to a result that suited their fancy, and then ignored this principle when it led to an inconvenient result. Under the circumstances, Jackson did not feel it appropriate to mention that his own preferences were for binding marriages and the interests of employers over those of workingmen. His petulant argument was, instead, that as long as the libertarian-dominated majority of the Court was going to insist upon the binding effect of ex parte divorce judgments, then he was going to insist upon the binding effect of ex parte[10] compensation awards.

By MR. *JUSTICE JACKSON:*

I concur with the opinion of the Chief Justice.

If the Court were to reconsider *Williams* v. *North Carolina,* 317 U.S. 287, in the light of the views expressed by Mr. Justice Black, I should adhere to the views I expressed in dissent there. Until we do so, I consider myself bound by that

---

[9] See my "Policy without Law: An Extension of the Certiorari Game," *Stanford Law Review,* XIV (1962), 284-327.

[10] The employer was not a party to the Texas compensation proceeding.

decision. Whatever might be the law if that case had never been decided, I am unable to see why the controlling principles it announced under the full faith and credit clause to reverse the North Carolina decision therein do not require reversal of the Louisiana decision under review. I agree with the dissent that Louisiana has a legitimate interest to protect in the subject matter of this litigation, but so did North Carolina in the *Williams* case. I am unable to see how Louisiana can be constitutionally free to apply its own workmen's compensation law to its citizens despite a previous adjudication in another state if North Carolina was not free to apply its own matrimonial policy to its own citizens after judgment on the subject in Nevada. Is Louisiana's social interest in seeing that its labor contracts carry adequate workmen's compensation superior constitutionally to North Carolina's interest in seeing that people who contract marriage there are protected in the rights they acquire? It is true that someone might have to take care of the Louisiana citizen who is injured but inadequately compensated in Texas, as it was true in the *Williams* case that someone might have to care for those deprived of their marriage status by the foreign divorce decree.

Overruling a precedent always introduces some confusion and the necessity for it may be unfortunate. But it is as nothing to keeping on our books utterances to which we ourselves will give full faith and credit only if the outcome pleases us. I shall abide by the *Williams* case until it is taken off our books, and for that reason concur in the decision herein.

B. DISTINGUISHING PRECEDENTS

UNITED STATES V. LILLIAN SPELAR
338 U.S. 217, 224 (November 7, 1949)

To understand the *Spelar* decision, it is necessary to briefly recount the Court's action of the previous term[11] when a majority dominated by the four libertarians interpreted the Fair Labor Standards Act of 1938 to apply to labor relations of an American contractor working on one of the bases leased by the United States from Great Britain as a consequence of the Destroyer Deal. Obviously, Congress in 1938 had no such intent with regard to such unanticipated territorial acquisitions as the leased Atlantic military bases which came under partial American control in 1941. Although Jackson's dissenting opinion in *Vermilya-Brown* does not

[11] *Vermilya-Brown* v. *Connell,* 335 U.S. 377 (December 6, 1948).

explicitly point this out, he makes oblique reference to events in which he had participated as the Attorney General who advised the President that the proposed executive agreement, to trade fifty "overage" destroyers for the leasehold rights, was constitutional.[12] And it was Jackson who, as the Nuremberg prosecutor, had exposed the record that verified the military assumption underlying the leased bases—that the Nazis planned to use them as stepping stones to an invasion of the United States. Objecting strenuously to the Court's construction of the word "possession" of the Fair Labor Standards Act to include the leased bases, Jackson argued that "it was settled American policy, grounded, as I think on the highest wisdom, that, whatever technical form the transaction should take, we should acquire no such responsibilities as would require us to import to those islands our laws, institutions and social conditions beyond the necessities of controlling a military base and its garrison, dependents and incidental personnel."[13] There was no doubt, he said, that Congress could legislate regarding wages and hours of employees of American contractors on the leased bases, but Congress, rather than the Court, should make the policy decision that this should be done.

But Murphy and Rutledge died during the summer following *Vermilya-Brown;* and the *Spelar* case, which came next, raised before a quite differently composed Court the question whether statutory exceptions to the principle of sovereign immunity from tort liability should be liberally or strictly construed. Black was the only libertarian to participate because Douglas had just fallen off his horse and his injury prevented him from taking part. The decision was unanimous, with six joining in the majority opinion and Frankfurter and Jackson concurring, each separately.

Spelar, a flight engineer, employed by American Overseas Airlines, was killed on October 3, 1946, during a takeoff crash at Harmon Field, Newfoundland. Harmon Field was leased by the United States for ninety-nine years. Spelar's administrator initiated an action under the Federal Tort Claims Act of 1946, alleging that the accident was the result of negligent operation of the airfield by employees of the government of the United States. The local law on which the claim was based, in accordance with the requirements of the Federal Tort Claims Act, was the Newfoundland wrongful death statute. A decision of a federal court of appeals reversed the decision of a federal district court which had dismissed the suit for lack of jurisdiction. This, in turn, was reversed by the Supreme Court.

[12] *Opinions of the Attorney General of the United States,* XXXIX (August 27, 1940), 484.

[13] 335 U.S. 377, 394.

The opinion of the Court stated that an examination of the face of the statute, the Federal Tort Claims Act, showed in express words that the intent of Congress had been to waive the principle of sovereign immunity from suit only in areas subject to American sovereignty; and the arrangement here continued to recognize *British* sovereignty over the base. It was clear, therefore, from the letter of the act that the statute did not apply to leased bases such as this. Moreover, an examination (which the majority opinion undertook, *ex abundanti cautella*) of the legislative history of the act made it indisputably clear that Congress had shown no willingness to subject the United States to liabilities arising under the laws of a foreign country such as Newfoundland. Because of these fundamental differences between the Fair Labor Standards Act and the Federal Tort Claims Act, *Vermilya-Brown* was not a relevant precedent for the problem raised by Mrs. Spelar. Of course, Jackson agreed with this outcome, but seized the opportunity that the occasion provided to argue against the Court's attempt to distinguish *Vermilya-Brown,* and, thereby, reinforced and added a footnote to his dissent in that case. That battle may have been over, but the ideological warfare with his colleagues continued.

MR. *JUSTICE JACKSON, concurring.*

I reach the same result; but I could hardly do so, as does the Court, by reiteration of the prevailing opinion in *Vermilya-Brown Co.* v. *Connell,* 335 U.S. 377. That decision, taken with the present one, adds up to this: If an employee should chance to work overtime on a leased air base, he can maintain an action for extra wages, penalties and interest, because the Court finds the air base to be a "possession" of the United States. However, if he is injured at the same place, he may not proceed under the Tort Claims Act to recover, because the Court finds the air base then to be a "foreign country." To those uninitiated in modern methods of statutory construction it may seem a somewhat esoteric doctrine that the same place at the same time may legally be both a possession of the United States and a foreign country. This disparity results from holding that Congress, when it refers to our leased air bases, at one time calls them "possessions" and at another "foreign countries." While congressional incoherence of thought or of speech is not unconstitutional and Congress can use a contrariety of terms to describe the same thing, we should pay Congress the respect of not assuming lightly that it indulges in inconsistencies of speech which make the English language almost meaningless. There is some reason to think the inconsistency lies in the Court's rendering of the statutes rather than in the way Congress has written them. At all events, the present decision seems to me correct, and, so far as it is contradicted by the effect of *Vermilya-Brown,* I think we should retreat from the latter.

C. OVERRULING PRECEDENTS

UNITED STATES V. HELEN R. BRYAN
339 U.S. 323 (May 8, 1950)

Less than a year earlier, on the closing day of the 1948 Term, the final group of decisions to be participated in by Murphy and Rutledge was announced. One of these was *Christoffel* v. *United States*,[14] in which Frankfurter joined the four libertarians in a 5-4 decision that reversed the conviction of a labor leader who had been found guilty of having perjuriously denied Communist affiliations, on the ground that, at the time of his testimony, there had been no quorum present of the House Committee on Education and Labor, before whom Christoffel had been compelled to appear. Through Jackson, the four dissenters had vigorously protested what they considered to be the unwise policy result. When the Court reconvened in the fall sans Murphy and Rutledge but plus Clark and Minton, the government sought certiorari for a reconsideration of this issue.

The instrument that brought the issue back to the Court so quickly was the case of Helen Bryan, an officer of an organization designated as communist by the Attorney General.[15] She had refused to comply with a subpoena that directed her to turn over to the Committee on Un-American Activities certain records of her organization. The Court of Appeals of the District of Columbia had faithfully followed the Supreme Court's decision in *Christoffel,* and had reversed Miss Bryan's conviction for contempt of Congress. It was clear to close observers of the Court that the new majority was never going to follow *Christoffel*—a decision, incidentally, much criticized at the time, and not at all popular with either Senator McCarthy or his followers—and the only question was what form the rationalization for the new tune should take. Discussion at conference no doubt revealed that there was going to be articulate criticism of the overruling decision, no matter which alternative of rhetoric the new majority might select; so they evidently opted to suffer the insider critique from concurrers and dissenters, as a lesser evil (and one which in substantial measure could not be avoided anyhow) than the agitation that would be aroused among the Court's external critics if it were to overrule yet another precedent in the latter's infancy. (The ideological orientation among external critics was—and is—sufficiently naive, or hypocritical, or both, that no hue and cry is raised when the Court "merely distinguishes" its

[14] 338 U.S. 84 (June 27, 1949).
[15] Cf. *Joint Anti-Fascist Refugee Committee* v. *McGrath,* 341 U.S. 123 (1951).

precedents; it is only the open disclosure that the feet of the justices are molded from political clay that cannot be tolerated as a public stance.)

Clark, who agreed with the new majority, and Douglas, who did not, were paired in nonparticipation, for reasons which are by now quite familiar to us. But Minton joined the Jackson group, leaving only Black and Frankfurter to dissent from the Court's changed policy toward the autonomy of congressional committees. Nobody, of course, took seriously Chief Justice Vinson's opinion for the Court, which suggested that the different results in the two cases could best be explained by the circumstance that Christoffel had been convicted for violating a statute defining perjury, whereas Bryan came under another statute governing contempt of Congress by willful failure to produce documents that a committee sought to examine. The Chief Justice went on to offer the dictum that Bryan's case raised a very different problem than had Christoffel's, because perjury could be committed only in the presence of a committee, whereas one could fail to comply with a subpoena irrespective of whether the committee convened in formal session. (Miss Bryan *had* appeared before the committee which cited her for contempt.) Other statutory language, which seemed at face value to preclude Bryan's conviction on the basis of her testimony before the committee,[16] was explained—on the basis of the Court's inquiry into what it deemed to be the relevant materials of legislative history—to have a very different meaning than the literal sense which Vinson agreed was conveyed by a mere reading of the words of the statute.

Dissenters Black and Frankfurter each protested the deviousness of the Court's distinguishment of the above statute, which would have provided a ground for reversal of Bryan's conviction quite independent of the *stare decisis* issue. Jackson, of course, was troubled not at all by the majority's failure to accord "full faith and credit" to *that* statute; he argued, instead—and, necessarily, somewhat self-righteously—that *Christoffel* had been a mistake, that it was clear that a majority of the incumbent Court did not agree with the policy result that *Christoffel* represented, and that the only honest thing to do was to admit the mistake and bring the Court openly into support of the policy that it did now favor.

MR. JUSTICE JACKSON, concurring.

With the result I am in agreements, but I do not see how this decision and that in the *Christoffel* case, 338 U.S. 84, can coexist.

The Court is agreed that this defendant could rightly demand attendance of

[16] "No testimony given by a witness before ... any Committee of either house, ... shall be used as evidence in any criminal proceeding against him in any court, except in a prosecution for perjury committed in giving such testimony...." 18 U.S.C.A. s. 3486.

a quorum of the Committee and decline to testify or to produce documents so long as a quorum was not present. Therefore the real question here is whether, without making any demand, the issue may be raised for the first time long afterwards in a trial for contempt.

This case is the duplicate of *Christoffel* in this respect: in both cases defendants have sought to raise the question of no quorum for the first time in court, when they are on trial for an offense, without having raised it in any manner before the Committee while there was time to remedy it. The Court is now saying, quite properly I think, that this question must be raised at the time when it can be corrected, and proper records made, and cannot be kept as an ace up the sleeve to be produced years later at a trial. But in *Christoffel*, the majority took the opposite view and said, "In a criminal case affecting the rights of one not a member, the occasion of trial is an appropriate one for petitioner to raise the question." . . . If this statement of the law is to be left standing, I do not see how we can say that what was timely for Christoffel is too late for Bryan. It is plain we are not following the *Christoffel* decision and so I think we should candidly overrule it.

The practice of withholding all objection until time of trial is not helpful in protecting a witness' right to a valid Committee. It prevents correction of any error in that respect and profits only the witness who seeks a concealed defect to exploit. Congressional custom, whether written or not, has established that Committee members may indulge in temporary absences, unless there is objection, without disabling those remaining from continuing work as a Committee. Members may step out to interview constituents, consult members of their staffs, confer with each other, dictate a letter, or visit a washroom, without putting an end to the Committee—but always subject to call whenever the point of no quorum is raised; that is notice that someone deems their personal presence important. This is the custom *Christoffel*, in effect, denied to members of Congress. A member now steps out of a committee room at risk of nullifying the whole proceeding.

It is ironic that this interference with legislative procedures was promulgated by exercise within the Court of the very right of absentee participation denied to Congressmen. Examination of our journal on the day *Christoffel* was handed down shows only eight Justices present and that four Justices dissented in that case. The prevailing opinion does not expressly indicate the Justices who joined in it, but only four nondissenting Justices were present to do so. On the record this would show only an equally divided Court, which would affirm the judgment below. The only way the four who were present and for a reversal could have prevailed was by counting for it one shown by the record to be absent. There is not even any public record to show that *in absentia* he joined the decision, or approved the final opinion, or considered the matter after the dissent was circulated; nor is there any written rule or law which permitted him to do so.

I want to make it clear that I am not criticizing any Justice[17] or suggesting the slightest irregularity in what was done. I have no doubt that authorization to include the absent Justice was given; and I know that to vote and be counted *in absentia* has been sanctioned by practice and was without objection by anyone. It is the fact that it is strictly regular and customary, according to our unwritten practice, to count as present for purposes of Court action one physically absent that makes the denial of a comparable practice in Congress so anomalous. Of course, there is this difference: The absent Congressman was only necessary to a quorum, the absent Justice was necessary to a decision. No Committee action was dependent upon the Representatives presumed to be absent in the *Christoffel* case. All they could have done if present was to listen. In our own case, personal judgment and affirmative action of the absent member was necessary to make the *Christoffel* opinion a decision of the Court.

The ruling of the Court today seems irreconcilable with the Court's decision in that case. True, the ink on *Christoffel* is hardly dry. But the principle of *stare decisis*, which I think should be the normal principle of judicial action, is not well served by failing to make explicit an overruling which is implicit in a later decision. Unless we really accede to its authority, it were far better to undo *Christoffel* before it becomes embedded in the law as a misleading influence with the profession. Of course, it is embarrassing to confess a blunder; it may prove more embarrassing to adhere to it. In view of the holding today, I think that the decision in the *Christoffel* case should be forthrightly and artlessly overruled.

D. THE LETTER KILLETH

UNITED STATES V. HARRISS
347 U.S. 612, 633 (June 7, 1954)

A common technique of judicial legislation is for the Court to "interpret" statutes to mean something quite different from either the literal statutory language or the expressed intent of the Congress. One theory on which the Court relies to justify such action is, first, that the Court has an obligation to avoid the decision of constitutional questions if this is at all possible; and second, that it has a correlative obligation to "save" from judicial invalidation acts of Congress by interpreting them to mean what-

---

[17] This is a thinly veiled reference to William O. Douglas. As Jackson was well aware, most regular readers of the Court's opinions would know that a two-minute check of *United States Law Week: Supreme Court Section* would divulge the identity of the absentee justice. [Ed.]

ever the Court is willing to approve as within the permissible limits of the "Constitution." Of course, it has been argued that judicial review and judicial interpretation of statutes are merely alternative forms of judicial legislation.[18] This, however, is not the orthodox theory. In the case that follows, Jackson accepts the orthodox theory of judicial review while challenging the orthodox explanation of judicial interpretation as constituting a means of *upholding* the authority of Congress.

This case considered various challenges, on constitutional grounds, to the Federal Regulation of Lobbying Act. A majority of five justices, in an opinion written by Warren, construed the statute strictly so that the range of activities subject to regulation became very narrowly defined. The probable effect of this would be to defeat the prosecution of these and many other defendants, but it preserved the skeleton of the statute and resulted in the avoidance, so far as the Court was concerned, of the publicity and criticism that would have been certain to attend a ruling that the statute was unconstitutional. Clark, as the former Attorney General who had been responsible for the enforcement of the statute, did not participate. Douglas and Black dissented on the grounds that the statute, even as narrowly construed by the majority, still was unconstitutional. Jackson dissented on the alternative ground that, if a new statute were needed to replace the one that Congress had enacted, the Congress was a more competent body to write such a statute than was the Court. As it turned out, this was his last opinion as an Associate Justice of the United States Supreme Court,[19] and this decision was one of the very few in which he ever voted to hold unconstitutional an act of Congress.

MR. JUSTICE JACKSON, *dissenting*.

Several reasons lead me to withhold my assent from this decision.

The clearest feature of this case is that it begins with an Act so mischievously vague that the Government charged with its enforcement does not understand it, for some of its important assumptions are rejected by the Court's interpretation. The clearest feature of the Court's decision is that it leaves the country under an Act which is not much like any Act passed by Congress. Of course, when such a question is before us, it is easy to differ as to whether it is more appropriate to

---

[18] Fred V. Cahill, Jr., *Judicial Legislation* (New York: The Ronald Press Company, 1952), *passim*. "I believe," Jackson confided to his biographer, "in *liberal* legislation *conservatively* construed." Eugene C. Gerhart, *United States Supreme Court Justice Robert H. Jackson: Lawyer's Judge*, (Albany: Q Corporation, 1961), p. 99 and n. 248.

[19] Jackson's final opinion, in *Knickerbocker Printing Co.* v. *United States*, 75 S.Ct. 212 (September 3, 1954), was a memorandum written in his capacity as Circuit Justice for the Second Circuit, barely a month before his death on October 9 on the threshold of a new term of the Court.

strike out or to strike down. But I recall few cases in which the Court has gone so far in rewriting an Act.

The Act passed by Congress would appear to apply to all persons who (1) solicit or receive funds for the purpose of lobbying, (2) receive and expend funds for the purpose of lobbying, or (3) merely expend funds for the purpose of lobbying. The Court at least eliminates this last category from coverage of the Act, though I should suppose that more serious evils affecting the public interest are to be found in the way lobbyists spend their money than in the ways they obtain it. In the present indictments, six counts relate exclusively to failures to report expenditures while only one appears to rest exclusively on failure to report receipts.

Also, Congress enacted a statute to reach the raising and spending of funds for the purpose of influencing congressional action *directly* or *indirectly*. The Court entirely deletes "indirectly" and narrows "directly" to mean "direct communication with members of Congress." These two constructions leave the Act touching only a part of the practices Congress deemed sinister.

Finally, as if to compensate for its deletions from the Act, the Court expands the phrase "the principal purpose" so that it now refers to any contribution which "in substantial part" is used to influence legislation.

I agree, of course, that we should make liberal interpretations to save legislative Acts, including penal statutes which punish conduct traditionally recognized as morally "wrong." Whoever kidnaps, steals, kills, or commits similar acts of violence upon another is bound to know that he is inviting retribution by society, and many of the statutes which define these long-established crimes are traditionally and perhaps necessarily vague. But we are dealing with a novel offense that has no established bounds and no such moral basis. The criminality of the conduct dealt with here depends entirely upon a purpose to influence legislation. Though there may be many abuses in pursuit of this purpose, this Act does not deal with corruption. These defendants, for example, are indicted for failing to report their activities in raising and spending money to influence legislation in support of farm prices, with no charge of corruption, bribery, deception, or other improper action. This may be a selfish business and against the best interests of the nation as a whole, but it is in an area where legal penalties should be applied only by formulae as precise and clear as our language will permit.

The First Amendment forbids Congress to abridge the right of the people "to petition the Government for a redress of grievances." If this right is to have an interpretation consistent with that given to other First Amendment rights, it confers a large immunity upon activities of persons, organizations, groups and classes to obtain what they think is due them from government. Of course, their conflicting claims and propaganda are confusing, annoying and at times, no doubt, deceiving and corrupting. But we may not forget that our constitutional system is to allow the greatest freedom of access to Congress, so that the people may press for their selfish interests, with Congress acting as arbiter of their demands and conflicts.

In matters of this nature, it does not seem wise to leave the scope of a criminal Act, close to impinging on the right of petition, dependent upon judicial construction for its limitations. Judicial construction, constitutional or statutory, always is subject to hazards of judicial reconstruction. One may rely on today's narrow interpretation only at his peril, for some later Court may expand the Act to include, in accordance with its terms, what today the Court excludes. This recently happened with the antitrust laws, which the Court cites as being similarly vague. This Court, in a criminal case, sustained an indictment by admittedly changing repeated and long-established constitutional and statutory interpretations. *United States* v. *South-Eastern Underwriters Assn.*, 322 U.S. 533 [1944]. The *ex post facto* provision of our Constitution has not been held to protect the citizen against a retroactive change in decisional law, but it does against such a prejudicial change in legislation. As long as this statute stands on the books, its vagueness will be a contingent threat to activities which the Court today rules out, the contingency being a change of views by the Court as hereafter constituted.

The Court's opinion presupposes, and I do not disagree, that Congress has power to regulate lobbying for hire as a business or profession and to require such agents to disclose their principals, their activities, and their receipts. However, to reach the real evils of lobbying without cutting into the constitutional right of petition is a difficult and delicate task for which the Court's action today gives little guidance. I am in doubt whether the Act as construed does not permit applications which would abridge the right of petition, for which clear, safe and workable channels must be maintained. I think we should point out the defects and limitations which condemn this Act so clearly that the Court cannot sustain it is written, and leave its rewriting to Congress. After all, it is Congress that should know from experience both the good in the right of petition and the evils of professional lobbying.

E.   THE SPIRIT GIVETH LIFE

UNITED STATES EX REL MARCUS V. HESS
317 U.S. 537, 556 (January 18, 1943)

One of the ancient games played by American courts involves what is considered to be the necessity of choosing between the horns of a dilemma: In interpreting a statute, should the court give effect to the spirit or to the letter of the law? (There is some indication, from the fact that English courts follow only the literal rule, that the dilemma may be one of choice rather than necessity.) One of Jackson's strongest statements in behalf of the Court's obligation to give effect to legislative intent and to the latent policy underlying statutory law came in his opinion in this relatively insignificant case.

The major question was whether a statutory provision of general applicability, which prohibited the United States Government to present claims known to be fraudulent, could be relied upon to support the present civil suit for indemnity. The respondents were electrical contractors who had acquired, through collusive bidding, contracts with local governments; the federal government paid most of the bill through a grant-in-aid program. The legal question was whether the fraudulent claim section applied to indirect, as well as to direct, presentation of claims to the federal government. The Court, speaking through Black, unanimously agreed that it did so apply.

But there was a second question, and it was on this point that Jackson differed with the rest of the Court. Could an informer, whose research in the matter appeared to be limited to copying a public record—the indictment in an earlier criminal action against these same defendants—bring his own suit against the contractors? Notwithstanding the fact that the respondents already had paid substantial fines in the settlement of the criminal action brought against them by the government, the Court decided that the statute clearly permitted recourse to a civil remedy, such as the present suit, in lieu of or in addition to any criminal action that might be taken. Moreover, said the Court, the monetary judgment that had been secured from the trial (federal district) court was to be shared by the informer with the government. According to Black, this proved that the statute, under the interpretation that the Court was now giving to it, was being used to realize the objectives that Congress had envisaged—the recompense of the government for its financial loss. In a thrust intended for Jackson, who was the only dissenter, Black suggested that arguments against the wisdom of the plain statutory policy should be directed to the Congress, not to the judiciary.[20]

MR. JUSTICE JACKSON, dissenting....

I cannot deny that on a literal reading the statute says what the Court's opinion renders it to say. That being the case, one cannot be critical of those who stay close to the words of the statute because guiding principles as to where to depart and in what direction to depart from the literal words of a statute are so conflicting.

But that we have in these matters considerable, although ill-defined, freedom is certain. I could not better state my attitude toward the present statute as applied to this case than in the language of the present Chief Justice ... :

[20] Whatever Jackson's intent, his dissent apparently was more persuasive with the Congress than with his colleagues; a statutory change which overruled the Court by repealing 31 U.S.C.A. s. 234 was promptly adopted later in the year. See 57 *Stat.* 609.

"All laws are to be given a sensible construction; and a literal application of a statute, which would lead to absurd consequences, should be avoided whenever a reasonable application can be given to it, consistent with the legislative purpose."

Nor was he announcing unorthodox or unconventional doctrine. . . . [As] Mr. Justice Day said:

"But in construing a statute we are not always confined to a literal reading, and may consider its object and purpose, the things with which it is dealing, and the condition of affairs which led to its enactment so as to effectuate rather than destroy the spirit and force of the law which the legislature intended to enact. . . ."

If ever we are justified in reading a statute, not narrowly as through a keyhole but in the broad light of the evils it aimed at and the good it hoped for, it is here. The only disadvantage therefrom falls on one who sues, not to be made whole for injuries he has sustained, or to recover for goods he has delivered, or services he has performed, but solely to make profitable to himself the wrong done by others. We should, of course, fully sustain informers in proceedings where Congress has utilized their self-interest as an aid to law enforcement. Informers who disclose law violations even for the worst of motives play an important part in making many laws effective. But there is nothing in the text or history of this statute which indicates to me that Congress intended to enrich a mere busybody who copies a Government's indictment as his own complaint and who brings to light no frauds not already disclosed and no injury to the Treasury not already in process of vindication.

In this case the Government investigated respondents and on November 3, 1939, indicted them for conspiracy to defraud. On January 5 and February 6, 1940, the defendants named in the indictment entered pleas of *nolo contendere*, and fines were imposed. While the criminal case was still pending, and on January 25, 1940, petitioner commenced his informer proceeding, the averments in his complaint being substantially a copy of the indictment. It is not shown that he had any original information, that he had added anything by investigations of his own, or that his recovery is based on any fact not disclosed by the government itself. . . .

I am sure it was never in the mind of Congress to authorize this misuse of the statute. If ever there was a case where the letter killeth but the spirit giveth life, it is this. Construed to the letter as the Court does, it becomes an instrument of abuse and corruption which can only be stopped by the timely intervention of Congress. If it were construed according to its spirit to reward those who disclose frauds otherwise concealed or who prosecute frauds otherwise unpunished, it would serve a useful purpose in the enforcement of the law and protection of the Treasury.

Since 1863, this law has been upon the statute books. Never until now has the bar dreamed that it permitted such use. When once it was attempted to commence an informer action under a similar statute after the government had brought a civil action, this Court promptly limited the statute to preclude that sort of abuse. *Francis* v. *United States,* 5 Wall. 338 [1867]. There was no specific language in the statute to support that court-made limitation, and although I find no specific language in this statute to support another, I should now say that the same limitation exists where the Government has already possessed itself of the facts and disclosed them in criminal proceedings. This is what I think the profession has generally assumed this statute to mean. If the statute has all these eighty years authorized this sort of proceeding, the legal profession of the United States has been strangely unresponsive to a Congressional proffer of windfall income.

We are justified in determining whether we will accept a new interpretation not before sustained in the history of this statute by reference to the condition of our own times rather than to those of former ones. Nothing better illustrates the difference between the conditions of 1863 and the present than the statement quoted by the Court, made by the Senate sponsor of the Informer Act, "Even the district attorney, who is required to be vigilant in the prosecution of such cases, may be also the informer, and entitle himself to one half the forfeiture under the qui tam clause, and to one half the double damages which may be recovered against the persons committing the act." I do not understand the Court to hold that a prosecuting attorney may now sue, but in construing the statute as applied to the plaintiff now before us, we must not forget that the Senator was then speaking of law-enforcement in a nation which had not yet established a Federal Department of Justice, which did not then have a Federal Bureau of Investigation, or a Treasury investigating force, and in which the activities of the Federal Government were so circumscribed that they had not been found necessary. To accept the view of 1863 to mean that today law-enforcement officials could use information gleaned in their investigations to sue as informers for their own profit, would make the law a downright vicious and corrupting one. Fortunately, no one in the executive department has ever suspected that such an interpretation as the Court now indulges could be placed upon this statute. If we were to add motives of personal avarice to other prompters of official zeal the time might come when the scandals of law-enforcement would exceed the scandals of its violation.

F. STATUTORY RECONSTRUCTION

SCHWEGMANN BROTHERS V. CALVERT DISTILLERS CORPORATION
341 U.S. 384, 395 (May 21, 1951)

All of the justices agreed that the question in this case concerned how the Court should construe an act of Congress that authorized state legislation regulating resale price maintenance, in relation to earlier congressional legislation under which such state legislation clearly would have been illegal. The state statute in this case permitted the distributor of a product in interstate commerce, who entered into a contract establishing minimum retail prices with a single retailer in the state, to bind thereby all other retailers of the product within the state, whether or not they were willing to make such contracts with the distributor. Unless permitted by the Miller-Tydings Act, such legislation and contracts of such effect would clearly be in violation of the Sherman Anti-Trust Act.

Both Douglas, who wrote for a plurality of the six-man majority, and Frankfurter, who dissented for Black and Burton as well as for himself, engaged in discursive examinations of the legislative history of the Miller-Tydings Act; and each emerged with what was proffered as conclusive proof that Congress intended opposite results. Pointing out that no less than forty-two of the states already had nonsigner provisions in their fair-trade laws at the time the Miller-Tydings Act was passed, Frankfurter's dissent argued that, "Where both the words of a statute and its legislative history clearly indicate the purpose of Congress, it should be respected. We should not substitute our notion of what Congress should have done." The majority, speaking through Douglas in what seemed to be an endeavor to rebut the dissent, and on the basis of the very same evidence that Frankfurter had relied upon, argued that *they* had discovered the true intent of Congress; and that it was the dissenters who sought to substitute their own personal notions of wise economic policy for the will of Congress.

Because their colleagues were divided into the four-justice Douglas group, and the three-man Frankfurter group, Jackson and Minton were clearly in a position to determine the outcome, in either direction. As it happened, these two took the stance that all seven of their colleagues were wrong, in their respective endeavors to divine congressional intent by delving into so-called legislative history. Their own more limited examination of the face of the statute convinced Jackson and Minton that the evident and manifest intent of Congress had *not* been to authorize state laws such as Louisiana's. Therefore, they joined in voting with the Douglas group to form a majority which upheld the position of the price-cutting retailer.

When Jackson argued against recourse to legislative history, as in this opinion, he was often concerned with the plight of the small-town lawyer whose county law library could not hope to compete with the Library of Congress available to the Solicitor General of the United States and his staff. Jackson understood the point of view of both the country lawyer and the Solicitor General, for he had lived the life of both; but his basic sympathy as a judge was with the Jamestown, not the Washington, attorney.[21]

MR. JUSTICE JACKSON, *whom* MR. JUSTICE MINTON *joins, concurring.*

I agree with the Court's judgment and with its opinion insofar as it rests upon the language of the Miller-Tydings Act. But it does not appear that there is either necessity or propriety in going back of it into legislative history.

Resort to legislative history is only justified where the face of the Act is inescapably ambiguous, and then I think we should not go beyond Committee reports, which presumably are well considered and carefully prepared. I cannot deny that I have sometimes offended against that rule. But to select casual statements from floor debates, not always distinguished for candor or accuracy, as a basis for making up our minds what law Congress intended to enact is to substitute ourselves for the Congress in one of its important functions. The Rules of the House and Senate, with the sanction of the Constitution, require three readings of an Act in each House before final enactment. That is intended, I take it, to make sure that each House knows what it is passing and passes what it wants, and that what is enacted was formally reduced to writing. It is the business of Congress to sum up its own debates in its legislation. Moreover, it is only the words of the bill that have presidential approval, where that approval is given. It is not to be supposed that, in signing a bill, the President endorses the whole Congressional Record. For us to undertake to reconstruct an enactment from legislative history is merely to involve the Court in political controversies which are quite proper in the enactment of a bill but should have no place in its interpretation.

Moreover, there are practical reasons why we should accept whenever possible the meaning which an enactment reveals on its face. Laws are intended for all of our people to live by; and the people go to law offices to learn what their rights under those laws are. Here is a controversy which affects every little merchant in many States. Aside from a few offices in the larger cities, the materials of legislative history are not available to the lawyer who can afford neither the cost of acquisition, the cost of housing, or the cost of repeatedly examining the whole congressional history. Moreover, if he could, he would not know any way of anticipating what would impress enough members of the Court to be controlling. To accept legislative debates to modify statutory provisions is to make the law inaccessible to a large part of the country.

By and large, I think our function was well stated by Mr. Justice Holmes: "We do not inquire what the legislature meant; we ask only what the statute

---

[21] See, for example, Jackson's "The County-Seat Lawyer," *American Bar Association Journal,* XXXVI (1950), 497. Cf. Francis Lyman Windolph, *The Country Lawyer* (Philadelphia: University of Pennsylvania Press, 1938).

means." Holmes, Collected Legal Papers, 207. . . . And I can think of no better example of legislative history that is unedifying and unilluminating than that of the Act before us.

G. PSYCHOANALYZING THE COURT

UNITED STATES V. PUBLIC UTILITIES COMMISSION OF CALIFORNIA
345 U.S. 295, 319 (April 6, 1953)

The question in this case was whether the Federal Power Commission had exclusive authority, under the Federal Power Act, to regulate rates charged by the California Electric Power Company for the resale of whole-sale hydroelectric energy transmitted through interstate commerce to the United States Navy Department and to Mineral County, Nevada. A typical facet of American federalism is revealed in that, after a joint hearing, both the Federal Power Commission and the Public Utilities Commission of California each asserted exclusive jurisdiction over rates; and, upon appeal of their respective orders, a federal court of appeals upheld the authority of the federal administrative agency whereas the California state courts upheld the authority of the state administrative agency. The legal issue presumably hinged upon the proper interpretation of certain language in the Federal Power Act, in order to determine whether Congress intended such rates to be subject to national or to state regulation.

There was no question of the authority of Congress to have decided the matter in either way. With the exception of Frankfurter, who found Jackson's caveats so persuasive that he withdrew from participation in the decision, the Court was unanimously agreed that the relevant federal statutes supported the position of the Federal Power Commission rather than that of the state utilities commission. Jackson's quarrel, as in the *Schwegmann* case, was not with the outcome of the case, but rather with the process by which Reed's opinion for the majority determined the meaning of the statute.

Although Jackson's opinion in this case portrays the fundamental problem as the difficulty lawyers have in attempting to postcast the intent of Congress, the evidence that Jackson presents suggests that the real difficulty, at least from a functional point of view, is how anybody else can forecast the intent of the Supreme Court. That would, of course, be a serious difficulty if most lawyers were interested primarily in predicting the form of the Court's rhetorical formulations. It is perhaps lucky for lawyers that most of them are much more interested in the mundane enterprise of trying to predict the Court's decisional outcomes.[22]

MR. JUSTICE JACKSON, *concurring.*

I should concur in this result more readily if the Court could reach it by analysis of the statute instead of by psychoanalysis of Congress. When we decide from legislative history, including statements of witnesses at hearings, what Congress probably had in mind, we must put ourselves in the place of a majority of Congressmen and act according to the impression we think this history should have made on them. Never having been a Congressman, I am handicapped in that weird endeavor.[23] That process seems to me not interpretation of a statute but creation of a statute.

I will forego repeating what I have said about this practice in *Schwegmann Bros.* v. *Calvert Corp.,* 341 U.S. 384, 395. But I do point out that this case is a dramatic demonstration of the evil of it. Neither counsel who argued the case for the State Commission nor the Supreme Court of California had access to the material used by the Court today. Counsel for the Public Utilities Commission of that State stated at the bar, and confirmed by letter, that he had tried without success over a period of four months to obtain the legislative history of §20 of Part I of the Federal Power Act. He obtained it only four days before argument, in Washington at the Library of this Court. He stated that the City and County Library of San Francisco, the Library of the University of California, and the library of the largest law office in San Francisco were unable to supply it. The City and County Library tried to obtain the material by interlibrary loan from the Library of Congress, but the request was refused. Counsel then attempted to obtain the material from the Harvard Law School Library, but it advised that "our rules do not permit this kind of material to be sent out on loan."

The practice of the Federal Government relying on inaccessible law has heretofore been condemned. Some of us remember vividly the argument in *Panama Refining Co.* v. *Ryan,* 293 U.S. 388 [1935], in which the Government was obliged to admit that the Executive Orders upon which it had proceeded below had been repealed by another Executive Order deposited with the State Department. No regularized system for their publication had been established. Copies could be obtained at nominal cost by writing to the Department. Having discovered the error, the Government brought it to the attention of the Court. At the argument,

22 Underhill Moore and Gilbert Sussman, "The Lawyer's Law," *Yale Law Journal,* XLI (1932), 566-576.

23 This probably *was* a significant gap in Jackson's experience, because his naive theory that congressional inaction should be considered as holding equal weight with congressional action in approving legislative proposals is certainly unsupported—indeed, it is flatly contradicted—by what is by now a substantial body of political science research in the legislative process. [Ed.]

however, the Court, led by Mr. Justice Brandeis, subjected government counsel to a raking fire of criticism because of the failure of the Government to make Executive Orders available in official form. The Court refused to pass on some aspects of the case, and the result was the establishment of a Federal Register.

Today's decision marks a regression from this modern tendency. It pulls federal law, not only out of the dark where it has been hidden, but into a fog in which little can be seen if found. Legislative history here as usual is more vague than the statute we are called upon to interpret.

If this were an action to enforce a civil liability or to punish for a crime, I should protest this decision strenuously. However, the decision seems to have operation in the future only. If Congress does not like our legislation, it can repeal it—as it has done a number of times in the past. I therefore concur in the interpretation unanimously approved by the members of the Court who have had legislative experience.

H. CAVEAT EMPTOR

FEDERAL CROP INSURANCE CORP. V. MERRILL
332 U.S. 380, 386 (November 10, 1947)

One gathers, from a reading of Jackson's opinion in the preceding case, that the government erred in that it failed to publish the legislative history of the Federal Power Act, either in the *Federal Register* or in another publication akin to it. One gets the impression from the present case, however, that the government is damned if it doesn't, and damned anyhow even if it does: here the government erred by relying upon regulations which it *had* published in the *Federal Register*. Some readers might well agree with Jackson's quotation (in *Chenery*) of Samuel L. Clemens: "The more you explain it, the more I don't understand it."

A favorite epigram of the legal profession is that "Hard cases make bad law." *Federal Crop Insurance Corp.* v. *Merrill* was a hard case, and Jackson tried without success to use it as the basis for making bad law. Oblique evidence of this is found in the unusual division of the Court, with Frankfurter writing for a majority of five that included Murphy, and Jackson joining the three remaining libertarians in dissent. Only Murphy's deviation stood between the dissenting libertarians and what Jackson liked to call "the power of decision" in the case, because they were able to enlist Jackson's sympathies. Unlike those of the other dissenters, however, his sympathies lay with a legal principle rather than with the plight of drought-stricken farmers.

The issue in the case was whether, on the basis of private law principles governing the responsibility of a principal for the acts of his agent,
the Court should attribute governmental contract liability contrary to
the express terms of the applicable act of Congress and administrative
regulations. The facts were these. A local committee, which was part
of the official decision-making apparatus of the Federal Crop Insurance
Corporation (a subordinate agency of the United States Department of
Agriculture), had advised the respondents that their entire wheat crop was
insurable under the applicable regulations, and the corporation subsequently approved in writing their application for insurance. The local
committee was made up of a representative group of farmers resident in
the county in which the crop was grown. Part of the respondents' crop
was reseeded winter wheat acreage, and neither they, nor the local committee, were aware at the time the application for drought insurance was
filed and accepted that the corporation's regulations, for that crop year,
prohibited the insurance of reseeded winter wheat crops. These regulations
had been duly published in the *Federal Register,* and they were declared
by statute to be an implied part of all crop insurance contracts. A summer
drought had destroyed the respondents' entire wheat crop, and they sued
for recovery on the contract. The F.C.I.C. had obtained certiorari from
the Court to review a decision of the state supreme court affirming a jury
verdict in favor of the farmers.

The majority ruled that contracts with the government must be conducted in the light of all legally promulgated regulations, and that failure
to observe or to be cognizant of such regulations, on the part of either the
individual or the government's representative, does not bind the government as it would a private insurance company. Anyone entering into an
arrangement with the government, said Frankfurter, takes the risk of
having to ascertain accurately that the government's agent is acting within
the bounds of his authority. Moreover, Congress has explicitly provided
that publication in the *Federal Register* gives to all legal notice of its contents; so these regulations must be deemed binding in law regardless of actual knowledge, or of any hardships that might result from ignorance in
fact.

As in the two preceding cases, Jackson expressed concern for both
the citizen and the small-town lawyer who are placed at an unfair disadvantage in their dealings with a government that relies upon laws that (in
this instance) were published but which, for all practical purposes, remained "inaccessible." Certainly the government relied upon a blatant
legal fiction when it argued that these farmers had had adequate notice of
the limitations to the government's contracting authority, and, therefore,
to its liability as an insurer. He felt that the Court should, under these

circumstances, formulate a more reasonable policy to govern this kind of relationship, irrespective of the explicit command of Congress. If Jackson's view had prevailed, the Court would have amended the ancient legal aphorism to make it read: "Ignorance of the law is no excuse, except for farmers and country lawyers."

MR. JUSTICE JACKSON, dissenting.

I would affirm the decision of the court below. If crop insurance contracts made by agencies of the United States Government are to be judged by the law of the State in which they are written, I find no error in the court below. If, however, we are to hold them subject only to federal law and to declare what that law is, I can see no reason why we should not adopt a rule which recognizes the practicalities of the business.

It was early discovered that fair dealing in the insurance business required that the entire contract between the policyholder and the insurance company be embodied in the writings which passed between the parties, namely, the written application, if any, and the policy issued. It may be well enough to make some types of contracts with the Government subject to long and involved regulations published in the Federal Register. To my mind, it is an absurdity to hold that every farmer who insures his crops knows what the Federal Register contains or even knows that there is such a publication. If he were to peruse this voluminous and dull publication as it is issued from time to time in order to make sure whether anything has been promulgated that affects his rights, he would never need crop insurance, for he would never get time to plant any crops. Nor am I convinced that a reading of technically-worded regulations would enlighten him much in any event.

In this case, the Government entered a field which required the issuance of large numbers of insurance policies to people engaged in agriculture. It could not expect them to be lawyers, except in rare instances, and one should not be expected to have to employ a lawyer to see whether his own Government is issuing him a policy which in case of loss would turn out to be no policy at all. There was no fraud or concealment, and those who represented the Government in taking on the risk apparently no more suspected the existence of a hidden regulation that would render the contract void than did the policyholder. It is very well to say that those who deal with the Government should turn square corners. But there is no reason why the square corners should constitute a one-way street.

The Government asks us to lift its policies out of the control of the States and to find or fashion a federal rule to govern them. I should respond to that request by laying down a federal rule that would hold these agencies to the same fundamental principles of fair dealing that have been found essential in progressive states to prevent insurance from being an investment in disappointment.

8 COMITY

There are many different ways in which federal constitutional polities, including the former colonies of the British Empire, structure their judicial systems. In Canada there are, except at the level of local government, only judges selected by the national government; in Australia, to the contrary, each state has its own independent judicial system, and the only national court of general jurisdiction is the High, or supreme, Court. Only in the United States is there complete duplication of judicial resources, with each of the fifty states maintaining its own judiciary, and, at the same time, with the national court system dispersed throughout the land, with one or more United States district (trial) courts in each state.[1] One consequence of the existence of fifty-one different judicial structures, which respond to as many different patterns of political influence and control, is that relationships at and across the boundaries[2] of these manifold judicial systems are continuous for many of the judges who staff them. As events of the past decade in regard to lower court "enforcement" of the Supreme Court's decisions concerning racial integration[3] and legislative reapportionment amply demonstrate, both indirect and direct relationships between federal circuit and district judges, and between them and state judges, are a critical aspect of accommodation when local interests are reshaped in the crucible of Supreme Court policy making (and vice versa). Conflicts in judicial interests, associated with such boundary relationships, are frequently bucked up to the Supreme Court for reinforcement, reconsideration, delay, or other action (or inaction).

"It is the maintenance of the constitutional equilibrium between the states and the Federal Government that has brought the most vexatious questions to the Supreme Court," said Robert Jackson.[4] Both inter-

1 Glendon Schubert, *Judicial Policy-Making* (Chicago: Scott, Foresman and Company, 1965), Chaps. 2 and 3.

2 "Boundary" is used here in an analytical rather than a territorial sense.

3 See Kenneth Vines: "The Role of Circuit Courts of Appeals in the Federal Judicial Process," *Midwest Journal of Political Science,* VII (1963), 305-319; "Federal District Judges and Race Relations Decisions in the South," *Journal of Politics,* XXVI (1964), 337-357; and "Southern State Supreme Courts and Race Relations," *Western Political Quarterly,* XVIII (1965), 5-18.

4 Robert Jackson, *The Supreme Court in the American System* (Cambridge: Harvard University Press, 1955), p. 65. Cf. William B. Lawless, "Mr. Justice Jackson: The Struggle for Federal Supremacy," *Notre Dame Lawyer,* XXXVII (1962), 489-498.

action between the federal and state judiciaries, and that concerning what
Jackson conceptualized as relationships between the national and state
"units" in a federal governmental system, were in his view aspects of this
constitutional equilibrium. Because of the substantial overlap in the national and state lego-policy jurisdictions, state judges participate in many
decisions which "interpret" legal norms that are products or by-products
of the national political system; judges of the lower federal courts decide
—legal fiction to the contrary notwithstanding—many questions which
interpret counterpart "state laws"; and state judges are continuously involved in the interpretation of legal norms of other states. Appeals from
the decisions of lower judges, in all three of the above situations, are carried
to the Supreme Court, and with frequencies corresponding to the order
in which the three types are listed above.

Jackson's position was more subtle than it might appear from the first
reading of the above quotation gleaned from his final testament, however. His own bureaucratic service, as Solicitor and as Attorney General,
came on the heels of a period during which the Court had employed the
commerce clause of the Constitution as a principal instrument for frus-
trating the major socioeconomic policies of the New Deal—or at least so it
seems to have appeared to Jackson.[5] It is hardly surprising, therefore, to
find him worrying, particularly during his freshman year on the Court,
about what today (with the benefit of several decades of hindsight) appears to have been a dead issue by the time he joined the Court. As we
have seen, however, Jackson was also sympathetic to the plight of American businessmen in their continuing battles not only with each other but
with bureaucrats and unions as well. Freedom of commerce was for him
a positive verbal symbol of the freedom of American enterprise to seek out
and realize the potentialities that are a major part of the economic promise
of the American way of life. Therefore, his generally sympathetic remarks
about national and state regulation of commerce were often admixed with
his economically conservative hostility toward both governmental and
union bureaucrats. On the whole, however, he tended to support *both*
national and state regulation of interstate commerce.

What may seem a surprise was his general tendency to give even
stronger verbal support to *state* than to national regulation of the national
economy, particularly in the light of his valedictory statement on this
subject. "I make no concealment of and offer no apology," he remarked as
his time on the Court drew to a close, "for my philosophy that the federal
interstate commerce power should be strongly supported and that the
impingement of the states upon that commerce which moves among them

[5] Robert Jackson, *The Struggle for Judicial Supremacy* (New York: Alfred A. Knopf,
Inc., 1941).

should be restricted to narrow limits."[6] This may well have been his ultimate point of view and his "philosophy" at the time he wrote these words,
but his opinion behavior belies the assertion. His overall support of state
regulation of business was about twice as great as the ratio of his overall
support of national regulation, which was consistent with his tendency to
slightly favor states' rights over those of the national government in arguing issues that he did conceptualize and verbalize as aspects of federalism.[7]

His ambivalence toward the competing values of the national market,
freedom of commerce, and decentralized politics resulted in a course of
judicial action on his part that can perhaps best be described as pragmatic.
Thus, he felt that if national regulation of wheat production was demon-
strably necessary in order to keep small farmers in the business of agricultural production—and there were, he thought, important ancillary social
reasons why the family farm should be retained, as an economic unit, as
long as possible—then farmers who wanted to compete in the national
market would have to put up with the regulations which alone made possible such a market. Jackson wrote for a unanimous Court what is surely
the coup de grâce to the use of the commerce clause as a device for rationalizing limits upon national regulation of the economy.[8] This was
Jackson's first opinion in his second term on the Court; less than two
years later, however, in his final opinion of the following term, he dissented
vigorously against the Court's decision that the insurance business in the
United States was "in" interstate commerce, and, therefore, subject to
national regulation by act of Congress.[9] There was no point, he argued,
in disturbing the equilibrium of the national economy by forcing a Congress, preoccupied with the problems of prosecuting World War II, to
substitute national regulation, when the states long had been and were
doing what Jackson described as a satisfactory job of regulating the insurance industry.

Particularly during his early days on the Court, Jackson devoted considerable ingenuity to creative suggestions for novel alternatives to the
stereotyped rationales—especially to those invoking or rejecting the commerce clause as a limitation upon state regulatory powers—that were satisfactory to the Court's majorities. Possibly this tactic was merely the ploy
by which a freshman justice attracted more attention to himself than

[6] Jackson, *The Supreme Court in the American System*, p. 67.

[7] See my "Jackson's Judicial Philosophy," *American Political Science Review*, LIX
(1965), 949.

[8] *Wickard* v. *Filburn*, 317 U.S. 111 (November 9, 1942).

[9] *United States* v. *South-Eastern Underwriters Association*, 322 U.S. 533, 584 (June
5, 1944).

might otherwise have been his lot; in any event, the "forgotten clause" approach to resolving the Court's jurisprudential problems largely disappeared from Jackson's repertoire after his initial term of service.[10] This is well illustrated by the first two cases in this chapter, which are the second and fourth of his opinions as a justice. One argues for the resurrection of the privileges and immunities clause as an alternative to relying upon the commerce clause as a *limitation* upon state regulatory power; whereas, the other seeks to baptize the Twenty-first Amendment in order to avoid an *expansion* of state power to regulate interstate commerce. Either outcome, and therefore either Jackson's or the Court's position, assumes the propriety of having the judiciary in general, and the Supreme Court in particular, determine the scope of state authority to regulate interstate commerce, that is, to control in part transactions that judges deem important components of the national economy. The significant federal relationship in these decisions is not, therefore, well described as the resolution of conflict ("in jurisdiction") between the national and state governments by the Supreme Court as the Keeper of the Keys to the Constitution. It is better conceptualized as an accommodation between the policy choices of earlier but still dominant political majorities according to state groupings, and the pattern of values represented on the Court at the time it makes relevant decisions. That is to say, the functional federal relationship is between Supreme Court justices on one hand, and state law makers, on the other.

In the second group of cases (C, D, and E), the same federal relationship obtains, but in the somewhat more complex form of a triangle: here the Court is cast in the role of arbitrator between conflicting state policies. No doubt the values acceptable to Supreme Court majorities remain the critical consideration in the accommodations that are struck, but the format of the associated rationale has changed. Instead of the commerce clause serving as the formal restraint upon state power, it is now the policy of one state that restrains another state or, because the relationship sometimes is at least partially reciprocal, vice versa. This issue can be raised by cases representing a variety of legal subjects,[11] but the three decisions that we shall examine all concern property settlements entailed by divorce decrees which had effects in interstate commerce. Jackson found it easy to jump from his favored concept of "the national market" to the analogy of a "national legal system." His vocal enthusiasm

[10] The exception was the "full faith and credit" clause, which he discussed in lectures that subsequently were published as a small book. See his *Full Faith and Credit: The Lawyer's Clause of the Constitution* (New York: Columbia University Press, 1945).

[11] As illustrated, for example, by *Magnolia Petroleum* v. *Hunt,* 320 U.S. 430, 446 (1943) and Chap. 7A, *supra.*

for the notion should not be understood to signify, however, that his support was given strongly either to having the Supreme Court make policies that would resolve the conflict-of-laws problems of the states, or to the observance, in practice, of the full faith and credit about which he so often talked. In regard to the extraterritorial effect of state adjudications, Jackson showed at best a slight tendency, more in his later than in his earlier years on the Court, to uphold a policy of strict rather than lax requirement for the "lawyer's clause" of the Constitution.

The remaining two opinions in this chapter (F and G) discuss a third kind of federal relationship: that between the lower federal and state judges who hold court over the same people in the same territory. Both the diversity (of citizenship, as among the states) clause of the Constitution and many acts of Congress give a plaintiff the choice of taking his suit to a state or a federal court; and many, particularly corporate, plaintiffs have an additional choice among state judiciaries. Defendants, however, may seek to transfer the suit to an alternative forum, or even better, to persuade that forum to quash proceedings in the court of plaintiff's choice. Usually, these options are available only when the plaintiff begins in a state court, and the defendant invokes the aid of a federal district court. Both of the cases below illustrate facets of this increasingly typical kind of boundary relationship between state and federal judges.

A.   BURDENING INTERSTATE COMMERCE

EDWARDS V. CALIFORNIA
314 U.S. 160, 181 (November 24, 1941)

In 1868, a few months before the Fourteenth Amendment was adopted, the Supreme Court first confronted the issue of state limitations upon the right of American citizens to travel freely throughout the Union. No question could be raised then as yet about the right to national citizenship posited by the imminent amendment; nevertheless, the Court decided that a Nevada statute, that placed a special tax upon all persons leaving the state by railroad, stage, or coach, was an unconstitutional violation of the rights of a national citizenship that, as most of the justices thought, was clearly implied by the Constitution. Only two of the justices concurred, arguing that the Nevada tax burdened the commerce clause rather than any inferred right of citizenship in the Union.[12]

12 *Crandall* v. *Nevada,* 6 Wall. 35 (1868).

The next three-quarters of a century brought no great progress in this particular sector of legal rationalization. When the question returned to the Supreme Court, the Fourteenth Amendment was as old as the commerce clause had been in the days of Reconstruction; FDR already had succeeded in packing the Court with a majority of his own choice; and the policy issue arose as one of the fruits of the grapes of wrath. Fred F. Edwards, a citizen of the United States and resident of California, motored to Texas and returned to his home in California accompanied by his brother-in-law, one Frank Duncan, a citizen of the United States who had been a resident of Texas. Edwards knew that Duncan was without funds and that he had no job waiting for him in California. Ten days after the arrival of the two men at Edwards' home, Duncan applied for and received assistance from the Farm Security Administration. The state of California, in turn, prosecuted and secured the conviction of Edwards under Section 2615 of the California Welfare and Institutions Code (the so-called "anti-Okie" law), which made it a penal offense knowingly to import indigent persons into the state and thus add to the burden of the state's public assistance program.

The simple and most obvious course for the Court would have been to have viewed *Crandall* v. *Nevada* as a direct, relevant, and controlling precedent, for the justices were unanimously agreed now, as they had been then, that the state law was invalid. Instead, they continued to disagree over the rationale, except that now the division was much closer. When the case was first argued in late April, 1941, there appears to have been a 4-4 deadlock between those favoring the rights of national citizenship, and those favoring the commerce clause, as a basis for reversing Edwards' conviction and declaring unconstitutional the California anti-Okie law. The deadlock was possible because the McReynolds seat, which he had resigned in January, remained vacant. It is easy to infer, from the subsequent decision in the case, that the four pro-commerce clause group must have included Stone, Roberts, Reed, and Frankfurter; conversely, the justices who preferred to justify the decision on grounds of civil liberties rather than economics included Murphy, Black, and Douglas. The remaining libertarian vote must have been provided by Chief Justice Hughes whose intention to retire later in the month, at the end of the term, was announced on June 3.

Given the deadlock, the case was set down for reargument in the fall. In the interim, Stone was promoted to replace Hughes as Chief Justice, and Byrnes and Jackson were appointed during the summer to fill the two vacancies that then existed. Presumably, the rest of the justices stood pat in their 4-3 division, with the majority favoring the commerce clause after reargument; and the two freshman justices divided. Byrnes joined, and thereby preserved the majority, and was rewarded with the assignment to write the opinion of the Court which took an immense leap backward by embracing the commerce clause rationale. Douglas, Murphy, and Black concurred in behalf of the privileges and immunities clause, as did Robert Jackson although in a separate opinion. Because this particular policy issue has almost the identical periodicity, in its appearances before the Supreme Court, as does Halley's Comet in its visitations near Earth, it is perhaps ironic to note that Byrnes' service on the Court was limited to the 1941 Term, and if only Edwards' case had been delayed for another fifteen months when Wiley Rutledge replaced Byrnes, the norm outcome might have been very different indeed. For then, assuming that the Libertarian Four stuck together, Jackson would have had the opportunity for which he pleaded, to make of "our heritage of constitutional privileges and immunities" something more than "a promise to the ear to be broken to the hope"; and no longer, then, would the first section of the Fourteenth Amendment have remained, as apparently it still does, merely "a teasing illusion like a munificent bequest in a pauper's will."

MR. JUSTICE JACKSON, *concurring:*

I concur in the result reached by the Court, and I agree that the grounds of its decision are permissible ones under applicable authorities. But the migrations of a human being, of whom it is charged that he possesses nothing that can be sold and has no wherewithal to buy, do not fit easily into my notions as to what is commerce. To hold that the measure of his rights is the commerce clause is likely to result eventually either in distorting the commercial law or denaturing human rights. I turn, therefore, away from principles by which commerce is regulated to that clause of the Constitution by virtue of which Duncan is a citizen of the United States and which forbids any State to abridge his privileges or immunities as such.

This clause was adopted to make United States citizenship the dominant and paramount allegiance among us. The return which the law had long associated with allegiance was protection. The power of citizenship as a shield against oppression was widely known from the example of Paul's Roman citizenship, which sent the centurion scurrying to his higher-ups with the message: "Take heed what thou doest: for this man is a Roman." I suppose none of us doubts that the hope of imparting to American citizenship some of this vitality was the purpose of declaring in the Fourteenth Amendment: "All persons born or naturalized in the United States, and subject to the jurisdiction thereof, are citizens of the United States and of the state wherein they reside. No state shall make or enforce any law which shall abridge the privileges or immunities of citizens of the United States. . . ."

But the hope proclaimed in such generality soon shriveled in the process of judicial interpretation. For nearly three-quarters of a century this Court rejected every plea to the privileges and immunities clause. The judicial history of this clause and the very real difficulties in the way of its practical application to specific cases have been too well and recently reviewed to warrant repetition.

While instances of valid "privileges or immunities" must be but few, I am convinced that this is one. I do not ignore or belittle the difficulties of what has been characterized by this Court as an "almost forgotten" clause. But the difficulty of the task does not excuse us from giving these general and abstract words whatever of specific content and concreteness they will bear as we mark out their application, case by case. That is the method of the common law, and it has been the method of this Court with other no less general statements in our fundamental law. This Court has not been timorous about giving concrete meaning to such obscure and vagrant phrases as "due process," "general welfare," "equal protection," or even "commerce among the several States." But it has always hesitated to give any real meaning to the privileges and immunities clause lest it improvidently give too much.

This Court should, however, hold squarely that it is a privilege of citizenship of the United States, protected from state abridgment, to enter any state of the Union, either for temporary sojourn or for the establishment of permanent residence therein and for gaining resultant citizenship thereof. If national citizenship means less than this, it means nothing.

The language of the Fourteenth Amendment declaring two kinds of citizenship is discriminating. It is: "All persons born or naturalized in the United States and subject to the jurisdiction thereof, are citizens of the United States and of the State wherein they reside." While it thus establishes national citizenship from the mere circumstance of birth within the territory and jurisdiction of the United States, birth within a state does not establish citizenship thereof. State citizenship is ephemeral. It results only from residence and is gained or lost therewith. That choice of residence was subject to local approval is contrary to the inescapable implications of the westward movement of our civilization.

Even as to an alien who had "been admitted to the United States under the Federal Law," this Court, through Mr. Justice Hughes, declared that "He was thus admitted with the privilege of entering and abiding in the United States, and hence of entering and abiding in any State in the Union." *Truax* v. *Raich*, 239 U.S. 33, 39 [1915]. Why we should hesitate to hold that federal citizenship implies rights to enter and abide in any state of the Union at least equal to those possessed by aliens passes my understanding. The world is even more upside down than I had supposed it to be, if California must accept aliens in deference to their federal privileges but is free to turn back citizens of the United States unless we treat them as subjects of commerce.

The right of the citizen to migrate from state to state which, I agree with MR. JUSTICE DOUGLAS, is shown by our precedents to be one of national citizenship is not, however, an unlimited one. In addition to being subject to all constitutional limitations imposed by the federal government, such citizen is subject to some control by state governments. He may not, if a fugitive from justice, claim freedom to migrate unmolested, nor may he endanger others by carrying contagion about. These causes, and perhaps others that do not occur to me now, warrant any public authority in stopping a man where it finds him and arresting his progress across a state line quite as much as from place to place within the State.

It is here that we meet the real crux of this case. Does "indigence" as defined by the application of the California statute constitute a basis for restricting the freedom of a citizen, as crime or contagion warrants its restriction? We should say now, and in no uncertain terms, that a man's mere property status, without more, cannot be used by a state to test, qualify, or limit his rights as a citizen of the United States. "Indigence" in itself is neither a source of rights nor a basis for denying them. The mere state of being without funds is a neutral fact—constitutionally an irrelevance, like race, creed, or color. I agree with what I understand to be the holding of the Court that cases which may indicate the contrary are overruled.

Any measure which would divide our citizenry on the basis of property into one class free to move from state to state and another class that is poverty-bound to the place where it has suffered misfortune is not only at war with the habit and custom by which our country has expanded, but is also a short-sighted blow at the security of property itself. Property can have no more dangerous, even if unwitting, enemy than one who would make its possession a pretext for unequal or exclusive civil rights. Where those rights are derived from national citizenship no state may impose such a test, and whether the Congress could do so we are not called upon to inquire.

I think California had no right to make the condition of Duncan's purse, with no evidence of violation by him of any law or social policy which caused it, the basis of excluding him or of punishing one who extended him aid.

If I doubted whether his federal citizenship alone were enough to open the gates of California to Duncan, my doubt would disappear on consideration of the obligations of such citizenship. Duncan owes a duty to render military service, and this Court has said that this duty is the result of his citizenship. Mr. Chief Justice White declared in the *Selective Draft Law Cases,* 245 U.S. 366, 378 [1918]: "It may not be doubted that the very conception of a just government and its duty to the citizen includes the reciprocal obligation of the citizen to render military service in case of need and the right to compel it." A contention that a citizen's duty to render military service is suspended by "indigence" would meet with little favor. Rich or penniless, Duncan's citizenship under the Constitution pledges his strength to the defense of California as a part of the United States, and his right to migrate to any part of the land he must defend is something she must respect under the same instrument. Unless this Court is willing to say that citizenship of the United States means at least this much to the citizen, then our heritage of constitutional privileges and immunities is only a promise to the ear to be broken to the hope, a teasing illusion like a munificent bequest in a pauper's will.

B. BALKANIZING INTERSTATE COMMERCE

DUCKWORTH V. ARKANSAS
314 U.S. 390, 397 (December 15, 1941)

Duckworth was a bootlegger who transported liquor by motor vehicle through Arkansas from Illinois en route to Mississippi. Arkansas law, as construed by the state supreme court, required Duckworth to apply for a license before bringing any liquor into the state. His claim was that, because his journey unquestionably was in interstate commerce, Arkansas was forbidden by the federal constitution from "burdening" that commerce by requiring him to submit to its licensing system. Eight members of the Court disagreed, joining in an opinion written by the Chief Justice to uphold the Arkansas regulation as a legitimate exercise of the state's police power, especially because Congress had not acted to regulate such interstate transportation of liquor and the state regulations did not "materially obstruct the free flow of commerce." The Court added that the decision in this case was limited to its own facts, and did not purport to settle all questions concerning the Arkansas licensing system, or the state's authority to regulate other commodities not as potentially injurious to the public interest as liquor.

Jackson voted to uphold Duckworth's conviction, but otherwise his opinion is devoted to the grounds for his disagreement with his brethren. Bespeaking once again that legal parochialism by means of which he so frequently sought to emphasize the dissimilarities and discontinuities of life, Jackson argued that liquor—like Kovacs' sound truck, or the water preemption practices of gold miners in the High Sierra—was unique in its essential characteristics so that it required and merited a "law unto itself." This analogistic form of argument was one which he subsequently found an opportunity to develop most consistently, and repeatedly, in regard to air travel. Since the air was (like fire? or water?) a unique substance, airplanes needed a law unto themselves; and the one favored by Jackson was exclusive federal control pegged to the commerce clause:

> We are at a stage in development of air commerce roughly comparable to that of steamship navigation in 1824 when Gibbons v. Ogden, 9 Wheat. 1, came before this Court. Any

authorization of local burdens on our national air commerce will lead to their multiplication in this country. . . . Aviation has added a new dimension to travel and to our ideas. The ancient idea that landlordism and sovereignty extend from the center of the world to the periphery of the universe has been modified. Today the landowner no more possesses a vertical control of all the air above him than a shore owner possesses horizontal control of all the sea before him. . . . Air as an element in which to navigate is even more inevitably federalized by the commerce clause than is navigable water. Local exactions and barriers to free transit in the air would neutralize its indifference to space and its conquest of time.

Congress has recognized the national responsibility for regulating air commerce. Federal control is intensive and exclusive. Planes do not wander about in the sky like vagrant clouds. They move only by federal permission, subject to federal inspection, in the hands of federally certified personnel and under an intricate system of federal commands.[13]

Later he added that:

Of course, air transportation, water transportation, rail transportation, and motor transportation all have a kinship in that all are forms of transportation and their common features of public carriage for hire may be amenable to kindred regulations. But these resemblances must not blind us to the fact that legally, as well as literally, air commerce, whether at home or abroad, soared into a different realm than any that had gone before.[14]

In the present case, the law that the Court should have applied to Duckworth is one that could not subsequently—or by other judges—be used to encourage unwonted interference with the freedom of commerce which Jackson posited as the primary goal at stake in this decision. The "Balkanization" of American economic enterprise had already gone much too far; and what his colleagues somehow failed to appreciate was that the greatest danger came from the cumulative effects of a thousand petty usufructs.[15] "If it is interstate commerce that feels the pinch," as he subsequently put it in another case, "it does not matter how local the operation which applies the squeeze."[16]

MR. JUSTICE JACKSON, concurring in result:

I agree that this Court should not relieve Duckworth of his conviction, but I would rest the decision on the constitutional provision applicable only to the transportation of liquor, and refrain from what I regard as an unwise extension of state power over interstate commerce.

---

[13] *Northwest Airlines* v. *Minnesota,* 322 U.S. 292, 302-303 (1944).

[14] *Chicago and Southern Air Lines* v. *Waterman Steamship Corp.,* 333 U.S. 103, 107 (1948).

[15] "Balkanism," he had remarked a year or so earlier, before joining the Court, "is as much a state of mind as a condition of geography." Robert H. Jackson, "The Supreme Court and Interstate Barriers," *Annals of the American Academy of Political and Social Science,* CCVII (January, 1940), 78.

[16] *United States* v. *Women's Sportswear Association,* 336 U.S. 460, 464 (1949).

I

Appellant was convicted for transporting a load of intoxicating liquor through Arkansas, without permit from that State, on the way from Illinois to Mississippi. The owner of the liquor testified, and his testimony was treated as a stipulation of fact, "that the liquor was intended to be sold in the State of Mississippi in violation of the state laws of Mississippi."

The Twenty-first Amendment provides:

"The transportation or importation into any State, Territory, or possession of the United States for delivery or use therein of intoxicating liquors, in violation of the laws thereof, is hereby prohibited."

Duckworth now contends that it is our duty to assure him safe conduct as against the action of Arkansas, although his goal is to violate both the laws of Mississippi and the Federal Constitution. He asks us to hold that one provision of the Constitution guarantees him an opportunity to violate another. The law is not that tricky.

Whether one transporting liquor across Arkansas to a legal destination might not have some claim to federal protection, we do not need to consider. One who assails the constitutionality of a statute must stand on his own right to relief. Since this appellant had no rightful claim to constitutional protection for his trip, the whole purpose of which was to violate the Constitution which he invokes, we should leave him where we find him, and for this reason I concur in the judgment of this Court affirming the conviction.

II

If we yield to an urge to go beyond this rather narrow but adequate ground of decision, we should then consider whether this liquor controversy cannot properly be determined by guidance from the liquor clauses of the Constitution. These clauses of the Twenty-first Amendment create an important distinction between state power over the liquor traffic and state power over commerce in general. The people of the United States knew that liquor is a lawlessness unto itself. They determined that it should be governed by a specific and particular Constitutional provision. They did not leave it to the courts to devise special distortions of the general rules as to interstate commerce to curb liquor's "tendency to get out of legal bounds." It was their unsatisfactory experience with that method that resulted in giving liquor an exclusive place in constitutional law as a commodity whose transportation is governed by a special, constitutional provision.

Transportation itself presented no special dangers or hazards, but it might be a step in evading and undermining a policy as to use and sale of liquor which the state has a right to prescribe for itself. Regulated transportation of liquor is a necessary incident of regulated consumption and distribution. So the Twenty-first Amendment made the laws as to delivery and use in the state of destination the test of legality of interstate movement. This obviously gives to state law a much greater control over interstate liquor traffic than over commerce in any other commodity.

If the Twenty-first Amendment is not to be resorted to for the decision of liquor cases, it is on the way to becoming another "almost forgotten" clause of the Constitution. Compare *Edwards* v. *California, ante,* p. 183. It certainly applies to nothing else. We should decide whether this Arkansas statute is sustainable under the Twenty-first Amendment. Does it authorize a state to exact some assurance that all liquor entering its territory either is imported for lawful delivery under its own laws or will pass through without diversion? The Amendment might bear a construction that would allow a state to prohibit liquor from entering its borders at all unless by responsible carrier under consignment to some lawful destination within or beyond the state. I should not at all object to considering all of the potential evils which the Court's opinion associates with the liquor traffic, and some more that I could supply, to be sufficient reasons for giving a liberal interpretation to the Twenty-first Amendment as to state power *over liquor.* But the Court brushes aside the liquor provisions of the Twenty-first Amendment.

III

The opinion of the Court solves the present case through a construction of the interstate commerce power. It regards this liquor as a legitimate subject of a lawful commerce, and then, because of its special characteristics, approves this admittedly novel permit system and thus expands the power of the state to regulate such lawful commerce beyond anything this Court has yet approved.

The extent to which state legislation may be allowed to affect the conduct of interstate business in the absence of Congressional action on the subject has long been a vexatious problem. Recently the tendency has been to abandon the earlier limitations and to sustain more freely such state laws on the ground that Congress has power to supersede them with regulation of its own. It is a tempting escape from a difficult question to pass to Congress the responsibility for continued existence of local restraints and obstructions to national commerce. But these restraints are individually too petty, too diversified, and too local to get the attention of a Congress hard pressed with more urgent matters. The practical result is that in default of action by us they will go on suffocating and retarding and Balkanizing American commerce, trade and industry.

I differ basically with my brethren as to whether the inertia of government shall be on the side of restraint of commerce or on the side of freedom of commerce. The sluggishness of government, the multitude of matters that clamor for attention, and the relative ease with which men are persuaded to postpone troublesome decisions, all make inertia one of the most decisive powers in determining the course of our affairs and frequently gives to the established order of things a longevity and vitality much beyond its merits. Because that is so, I am reluctant to see any new local systems for restraining our national commerce get the prestige and power of established institutions. The Court's present opinion and tendency would allow the states to establish the restraints and let commerce struggle for Congressional action to make it free. This trend I am unwilling to further in any event beyond the plain requirements of existing cases.

If the reaction of this Court against what many of us have regarded as an excessive judicial interference with legislative action is to yield wholesome results, we must be cautious lest we merely rush to other extremes. The excessive use for insufficient reason of a judicially inflated due process clause to strike down states' laws regulating their own internal affairs, such as hours of labor in industry, minimum wage requirements, and standards for working conditions, is one thing. To invoke the interstate commerce clause to keep the many states from fastening their several concepts of local "well-being" onto the national commerce is a wholly different thing.

Our national free intercourse is never in danger of being suddenly stifled by dramatic and sweeping acts of restraint. That would produce its own antidote. Our danger, as the forefathers well knew, is from the aggregate strangling effect of a multiplicity of individually petty and diverse and local regulations. Each may serve some local purpose worthy enough by itself. Congress may very properly take into consideration local policies and dangers when it exercises its power under the commerce clause. But to let each locality conjure up its own dangers and be the judge of the remedial restraints to be clamped onto interstate trade inevitably retards our national economy and disintegrates our national society. It is the movement and exchange of goods that sustain living standards, both of him who produces and of him who consumes. This vital national interest in free commerce among the states must not be jeopardized. I do not suppose the skies will fall if the Court does allow Arkansas to rig up this handy device for policing liquor on the ground that it is not forbidden by the commerce clause, but in doing so it adds another to the already too numerous and burdensome state restraints of national commerce and pursues a trend with which I would have no part.

C. *EX PARTE* BIGAMY

WILLIAMS V. NORTH CAROLINA
317 U.S. 287, 311 (December 21, 1942)

It is understandable that a farm lad who was almost twelve when, at Kitty Hawk, North Carolina, Orville Wright became the first man to fly an airplaine, should have grown up to be a judge impressed with the idea that air travel is different. It is perhaps equally understandable that this same farm boy should grow up believing that Americans "belong" in some one particular place. In the opinion below, Robert Jackson frequently invokes this image by speaking of a state's "permanent population," of "its own permanent inhabitants," and of "domicile" as referring to the one place where a man "has his roots and his real, permanent home." In particular, he characterizes the two defendants in this case as "North Carolina people"; and the clear implication of his argument is that if they had never left home, they would never have gotten into trouble—which is certainly a truism of sorts.

Jackson's is a tolerable opinion, but one better suited to the rural America of the century of his birth than to the megalopolitan America of the century of his death. One might have expected that his participation in the *Edwards* decision, barely thirteen months earlier and a scant two weeks prior to Pearl Harbor, would have sensitized Jackson to the sweeping changes in population mobility which, having been catalyzed by the Depression, were in the process of acceleration when this case was decided in the midst of the demographic dislocations consequent upon World War II. But it is the role of the true conservative to be the last, not the first, to give up the mainsprings of his former way of life; and so we find Jackson setting his face vehemently against the full faith and credit demanded by the lawyer's clause, when to respect it would have meant to support a decision certain to encourage a trend that already had gone too far in the direction of weakening both the marriage contract and the stability of the home in which it is sanctified. Frank Murphy, the only Roman Catholic justice at this time, also protested against the Court's new and libertine policy of putting its imprimatur upon Reno divorces. It appears that, at this time, Murphy was without question the colleague whom Jackson disliked most;[17] and their written opinions, like their reasons for dissenting, remained quite independent.

The explicit question before the Court was whether it should affirm the conviction of O. B. Williams and Lillie S. Hendrix on a charge of bigamous cohabitation, in that they openly set up housekeeping and lived together as though they were man and wife, while their respective lawfully wedded spouses were not only alive but still living in the same North Carolina rural (Brushy Mountains) community. In approving their convictions, the North Carolina Supreme Court had relied upon *Haddock* v. *Haddock*, a thirty-six-year-old precedent in which the Supreme Court had ruled that *ex parte* divorces—and the Reno decrees of Mr. Williams and

---

[17] Eugene C. Gerhart, *America's Advocate* (Indianapolis: The Bobbs-Merrill Company, Inc., 1958), Chap. 11.

Mrs. Hendrix were surely that—did not merit the full faith and credit that the Constitution requires to be given to valid laws and judgments. A majority of the present Court joined in an opinion by Douglas which overruled the *Haddock* precedent and reversed the decision of the state court in the case of Williams and Hendrix.

The opinion of the Court did note, however, that the relevant Nevada statutes require a plaintiff in a divorce action to "reside" in the state, and the Court presumed that what this really meant was a legal domicile. Moreover, no question had been raised (said Douglas) of whether North Carolina might have refused to give full faith and credit to the Nevada decrees *if* the trial court in North Carolina had made its own independent determination that the purported Nevada residence of these defendants was not a bona fide domicile. It was true that the adoption of liberal policies in one state might have an effect upon the stricter policies adhered to in other states, but this was part of the price of a federal system of government. Murphy argued that neither Nevada nor North Carolina should be forced to accept the other's requirements in regard to divorce, because "The fair result is to leave each free to regulate within its own area the rights of its own citizens." Jackson also thought that neither faith nor credit should be accorded to the Nevada divorces, under the circumstances in this case.

MR. JUSTICE JACKSON, *dissenting:*

I cannot join in exerting the judicial power of the Federal Government to compel the State of North Carolina to subordinate its own law to the Nevada divorce decrees. The Court's decision to do so reaches far beyond the immediate case. It subjects matrimonial laws of each state to important limitations and exceptions that it must recognize within its own borders and as to its own permanent population. It nullifies the power of each state to protect its own citizens against dissolution of their marriages by the courts of other states which have an easier system of divorce. It subjects every marriage to a new infirmity, in that one dissatisfied spouse may choose a state of easy divorce, in which neither party has ever lived, and there commence proceedings without personal service of process. The spouse remaining within the state of domicile need never know of the proceedings. Or, if they come to one's knowledge, the choice is between equally useless alternatives: one is to ignore the foreign proceedings, in which case the marriage is quite certain to be dissolved; the other is to follow the complaining spouse to the state of his choice and there defend under the laws which grant the dissolution on relatively trivial grounds. To declare that a state is powerless to protect either its own policy or the family rights of its people against such consequences has serious constitutional implications. It is not an exaggeration to say that this decision repeals the divorce laws of all the states and substitutes the law of Nevada as to all marriages one of the parties to which can afford a short trip there. . . .

From the viewpoint of North Carolina, this is the situation: The Williamses, North Carolina people, were married in North Carolina, lived there twenty-five years and have four children. The Hendrixes were also married in North Carolina and resided there some twenty years. In May of 1940, Mr. Williams and Mrs. Hendrix left their homes and respective spouses, departed the state, but after an absence of a few weeks reappeared and set up housekeeping as husband and wife. North Carolina then had on its hands three marriages among four people in the form of two broken families, and one going concern. What problems were thereby created as to property or support and maintenance, we do not know. North Carolina, for good or ill, has a strict policy as to divorce. The situation is contrary to its laws, and it has attempted to vindicate its own law by convicting the parties of bigamy.

The petitioners assert that North Carolina is made powerless in the matter, however, because of proceedings carried on in Nevada during their brief absence from North Carolina. We turn to Nevada for that part of the episode.

Williams and Mrs. Hendrix appear in the state of Nevada on May 15, 1940. For barely six weeks they made their residences at the Alamo Auto Court on the Las Vegas-Los Angeles Road. On June 26, 1940, both filed bills of complaint for divorce through the same lawyer, and alleging almost identical grounds. No personal service was made on the home-staying spouse in either case; and service was had only by publication and substituted service. Both obtained divorce decrees. The Nevada policy of divorce is reflected in Mrs. Hendrix's case. Her grounds were "extreme mental cruelty." She sustained them by testifying that her husband was "moody"; did not talk or speak to her "often"; when she spoke to him he answered most of the time by a nod or shake of the head and "there was nothing cheerful about him at all." The latter of the two divorces was granted on October 4, 1940, and on that day in Nevada they had benefit of clergy and emerged as man and wife. Nevada having served its purpose in their affairs, they at once returned to North Carolina to live.

The question is whether this court will now prohibit North Carolina from enforcing its own policy within that State against these North Carolinians on the ground that the law of Nevada under which they lived a few weeks is in some way projected into North Carolina to give them immunity.

I. OUR FUNCTION IN THE MATTER

There is confided to the Court only the power to resolve constitutional questions raised by these divorce procedures, and not moral, religious, or social questions as to divorce itself. I do not know with any certainty whether in the long run strict or easy divorce is best for society or whether either has much effect on moral conduct. It is enough for judicial purposes that to each state is reserved constitutional power to determine its own divorce policy. It follows that a federal court should uphold impartially the right of Nevada to adopt easy divorce laws and the right of North Carolina to enact severe ones. No difficulties arise so long as each state applies its laws to its own permanent inhabitants. The complications begin when one state opens its courts and extends the privileges of its laws to persons who never were domiciled there and attempts to visit disadvantages therefrom upon persons who have never lived there, have never submitted to the jurisdiction of its courts, and have never been lawfully summoned by personal service of process. This strikes at the orderly functioning of our federal constitutional system, and raises questions for us. . . .

II. Lack of Due Process of Law

Thirty-seven years ago this Court decided that a state court, even of the plaintiff's domicile, could not render a judgment of divorce that would be entitled to federal enforcement in other states against a nonresident who did not appear, and was not personally served with process. *Haddock* v. *Haddock,* 201 U.S. 562 (1905 Term). The opinion was much criticized, particularly in academic circles. Until today, however, it has been regarded as law, to be accepted and applied, for good or ill, depending on one's view of the matter. The theoretical reasons for the change are not convincing.

The opinion concedes that Nevada's judgment could not be forced upon North Carolina in absence of personal service if a divorce proceeding were an action *in personam.* In other words, settled family relationships may be destroyed by a procedure that we would not recognize if the suit were one to collect a grocery bill.

We have been told that this is because divorce is a proceeding *in rem.* The marriage relation is to be reified and treated as a *res.* Then it seems that this *res* follows a fugitive from matrimony into a state of easy divorce, although the other party to it remains at home where the *res* was contracted and where years of cohabitation would seem to give it local situs. Would it be less logical to hold that the continued presence of one party to a marriage gives North Carolina power to protect the *res,* the marriage relation, than to hold that the transitory presence of one gives Nevada power to destroy it? Counsel at the bar met this dilemma by suggesting that the *res* exists in duplicate—one for each party to the marriage. But this seems fatal to the decree, for if that is true the dissolution of the *res* in transit would hardly operate to dissolve the *res* that stayed in North Carolina. Of course this discussion is only to reveal the artificial and fictional character of the whole doctrine of a *res* as applied to a divorce action.

I doubt that it promotes clarity of thinking to deal with marriage in terms of a *res,* like a piece of land or a chattel. It might be more helpful to think of marriage as just marriage—a relationship out of which spring duties to both spouse and society and from which are derived rights,—such as the right to society and services and to conjugal love and affection—rights which generally prove to be either priceless or worthless, but which none the less the law sometimes attempts to evaluate in terms of money when one is deprived of them by the negligence or design of a third party.

It does not seem consistent with our legal system that one who has these continuing rights should be deprived of them without a hearing. Neither does it seem that he or she should be summoned by mail, publication, or otherwise to a remote jurisdiction chosen by the other party and there be obliged to submit marital rights to adjudication under a state policy at odds with that of the state under which the marriage was contracted and the matrimonial domicile was established.

Marriage is often dealt with as a contract. Of course a personal judgment could not be rendered against an absent party on a cause of action arising out of an ordinary commercial contract, without personal service of process. I see no reason why the marriage contract, if such it be considered, should be discriminated against, nor why a party to a marriage contract should be more vulnerable to a foreign judgment without process than a party to any other contract. I agree that the marriage contract is different, but I should think the difference would be in its favor. . . .

III. LACK OF DOMICILE

We should, I think, require that divorce judgments asking our enforcement under the full faith and credit clause, unlike judgments arising out of commercial transactions and the like, must also be supported by good-faith domicile of one of the parties within the judgment state. Such is certainly a reasonable requirement. A state can have no legitimate concern with the matrimonial status of two persons, neither of whom lives within its territory.

The Court would seem, indeed, to pay lip service to this principle. I understand the holding to be that it is domicile in Nevada that gave power to proceed without personal service of process. That being the course of reasoning, I do not see how we avoid the issue concerning the existence of the domicile which the facts on the face of this record put to us. Certainly we cannot, as the Court would, bypass the matter by saying that "we must treat the present case for the purpose of the limited issue before us precisely the same as if petitioners had resided in Nevada for a term of years and had long ago acquired a permanent abode there." I think we should treat it as if they had done just what they have done.

The only suggestion of a domicile within Nevada was a stay of about six weeks at the Alamo Auto Court, an address hardly suggestive of permanence. . . .

While a state can no doubt set up its own standards of domicile as to its internal concerns, I do not think it can require us to accept and in the name of the Constitution impose them on other states. If Nevada may prescribe six weeks of indefinite permanent abode in a motor court as constituting domicile, she may as readily prescribe six days. Indeed, if the Court's opinion is carried to its logical conclusion, a state could grant a constructive domicile for divorce purposes upon the filing of some sort of declaration of intention. Then it would follow that we would be required to accept it as sufficient and to force all states to recognize mail-order divorces as well as tourist divorces. Indeed, the difference is in the bother and expense—not in the principle of the thing. . . .

Domicile means a relationship between a person and a locality. It is the place, and the one place, where he has his roots and his real, permanent home. . . .

In the application of the full faith and credit clause to the variety of circumstances that arise when families break up and separate domiciles are established, there are, I grant, many areas of great difficulty. But I cannot believe that we are justified in making a demoralizing decision in order to avoid making difficult ones.

IV. PRACTICAL CONSIDERATIONS

The Court says that its judgment is "part of the price of our federal system." It is a price that we did not have to pay yesterday and that we will have to pay tomorrow, only because this Court has willed it to be so today. This Court may follow precedents, irrespective of their merits, as a matter of obedience to the rule of *stare decisis*. Consistency and stability may be so served. They are ends desirable in themselves, for only thereby can the law be predictable to those who must shape their conduct by it and to lower courts which must apply it. But we can break with established law, overrule precedents, and start a new cluster of leading cases to define what we mean, only as a matter of deliberate policy. We therefore search a judicial pronouncement that ushers in a new order of matrimonial confusion and irresponsibility for some hint of the countervailing public good that is believed to be served by the change. Little justification is offered. And it is difficult to believe that what is offered is intended seriously.

The Court advances two "intensely practical considerations" in support of its present decision. One is the "complicated and serious condition" if "one is lawfully divorced and remarried in Nevada and still married to the first spouse in North Carolina." This of course begs the question, for the divorces were completely ineffectual for any purpose relevant to this case. I agree that it is serious if a Nevada court without jurisdiction for divorce purports to say that the sojourn of two spouses gives four spouses rights to acquire four more, but I think it far more serious to force North Carolina to acquiesce in any such proposition. The other consideration advanced is that if the Court doesn't enforce divorces such as these it will, as it puts it, "bastardize" children of the divorcees. When thirty-seven years ago Mr. Justice Holmes perpetrated this quip, it had point, for the Court was then holding divorces invalid which many, due to the confused state of the law, had thought to be good. It is difficult to find that it has point now that the shoe is on the other foot. In any event, I had supposed that our judicial responsibility is for the regularity of the law, not for the regularity of pedigrees.

The various opinions of the Supreme Court justices in the *Williams* case made it perfectly clear that North Carolina's mistake had been in

failing to question the *jurisdiction* of Nevada over these particular defendants at the time the decrees were entered. North Carolina's blunder was,
of course, the foolish assumption that the United States Supreme Court
would continue to follow the rule of *stare decisis* on this issue; and, as a
consequence, the state failed to prove and to get affirmatively into the
record a point which there was no apparent need to establish. So the defendants were put on trial a second time, at which time the prosecutor was
careful to prove, to the satisfaction of a North Carolina jury, that neither
Mr. Williams nor Mrs. Hendrix had ever intended to live permanently in
Nevada. And so they were convicted again, and North Carolina again refused to give full faith and credit to the Nevada divorces; but this time the
Supreme Court approved the conviction by a majority just as large as that
which only two and a half years earlier had seemingly come to a somewhat
opposite conclusion.[18] The former dissenters, Murphy and Jackson, were
joined by four of the former majority (Frankfurter, Reed, Roberts, and
Stone) so that only the three remaining libertarians—Douglas, Black,
and Rutledge—were left to dissent.

Only six months before, on the third anniversary of Pearl Harbor,
Robert Jackson had delivered the fourth annual Benjamin N. Cardozo Lecture before the Association of the Bar of the City of New
York. His subject was "full faith and credit," and he stated that only
recently had he undertaken the research upon which his lecture was based,
which may account, at least in part, for the seeming hiatus between the
attitudes which he now articulated and the views that he expressed in the
first *Williams* decision.

Jackson's lawyer-like approach to constitutional interpretation is nowhere more evident than in his concern about the "dead letter" clauses of
the Constitution. The existence of such lacunae in the *corpus constitution-
alis* was pathological, from his point of view, and the Court's obligation
was to give meaning and content to these great silences of the Constitution.[19] There was no doubt, in Jackson's mind, what the Constitutional
fathers had intended to accomplish by the inclusion of this clause: "By
the full faith and credit clause they sought to federalize the separate and
independent state legal systems by the overriding principle of reciprocal
recognition."[20] The aspirations of the fathers, however, remained far from
fulfillment; in comparison with the other two English-speaking federa-

[18] *Williams* v. *North Carolina*, 325 U.S. 226 (May 21, 1945).

[19] The concluding sentence of his lecture was: "If I have any message to the legal
profession worthy of the occasion, it is this: that you must not suffer this lawyer's clause to
become the orphan clause of the Constitution." Jackson, *Full Faith and Credit*, p. 60. The
lectures were also published, under the same title, as an article in *Columbia Law Review*,
XLV (1945), 1-34; references herein are to the pagination of the book.

[20] *Ibid.*, p. 29.

tions, Canada and Australia, "We alone in a century and a half have made no effort better to integrate our judicial systems."[21] Commenting upon Dicey's observation that the United States is "a nation concealed under the form of a federation," Jackson said that:

> However true this may be as to political power and economic control, it is far wide of the truth as to administration of internal justice among our forty-eight state legal systems. Indeed, today in respect of our legal administrations we have not achieved a much "more perfect union" than that of the colonies under the Articles of Confederation. We have so far as I can ascertain the most localized and conflicting system of any country which presents the external appearance of nationhood.[22]

Perhaps, he suggested, a basic reason for this lamentable situation was the circumstance that neither Congress nor the Supreme Court had been alerted to the potential utility of the full faith and credit clause. Because there was no federal legislative or administrative program that established a policy of national responsibility for the creation of a better integrated legal system, men who became Supreme Court justices were not exposed to the kind of personal experience that would sensitize them to the need and opportunity for positive leadership by the Supreme Court in this field.[23] "The federalism of the faith and credit clause," he pointed out, "depends generally on private advocacy, not always supported by the best research and understanding, and often finds the perception of the Justices unsharpened and their perspective uninformed by any extensive experience or investigation of this subject."[24] As a consequence, it was inevitably—but most regrettably—true that members of the Court had to fall back upon mere personal predilections in attempting to cope with the constitutional problems that faced them under this clause:

> Certainly the personal preferences of the Justices among the conflicting state policies is not a permissible basis of determining which shall prevail in a case. But only a singularly balanced mind could weigh relative state interests in such subject matter except by resort to what are likely to be strong preferences in sociology, economics, governmental theory, and politics. There are no judicial standards of valuation of such imponderables.[25]

Jackson's own personal preference, which he proffered in the raiment of the intent of the fathers of the Constitution, was nothing less than a national legal system. The time might be ripe, he thought, "to utilize this clause to realize its purpose as a principle of order in our federated

[21] *Ibid.*, p. 35.

[22] *Ibid.*, p. 31.

[23] "It seems easier," he said, "for the Court to put aside parochialism and to think in terms of a national economy or of a national social welfare than to think in terms of a truly national legal system." *Ibid.*, pp. 58-59.

[24] *Ibid.*, p. 59.

[25] *Ibid.*, p. 49.

legal systems."[26] Indeed, "the full faith and credit clause is the foundation of any hope we may have for a truly national system of justice."[27] There were, as Jackson saw it, three alternatives open to the Court. The first was "for us to leave choice of law in all cases to the local policy of the state."[28] This was obviously unacceptable, both to him and to the rest of the Court. "A second course," he suggested, "is for us to adopt no rule, permit a good deal of overlapping and confusion, but interfere now and then without imparting to the bar any reason by which the one or the other course is to be guided or predicted. This seems to me," he added, "about where our present decisions leave us."[29] The third, and the only desirable course, would be for the Court to use the clause as a positive instrument, and "at least to mark out reasonably narrow limits of permissible variation in areas where there is confusion"[30] in choice-of-law questions.

What Jackson meant was that the Supreme Court should insist upon *full* faith and credit: that the courts of all the states must, on pain of reversal by the United States Supreme Court, accept as the basis for their decisions the relevant and prior judicial decisions of any of the states. At least, such out-of-state decisions should be entitled to the same respect by any state as it would accord to the corresponding decisions of its own courts. But how doing this would lead to the "establishment of a more unified system of law" is by no means self-evident, nor does Jackson explain how and why such a result would be the necessary consequence of having the Supreme Court enforce the rule that the might of the priority of decision makes for right in the resolution of policy conflicts among the states.

D. *EX PARTE* DIVORCE

ESTIN V. ESTIN
334 U.S. 541, 553 (June 7, 1948)

From a legal point of view, it might be said that the Court's pragmatic solution in this case reflected the complexity of the reciprocal full faith and credit problems with which it was confronted. A New York court granted a separation decree, with alimony, to an abandoned wife. The husband appeared by counsel, to defend the suit, but he lost. He then went to Nevada, where he was granted an absolute divorce that his wife

---

[26] *Ibid.*, p. 45.
[27] *Ibid.*, pp. 59-60.
[28] *Ibid.*, p. 46.
[29] *Idem.*
[30] *Ibid.*, p. 47.

did not contest. Thus, two separate full faith and credit problems were presented: (1) Should Nevada have granted full faith and credit to the New York decree of separation? (2) Should New York have granted full faith and credit to the Nevada decree of divorce? Douglas, writing for a majority of seven, said that because the answer to the first question was "yes," the answer to the second question was a qualified "no." The Court did not decide that the Nevada divorce was invalid; but it did decide that to the extent that the decrees were incompatible, the earlier New York decree, granting alimony, "survived" the Nevada decree. A majority of the justices upheld the interests of the wife; and only the two most economically conservative members of the Court, Frankfurter and Jackson, voted to relieve the ex-husband of the obligation to pay alimony to his former spouse.

Frankfurter dissented, because of doubts whether the New York courts had ruled that, as a matter of New York law, an alimony award incident to a contested separation action survived *any ex parte* divorce decree—including such a decree by a New York court—or merely out-of-state decrees. He thought that the first position would be compatible with the first *Williams* decision, but that the second would not. Jackson's view, which constituted a complete volte-face from his position in the *Williams* decisions, was that the Nevada decree was either all good or all bad. Because the Court refused to overrule the first *Williams* decision, and, therefore, upheld the validity of the Nevada decree, Jackson now argued that the Nevada decree should be given full faith and credit by New York. Appropriately enough, since he had changed his tune, Jackson made corresponding changes in the lyrics, substituting now an emphasis upon the mobility of America's "nomadic" society in place of the feudal notion of belonging to the land with which he had embellished his *Williams'* dissent just a few years earlier.

MR. JUSTICE JACKSON, *dissenting*.

If there is one thing that the people are entitled to expect from their lawmakers, it is rules of law that will enable individuals to tell whether they are married and, if so, to whom. Today many people who have simply lived in more than one state do not know, and the most learned lawyer cannot advise them with any confidence. The uncertainties that result are not merely technical, nor are they trivial; they affect fundamental rights and relations such as the lawfulness of their cohabitation, their children's legitimacy, their title to property, and even whether they are law-abiding persons or criminals. In a society as mobile and nomadic as ours, such uncertainties affect large numbers of people and create a social problem of some magnitude. It is therefore important that, whatever we do, we shall not add to the confusion. I think that this decision does just that.

These parties lived together in New York State during their entire married life. Courts of that State granted judgment of separation, with award of alimony to the wife, in October 1943. Three months later the husband journeyed to Nevada and in three more months began a divorce action. No process was served on the wife in Nevada; she was put on notice only by constructive service through publication in New York. Notified thus of what was going on, she was put to this choice: to go to Nevada and fight a battle, hopeless under Nevada laws, to keep her New York judgment, or to do nothing. She did nothing, and the Nevada court granted the husband a divorce without requiring payment of alimony.

Now the question is whether the New York judgment of separation or the Nevada judgment of divorce controls the present obligaton to pay alimony. The New York judgment of separation is based on the premises that the parties remain husband and wife, though estranged, and hence the obligation of support, incident to marriage, continues. The Nevada decree is based on the contrary premise that the marriage no longer exists and so obligations dependent on it have ceased.

The Court reaches the Solomon-like conclusion that the Nevada decree is half good and half bad under the full faith and credit clause. It is good to free the husband from the marriage; it is not good to free him from its incidental obligations. Assuming the judgment to be one which the Constitution requires to be recognized at all, I do not see how we can square this decision with the command that it be given *full* faith and credit. For reasons which I stated in dissenting in *Williams* v. *North Carolina*, 317 U.S. 287, I would not give standing under the clause to constructive service divorces obtained on short residence. But if we are to hold this divorce good, I do not see how it can be less good than a divorce would be if rendered by the courts of New York.

As I understand New York law, if, after a decree of separation and alimony, the husband had obtained a New York divorce against his wife, it would terminate her right to alimony. If the Nevada judgment is to have *full* faith and credit, I think it must have the same effect that a similar New York decree would have. I do not see how we can hold that it must be accepted for some purposes and not for others, that he is free of his former marriage but still may be jailed, as he may in New York, for not paying the maintenance of a woman whom the Court is compelled to consider as no longer his wife.

E. *EX PARTE* MARRIAGE

HERMOINE P. RICE V. LILLIAN P. RICE
336 U.S. 674, 676 (April 18, 1949)

The Court vacillated once again in this case that involved two widows who both claimed rights to the same estate. Both the former majority and the two dissenters in *Estin* were reshuffled in the process of reaching a decision; the new majority included Murphy (who alone, among the justices, remained consistently anti-divorce no matter what the context), Burton, Reed, and Vinson, together with Frankfurter. Black, Douglas, and Rutledge dissented without opinion, but their votes at least had the same effect as in the second *Williams* decision, when they sought to uphold the extraterritorial validity of a Nevada divorce decree. So the majority favored Lillian, the wife back home, while the three libertarians supported the claims of the more recent wife, Hermoine; and the *per curiam* opinion of the Court pointed out that it was merely following the second *Williams* decision in upholding Connecticut's right to challenge, as it had, the bona fides of Rice's divorce, in view of the fact that a Connecticut trial judge had found, with ample support in the evidence, that Rice never had established a domicile in Nevada.

Jackson took advantage of the opportunity to ridicule his brethren, and their somewhat less than consistent pattern of decisions in regard to *ex parte* divorce and marriage. His own view, as he stated it, was that the Court ought to follow the path charted by his own dissent in the first *Williams* decision; but if the majority were not (as they did not seem to be) prepared to join him in a policy of neither faith nor credit for *ex parte* divorces, then there was no point in the Court's undertaking to decide such cases as this one, because determination of domicile on a particular set of facts presented the Court with no legal or policy problem appropriate for it to resolve. The first position should have led him to join the majority in this decision; and the second to abstain from participation expressing himself, perhaps, as *dubitante,* as his colleague Frankfurter did from time to time. Instead, Jackson said that if everybody else was going to involve himself in the inappropriate task of weighing the evidence on the mere fact question of domicile, then he would also. On that basis, he came to the apparently unique conclusion that there was nothing wrong with Rice's Nevada domicile. It was on this petulant tone, and dubious basis, that Jackson opted for Hermoine, and went into dissent in the company of the three libertarians.[31] But as in *Estin,* the effect of Jackson's vote was to uphold the constitutional command of *full* faith and credit.

MR. JUSTICE JACKSON, dissenting.

Since this case involves only reappraisal of evidence, and we decline to do that, it is hard to see a reason for granting certiorari unless it was to record in our reports an example of the manner in which, in the law of domestic relations, "confusion now hath made his masterpiece." The question is whether property owned

---

[31] After having completed a searching lawyerlike analysis of Jackson's opinions in this and in a closely related policy sector, a Stanford University law professor concluded: "Mr. Justice Jackson appears to have found these problems interesting, but not to have contributed

in Connecticut by one who has obtained a Nevada divorce and remarried in that State can be taken from his acting widow and bestowed upon the woman she superseded. The facts are these:

After twenty years of married life in Connecticut with Lillian, Rice arrived at Reno, Nevada, on March 23, 1944, and began a divorce action on May 5. The complaint and process were handed to Lillian at her home in Connecticut. She was not served with process in Nevada. She was teaching school in Connecticut, never had lived in Nevada, and did not appear personally or by attorney in the action, which she claims was a surprise maneuver on the part of Rice.

Rice had rented a furnished room in Reno and testified that he intended to remain there "indefinitely." He was awarded a divorce from Lillian on June 13 and wired Hermoine, who arrived there on July 3. They were immediately married and never returned to Connecticut. They retained the room in Reno, which they occupied from time to time, and both obtained war employment in California where six months later Rice died.

Lillian brought an action in Connecticut to have herself declared his widow insofar as Connecticut real estate was concerned. The court reviewed the evidence as to whether Rice established a good faith domicile in Nevada and held that he had not and was not entitled to maintain an action there for divorce. The question comes here as to whether this holding by Connecticut courts gave full faith and credit to the Nevada decree of divorce as required by the Constitution.

In *Williams* v. *North Carolina,* 317 U.S. 287, this Court rode roughshod over the precedents and held that a state court, without personal service of process on the defendant, can on short residence grant a divorce which is valid and entitled to faith and credit in all states. If Rice could have relied on that pronouncement, his divorce from Lillian and his marriage to Hermoine would be without legal flaw, and the latter's widowhood clear.

But in the second case of *Williams* v. *North Carolina,* 325 U.S. 226, the Court held that jurisdictional findings by the Nevada court in such a case do not preclude reexamination and a different conclusion on the part of another state. And in *Estin* v. *Estin,* 334 U.S. 541, the Court held that the second state is free to arrive at its own determination as to plaintiff's domicile in determining property rights, even though required, under the *Williams* cases or either of them, to recognize the divorce judgment as terminating the marriage. Now comes *Rice* v. *Rice* to demonstrate the consequences of these doctrines.

Congress, as it is empowered to do by the Full Faith and Credit Clause of the Constitution, has enacted that judgments "shall have such faith and credit given to them in every court within the United States, as they have by law or usage in

significantly to their analysis or solution." John R. McDonough, Jr., "Mr. Justice Jackson and Full Faith and Credit to Divorce Decrees: A Critique," *Columbia Law Review,* LVI (1956), 886.

the courts of the state from whence the said records are or shall be taken." 1 Stat. 122. There is no doubt that under the law and usage of Nevada, Hermoine was wife and widow of Rice, and on its face the statute would seem to require that she be recognized as such elsewhere. But things sometimes are not what they seem.

In order to have anything which courts of the Western World recognize as a judgment, except in an action *in rem*, it is necessary that the rendering court have within its power both the party who seeks relief and the one against whom relief is sought.

This Court, while acknowledging that personal service of process on the defendant ordinarily is necessary to a valid judgment in a personal action, held in the first *Williams* case that a state could bring a nonresident defendant within its power merely by publication or out-of-state service of its summons. It overruled former decisions to introduce what it has aptly characterized in *Sherrer* v. *Sherrer*, 334 U.S. 343, 349 n. 11, and 356, as the *"ex parte* divorce." To me *ex parte* divorce is a concept as perverse and unrealistic as an *ex parte* marriage. The vice of the system sanctioned in *Williams* v. *North Carolina*, 317 U.S. 287, is that one of the parties may leave the state where both for years have made their home, seek a forum of his choice, and pretty much on his own terms alter the pattern of two lives without affording the other even a decent chance to be heard—as this case illustrates. Lillian either had to leave her teaching and means of support to follow her husband two thousand miles from any place where she ever had lived, or let her marriage go by default. If she chose to follow and contest under Nevada law, she had little real chance to succeed. But this Court had called this due process of law for Lillian.

Hermoine relied on the Nevada court, which did only what this Court authorized it to do—grant an *ex parte* divorce. She married a man whom this Court says Nevada had a right to make free by such process. She had every right to believe her marriage complete and valid in all places and for all purposes. Certainly under the law of Nevada where she continued to reside it was valid, and this Court had held the out-of-state service sufficient to empower Nevada to take jurisdiction of Lillian for the purpose of dissolving her marriage. But now we say that Connecticut may find that Rice was not sufficiently domiciled in Nevada to give that State power to act on his complaint. This presents a study in contrasts.

We have said that Nevada does have power to dissolve the marriage of a woman who never was there in her life, never invoked its law or its courts, did not submit herself to its jurisdiction, refused to answer its summons, and took no benefits from its judgments.

On the other hand, we say that courts of any state may find that Nevada does not get power to dissolve the marriage of a man who went to that State and never came back, who invoked its law, went into its court and submitted himself to its jurisdiction, testified he was domiciled there, and during the rest of his life held quarters within that State.

But even under the two *Williams* cases, a quick Nevada divorce was either conclusive (first *Williams* case) or vulnerable (second *Williams* case) in its entirety. However, in addition to the rights grouped under the term *consortium,* which are terminated by divorce, there are subsidiary rights of a property nature such as support, alimony, distributive interests in personalty, dower, and inheritance. These presented difficulties in case of the divorce on constructive service of process on a nonresident dependent in which there was no real chance to defend. So the Court improvised the concept of "divisible" divorce, *Estin* v. *Estin,* 334 U.S. 541, 549, a divorce good to end a marriage but invalid to affect dependent property rights.

I think that the judgment of the Connecticut court, but for the first *Williams* case and its progeny, might properly have held that the *Rice* divorce decree was void for every purpose because it was rendered by a state court which never obtained jurisdiction of the nonresident defendant and which had no power to reach into another state and summon her before it.

But if we adhere to the holdings that the Nevada court had power over her for the purpose of blasting her marriage and opening the way to a successor, I do not see the justice of inventing a compensating confusion in the device of a divisible divorce by which the parties are half-bound and half-free and which permits Rice to have a wife who cannot become his widow and to leave a widow who was no longer his wife. Lillian's standing as the relict of Rice is invulnerable, while her standing as his wife could be blasted by a Nevada decree in an action to which she did not need to even become a party.

This Court is not responsible for all the contradictions and conflicts resulting from our federal system or from our crazy quilt of divorce laws, but we are certainly compounding those difficulties by repudiating the usual requirements of procedural due process in divorce cases and compensating for it by repudiating the Full Faith and Credit Clause. My dissenting views in the *Williams* and *Estin* cases would lead me to affirm the judgment below, because I believe this divorce was always and in all places invalid on due process grounds for want of jurisdiction of the defendant. However, if it was valid on that ground and nothing but a review of the evidence of domicile by the second state court is involved, we should not grant writs in this class of cases; but if I am to review the evidence here, I think the Nevada court's finding of jurisdiction was based on substantial evidence of domicile, not overcome by any new evidence before the Connecticut court, and the Nevada judgment should be given full faith and credit as the Congress has commanded.[32]

[32] Jackson's panoply of mutually inconsistent alternative outcomes is reminiscent of common law pleading of ancient vintage. Perhaps the classic parody is "the famous 'Codd's Puzzle,' in which Codd, counsel for a defendant charged with stealing a duck, pleaded (1) that his client had bought the bird; (2) that he had found it; (3) that it had flown into his garden; (4) that its owner had made him a present of it; (5) that some person or persons

F. FORUM SHOPPING

MILES V. ILLINOIS CENTRAL RAILROAD CORPORATION
315 U.S. 698, 705 (March 30, 1942)

The late Paul H. Miles, an employee of the Illinois Central Railroad, had a fatal on-the-job accident in Memphis. The Federal Employers Liability Act provided no direct compensation to his widow Jessie for her loss of her husband, but it did preclude for the railroad certain common law defenses, upon which employers had been wont to rely since the early days of the industrial revolution, and grant her the right to bring a lawsuit for damages in any federal or a state court that might have jurisdiction over the defendant railroad. She chose to bring suit in St. Louis, across the river and a bit upstream from her own residence and the locale of her husband's misfortune. The railroad chose to make its principal defense, however, in the Tennessee, rather than Missouri, state courts; and it induced a trial court to issue a temporary injunction, which was made permanent by the Tennessee Court of Appeals, to forbid her to press her in-state cause of action in an out-of-state forum. The Tennessee Supreme Court denied Mrs. Miles' appeal, so she brought it to the United States Supreme Court, which divided into two opposing groups of four justices each, with Jackson—again, the loner—casting the decisive vote in her behalf.

Reed's opinion of the Court, in which Douglas, Black, and Murphy joined, noted that "The grounds for the injunction were the inconvenience and expense to the Illinois Central of taking its Memphis employees to St. Louis, and the resulting burden upon *interstate commerce.*" (Emphasis added.) This finding of the trial judge was expressly abandoned, by the Illinois Central, upon appeal. But the Supreme Court majority was no more impressed by the burden of the suit upon the railroad itself. Because of the supremacy clause of the Constitution, the Tennessee policy against vexatious suits must yield, said Reed, to the explicit requirements of the Federal Employers Liability Act. Moreover, the statute permitted suit in either a federal or a state court, wherever the rail carrier "is doing substantial business"; and there was no question that this was true of Illinois Central's operations in Missouri. Therefore, "The Missouri court

---

unknown had stuffed it into his pocket while he was asleep; (6) that there had never been any duck in existence at any material time; and (7) that his client would if necessary make a full confession. For one version of this old story see Theo Ruoff in 30 *Aust. L. J.* 512 (1957); for a slightly different version, Megarry, *Miscellany-at-law* 46 (revised imp. 1956)." Anthony R. Blackshield, " 'Fundamental Rights' and the Institutional Viability of the Indian Supreme Court," *Journal of the Indian Law Institute,* VIII (1966), 146n. 19.

here involved must permit this litigation. To deny citizens from other states, suitors under F.E.L.A., access to its courts would, if it permitted access to its own citizens, violate the Privileges and Immunities Clause" (Article IV, Section 2) of the Constitution. (The Full Faith and Credit Clause is Section 1 of that same article).

Frankfurter's dissent, with which Stone, Roberts, and Byrnes agreed, was a strong plea for states' rights, based upon a lengthy excursion into the legislative history of the federal statutes of 1908 and 1910. From these he concluded that Congress had intended that the states *could*, not that they *had to*, exercise concurrent jurisdiction with federal courts in F.E.L.A. claims. What was more, Tennessee very properly was following precedent that went back a full third of a millenium: "The power invoked by Tennessee in this case was a familiar head of equity jurisdiction long before the Constitution. Injunctions by the [English] chancellor against suits in other courts go back to at least the late sixteenth century."

The blatant legal scholasticism indulged in by both the opinion of the Court and the dissent provided Jackson with the sort of opportunity in which he delighted, to cut candidly through the legal impedimenta and focus upon the policy choices which the case presented.

MR. JUSTICE JACKSON, *concurring*:

I agree with the conclusion and, with exceptions stated herein, with the opinion of MR. JUSTICE REED, though I am not able to sublimate the conflict that underlies this case to the level of either of the conflicting opinions. Realistically considered, the issue is earthy and unprincipled. So viewed, the real issue is whether a plaintiff with a cause of action under the Federal Employers' Liability Act may go shopping for a judge or a jury believed to be more favorable than he would find in his home forum. An advantage which it is hoped will be reflected in a judgment is what makes plaintiffs leave home and incur burdens of expense and inconvenience that would be regarded as oppressive if forced upon them. And that is what makes railroads seek injunctions such as this one.

The judiciary has never favored this sort of shopping for a forum. It has sought to protect its own good name as well as to protect defendants by injunctions against the practice of seeking out soft spots in the judicial system in which to bring particular kinds of litigation. But the judges, with lawyerly indirection, have not avowed the interest of the judiciary in orderly resort to the courts as a basis for their decision, and have cast their protective doctrines in terms of sheltering defendants against vexatious and harassing suits. This judicial treatment of the subject of venue leads Congress and the parties to think of the choice of a forum as a private matter between litigants, and in cases like the present obscures the public interest in venue practices behind a rather fantastic fiction that a widow is harassing the Illinois Central Railroad. If Congress had left us free to consult the ultimate public interest in orderly resort to the judicial system, I should agree with MR. JUSTICE FRANKFURTER's conclusion. But the plaintiffs say that they go shopping, not by leave of the courts themselves, but by the authority of Congress. Whether the Congress has granted such latitude is our question.

Unless there is some hidden meaning in the language Congress has employed, the injured workman or his surviving dependents may choose from the entire territory served by the railroad any place in which to sue, and in which to choose either a federal or a state court of which to ask his remedy. There is nothing which requires a plaintiff to whom such a choice is given to exercise it in a self-denying or large-hearted manner. There is nothing to restrain use of that privilege, as all choices of tribunal are commonly used by all plaintiffs to get away from judges who are considered to be unsympathetic, and to get before those who are considered more favorable; to get away from juries thought to be small-minded in the matter of verdicts, and to get to those thought to be generous; to escape courts whose procedures are burdensome to the plaintiff, and to seek out courts whose procedures make the going easy.

That such a privilege puts a burden on interstate commerce may well be admitted, but Congress has the power to burden. The Federal Employers' Liability Act itself leaves interstate commerce under the burden of a medieval system of compensating the injured railroad worker or his survivors. He is not given a remedy, but only a lawsuit. It is well understood that in most cases he will be unable to pursue that except by splitting his speculative prospects with a lawyer. The functioning of this backward system of dealing with industrial accidents in interstate commerce burdens it with perhaps two dollars of judgment for every dollar that actually reaches those who have been damaged, and it leaves the burden of many injuries to be borne by them utterly uncompensated. Such being the major burden under which the workmen and the industry must function, I see no reason to believe that Congress could not have intended the relatively minor additional burden to interstate commerce from loading the dice a little in favor of the workman in the matter of venue. It seems more probable that Congress intended to give the disadvantaged workman some leverage in the choice of venue, than that it intended to leave him in a position where the railroad could force him to try one lawsuit at home to find out whether he would be allowed to try his principal lawsuit elsewhere. This latter would be a frequent result if we upheld the contention made in this case. . . . I think, therefore, that the petitioner had a right to resort to the Missouri court under the circumstances of this case for her remedy.

I do not, however, agree with the statement in MR. JUSTICE REED's opinion that "the Missouri court here involved must permit this litigation." It is very doubtful if any requirement can be spelled out of the Federal Constitution that a state must furnish a forum for a nonresident plaintiff and a foreign corporation to fight out issues imported from another state where the cause of action arose. It seems unnecessary to decide now whether this litigation could be imposed on the Missouri court, for it appears to have embraced the litigation. Even if Missouri, by reason of its control of its own courts might refuse to open them to such a case, it does not follow that another state may close Missouri's courts to one with a federal cause of action. If Missouri elects to entertain the case, the courts of no other state can obstruct or prevent its exercise of jurisdiction as conferred by the federal statute or its right to obtain evidence and to distribute the proceeds, if any, in accordance with the Federal Employers' Liability Act. I therefore favor reversal.

G. *HABEAS CONVICTUS*

BROWN V. ALLEN
344 U.S. 443, 533 (February 9, 1953)

This decision concerned three cases that were grouped for common disposition. All involved Negroes who had been convicted by North Carolina courts of serious crimes, for which they had been sentenced to death. In each case, the Supreme Court had previously refused to review the judgments of the state courts on direct appeal, that is, petition for certiorari, and the defendants (petitioners for the writ of habeas corpus in the present proceedings) then had attempted collaterally to attack in a federal district court the judgments of their conviction. All of the justices except Jackson reached the merits of the substantive issue whether these petitioners had been denied, as they claimed, due process of law or equal protection of the laws to which they were entitled under the Fourteenth Amendment.

The Court, however, focused upon another question, which apparently explains why it agreed to review these cases. The Court's interest was not in whether these petitioners were guilty of the crimes of which they had been convicted, nor even in whether they had been denied their constitutional rights; the Court's interest was in its supervisory relationship over lower federal courts, and the manner in which decisions of state courts should be subject to review in the *lower* federal courts.

From this perspective, there were two relevant questions:

A. What weight, if any, should be given to a previous denial of certiorari by the Supreme Court on direct review, by a federal district court ruling upon a subsequent habeas corpus application?

B. In view of the circumstance that the federal district judge in each of these cases did weigh, in coming to his decision to deny the writs, the Supreme Court's previous denials of certiorari in the cases of these petitioners, was this error? If so, should the Supreme Court reverse and remand for reconsideration by the federal district court?

A majority of five members of the Court agreed that the answer to Question A was "None." These justices did not control the Court's decision, however, because a different majority of six justices were of the opinion that either (a) no error had been committed; or (b) only a harmless error had been committed by the federal district court; and because these six justices agreed that the judgments of the lower federal courts, denying the writ, should be affirmed, this was the effective decision, so far as the petitioners were concerned. But as far as federal judges and state prisoners generally were concerned, the significant ruling was the answer to Question A, which was supplied by the majority of a majority of the Court (that is, the minority of three) who wrote the dissenting opinions in *Brown* v. *Allen!*

There may be confusion here, but there is no paradox. The Court was splintered into four different groups for purposes of decision making in this case. One group of three justices (Reed, Vinson, and Minton), a majority of the Question B majority, thought that a previous denial of certiorari by the Court did mean something (although not much); on the other hand, because they were bound by a contrary decision of a majority of other members of the Court on this point, and assuming that error had been committed by the federal district court (with whom these three justices agreed), it was a harmless error, that had not really prejudiced the rights of these petitioners. Another group of three justices (Frankfurter, Black, and Douglas), a majority of the Question A majority, thought that a previous denial of certiorari meant nothing relevant to the decision of a federal district court on an application for habeas corpus; error had been committed, and it was not a harmless error. On the merits of substantive issues, these petitioners appeared to have been deprived of their constitutional rights. Burton and Clark were the two voters who converted these conflicting minority groups of justices into the differing majorities. These two justices agreed with Frankfurter, Black, and Douglas that denial of certiorari is legally meaningless; but they also agreed with Reed, Minton, and Vinson that the federal district court's misunderstanding and, therefore, disregard of this useful legal fiction was harmless error.

Jackson was typically in a group all by himself. He thought that the denial of certiorari means a lot; consequently, no error had been committed by the federal district court;[33] and, therefore, the decisions of the lower federal courts, dismissing the applications for the writ, were properly affirmed. His separate concurrence reflects the difference in emphasis that Jackson wanted to give in defining the extent to which the lower federal courts should undertake to review the judgments of state courts in criminal cases. None of the other members of the Court appeared to be particularly disturbed by the lack of deference for state courts implicit in the federal habeas corpus procedure, but Jackson made this point the central theme of his opinion.

MR. JUSTICE JACKSON, *concurring in the result.*

Controversy as to the undiscriminating use of the writ of habeas corpus by federal judges to set aside state court convictions is traceable to three principal causes: (1) this Court's use of the generality of the Fourteenth Amendment to subject state courts to increasing federal control, especially in the criminal law field; (2) *ad hoc* determination of due process of law issues by personal notions of justice instead of by known rules of law; and (3) the breakdown of procedural safeguards against abuse of the writ.

1. In 1867, Congress authorized federal courts to issue writs of habeas corpus to prisoners "in custody in violation of the Constitution or laws or treaties of the United States." At that time, the writ was not available here nor in England to challenge any sentence imposed by a court of competent jurisdiction. The historic purpose of the writ has been to relieve detention by executive authorities without judicial trial. It might have been expected that if Congress intended a reversal of this traditional concept of habeas corpus it would have said so. However, this one sentence in the Act eventually was construed as authority for federal judges to entertain collateral attacks on state court criminal judgments. Whatever its justification, it created potentialities for conflict certain to lead to the antagonisms we have now, unless the power given to federal judges were responsibly used according to lawyerly procedures and with genuine respect for state court fact finding.

But, once established, this jurisdiction obviously would grow with each expansion of the substantive grounds for habeas corpus. The generalities of the Fourteenth Amendment are so indeterminate as to what state actions are forbidden that this Court has found it a ready instrument, in one field or another, to magnify federal, and incidentally its own, authority over the states. The expansion now has reached a point where any state court conviction, disapproved by

---

33 A clue to Jackson's attitudes on the merits of the defendants' guilt, which he alone purported not to reach, is perhaps suggested by his choice of the epithet "convicts" which he used no less than half a dozen times (in addition to the less pejorative term "prisoners") to describe habeas corpus petitioners of federal district courts.

a majority of this Court, thereby becomes unconstitutional and subject to nullifi-
cation by habeas corpus.

This might not be so demoralizing if state judges could anticipate, and so
comply with, this Court's due process requirements or ascertain any standards to
which this Court will adhere in prescribing them. But they cannot. Of course, considerable uncertainty is inherent in decisional law which, in changing times,
purports to interpret implications of constitutional provisions so cryptic and vagrant. How much obscurity is inevitable will be a matter of opinion. However,
in considering a remedy for habeas corpus problems, it is prudent to assume that
the scope and reach of the Fourteenth Amendment will continue to be unknown
and unknowable, that what seems established by one decision is apt to be unsettled
by another, and that its interpretation will be more or less swayed by contemporary intellectual fashions and political currents.

We may look upon this unstable prospect complacently, but state judges
cannot. They are not only being gradually subordinated to the federal judiciary
but federal courts have declared that state judicial and other officers are personally liable to federal prosecution and to civil suit by convicts if they fail to carry
out this Court's constitutional doctrines.

2. Rightly or wrongly, the belief is widely held by the practicing profession
that this Court no longer respects impersonal rules of law but is guided in these
matters by personal impressions which from time to time may be shared by a majority of Justices. Whatever has been intended, this Court also has generated an
impression in much of the judiciary that regard for precedents and authorities
is obsolete, that words no longer mean what they have always meant to the profession, that the law knows no fixed principles.

A manifestation of this is seen in the diminishing respect shown for state
court adjudications of fact. Of course, this Court never has considered itself foreclosed by a state court's decision as to the facts when that determination results
in alleged denial of a federal right. But captious use of this power was restrained
by observance of a rule, elementary in all appellate procedure, that the findings of
fact on a trial are to be accepted by an appellate court in absence of clear showing
of error. The trial court, seeing the demeanor of witnesses, hearing the parties,
giving to each case far more time than an appellate court can give, is in a better
position to unravel disputes of fact than is an appellate court on a printed tran-
script. Recent decisions avow no candid alteration of these rules, but revision of
state fact finding has grown by emphasis, and respect for it has withered by disregard.

3. The fact that the substantive law of due process is and probably must remain so vague and unsettled as to invite farfetched or borderline petitions make it
important to adhere to procedures which enable courts readily to distinguish a
probable constitutional grievance from a convict's mere gamble on persuading
some indulgent judge to let him out of jail. Instead, this Court has sanctioned pro-

gressive trivialization of the writ until floods of stale, frivolous and repetitious petitions inundate the docket of the lower courts and swell our own. Judged by our own disposition of habeas corpus matters, they have, as a class, become peculiarly undeserving. It must prejudice the occasional meritorious application to be buried in a flood of worthless ones. He who must search a haystack for a needle is likely to end up with the attitude that the needle is not worth the search. Nor is it any answer to say that few of these petitions in any court really result in the discharge of the petitioner. That is the condemnation of the procedure which has encouraged frivolous cases. In this multiplicity of worthless cases, states are compelled to default or to defend the integrity of their judges and their official records, sometimes concerning trials or pleas that were closed many years ago. State Attorneys General recently have come habitually to ignore these proceedings, responding only when specially requested and sometimes not then. Some state courts have wearied of our repeated demands upon them and have declined to further elucidate grounds for their decisions. The assembled Chief Justices of the highest courts of the states have taken the unusual step of condemning the present practice by resolution. . . .

Conflict with state courts is the inevitable result of giving the convict a virtual new trial before a federal court sitting without a jury. Whenever decisions of one court are reviewed by another, a percentage of them are reversed. That reflects a difference in outlook normally found between personnel comprising different courts.[34] However, reversal by a higher court is not proof that justice is thereby better done. There is no doubt that if there were a super-Supreme Court, a substantial proportion of our reversals of state courts would also be reversed. We are not final because we are infallible, but we are infallible only because we are final. . . .

Since the Constitution and laws made pursuant to it are the supreme law and since the supremacy and uniformity of federal law are attainable only by a centralized source of authority, denial by a state of a claimed federal right must give some access to the federal judicial system. But federal interference with state administration of its criminal law should not be premature and should not occur where it is not needed. Therefore, we have ruled that a state convict must exhaust all remedies which the state affords for his alleged grievance before he can take it to any federal court by habeas corpus.

The states all allow some appeal from a judgment of conviction which permits review of any question of law, state or federal, raised upon the record. No state is obliged to furnish multiple remedies for the same grievance. Most states, and with good reason, will not suffer a collateral attack such as habeas corpus to

[34] "An appeal, Hinnissy," as Finley Peter Dunne once had Mr. Dooley remark, "is where ye ask wan coort to show its contempt f'r another coort." "The Law's Delays" in *Mr. Dooley on the Choice of Law,* ed. Edward J. Bander (Charlottesville, Virginia: The Michie Company, 1963), p. 42. [Ed.]

be used as a substitute for or duplication of the appeal. A state properly may deny habeas corpus to raise either state or federal issues that were or could have been considered on appeal. Such restriction by the state should be respected by federal courts.

Assuming that a federal question not reachable on appeal is properly presented by habeas corpus and decided adversely by the highest competent court of the state, should the prisoner then come to this Court and ask us to review the record by certiorari or should he go to the district court and institute a new federal habeas corpus proceeding? *Darr* v. *Burford,* 339 U.S. 200 [1950], as I understand it, held that in these circumstances the prisoner must apply to this Court for certiorari before he can go to any other federal court, because only by so doing could he exhaust his state remedy. Whatever one may think of that result, it does not seem logical to support it by asserting that this Court's certiorari power is any part of a state's remedy. An authority outside of the state imposes a duty upon the state to turn the case over to it, in a proceeding which makes the state virtually a defendant. To say that our command to certify the case to us is a state remedy is to indulge in fiction, and the difficulty with fictions is that those they are most apt to mislead are those who proclaim them.

But now it is proposed to neutralize the artificiality of the process and counterbalance the fiction that our certiorari is a state remedy by holding that this step which the prisoner must take means nothing to him or the state when it fails, as in most cases it does.

The Court is not quite of one mind on the subject. Some say denial means nothing, others say it means nothing much. Realistically, the first position is untenable and the second is unintelligible. How can we say that the prisoner must present his case to us and at the same time say that what we do with it means nothing to anybody. We might conceivably take either position but not, rationally, both, for the two will not only burden our own docket and harass the state authorities but it makes a prisoner's legitimate quest for federal justice an endurance contest.

True, neither those outside of the Court, nor on many occasions those inside of it, know just what reasons led six Justices to withhold consent to a certiorari. But all know that a majority, larger than can be mustered for a good many decisions, has found reason for not reviewing the case here. Because no one knows all that a denial means, does it mean that it means nothing? Perhaps the profession could accept denial as meaningless before the custom was introduced of noting dissents from them. Lawyers and lower judges will not readily believe that Justices of this Court are taking the trouble to signal a meaningless division of opinion about a meaningless act. It is just one of the facts of life that today every lower court does attach importance to denials and to presence or absence of dissents from denials, as judicial opinions and lawyer's arguments show.

The fatal sentence that in real life writes *finis* to many causes cannot in legal theory be a complete blank. I can see order in the confusion as to its meaning only by distinguishing its significance under the doctrine of *stare decisis*, from its effect under the doctrine of *res judicata*. I agree that, as *stare decisis*, denial of certiorari should be given no significance whatever. It creates no precedent and approves no statement of principle entitled to weight in any other case. But, for the case in which certiorari is denied, its minimum meaning is that this Court allows the judgment below to stand with whatever consequences it may have upon the litigants involved under the doctrine of *res judicata* as applied either by state or federal courts. . . . But call it *res judicata* or what one will, courts ought not to be obliged to allow a convict to litigate again and again exactly the same question on the same evidence. Nor is there any good reason why an identical contention rejected by a higher court should be reviewed on the same facts in a lower one.

The chief objection to giving this limited finality to our denial of certiorari is that we pass upon these writs of habeas corpus so casually or upon grounds so unrelated to their merits that our decision should not have the weight of finality. No very close personal consideration can be given by each Justice to such a multiplicity of these petitions as we have had and, as a class, they are so frivolous, so meaningless, and often so unintelligible that this worthlessness of the class discredits each individual application. If this deluge were reduced by observance of procedural safeguards to manageable proportions so that it would be possible to examine the cases with some care and to hear those that show merit, I think this objection would largely disappear. The fact is that superficial consideration of these cases is the inevitable result of depreciation of the writ. The writ has no enemies so deadly as those who sanction the abuse of it, whatever their intent.

If a state is really obtaining conviction by laws or procedures which violate the Federal Constitution, it is always a serious wrong, not only to a particular convict, but to federal law. It is not probable that six Justices would pass up a case which intelligibly presented this situation. But an examination of these petitions will show that few of them, tested by any rational rules of pleading, actually raise any question of law on which the state court has differed from the understanding prevailing in this Court. The point on which we are urged to overrule state courts almost invariably is in their appraisal of facts. For example, the jury, the trial judge, and one or more appellate courts below have held that conflicting evidence proves a confession was voluntary; the prisoner wants us to say the evidence proves it was coerced. The court below found that the prisoner waived counsel and voluntarily pleaded guilty; he wants us to find that he did not. The jury and the trial judge below believed one set of witnesses whose testimony showed his guilt; he wants us to believe the other and to hold that he has been convicted by perjury. That is the type of factual issue upon which this Court and other federal courts are asked to intervene and upset state court convictions. There are plenty of good reasons why we should rarely do that, and even better reasons why the district court should not undertake to do it after we have declined to.

My conclusion is that whether or not this Court has denied certiorari from a state court's judgment in a habeas corpus proceeding, no lower federal court should entertain a petition except on the following conditions: (1) that the petition raises a jurisdictional question involving federal law on which the state law allowed no access to its courts, either by habeas corpus or appeal from the conviction, and that he therefore has no state remedy; or (2) that the petition shows that although the law allows a remedy, he was actually improperly obstructed from making a record upon which the question could be presented, so that his remedy by way of ultimate application to this Court for certiorari has been frustrated. There may be circumstances so extraordinary that I do not now think of them which would justify a departure from this rule, but the run-of-the mill case certainly does not.

Whether one will agree with this general proposition will depend, I suppose, on the latitude he thinks federal courts should exercise in retrying *de novo* state court criminal issues. . . .

If this Court were willing to adopt this doctrine of federal self-restraint, it could settle some procedures, rules of pleading and practices which would weed out the abuses and frivolous causes and identify the worthy ones. I know the difficulty of formulating practice rules and their pitfalls. Nor do I underestimate the argument that the writ often is petitioned for by prisoners without counsel and that they should not be held to the artificialities in pleading that we expect in lawyers. But I know of no way that we can have equal justice under law except we have some law . . . some general principles which, if adhered to, would reduce the number of frivolous petitions, make decision upon them possible at an earlier time and alleviate some of the irritation that is developing over ill-considered federal use of the writ to slap down state courts.

9 ADVOCACY

The profession of law was a passion with Robert Jackson, and a major theme of his writing both on and off the Court.[1] His career as a Supreme Court justice was a direct function of his political career as a New Dealer, which in turn stemmed directly from his leadership role in the smaller-scale political arena of organizing a regional enclave of the New York State Bar. And the bar association work was an outgrowth of his early and rapid success in the role of a small-town trial lawyer. All of his experience as a Washington bureaucrat was in what were explicitly defined as professional legal roles, for which no man untrained in law could possibly have been considered: General Counsel of the Bureau of Internal Revenue; Assistant Attorney General, first of the Tax Division and later of the Anti-Trust Division; Solicitor General; and Attorney General. But the biggest and best job, in his own opinion, was his international legal role as Chief American counsel at the war crimes trials: "[T]he hard months at Nuremberg," he wrote only six months before his death, "were well spent in the most important, enduring and constructive work of my life."[2] For over forty years, from late adolescence until the very day of his death, his was the life of a law-man.[3]

The manner of his socialization into the legal profession, and the mode of his formal education, help to explain his unusually strong need for a sense of identification with his profession. He took a post-graduate year at high school, a not uncommon action for a bright young man to take at that time and in that region, but he never went to college. Therefore, his liberal education in the arts, sciences, and humanities, beyond high school, was informal. His legal training is best described in his own words, spoken on the occasion of the dedication of a new building for the Stanford University School of Law:

Considerations of an autobiographical nature would make it immodest for me to suggest what a law school should teach and how best to teach it. I am a vestigial remnant

---

[1] Of his first eleven articles and speeches (1926-35), eight (73%), and of his last sixteen (1949-54), eleven (69%), dealt explicitly with professional subjects (advocacy, the relationships of lawyers with each other [bar associations] and with clients, political roles for lawyers, legal education, the history of the bar as a profession, legal research) as distinguished from the substantive legal topics (due process, freedom of speech, tax policy) which constitute the content of most discourse in legal periodicals.

[2] Introduction to Whitney R. Harris, *Tyranny on Trial* (Dallas: Southern Methodist University, 1954), p. xxxvii.

[3] The idiom is that of Karl Llewellyn rather than that of Matt Dillon.

of the system which permitted one to come to the Bar by way of apprenticeship in a law office. Except for one term at law school, I availed myself of that method of preparation which already was causing uneasiness—to which feeling I must have added, for the system was almost immediately abolished. You may be comforted to realize that I am the last relic of that method likely to find a niche on the Supreme Court.[4]

So his own son prepared at St. Albans, took an A.B. at Yale, and an LL.B. at Harvard; and Jackson compensated for his lack of such amenities both by becoming a Master of his chosen Guild—he not only belonged to the bar; he exemplified it[5]—and by returning again and again, in his writing, to praise apprenticeship as a method for training the best law-men for the most important law-jobs.[6]

His off-the-bench speaking and writing extends, of course, to a much broader array of legal roles[7] than do his opinions as a Supreme Court Justice. The latter tend to focus, however, upon four of the five most basic types of legal roles ("law-jobs"), at least as viewed from the perspective of a Supreme Court justice: the trial advocate, the trial judge, the advocate before the Supreme Court,[8] and the Supreme Court justice. Conspicuously missing is a discussion of the role of the appellate judge, because it is with lawyers in this type of role that Supreme Court justices primarily interact (excepting, of course, interaction among themselves and with the Supreme Court bar) rather than with trial advocates and trial judges. But the explanation for this striking omission is not hard to deduce, and it has nothing to do with the lack of opportunity. Jackson had acted on an advocate before the New York State appellate courts, it is true, but he was never an appellate judge; and so his opinions discussed what he had ex-

[4] Robert H. Jackson, "The Advocate: Guardian of Our Traditional Liberties," *American Bar Association Journal*, XXXVI (1950), 608.

[5] Norman Birkett, Foreword to Eugene C. Gerhart, *America's Advocate* (Indianapolis: The Bobbs-Merrill Co., Inc., 1958).

[6] For example, "The Advocate," pp. 610, 698-699; and two decades earlier, in "The Future of the Bar," *Lincoln Law Review*, III (1930), 42-43.

[7] See the bibliography in *Stanford Law Review*, VIII (1955), 71-76. On the roles of the trial advocate, and of the advocate before the Supreme Court, see his "Advocacy as a Specialized Career," *New York Law Review*, VII (1929), 77-82, and "Advocacy before the Supreme Court," *American Bar Association Journal*, XXXVII (1951), 801-804, 861-864.

[8] Most of Jackson's advocacy before the Supreme Court was in his capacity as Solicitor General, of course. However, "while still with the Antitrust Division, [he] was well into the swing of his career as advocate extraordinary and barrister at large. In his year and a half in the Antitrust Division, Assistant Attorney General Jackson argued ten cases to the Supreme Court, only one of which related to the responsibilities of the Antitrust Division." Warner W. Gardner, "Robert H. Jackson, 1892-1954: Government Attorney," *Columbia Law Review*, LV (1955), 440. "Few attorneys in private practice ever got to argue a case before the Supreme Court; Jackson had one such opportunity." Gerhart, *America's Advocate*, p. 44.

perienced and knew and understood best: the interlocking roles of trial
counsel with those of trial judges, and of Supreme Court justices with each
other. Of the opinions included in the present chapter, the first two (A
and B) discuss the role of the trial advocate, and the status of a member
of the Supreme Court bar; the third (C) deals with the decision-making
role of trial judges; and the last two opinions (D and E) with the decision-
making role of Supreme Court justices.

Typically, Jackson referred to lawyers with both favor and fervor.
His opinions are sprinkled with remarks such as "The welfare and tone of
the legal profession is of prime consequence to society."[9] Over and over,
he reminded his colleagues that lawyers and law offices are indispensable
parts of the administration of justice. The Court ought not, therefore,
to permit lawyers to be discriminated against by zealous administrators (as
in the first case below). On the other hand, the Court should be tolerant
of the contentiousness of other lawyers. In fact, it is perfectly proper for
lawyers themselves to be zealous in trying to win their cases; and the Supreme Court should recognize that hyperbolic expressions are a working
tool of the art of advocacy. ("Our profession," he would say, "necessarily
is a contentious one and they respect the lawyer who makes a strenuous
effort for his client.") Nor should the Court lean too far backward in an
attempt to avoid all suspicion of partiality toward fellow-lawyers.[10] In
particular the Court should not approve policies which might prove pro-
fessionally embarrassing to practicing attorneys, by taking them out of
their accustomed role. The Court itself should, of course, behave in a
"lawyerly" way by making its orders "specific, positive, and concrete."

Probably the most polished and extended statement of Jackson's
image of the advocate occurs in his idealized portrait of the small-town
lawyer, published in the *American Bar Association Journal* at the close of
the 1949 Term[11] when he reached the two-thirds mark of his judicial tenure. (Initially his remarks had comprised the latter part of a review that
he had written, over half a dozen years earlier for the same journal, of the

9 "But it too often is overlooked," he said in the same concurring opinion, "that the
lawyer and the law office are indispensable parts of our administration of justice. Law-
abiding people can go nowhere else to learn the ever changing constantly multiplying rules
by which they must behave and to obtain redress for their wrongs." *Hickman* v. *Taylor*, 329
U.S. 495, 514-515 (1947).

10 "It seems to me," he once wrote, "that the Court is converting a provision of the
Bankruptcy Act designed to prevent lawyers from overreaching stockholders into an authority for stockholders to swindle lawyers. It may appear like an instance of man biting
dog, but the case before us is actually one of client snaring lawyer." Dissenting in *Leiman*
v. *Guttman*, 336 U.S. 1, 11 (1949).

11 Robert H. Jackson, "The County-Seat Lawyer," *American Bar Association Journal*,
XXXVI (1950), 497.

autobiography of a southwest Georgian country lawyer.[12]) Like the explicit references to his own farm boyhood, in that part of his review that samples the Powell narrative, this more generalized and public portion of his essay is marked with a pungent nostalgia:

The county-seat lawyer, counsellor to railroads and to Negroes, to bankers and to poor whites, who always gave to each the best there was in him—and was willing to admit that his best was good. That lawyer has been an American institution—about the same in South and North and East and West. Such a man understands the structure of society and how its groups interlock and interact, because he lives in a community so small that he can keep it in all view. Lawyers in large cities do not know their cities; they know their circles, and urban circles are apt to be made up of those with a kindred outlook on life; but the circle of the man from the small city or town is the whole community and embraces persons of every outlook. He sees how this society lives and works under the law and adjusts its conflicts by its procedures. He knows how disordered and hopelessly unstable it would be without law. He knows that in this country the administration of justice is based on law practice. Paper "rights" are worth, when they are threatened, just what some lawyer makes them worth. Civil liberties are those which some lawyer, respected by his neighbors, will stand up to defend. Any legal doctrine which fails to enlist the support of well-regarded lawyers will have no real sway in this country.

It has been well said that "The life of the law has not been logic: it has been experience." The experience that gave life to our judge-made and statutory law, at least until the last few years, was this type of country life. From such homes came the lawyers, the judges and the legislators of the nineteenth century. Their way of living generated independence and amazing energy, and these country boys went to the cities and dominated the professions and business as well. They controlled the country courthouses and the state houses and the Nation's capitol as well, and they weighed legal doctrines, political theories and social policies in the light of the life they knew. If we would understand the product of those courthouses and state houses, we must understand that life and the impression it made on the minds of men. Much of the changing trend of law and of political and social policy is due to the declining number of men who have shared this experience. More men now come to the profession from the cities, fewer from farms. There isn't a whiff of the stable in a carload of college freshmen. More and more those who in court and classroom and legislative body restate our legal principles are men who have not experienced the country life of which our law was so largely the expression.

The county-seat lawyer and the small-town advocate are pretty much gone, and the small-city lawyer has a struggle to keep his head above water. Control of business has been concentrated in larger cities, and the good law business went to the city with it. The lawsuit has declined in public interest before the tough competition of movie and radio. Most rural controversies are no longer worth their cost to litigate. Much controversy has now shifted to the administrative tribunal, and the country lawyer hates it and all its works.

But this vanishing country lawyer left his mark on his times, and he was worth knowing.

---

[12] Robert H. Jackson, "Tribute to Country Lawyers: A Review" [of Arthur Gray Powell, *I Can Go Home Again* (Chapel Hill: University of North Carolina, 1943)], *American Bar Association Journal*, XXX (1944), 136-139. "Sometimes one is tempted," as he later remarked, "to quote his former self, not only to pay his respects to the author but to demonstrate the consistency of his views, if not their correctness." *The Supreme Court in the American System* (Cambridge: Harvard University Press, 1955), p. 82.

He "read law" in the *Commentaries* of Blackstone and Kent and not by the case system. He resolved problems by what he called "first principles." He did not specialize, nor did he pick and choose clients. He rarely declined service to worthy ones because of inability to pay. Once enlisted for a client, he took his obligation seriously.[13] He insisted on complete control of the litigation—he was no mere hired hand. But he gave every power and resource to the cause. He identified himself with the client's cause fully, sometimes too fully. He would fight the adverse party and fight his counsel, fight every hostile witness, and fight the court, fight public sentiment, fight any obstacle to his client's success. He never quit. He could think of motions for every purpose under the sun, and he made them all. He moved for new trials, he appealed; and if he lost out in the end, he joined the client at the tavern in damning the judge—which is the last rite in closing an unsuccessful case, and I have officiated at many. But he loved his profession, he had a real sense of dedication to the administration of justice, he held his head high as a lawyer, he rendered and exacted courtesy, honor and straightforwardness at the Bar. He respected the judicial office deeply, demanded the highest standards of competence and disinterestedness and dignity, despised all political use of or trifling with judicial power, and had an affectionate regard for every man who filled his exacting prescription of the just judge. The law to him was like a religion, and its practice was more than a means of support; it was a mission. He was not always popular in his community, but he was respected. Unpopular minorities and individuals often found in him their only mediator and advocate. He was too independent to court the populace—he thought of himself as a leader and lawgiver, not as a mouthpiece. He "lived well, worked hard, and died poor." Often his name was, in a generation or two, forgotten. It was from this brotherhood that America has drawn its statesmen and its judges. A free and self-governing Republic stands as a monument for the little known and unremembered as well as for the famous men of our profession.

Jackson exhibited considerable, if paternalistic, sympathy even for the lawyer who overstepped the ethical canons of the profession, providing that his fault stemmed from the excessive zeal of an earnest and skillful advocate. Such tolerance stands in sharp contrast to the low boiling point which, as we observed in Chap. 6, Jackson entertained for bureaucratic zeal; and there is his suggestion in the quotation above that the underlying basis for his discrimination between good lawyerly and bad administrative zeal was crudely—indeed, crassly—economically motivated: "Most rural controversies," he says, "are no longer worth their cost to litigate. Much controversy has now shifted to the administrative tribunal,

[13] Such claims of professional independence occur time and again in his speeches to legal audiences. But so, also, do wisecracks about the solace that retainers bring to counsellors; and such a wisecrack marks the invocation of what turned out to be his final writing for an audience of lawyers, although he did not live to read it at the dedication of the new law building at Syracuse University on December 11, 1954. There are places in this address where for the first time in any of his writing, and in contrast to the ebullient tone of the also-posthumous Godkin Lectures, he sounds old, tired, and discouraged. In rather sharp contrast to his recollections of his youth, he now observes that: "The attorney usually has little choice in the principles he will advocate. He usually is confronted with a client in a predicament, or one who has some particular interest at stake. He may not be free to advocate the doctrine that, except for his retainer, he might think sound law." *Syracuse Law Review*, VI (1955), 223. [Ed.]

and the country lawyer hates it and all its works."[14] The rare lawyer whom Jackson criticized was the parasite who wanted something for nothing,[15] or the shirker who used his professional skills to avoid military service.[16]

A major conceptual distinction for Jackson lay in the dichotomy he frequently invoked to differentiate "law" from "politics." Law, of course, is good; and politics is bad. Typically he argued that the twain ought to be kept as separate as possible, not, as one might suppose, to protect the process of political decision-making from the irrationality of law, but rather to keep the law as free as possible from the impurities of politics. But his attitude toward law and politics, like his behavior as a lawyer and a judge, was ambivalent. He had served as President of the Jamestown Wilson Club during the 1912 campaign, while still a minor and a full year before he was admitted to the bar; he was increasingly active in Democratic politics throughout the next three decades of his life;[17] and although he aspired to both the top law-job, that of Chief Justice, and the top political job, the Presidency, it is clear that his preference was for the latter.[18] As he confesses in more than one of his opinions, he did not hesitate, as Solicitor General and as Attorney General, to sublimate legal to political considerations;[19] and he did this in matters both large and small

[14] Cf. his characterization during his days as a "country lawyer" of the administrative process as a form of *economic* competition with lawyers (who specialized in the "judicial method of fact finding"), in his "An Organized American Bar," *American Bar Association Journal*, XVIII (1932), 383-386.

[15] *United States* ex rel *Marcus* v. *Hess,* 317 U.S. 537, 556 (1943), and Chap. 7E, *supra.*

[16] *Boone* v. *Lightner,* 319 U.S. 561 (1943).

[17] "I believe," he wrote in the heyday of the New Deal, and in the very year of the Landon debacle, "in a strong party of opposition and believe that an unwieldy majority for any governing party is a blow to its prudence. But a party [the Republican] which has failed pathetically in every function of opposition cannot be prepared to assume the responsibility of governing under a coherent and clear alternative program." Robert H. Jackson, "The People's Business: The Truth About Taxes," *Forum,* XCV (January, 1936), 25-26.

[18] Jackson's preference was opposite to that of William Howard Taft, who not only held down both positions but was able to crown his career by ending his labors working at the one which he deemed far the more important, and loved best. Daniel S. McHargue, "President Taft's Appointments to the Supreme Court," *Journal of Politics,* XII (1950), 478-479, 491.

[19] As his assistant at the time commented subsequently, "the opinion which permitted the President to exchange over-age destroyers for military bases in Bermuda, Labrador, and other British possessions [39 *Ops. Att'y. Gen.* 484 (1940), and see also *Congressional Digest* XX (January, 1941), 19-21] ... bears every internal evidence of having received a great deal of the Attorney General's personal attention. It is brilliantly executed, and marshalls a number of debatable propositions into an array that is powerfully persuasive. One may suspect that the Allied cause owed much to the fact that the Attorney General in 1940 viewed himself not as guardian of The Law, but as legal advisor to the Government." Warner W. Gardner, "Government Attorney," *Columbia Law Review,* LV (1955), 444. In the opinion

when he was acting as an advocate (as the "President's lawyer," as he sometimes put it) in what was by his own understanding predominately a political role.[20]

No doubt if he *had* become President, Jackson's impulsion to advocacy in behalf of getting the job at hand done would have led him to a greater appreciation of the virtues of the political process; and there is, therefore, more than a hint of sour grapes in the ardor with which he came as a judge to repudiate the political horn, whilst impaling himself the more staunchly upon the legal horn, of his life-long dilemma. Of course, this is perfectly comprehensible: it is only human to take the cash and let the credit go. Nor do I intend to imply that Jackson was not absolutely "sincere" in his increasing self-enshroudment within his judicial toga; the question is one of personality adjustment, not of hypocrisy.

Jackson's antipathy for the political process was most acute when he directed his remarks to the behavior of his colleagues on the Court. Frequently, however, his definition of his colleagues' behavior as "political" seemed to reflect little more than his own frustration at having failed to persuade a majority of the Court to agree with his own views. Thus, he would complain that he had been "outvoted" by the majority; he be-

---

of another observer, "Attorney General Jackson all but threw the hollow shell of the Neutrality Act in the trash can when he advised the President, on August 27, 1940, that it would be legal for him to give Great Britain fifty over-age destroyers and a flock of 'mosquito' boats in return for a ninety-nine year lease on a handful of bases. Commentators cried outrage at the legal shenanigan. Jackson skillfully steered the President around three legal obstacles by ruling that the deal need not be ratified by the Senate (as a treaty), that the President had authority to transfer title of the vessels away from the United States and that Britain's status as a belligerent need not bother anyone. It was one of the fanciest bits of legal advice ever received by a President. Small wonder that Roosevelt found no need to seek amending or repealing legislation. Legal expediency, based on the idea that Hitler was not disposed to wait until Congress got through debating, accomplished more than new legislation. Jackson was attacked for prostituting his profession by finding means to justify the ends sought by Roosevelt. [But] how [does] that . . . differ from what a lawyer ordinarily does [?]" Wesley McCune, *The Nine Young Men,* (New York: Harper & Row, Publishers, 1947), pp. 183-184.

[20] Referring to his advice advocating Presidential seizure of industrial properties for purposes of national defense, as the Attorney General on the eve of World War II, Jackson remarked some dozen years later: "I should not bind present judicial judgment by earlier partisan advocacy." *Youngstown Sheet and Tube* v. *Sawyer,* 343 U.S. 579, 649n.17 (1952), and Chap. 6A *supra.* In Gardner's appraisal, "His earlier 'partisan advocacy' was exercised, in his eight years as government attorney, in behalf of many causes, large and small. A few of those causes look a little less resplendent now than they did in the heat of battle; most have stood the test of time very well indeed. But the advocacy by which they were furthered is impervious to afterthought. It was always skilled, always effective and almost always successful." "Government Attorney," 438. For further examples see Gerhart, *America's Advocate,* Chaps. 11 and 12.

moaned the fact that the majority had "the power of decision in this case"; he accused the majority of having indulged in an "extreme exertion of power." On other occasions, he charged that the majority had deliberately disregarded the law enacted by Congress, the record, the facts, or the evidence in the case. And he regretted what he considered to be the widespread belief that decisions of the Court vacillated according to fluctuations in the dominant majority of the Court.

It is, therefore, the more ironic that it was Jackson, more than any other Supreme Court justice of the contemporary era, who was responsible for revealing the political mysteries of the inner temple; for it was Jackson, in the cable from Nuremberg, who told the entire world about the feud on the Supreme Court between himself and Black. This, in turn, raised for open discussion in the press charges that Black had lobbied with Truman to keep Jackson from becoming Chief Justice, and that Truman had succumbed to such pressure, thereby welching on F.D.R.'s commitment to Jackson. Black himself, it was said, aspired to the Chief Justiceship. Jackson and the President openly disagreed in their statements to the press at the time, about their communications with each other immediately preceding the public release of Jackson's cable.[21] The entire *Jewell-Ridge* affair, both on and off the Court, but especially in its culmination in the cable, was supercharged with political overtones. It was a strange enterprise for a judge who took as jaundiced a view of judicial political activity as Jackson professed—for his colleagues.

He did recognize, of course, that his own policy differences with his colleagues, and their's with each other, were largely inescapable, just as disagreement between present and past majorities of the Court could not be avoided. The measure of his conservatism lay in the extent to which he deplored the prospect of such changes in constitutional policy; he was no Walt Whitman of the law, saluting the unfolding future with open arms and a smile of confidence. Contemporary change was unfortunate; the best that one could hope for would be some future swing of the political pendulum that might restore the status quo. Thus, he consoled himself with the thought that: "Whatever license of constitutional construction one group of judges may take in one direction a later group may take in an opposite direction, as they succeed to office from different political backgrounds and atmospheres."[22] Indeed, the virtue of judicial review is that it slows down the tempo of change in the "political branches of the government," while at the same time avoiding

[21] *Ibid.,* pp. 264-265.
[22] Robert H. Jackson, "The Task of Maintaining Our Liberties: The Role of the Judiciary," *American Bar Association Journal,* XXXIX (1953), 965; also in *Vital Speeches,* XIX (October 1, 1953) 759-762. This was the last of Jackson's many speeches before national conventions of the American Bar Association.

complete political stalemates which might lead to drastic revolutionary attacks upon the constitutional regime itself as well as upon the prevailing structure of socioeconomic values:

> Exclude as far as humanly possible the pressures of group opinion, but let us not deceive ourselves; long-sustained public opinion does influence the process of constitutional interpretation. Each new member of the ever-changing personnel of our courts brings to his task the assumptions and accustomed thought of a later period. The practical play of the forces of politics is such that judicial power has often delayed but never permanently defeated the persistent will of a substantial majority. Judicial review in practice therefore has proved less an obstacle to majority rule than the followers of Mr. Jefferson feared and less a guaranty of the *status quo* than the followers of Mr. Hamilton hoped.[23]

This is, of course, the orthodox view; and although Jackson doubtless would have derived little comfort from the knowledge, the conclusions that he stated were shortly to receive empirical confirmation in the researches of social scientists.[24]

"But we must recognize," he said, "the pliability of the process for what it is"—so that we can "strive to keep our liberty under law by keeping ourselves under law."[25] How is this to be done? Presumably by discerning the true nature of law, and especially of constitutional law. This implies that "decisions will be reached so far as humanly possible by application of existing and ascertainable legal criteria and standards." Yet, as he confessed with characteristic candor,

> . . . as an advocate at the Supreme Court Bar in many constitutional cases, I never was able to determine what material would really be considered by the several Justices as controlling such issues.

---

23 *Ibid.,* 964.

24 Eloise C. Snyder, "The Supreme Court as a Small Group," *Social Forces,* XXXVI (1958), 232-238; Robert A. Dahl, "Decision-Making in a Democracy: The Role of the Supreme Court as a National Policy-Maker," *Journal of Public Law,* VI (1957), 279-295. In his earlier advices to law students and faculties, Jackson showed at least minimal tolerance toward the infusion of social science into the law school curriculum, and particularly for the purpose of better tracing the outcomes of judicial outputs. He did not, to be sure, advocate that young legal minds be exposed directly to the teachings of social scientists included in law faculties; he thought, rather, that law professors might work social science material into their own courses. (Cf. my "The Future of Public Law," *George Washington Law Review,* XXXIV (1966), 593-614.) But he became disillusioned with such endeavors; and in his parting shot on the subject, he remarked that: "there is a school of commentators [many of whom are law professors] who regale [our young lawyers] with statistical and other material to prove that results show only the judge's predilections, prepossessions and prejudices. Of course we have them, and where we differ from these commentators is that it is their privilege to exploit theirs." Address prepared for the dedication of Ernest I. White Hall, *Syracuse Law Review,* VI (1955), 224. "The fact is," he added superciliously, "that most of these critics never had experience in advocacy or in the practice of law." They never, that is to say, had even met a payroll!

25 Jackson, "The Task of Maintaining Our Liberties," *American Bar Association Journal,* XXXIX (1953), 964.

And I am bound to admit that a decade of experience as a judge throws little more light on the problem. Nothing has more perplexed generations of conscientious judges than the search in juridical science, philosophy and practice for objective and impersonal criteria for solution of politicolegal questions put to our courts. Few judges like to be accused of acting from merely personal predilections. Yet, frequently that is the point of dissenting opinions. Confusion at the Bar and disagreement on the Bench usually begin in lack of an accepted system of weights and measures to mete out constitutional justice. Unfortunately, the conclusion of judges having the highest sense of professional responsibility is that the present state of our constitutional development provides no definitive principles of decision. . . . The result is that constitutional precedents are accepted only at their current valuation and have a mortality rate almost as high as their authors.[26]

Some earlier cases relied upon "natural justice" or the "laws of nature and of nature's God", which our Declaration of Independence invoked. But new schools of thought scorn that belief as a sort of legal superstition and propose, in the name of "realism", to rely upon "facts" to determine decisions. These they would select largely from sociology, political science, psychology and other nonlegal disciplines. Citations of weekly magazines, newspapers and an endless list of popular, scientific and professional books and reviews are now found in briefs and opinions. We need not enter the controversy between these schools, for this "realism" and "natural justice" have much in common; both shield the judge with an impersonal and probably unconscious camouflage for holdings that emerge out of the mists of preconception. Unfortunately, both also are alike in bewildering the profession and arousing suspicion that decisions may be reached from latent motives and policies not avowed. Thus we find standards of constitutional decision soft and transient.[27]

This was a most discouraging conclusion to be reached by a true believer in the ideal of dispassionate justice. It all comes back to the ideological biases of individual justices, and the constitutional politics of their decision making together.

A. THE PHANTOM ADVOCATE

KINGSLAND V. DORSEY
338 U.S. 318, 320 (November 21, 1949)

The question here was whether the Supreme Court should encourage, among lower federal judges and in those administrative agencies whose functions included a formal adjudication process, lax or tight standards in

[26] Only a decade earlier, however, he had put the shoe on the other foot: "Inertia is a factor so powerful as to be a real fourth department of our government. The constitutional history of the United States has been a relatively static one, nearly every great Power having extensively revised its institutions since ours were established. Judicial interpretation has been the chief method of adaptation to new problems. The responsibility which this casts upon the legal profession[,] on the Bench and at the Bar[,] is extraordinary." Robert H. Jackson, "The Law Above Nations," *American Journal of International Law*, XXXVII (1943), 300. [Ed.]

[27] Jackson, "The Task of Maintaining Our Liberties," 962.

the policing of codes of ethics for the many specialized subguilds of the legal profession. The Court took this particular case only to correct the views of a panel of the Court of Appeals for the District of Columbia. A majority of two of the circuit judges had made the mistake of reversing a federal district court's affirmance of the decision of the Commissioner of Patents, Kingsland, who had ruled that attorney Dorsey had been guilty of gross misconduct and barred him from further practice as a member of the patent bar. Six members of the Supreme Court agreed with Circuit Judge Henry Edgerton's dissent,[28] thinking that both policy and precedent on this issue were so clear that a brief *per curiam* opinion sufficed to justify their reinstatement of the decision of the patent commissioner and the trial court. Not only was there ample evidence in the record to support the disbarment action, but also, the Court noted that Congress had intended to place primary responsibility for the maintenance of a relationship of mutual trust and confidence, between the patent bar and the Patent Office, upon the Commissioner of Patents—not upon the federal judiciary. Because the rest of his colleagues (save Frankfurter, and Douglas who did not participate) disposed of this issue with such equanimity, the vigor of Jackson's dissent may perhaps be explained by the convergence of his strong feelings of antipathy for bureaucratic, and of empathy for lawyerly, dedication to the accomplishment of their respective, and disparate, missions.[29]

MR. JUSTICE JACKSON, *whom* MR. JUSTICE FRANKFURTER *joins, dissenting.*

I agree that the privilege of practicing before the Patent Office is one that may and should be withdrawn for professional misconduct. In defense of his privilege it also is true that the lawyer may not demand that conclusiveness of proof or invoke all of the protections assured to an accused by the criminal process. But while society may expect that his judges will show him no favor because he has lived respectably for eighty years and devoted fifty-nine of them to practice of his profession without blemish, an accused lawyer may expect that he will not be condemned out of a capricious self-righteousness or denied the essentials of a fair hearing.

---

[28] See the discussion in my *Constitutional Politics* (New York: Holt, Rinehart and Winston, 1960), pp. 86-87; and see Louis S. Loeb, "Judicial Blocs and Judicial Values in Civil Liberties Cases Decided by the Supreme Court and the United States Court of Appeals for the District of Columbia Circuit," *American University Law Review,* XIV (1965), 151, 154.

[29] An alternative and contemporary explanation is implied in "Ghostly Dissent," *Newsweek,* XXXIV (December 5, 1949), 19: "As Solicitor General and Attorney General in the late '30s and early '40s, he refused to submit to the Washington—and worldwide—custom of having his speeches and articles written by others."

The court below thought Dorsey had not been fairly judged and indignantly reversed his disbarment. *Dorsey* v. *Kingsland,* 84 U.S. App. D. C. 264, 173 F.2d 405. All questions of fact seem to have been resolved against Dorsey by his departmental triers, and I shall not here review all of those issues, even if on some of them Dorsey would seem entitled to prevail. Accepting the findings against him at their full face value, I think the disbarment order was properly set aside.

Back in 1926 the Hartford-Empire Co. conceived and executed a scheme to prepare and publish, over the signature of an apparently disinterested labor leader, an article to be published and then used in support of the company's pending patent application. Such a dissertation, entitled, "Introduction of Automatic Glass Working Machinery; How Received by Organized Labor," was prepared. It purported to be authored by one Clarke, president of a glassworkers' union. It was published in a trade journal and then presented to the Patent Office as recognition by a "reluctant witness" of the success of the device under consideration. Several years later, involved in litigation testing the validity of its patent, Hartford-Empire took steps to suppress evidence of the real authorship of the Clarke essay. It made a gift of $8,000 to Clarke, who had told investigators employed by Hartford-Empire's adversary that he had written the article and would so testify if called upon as a witness. Ultimately, this Court reviewed the actions of Hartford-Empire and held that the sum total of acts attributable to it constituted a fraud on the Patent Office and the Federal courts. *Hazel-Atlas Glass Co.* v. *Hartford-Empire Co.,* 322 U.S. 238 [1944]. . . .

Dorsey was one of counsel for Hartford-Empire in the 1926 patent application and, shortly following our decision in *Hazel-Atlas, supra,* proceedings to suspend or exclude him from further practice before the Patent Office were commenced under 35 U.S.C. 11. Identical but separate proceedings were instituted against three other members of the patent bar involved in the transactions. All were disbarred. Only the *Dorsey* case is here. . . .

A view of the facts least favorable to Dorsey indicates that he inspected and criticized a few details of an early draft of the Clarke article and that later, with knowledge that it had been prepared by a Hartford-Empire employee, he submitted it to the Patent Office as being what on its face it purported to be. This is the long and the short of the case against Dorsey. The case against Hartford-Empire, however, included much in which Dorsey is not shown to have had even a consenting part. In two respects only are his actions urged to be wrong-doing: first, in that he deceived the Patent Office as to the real author, and (second, not charged in the notice but advanced here), that Dorsey represented it as the work of a "reluctant witness."

While it is not decisive of the narrow issue of deception pressed against Dorsey, it should be noted as showing how narrow that issue really is, that it includes no claim that any statement in the Clarke article is false or misleading in any respect whatsoever. It stated facts truthfully, facts which a patent lawyer was entitled to bring to the attention of the Patent Office in any manner permitted by its practice. One might expect that the Patent Office would have required facts on which it issued a patent to be proved by affidavits whose truthfulness is encouraged, if not assured, by sanctions against perjury; but it was content to accept unsworn publications for its purposes. The worst that can be said of Dorsey is that he took advantage of this loose practice to use a trade journal article as evidence, without disclosing that it was ghost-written for the ostensible author.

Let us suppose the Patent Office had exacted more lawyerly standards of proof and had required such information to be laid before it in affidavit form. Clarke, let us say, was prevailed upon to make a deposition. Would it be deceit if the lawyer drafted every word of the affidavit, though it purported to be Clarke's testimony? I suppose that the practice is almost universal that the lawyer ascertains to what facts the witness can testify and puts them in presentable form and suitable words, and that the witness adopts the document as his testimony, with any correction necessary to convey his story. Nothing on the face of the usual affidavit discloses the fact that the composition is that of the attorney; on the contrary, it generally recites that it is the witness who "deposes and says. . . ." Is a different standard to be applied to a trade journal article intended and accepted to serve the same end?

I should suppose that, so far as the law is concerned, one may as effectively father statements by adoption as by conception and that sincerely subscribing to what another has written for him does not contitute legal deceit or grounds for disbarment, impeachment or other penalty. And in this case, not only is there no claim that the Clarke article contained one false statement, but there is no denial that, whoever was the scribe, Clarke believed and knowingly adopted as his own every word of it.

I should not like to be second to anyone on this Court in condemning the custom of putting up decoy authors to impress the guileless, a custom which as the court below cruelly pointed out flourishes even in official circles in Washington. Nor do I contend that Dorsey's special adaptation of the prevailing custom comports with the highest candor. Ghost-writing has debased the intellectual currency in circulation here and is a type of counterfeiting which invites no defense. Perhaps this Court renders a public service in treating phantom authors and ghost-writers as legal frauds and disguised authorship as a deception. But has any man before Dorsey ever been disciplined or even reprimanded for it? And will any be hereafter?

It is added, though as something of an afterthought, that Dorsey in his brief to the Patent Office characterized Clarke as a "reluctant witness." I had supposed that such adjectives were in the nature of argument or, at most, of conclusion rather than representation or warranty. The arsenal of every advocate holds two bundles of adjectives for witnesses—such ones as "reluctant," "unbiased," "disinterested," and "honest" are reserved for his own; others, such as "partisan," "eager," "interested," "hostile," and even "perjured," for those of his adversary. I have the greatest difficulty believing that a mischoice among these adjectives has deceived anyone fit to decide facts, or that in any case other than this it would subject the advocate to disbarment. But if wrong in this standard, I should think the use of "reluctant" as applied to Clarke was justified. I should not expect a union president to be other than reluctant to point out the advantages of automatic machinery which tends to throw his membership out of employment. At least I hope we have not come to the time when to urge this inference is even a makeweight in disbarment proceedings.

If, however, a lawyer is to be called upon to be the first example of condemnation for an offense so tenuous, vague and novel, the least courts should require is that the case against him be clearly proved. . . . Even though courts lean backward to avoid suspicion of partiality to men of our own profession, they should not fear to protect a lawyer against loss of his right to practice on such a record as this.

B. THE PASSIONATE ADVOCATE

IN RE ISSERMAN
345 U.S. 286, 290 (April 6, 1953)

Isserman's case was a latter-day fruit of the McCarthy era in American political life. In another two years, with both Warren and Brennan (who came from the New Jersey Supreme Court) on the Court, it almost certainly would have been decided differently. Isserman, together with Crockett, Gladstein, McCabe, and Sacher, was of counsel for the national leaders of the Communist Party who were defendants in the celebrated trial, before Judge Harold Medina, that lasted nine months in 1949. At the termination of the nominal trial, at which Eugene Dennis and his ten cohorts were found guilty of conspiracy to advocate violent overthrow of the United States Government, the then federal district Judge Medina promptly, and without benefit of trial or even notice of charges, found the five presumably Communist defense lawyers to be guilty of contempt of court for their behavior during the trial.[30] The Supreme Court of New Jersey, the state where Isserman was a resident, then acted to disbar him from practice in the courts of that state because of his conviction, for the offense of criminal contempt, in and by the federal courts. The third level of punishment for Isserman came in proceedings to disbar him from practice before the United States Supreme Court.

[30] See *Sacher* v. *United States,* 343 U.S. 1 (1952).

The Court's Rule 2 specified that any member of the Supreme Court bar who was disbarred from further practice of law in his state of residence was to be suspended at once and disbarred from practice before the Supreme Court unless, within forty days, he could show cause satisfactory to the Court why he should not be disbarred. Clark, who had been Attorney General at the time the Dennis trial began, disqualified himself from participating; and the remaining members of the Court divided equally and in perfect accord with the attitudinal scale for civil liberties for the 1952 Term.[31] Minton, Reed, Vinson, and Burton voted to enforce the rule, and Douglas, Black, Frankfurter, and Jackson voted in Isserman's behalf. The opinion of the Chief Justice announced the order of the Court, confirming Isserman's disbarment, because the effect of the tie vote was to reject Isserman's efforts to show cause:

> The contemptuous acts . . . consisted of repetitious and insolent objections and arguments after the trial judge made rulings and then ordered a halt to further argument on the points involved. . . .
> Our rule puts the burden upon respondent to show good cause why he should not be disbarred. . . . There is no vested right in an individual to practice law. Rather there is a right in the Court to protect itself, and hence society, as an instrument of justice. . . . [W]e do not lay down a rule of disbarment for mere contempt; rather we have considered the basic nature of the actions which were contemptuous and their relation to the functioning of the judiciary.

The other three justices joined in Jackson's dissenting opinion. The division of the Court in Isserman's case was almost the same as it had been a year earlier, when the contempt of court convictions were upheld. The exception was Jackson, who, when forced to choose between his somewhat inconsistent ideals of the dispassionate trial judge and the zealous trial advocate, had taken his stance on the side of law and order, and had been rewarded for his virtue by being assigned to write the opinion of the Court in *Sacher*. But the present disbarment proceeding presented no such conflict in values for Jackson; and so he now voted in behalf of the zealous trial advocate, and the *Sacher* dissenters were glad to coopt Jackson as their spokesman.

MR. JUSTICE JACKSON, *whom* MR. JUSTICE BLACK, MR. JUSTICE FRANKFURTER *and* MR. JUSTICE DOUGLAS *join, delivered the following opinion.*

This proceeding to disbar Abraham J. Isserman results from his being adjudged guilty of contemptuous conduct in the trial of *United States* v. *Dennis*,

---

31 In the order of from most to least sympathetic to civil liberties, the justices ranked: Douglas, Black, Frankfurter, Jackson, Burton, Clark, Vinson, Reed, and Minton. See Glendon Schubert, *The Judicial Mind,* p. 107.

183 F.2d 201, 341 U.S. 494. The trial judge found that his contemptuous acts were pursuant to a conspiracy among counsel to obstruct justice and sentenced him, with others, to jail. But the Court of Appeals, while affirming the counts charging specific acts of contempt, reversed the conspiracy count. *United States* v. *Sacher*, 182 F. 2d 416. This Court limited its review to questions of law and affirmed. *Sacher* v. *United States*, 343 U.S. 1.

Disciplinary proceedings were instituted before the United States District Court for the Southern District of New York, in which Isserman was given a full hearing, and again the conspiracy charge was not sustained. A period of suspension from practice at the bar of the court against which the contempt was committed was considered adequate to the offense. However, the courts of New Jersey have disbarred Isserman and under our rule he must be disbarred here unless he shows good cause to the contrary.

While we have expressed different views as to the merits of the contempt charges, and each adheres to his former expressions, we are agreed that there is good cause for withholding this Court's decree of disbarment.

Primarily because of these contempts, the Supreme Court of New Jersey disbarred Isserman. It also considered his conviction in that State of statutory rape in 1925. At the time of conviction, however, the New Jersey courts found such extenuating circumstances that only a small fine and a temporary suspension from practice were deemed to make the punishment fit the crime. Five years after this conviction, this Court, asking no question which would have called for disclosure of the conviction, admitted Isserman to its bar, it appearing that he was then in good standing before the courts of New Jersey. Under these circumstances, we do not think we can now attach any weight to this dereliction.

We think this Court should not accept for itself a doctrine that conviction of contempt *per se* is ground for a disbarment. It formerly held, in an opinion by Mr. Chief Justice Marshall, that a lawyer should be admitted to this bar even though for contempt he had been disbarred by a federal district court action—"... one which the court do not mean to say was not done for sufficient cause, or that it is not one of a serious character; but this court does not consider itself authorised to punish here for contempts which may have been committed in that court." *Ex parte Tillinghast*, 4 Pet. 108, 109 [1830]. The remedy for courtroom contempt should be prompt and direct punishment proportioned to the offense. Isserman has been severely punished. His penalty has included what is rare in the punishment of lawyers' contempts—a substantial jail sentence.

We do not recall any previous instance, though not venturing to assert that there is none, where a lawyer has been disbarred by any court of the United States or of a state merely because he had been convicted of a contempt. But we do know of occasions when members of the bar have been found guilty of serious contempt without their standing at the bar being brought into question. It will sufficiently illustrate the point to refer to the tactics of counsel for the defense of

William M. Tweed. Those eminent lawyers deliberately and in concert made an attack upon the qualifications of Presiding Judge Noah Davis, charging him with bias and prejudice. At the end of that trial, after he had pronounced sentence on Tweed, Judge Davis declared several defense counsel guilty of contempt. Not one of these lawyers, apparently, was subjected to disciplinary proceedings in consequence of that judgment. Among them was Elihu Root, later to become one of the most respected of American lawyer-statesmen, and Willard Bartlett, destined to become Chief Judge of the New York Court of Appeals. These two were excused from any penalty, beyond a lecture on their ethics, on the ground of youth and domination by their seniors—a rebuke perhaps more humiliating than a sentence. One of the seniors who participated in the contempt, and certainly one of its chief architects, was David Dudley Field. He later was elected president of the American Bar Association.

There has been hue and cry both for and against these lawyers for Communist defendants. There are those who think the respectability of the bar requires their expulsion. There are those who lament that any punishment of their conduct will so frighten the legal profession that it will not dare to discharge its duty to clients. We make common cause with neither. In defending the accused Communists, these men were performing a legitimate function of the legal profession, which is under a duty to leave no man without a defender when he is charged with crime. In performing that duty, it has been adjudged that they went beyond bounds that are tolerable even in our adversary system. For this, Isserman has paid a heavy penalty.

If the purpose of disciplinary proceedings be correction of the delinquent, the courts defeat the purpose by ruining him whom they would reform. If the purpose be to deter others, disbarment is belated and superflous, for what lawyer would not find deterrence enough in the jail sentence, the two-year suspension from the bar of the United States District Court, and the disapproval of his profession? If the disbarment rests, not on these specific proven offenses, but on atmospheric considerations of general undesirability and Communistic leanings or affiliation, these have not been charged and he has had no chance to meet them. We cannot take judicial notice of them. On the occasions when Isserman has been before this Court, or before an individual Justice, his conduct has been unexceptionable and his professional ability considerable.

We would have a different case here if the record stood that Isserman, with others, entered into a deliberate conspiracy or plans to obstruct justice. But that charge has been found by the Court of Appeals to lack support in the evidence, and again in the disciplinary proceeding in District Court it was not found to be proven. What remains is a finding that he was guilty of several unplanned contumacious outbursts during a long and bitter trial.

Perhaps consciousness of our own short patience makes us unduly considerate of the failing tempers of others of our contentious craft. But to permanently and wholly deprive one of his profession at Isserman's time of life, and after he has paid so dearly for his fault, impresses us as a severity which will serve no useful purpose for the bar, the court or the delinquent.

But that was not quite the end of the matter. Isserman had been disbarred by a legal presumption of the Court's rules, not by a majority vote; and the death of Vinson followed by Warren's appointment to succeed him resulted in a new majority of the full Court who disagreed with the decision against Isserman. When the Court's rules were revised effective July 1, 1954, Rule 8 (replacing the former Rule 2) stipulated that for disbarment from the Court to become effective, a *majority* of the participating justices must agree to such a decision. And on the very first day of the new term, October 15, 1954, a motion for rehearing was granted and the 1953 action against Isserman was rescinded for the reason that "A majority of the Justices participating do not find ground for disbarment of Isserman[32]—which was true notwithstanding Jackson's death a week earlier. Neither Warren nor Clark participated; Burton, Minton, and Reed now dissented; and Black, Douglas, and Frankfurter stood fast in the faith. With majority control, as augmented by Warren and Jackson, over the Court's rule-making process, three justices were thereby able to overrule the former decision of four; and a 3-3 deadlock displaced with opposite direction the outcome of an earlier 4-4 deadlock.

C. THE DISPASSIONATE JUDGE

CRAIG V. HARNEY
331 U.S. 367, 394 (May 19, 1947)

Although the circumstances of this case led Jackson to argue the essential humanity of judges, the decision found him on the side of local law and order. At issue, as he saw it, was the right to a fair trial, which in turn he identified with the role of the trial judge. This was a subject upon which he not long thereafter ventured a more detailed portrait:

I am convinced that the position in our profession which requires the most versatility of mind and firmness of character is the worthily occupied trial bench. I do not belittle the

[32] *In re Isserman*, 348 U.S. 1. He was nevertheless subsequently disbarred by the federal court for the Southern District of New York (New York City), *New York Times,* January 30, 1958, 12:2. The stated ground was his failure to disclose, at the time of his admission to the bar of that court three decades earlier, his prior conviction in New Jersey of the offense involving "moral turpitude." The newspaper report also states erroneously that he was at this time (1958) disbarred from practice before the United States Supreme Court.

very necessary and important role of the appellate court, but I think it has been exalted at the expense of the role of the trial judge.

The trial judge sits alone and does most of his work with the public looking on. He cannot lean on advice of associates or help from a law clerk. He works in an atmosphere of strife, with counsel, litigants and often witnesses and spectators bitter, biased, and partisan; and, if the presiding judge fails of his part, they become demonstrative and disorderly.

This lone trial judge must make a multitude of quick and important decisions as the case progresses. He must rule immediately and firmly on questions upon which appellate judges may deliberate for months and then divide. He is frequently attended by poorly prepared counsel, and even diligent counsel may be unprepared on questions that are not anticipated. In training lawyers the law schools are also training these future judges, for we do not think it compatible with democracy that the judiciary, as in some Continental countries, be a separate profession specially trained for the task of judging. Either to preside over a courtroom or helpfully and successfully to conduct cases at its bar is, perhaps, less a science than an art. Some of the best trial judges I have known were not distinguished for learning so much as for wisdom and common sense and a personality that enabled them unostentatiously to dominate the courtroom and be master of its proceedings. I do not know that it would be possible to teach that kind of art, but it seems to me that the unsolved problem of legal education is how to equip the law student for work at the bar of the court and for assumption, the politicians willing, of the work of the trial bench. The two are similar in many requirements.[33]

The explicit question here was whether a county judge—and a *layman* at that—could summarily imprison various journalists on a charge of criminal contempt because the local newspaper had criticized his recent decision in a case at a time when he had not yet announced his ruling on a motion asking that he vacate the decision and grant a new trial. The majority of the Court, which included the four libertarians plus Burton and Reed, stated that the Court's recent precedents, applying the clear and present danger doctrine of freedom of the press, controlled the disposition here. This was a point of view with which Jackson fundamentally disagreed and he took pains to reiterate his dissent, a couple of years later, in his advice to young lawyers-to-be:

[I]t seems obvious that if before or during a trial the right to publicize inadmissible evidence is inseparable from our freedoms, then the trend of trials to turn on evidence and influences beyond control of the judge may be expected to continue. The custom of prejudging guilt or innocence and of injecting evidence and opinions upon the trial by publicity can easily proceed to such a point that verdicts in highly publicized American cases will no more really represent the jurors' dispassionate personal judgment on the legal evidence than do those of "People's Courts" we so criticize abroad. The plain fact is that courts and the legal profession cannot make good the constitutional assurance of fair trial except with the

33 "The Advocate," 610. This was his usual position: that a good lawyer was interchangeable in the roles of attorney and of judge. But in the end, he confessed to misgivings, saying that "It is not true that a good trial lawyer always will make a good judge." *Syracuse Law Review*, VI (1955), 223. To say nothing, as he might well have added, of a good administrator, which Jackson evidently was not: see Telford Taylor, "The Nuremberg Trials," *Columbia Law Review*, LV (1955), 488-526 and Warner W. Gardner, "Government Attorney," *ibid.*, 438-444.

cooperation of the agencies that make and convey public opinion. If they do not respect the judicial process sufficiently to forego scooping it, pressuring it, or circumventing it, fair trial in this country is headed in the direction we so deplore when we see examples of farcical trials abroad.[34]

Frankfurter and Jackson were very much of the same mind on this issue so they divided the dissenting task by writing separate opinions and emphasizing different points, with Vinson joining in the Frankfurter statement. Frankfurter distinguished the precedents relied upon by the majority; and having thus exorcised the Court's presumed obligation to free these defendants, he indicated his preference for having the Court defer to the judgment of each state, on the policy question of how much summary power should be vested in trial judges in order to guarantee the orderly and dispassionate administration of justice, without fear or favor.

Douglas' opinion for the Court advised trial judges to be men of fortitude and to rise above the sound and fury that might be provoked by the local press, whilst the latter was exercising its constitutional right to report and to comment upon the work of judges. It was hardly consistent, Jackson's opinion suggests, that his colleagues should be offering this kind of advice to *state* judges in the very decision in which they were themselves yielding to the very kind of pressure—the threat of bad publicity—which they advised Judge Harney manfully to surmount!

MR. JUSTICE JACKSON, dissenting.

This is one of those cases in which the reasons we give for our decision are more important to the development of the law than the decision itself.

It seems to me that the Court is assigning two untenable, if not harmful, reasons for its action. The first is that this newspaper publisher has done no wrong. I take it that we could not deny the right of the state to punish him if he had done wrong and I do not suppose we could say that the traditional remedy was an unconstitutional one.

The right of the people to have a free press is a vital one, but so is the right to have a calm and fair trial free from outside pressures and influences. Every other right, including the right of a free press itself, may depend on the ability to get a judicial hearing as dispassionate and impartial as the weakness inherent in men will permit. I think this publisher passed beyond the legitimate use of press freedom and infringed the citizen's right to a calm and impartial trial. I do not think we can say that it is beyond the power of the state to exert safeguards against such interference with the course of trial as we have here.

This was a private lawsuit between the individuals. It involved an issue of no greater public importance than which of two claimants should be the tenant of

[34] *Ibid.*, 609.

the "Playboy Cafe." The public interest in the litigation was that dispassionate justice be done by the court and that it appear to be done.

The publisher had a complete monopoly of newspaper publicity in that locality. For reasons that are not apparent, the papers took an unusual interest in the proceeding. They first made what the court agrees was a "rather sketchy and one-sided report of a case." This is no overstatement. The former tenant had tendered a check and the newspaper report represented it as a payment of rent; it made no reference to the fact that the check was postdated and was therefore no payment at all. Reports played up the fact that its favorite among the litigants was a veteran. The community became aroused. Then the newspaper published editorials which attacked the judge while a motion for retrial was pending with what the prevailing opinion concedes was "strong language, intemperate language, and, we assume, an unfair criticism." The object of the publicity appears to have been to get the judge to reverse himself and to grant a new trial.

The fact that he did not yield to it does not prove that the attack was not an effective interference with the administration of justice. The judge was put in a position in which he either must appear to yield his judgment to public clamor or to defy public sentiment. The consequence of attacks may differ with the temperament of the judge. Some judges may take fright and yield while others become more set in their course if only to make clear that they will not be bullied. This judge was evidently of the latter type. He was diverted from the calm consideration of the litigation before him by what he regarded as a duty to institute a contempt proceeding of his own against his tormentors.

For this Court to imply that this kind of attack during a pending case is all right seems to me to compound the wrong. The press of the country may rightfully take the decision of this Court to mean indifference toward, if not approval of, such attacks upon courts during pending cases. I think this opinion conveys a wrong impression of the responsibilities of a free press for the calm and dispassionate administration of justice and that we should not hesitate to condemn what has been done here.

But even worse is that this Court appears to sponsor the myth that judges are not as other men are, and that therefore newspaper attacks on them are negligible because they do not penetrate the judicial armor. Says the opinion: "But the law of contempt is not made for the protection of judges who may be sensitive to the winds of public opinion. Judges are supposed to be men of fortitude, able to thrive in a hardy climate." With due respect to those who think otherwise, to me this is an ill-founded opinion, and to inform the press that it may be irresponsible in attacking judges because they have so much fortitude is ill-advised, or worse. I do not know whether it is the view of the Court that a judge must be thick-skinned or just thickheaded, but nothing in my experience or observation confirms the idea that he is insensitive to publicity. Who does not prefer good to ill report of his work? And if fame—a good public name—is, as Milton said, the "last infirmity of noble mind," it is frequently the first infirmity of a mediocre one.

From our sheltered position, fortified by life tenure and other defenses to judicial independence, it is easy to say that this local judge ought to have shown more fortitude in the face of criticism. But he had no such protection. He was an elective judge, who held for a short term. I do not take it that an ambition of a judge to remain a judge is either unusual or dishonorable. Moreover, he was not a lawyer, and I regard this as a matter of some consequence. A lawyer may gain courage to render a decision that temporarily is unpopular because he has confidence that his profession over the years will approve it, despite its unpopular reception, as has been the case with many great decisions. But this judge had no anchor in professional opinion. Of course, the blasts of these little papers in this small community do not jolt us, but I am not so confident that we would be indifferent if a news monopoly in our entire jurisdiction should perpetrate this kind of attack on us.

It is doubtful if the press itself regards judges as so insulated from public opinion. In this very case the American Newspaper Publishers Association filed a brief *amicus curiae* on the merits after we granted certiorari. Of course, it does not cite a single authority that was not available to counsel for the publisher involved, and does not tell us a single new fact except this one: "This membership embraces more than 700 newspaper publishers whose publications represent in excess of eighty per cent of the total daily and Sunday circulation of newspapers published in this country. The Association is vitally interested in the issue presented in this case, namely, the right of newspapers to publish news stories and editorials on cases pending in the courts."

This might be a good occasion to demonstrate the fortitude of the judiciary.

D.   PASSIONATE JUSTICE

HIROTA V. MACARTHUR
335 U.S. 876 (December 6, 1948)

Like *Isserman*, this was the rare case that arises under the original jurisdiction of the Supreme Court, and the justices were equally divided—unless, that is, Robert Jackson would be willing to participate in deciding a case that raised an issue about which he was, putatively, one of the most biased men in the entire world. The case was exceptional, but the problem to which it related dogged the Court during the period after World War II. When Jackson returned from Nuremberg, he came to a Court that was deadlocked on the question of the constitutionality of American participation in the trials of the German "war criminals." The Libertarian Four insisted that the Supreme Court should hear the appeals of the enemy defendants, and it appeared that no lower courts of the United States had (or would exercise) jurisdiction, so that such cases would have to come before the Court as a matter of original jurisdiction. The other four justices were convinced that the war crimes trials raised only political questions which were beyond the constitutional competence of the Supreme Court to adjudicate. Since Jackson was unquestionably disqualified from voting on this question because of his official role at Nuremberg, the deadlock continued—and somewhat notoriously—for several years. The trials of the Japanese war criminals, which lagged a couple of years behind those of the Nazi leaders, despite General MacArthur's attempts to hasten the process,[35] raised the question again, shortly after the convicted Nazis had gone to their fate without benefit of the Supreme Court's confirmation of the legitimacy of American participation in the process. Against this background, Jackson's strategy in the case of Hirota becomes readily understandable.

Although he was not *technically* disqualified in the Japanese case, his actual bias was so widely known and so well documented that there could be no doubt where he stood and how he would vote, if he were to participate. Because he felt so strongly that the Supreme Court should give its blessing to the war crimes trials, particularly in view of the doubts raised by the four libertarians, his reluctance to participate can be understood best against the background of the *Jewell Ridge* affair. What would the Black cabal, and their academic acolytes, have to say about Jackson's failure to disqualify himself on this issue? What would be the ethics of having the prosecutor of Herman Goering sit in judgment on Koki Hirota? Politics, the art of compromise, provided a way out of the dilemma. According to his own statement, Jackson negotiated a "deal" whereby he would join the four libertarians to create a majority favorable to hearing the argument in the case—that is, the Court would assume temporary jurisdiction for the purpose of considering the question whether it had jurisdiction to hear the case on the merits. (A majority of five justices, rather than a plurality of four, was necessary because the motion before the Court was for leave to file a petition for the writ of habeas corpus rather than a petition for certiorari.)

The deal was advantageous to both factions. From Jackson's point of view, the effect of hearing the case would be to force the libertarians to officially commit themselves on a question whose affirmative resolution

[35] A. Frank Reel, *The Case of General Yamashita* (Chicago: The University of Chicago Press, 1949).

seemed so fraught with legal and political difficulties that the odds of picking up at least one switched vote from among the libertarians seemed good. And, if this did not happen, Jackson made it clear that he himself reserved the right to vote, if his participation should become necessary (necessary, that is, in order for the case to come out the way he was determined that it should come out). The gamble seemed less advantageous from the libertarians point of view, but apparently it was the best deal they could make in a game where the cards were stacked against them. The libertarians could hope to pick up a single vote from among the other four members of the Court[36]—perhaps Frankfurter, or Burton—in which case they would control the outcome no matter what Jackson did.

The Court's decision was announced on what was for the parties to the case the seventh anniversary of Pearl Harbor. In its entirety, it read as follows:

Miscellaneous Orders
No. 239, Misc. HIROTA V. MACARTHUR ET AL.;
No. 240, Misc. DOHIHARA V. MACARTHUR ET AL.; and
No. 248, MISC. KIDO ET AL. V. MACARTHUR ET AL.
The Court desires to hear argument upon the questions presented by the motions for leave to file petitions for writs of habeas corpus. Action upon the motions for leave to file will be withheld meanwhile, and the motions are set down for oral argument on Thursday, December 16, 1948. THE CHIEF JUSTICE, MR. JUSTICE REED, MR. JUSTICE FRANKFURTER, and MR. JUSTICE BURTON are of the opinion that there is want of jurisdiction. U. S. Constitution, Article III, § 2, Clause 2. MR. JUSTICE JACKSON has filed a memorandum stating his views.

MR. JUSTICE JACKSON:

Four members of this Court feel that the Japanese convicted of war crimes should have some form of relief, at least tentative, from this Court. The votes of these are not enough to grant it but, if I refrain from voting, they constitute one-half of the sitting Court. As I understand it, these Justices do not commit themselves as to whether there is any constitutional power in this Court to entertain these proceedings but only feel that they would like to hear argument to enlighten them in reaching a determination of that issue. They feel it so strongly that they not only favored grant of relief in conference, but, having failed, announce their dissent to the public—an interested section of which consists of our late enemies and allies in the Orient. This perhaps is all that these Justices could do consistently with the course that they have already taken in several German cases. This is their right, and I point it out not to question the right but as one of the facts which confronts me in deciding my own course.

---

[36] See Glendon Schubert, "Policy Without Law: An Extension of the Certiorari Game," *Stanford Law Review*, XIV (1962), 284-327.

On the other hand, four other Justices are convinced, from their study of the question, that there is no constitutional jurisdiction whatever in this Court over the subject matter. To interfere and assume to review it would in that view constitute an unwarranted interference with delicate affairs that are in no way committed to the jurisdiction of this Court. These four Justices having satisfied themselves that this Court is without lawful power, have consistently refused to take action which would usurp it, even tentatively, in the German cases. Of course, they could not consistently, with equal justice under law, apply a different jurisdictional rule to these cases than they have to those of the Germans.

By reason of nonparticipation in the German cases, for reasons which are obvious, I remain uncommitted on the jurisdictional issues. My nonparticipation has prevented their resolution heretofore and I must decide whether another nonparticipation will prevent it now. The issue transcends the particular litigation.

This public division of the Court, equal if I do not participate, puts the United States before the world, and particularly before Oriental peoples, in this awkward position: Having major responsibility for the capture of these Japanese prisoners, it also has considerable responsibility for their fate. If their plea ends in stalemate in this Court, the authorities have no course but to execute sentences which half of this Court tells the world are on so doubtful a legal foundation that they favor some kind of provisional relief and fuller review. The fact that such a number of men so placed in the United States are of that opinion would for all time be capitalized in the Orient, if not elsewhere, to impeach the good faith and to discredit the justice of this country, and to comfort its critics and enemies.

The other possible course is to assert tentatively a jurisdiction in this Court to stay and order hearings in these proceedings. This is likewise bound to embarrass the United States. On American initiative, under direction of the President as Commander-in-Chief, this country invited our Pacific allies, on foreign soil, to cooperate in conducting a grand inquest into the alleged crimes, including the war guilt, of these defendants. Whatever its real legal nature, it bears the outward appearance of an international enterprise, undertaken on our part under the war powers and control of foreign affairs vested in the Executive. For this Court now to call up these cases for judicial review under exclusively American law can only be regarded as a warning to our associates in the trials that no commitment of the President or of the military authorities, even in such matters as these, has finality or validity under our form of government until it has the approval of this Court. And since the Court's approval or disapproval cannot be known until after the event—usually long after—it would substantially handicap our country in asking other nations to rely upon the word or act of the President in affairs which only he is competent to conduct.

In this equal division each side's position is taken after long and frequent consideration and repeated public announcement in the German cases. The one group of Justices can hardly fail to proffer to the Japanese an opportunity to argue reviewability which they have consistently announced should be allowed to the Germans. Neither can the other side extend to the Japanese opportunities which they have consistently denied to the Germans. The fact that neither side in good grace can retreat puts to me disagreeable alternatives as to whether I should break the deadlock or permit it to continue.

I do not regard myself as under a legal disqualification in these Japanese cases under the usages as to disqualification which prevail in this Court. While I negotiated the international Charter under which the Nazi war criminals were tried and also represented the United States in that Four-Power trial, the Japanese were not tried under that Charter but under a later and, in respects relevant to the present controversy, a somewhat different charter, promulgated by different authority. Of course, I participated in formulating basic rules on the subject of war crimes. But it is not the custom of this Court that a Justice disqualifies from passing on a particular case because he actively participated as a Senator or Representative in making the law under which it was tried. Nor has it been considered necessary to disqualify himself because he had handled cases which involved the same law or crimes as those involved in the case before him. I have had no participation either in the basic decision to hold war crimes trials in the Orient or as to the manner in which they should be conducted. Nevertheless, I have been so identified with the subject of war crimes that, if it involved my personal preferences alone, I should not sit in this case.

But the issues here are truly great ones. They only involve decision of war crimes issues secondarily, for primarily the decision will establish or deny that this Court has power to review exercise of military power abroad and the President's conduct of external affairs of our Government. The answer will influence our Nation's reputation for continuity of policy for a long time to come. For these reasons I decided at Saturday's conference to break the tie in the Japanese cases. The horns between which I must choose in the dilemma are such, as I have pointed out, that it is a choice between evils. The reasons which guide me to a choice are these:

If I add my vote to those who favor denying these applications for want of jurisdiction, it is irrevocable. The Japanese will be executed and their partisans will forever point to the dissents of four members of the Court to support their accusation that the United States gave them less than justice. This stain, whether deserved or not, would be impressed upon the record of the United States in Oriental memory. If, however, I vote with those who would grant temporary relief, it may be that fuller argument and hearing will convert one or more of the Justices on one side or the other from the views that have equally divided them in the German cases. In those cases I did not feel at liberty to cast the deciding vote and there was no course to avoid leaving the question unresolved. But here I feel that a tentative assertion of jurisdiction, which four members of the Court believe does not exist, will not be irreparable if they ultimately are right. To let the sentences be executed against the dissent of four members will be irreparably injurious even if they are wrong, and if their minds are open, as it is understood, to further persuasion, I would not want to be responsible for eliminating even a faint chance of avoiding dissents in this matter. Our allies are more likely to understand and to forgive any assertion of excess jurisdiction against this background than our enemies would be to understand or condone any excess of scruple about jurisdiction to grant them a hearing.

It is fair to counsel to say that I intent to sit and hear argument at the hearing which I am voting to grant. I shall hope not to participate in the final decision but as to that, I reserve full freedom of decision.

For the present, it is enough that I vote with JUSTICES BLACK, DOUGLAS, MURPHY and RUTLEDGE, who have consistently noted their dissent in war crimes cases, for whatever temporary restraints or writs they see fit to grant for the purpose of bringing on any hearings or arguments they want to hear as a basis for reaching their final decision on the merits. Needless to say, in doing this I express neither approval nor disapproval of the course they have taken and intimate no views on the constitutional issues involved. I have thought, however, that a candid disclosure of the considerations which influence me is due, not only to the litigants in these cases and to those in the previous German cases, but in justice to the Court and to myself.

Time is important in these cases. I notified the full Court of my position on December 4, as soon as I knew the positions others took on this case, in order that no delay may be chargeable to my indecisions. I hope these cases will now be set for the earliest possible hearing. I also indulge the hope that argument will produce a majority decision of the Court without further intervention from one who has been so identified with controversial phases of war crimes law that he cannot expect others to consider him as detached and dispassionate on the subject as he thinks himself to be.

Jackson's calculated risk paid off only two weeks later: the Supreme Court upheld Hirota's execution by ruling that the Court had no jurisdiction to review a decision of an international war crimes court, which was "not a tribunal of the United States."[37] Five justices, *including Black,* joined in the *per curiam* opinion of the Court; Douglas concurred; Murphy dissented; Rutledge reserved judgment; and Jackson did not participate.

---

[37] *Hirota* v. *MacArthur*, 388 U.S. 197 (December 20, 1948); and see Clinton Rossiter, *The Supreme Court and the Commander in Chief* (Ithaca: Cornell University, 1951), pp. 116-121.

E. DISPASSIONATE JUSTICE

MCGRATH V. KRISTENSEN
340 U.S. 162, 176 (December 11, 1950)

This case is an example of Jackson at his engaging best. Upon other occasions, demonstrations of his impish candor[38]—and this phrase was a favorite of his—were focused upon his colleagues, litigants before the Court, and other villains; but in this instance, his lash was turned, lightly and with mellow humor, upon himself. Indeed, neither the facts, the legal questions before the Court, nor the views of his colleagues are directly responsible for Jackson's writing a separate opinion; his quarrel was with himself (or, rather, with his former self), and he was in complete agreement with the majority as to the disposition of the case.

The question was one of statutory interpretation: whether a temporary visitor to the United States, whose stay had been unavoidably prolonged by the outbreak of World War II, was a "resident" of the United States liable to induction under the Selective Service Act.[39] The majority decided that such a person was not barred from naturalization (and was, therefore, eligible for suspension of deportation), since the alien's status as an involuntary resident in fact did not constitute residence in law within

[38] Of many other possible examples, the following two are typical: "I used to say that, as Solicitor General, I made three arguments of every case. First came the one that I planned —as I thought, logical, coherent, complete. Second was the one actually presented—interrupted, incoherent, disjointed, disappointing. The third was the utterly devastating argument that I thought of after going to bed that night." Jackson, as quoted by Attorney General Brownell in the *Memorial Proceedings,* 349 U.S. xliv.

On one occasion during oral argument, as the time for the luncheon break drew near, the attorney who was speaking "looked first at the clock in the front of the courtroom and then at the clock on the rear wall. 'Your Honors,' he said, 'I don't know whether the time has come to suspend or not. These clocks don't seem to be in agreement.' Quick as a flash Justice Jackson interjected from the bench: 'That's the influence of the Court.'" Gerhart, *America's Advocate,* p. 300.

[39] Kristensen, a citizen of Denmark, had entered the United States on August 17, 1939, on a sixty-day temporary visitor's visa to attend the New York World's Fair and visit relatives. The outbreak of World War II prevented his return to Denmark; and although he applied for and was granted a series of successive extensions, eventually his funds were exhausted and he was forced to seek employment, thereby violating the terms of his visitor status. Deportation proceedings against him on this ground, begun in May 1940 and subsequently suspended for the duration of the war, were reopened in 1946. In the meantime, he married an American citizen, and was relieved from military service when he claimed exemption as an alien. The question now was whether his refusal to perform military duty precluded his becoming naturalized, and, therefore, made him ineligible to request suspension of the deportation order which had been issued against him.

the meaning of the statute or the prevailing regulations. As Attorney General before he joined the Court, however, Jackson had given contrary advice to Secretary of War Stimson; and the present Attorney General had relied upon Jackson's earlier opinion in arguing the instant case. This circumstance apparently provoked Jackson to add the following footnote to the opinion of the Court.

MR. JUSTICE JACKSON, *concurring*.

I concur in the judgment and opinion of the Court. But since it is contrary to an opinion which, as Attorney General, I rendered in 1940, I owe some word of explanation. 39 Op. Atty. Gen. 504. I am entitled to say of that opinion what any discriminating reader must think of it—that it was as foggy as the statute the Attorney General was asked to interpret. It left the difficult borderline questions posed by the Secretary of War unanswered, covering its lack of precision with generalities which, however, gave off overtones of assurance that the Act applied to nearly every alien from a neutral country caught in the United States under almost any circumstances which required him to stay overnight.

The opinion did not at all consider aspects of our diplomatic history, which I now think, and should think I would then have thought, ought to be considered in applying any conscription Act to aliens.

In times gone by, many United States citizens by naturalization have returned to visit their native lands. There they frequently were held for military duty by governments which refused to recognize a general right of expatriation. The United States consistently has asserted the right of its citizens to be free from seizure for military duty by reason of temporary and lawful presence in foreign lands. Immunities we have asserted for our own citizens we should not deny to those of other friendly nations. Nor should we construe our legislation to penalize or prejudice such aliens for asserting a right we have consistently asserted as a matter of national policy in dealing with other nations. Of course, if an alien is not a mere sojourner but acquires residence here in any permanent sense, he submits himself to our law and assumes the obligations of a resident toward this country.

The language of the Selective Service Act can be interpreted consistently with this history of our international contentions. I think the decision of the Court today does so. Failure of the Attorney General's opinion to consider the matter in this light is difficult to explain in view of the fact that he personally had urged this history upon this Court in arguing *Perkins* v. *Elg*, 307 U.S. 325 [1939]. Its details may be found in the briefs and their cited sources. It would be charitable to assume that neither the nominal addressee nor the nominal author of the opinion read it. That, I do not doubt, explains Mr. Stimson's acceptance of an answer so inadequate to his questions. But no such confession and avoidance can excuse the then Attorney General.

Precedent, however, is not lacking for ways by which a judge may recede from a prior opinion that has proven untenable and perhaps misled others. See Chief Justice Taney, *License Cases*, 5 How. 504, recanting views he had pressed upon the Court as Attorney General of Maryland in *Brown* v. *Maryland*, 12 Wheat. 419. Baron Bramwell extricated himself from a somewhat similar embarrassment by saying, "The matter does not appear to me now as it appears to have appeared to me then." *Andrews* v. *Styrap*, 26 L.T.R., N.S. 704, 706. And Mr. Justice Story, accounting for his contradiction of his own former opinion, quite properly put the matter: "My own error, however, can furnish no ground for its being adopted by this Court. . . ." *United States* v. *Gooding*, 12 Wheat. 460, 478. Perhaps Dr. Johnson really went to the heart of the matter when he explained a blunder in his dictionary—"Ignorance, sir, ignorance." But an escape less self-depreciating was taken by Lord Westbury, who, it is said, rebuffed a barrister's reliance upon an earlier opinion of his Lordship: "I can only say that I am amazed that a man of my intelligence should have been guilty of giving such an opinion." If there are other ways of gracefully and good-naturedly surrendering former views to a better considered position, I invoke them all.

10 IDEOLOGY

1

"I came," said *Robert Jackson,* "from people too busy making a living to work life's annoyances up into a philosophy. . . . The way of life of the American is practical, hardheaded and concrete. . . . It's distinguishing ideology is that it has no 'ideology' except to get results."[1] This certainly sounds like plain talk about common sense; and Jackson often gave voice, as in this instance, to the antitheoretical bias of the empiricist. His typical stance was to embrace the fallacy of the practical man, as it has been called. But he was also a student of William James, and he was quite aware that pragmatism, too, is a philosophy. Indeed, it bloomed and flowered in phase with Jackson's own maturation, and became the dominant American ideology at the very time that he was growing up in the law. As an exceptionally intelligent craftsman whose highly developed skill took the characteristic form of imposing rational verbal structures upon less well ordered raw materials, he necessarily operated on the basis of an at least partially consistent cognitive structure of value preferences. Ideology is an appropriate concept to invoke, as a shorthand way of referring to the patterning of his values.

What has confused many commentators upon Jackson's ideology has been the extent to which he argued both sides of many questions. Thus, one finds a law professor asserting that:

> The most striking feature of Justice Jackson's judicial philosophy is that it can only with great difficulty be made to conform to any of the neat and currently-popular classifications of Supreme Court justices. . . . Jackson, for one, cannot be so readily pigeonholed.[2]

Similarly, a political scientist remarks that "in striving to associate Jackson's views with some doctrine or set of doctrines which will neatly explain them all, one is beset with difficulties."[3] And another political scientist, after having concluded from an initial encounter that his "figures . . . average out a certain unpredictability in Jackson's votes,"[4] returned to the fray with fresh data only to reach a similar conclusion again:

---

[1] As quoted by William L. Ransome, "Associate Justice Robert H. Jackson," *American Bar Association Journal,* XXVII (1941), 481, and apparently quoting from Jackson's speech, "Back to the American Way," before the Commonwealth Club of San Francisco, on America's Town Meeting of the Air (November 2, 1939).

[2] Paul A. Weidner, "Justice Jackson and the Judicial Function," *Michigan Law Review,* LIII (1955), 593-594.

[3] Vincent L. Barnett, "Mr. Justice Jackson and the Supreme Court," *Western Political Quarterly,* I (1948), 241.

[4] C. Herman Pritchett, *The Roosevelt Court* (New York: The Macmillan Company, 1948), p. 261.

[T]he rather erratic nature of his opinions ma[kes] it difficult to catalogue him. . . .
The unpredictability of Jackson's performance leads one to question whether he has developed any systematic theories about civil liberties or the judicial function.[5]

I have attempted to demonstrate elsewhere that, just as punishment
can be suited to the criminal as well as to (or in lieu of) the crime, so an
analysis of Jackson's ideology can be based inductively upon his own judicial behavior,[6] in preference to an attempt to analogize him to a criterion
based upon Holmes, Brandeis, Cardozo, Stone, or to some other judge's
(or person's) set of attitudes.

2

There are three major themes in Jackson's opinions in Chapter 2.
First and foremost is freedom of belief, the passive counterpart of what
in activist form is usually referred to as the set of First Amendment rights
of freedom of speech, press, and petition—in short, the right to communicate. Jackson's strong support for the right to be free from official invasion of *un*communicated beliefs stemmed from his deep attachment to
the ideology of individualism.

Second is free speech for labor *and* management. In general, Jackson
was no great supporter of activist claims to the right to communicate; to
the contrary, he usually argued and voted to deny such claims. But the
particular circumstances of *Thomas* v. *Collins* made it possible for Jackson
to vote for the right of unions to communicate with workers, while primarily arguing in support of "equal time" for employers. Jackson's position on this issue was a joint function of his attachment to the economic
content of the ideology of individualism, and to his strong support of the
social ideology of equalitarianism.

The remaining issue in this chapter concerns the secularity of public
education, which Jackson strongly supported. In voting to oppose the bus
subsidy for Catholic schools, and both in-school and released-time forms
of religious instruction for captive audiences of children in public schools,
and in the opinions through which he sought to justify these votes, Jackson took one of the most extreme positions of any of the justices, in favor

[5] C. Hermann Pritchett, *Civil Liberties and the Vinson Court* (Chicago: University of
Chicago Press, 1954), pp. 18, 228-229.

[6] See Glendon Schubert, "Jackson's Judicial Philosophy: An Exploration in Value
Analysis," *American Political Science Review,* LIX (1965), 940-963. A similar conclusion
was reached by Dorothy B. James, who examined both speeches and judicial opinions in her
"Judicial Philosophy and Accession to the Court: The Cases of Justices Jackson and Douglas"
(Columbia University Ph. D. dissertation in political science, 1966; University Microfilms
No. 66-12,571), and "Role Theory and the Supreme Court," *Journal of Politics,* XXX
(1968), 160-186.

of the segregation of religious instruction. Tax-supported secular public schools were a major political fruit of Jacksonian Democracy; and the relevant ideological dimension for Robert Jackson, in upholding free public education, was political libertarianism. It is noteworthy that Jackson thought of this value, like freedom of belief, as a passive virtue; it was not the right to *do* something, but rather it was the right to be *free from* the endeavors of proselyters to impose their minority views upon the majority.

3

Jackson's position in upholding the separation of school and state was closely related to his basis for upholding the convictions of various zealous political, religious, and economic evangelists who sought to use force to disseminate their views. The Jehovah's Witnesses defendants had succeeded, in the one instance, in staging a raid upon a peaceful community of workingmen (in Jackson's own preferred, but already antiquated, ascriptive idiom) on a Sunday morning of especial religious significance for many of its citizens, and then of forcibly invading the privacy of their homes. In the other instance, the invasion was of the public's right to privacy in a public place—and surely the phrase is no more involuted than the circumstances to which it related. The very word images—workingmen sleeping in their cottages on their one day of rest, and Sabbath picnickers on family outings in the park—are strongly reminiscent of the faded American culture, of the turn of the century, with which Jackson so strongly identified. And well they must have been so perceived—Jeanette lies only some two score leagues due south of Jamestown, as the crow flies, and Lockport only half that distance in the opposite direction. Both towns were too close to home for Jackson to need to consult the record to know that only three months of the year are available for family picnics in the vicinity of the forty-second parallel. The amplified voice of labor in itself presented no great threat to the urban community of Trenton; that decision functioned primarily, for Jackson, as a delayed vindication of his position in the first sound truck case, and as a means of taunting the Libertarian Four for having lost "the power of decision" over the issue.

The remaining three decisions in Chapter 3 were concerned with what to Jackson was the much more serious threat, to both local communities and to the national community, raised by passionate advocates of political extremism. Nuremberg was much too close, in social and psychological distance, for Jackson to accept the Marquis of Queensberry rules for free speech as the relevant criterion for appraising the Philippics of fascist rabblerousers. Nor did it matter whether the forum, in such cases, was a soap box in the park or a privately hired hall—neither of these classic arenas for the exercise of freedom of speech could be tolerated, in Jackson's view, when the *content* of the speaker's remarks was so inflammatory that it presented a clear and present danger of public disorder.

An even more dangerous threat to national survival was implicit in the Communist conspiracy to use constitutional liberties as a means of maneuvering themselves into positions where they could deny such liberties to *all* others (for Communist leaders never did allow such rights to their own followers.) For the leaders of such a conspiracy against the American way of life—political, economic, and social—no First Amendment rights should be recognized. There was a more fundamental right of national self preservation; and it was to this natural right that the Supreme Court owed allegiance.

4

At times it suited Jackson's purposes (as it did his colleagues) to indulge in the fiction that the Supreme Court's primary interest in hearing the appeals of criminal convictions is to assure justice to the individual defendants. But it is neither the institutional role, nor the function in fact, of the Supreme Court of the United States to sit as a court of criminal appeals, from either the federal or the state judiciaries; nor has it been so in this century. Almost without exception, therefore, the Court takes cases, nominally involving the question of guilt or innocence (or stated more accurately, whether the Court should approve or reverse a conviction below) in order to get at some auxiliary issue of legal policy—what happens to the individual defendant is quite incidental. All of the cases in Chapter 4 illustrate how decisions in criminal "appeals" (most of which were reviewed, speaking technically, on certiorari rather than by the legal process of statutory appeal) functioned for Jackson as instruments of policy making.

The effect, for example, of superimposing a judicial requirement of criminal intent, upon statutory definitions of crimes, designed to control behavior in an increasingly collectivized society, was to frustrate the possibility of effective enforcement of much modern social and economic policy. All of the arguments that Jackson himself raised in *Dalehite*, concerning appropriate standards of care in our "increasingly synthetic civilization," can be invoked against his position in *Morissette*. But in *Morissette*, the bureaucrats were on the other, and therefore wrong, side of the fence of "due care" than they were in *Dalehite*; and Morrissette himself symbolizes the enterprising, independent, small-scale but autonomous individual who populated the Jamestown of Jackson's remembrance of things past. It is hardly surprising that Jackson backed him to the hilt; all that is surprising is that all eight of his colleagues joined in the *marche derrière*.

In general, Jackson did not favor liberalizing changes in the norms that were supposed to guide police and prosecutors in the investigation of crime, and judges in the trial of accused defendants. In his view society has rights paramount over those of criminals, because without an orderly society in which crime can be and is punished, there could be no liberty for anyone. Hence, it was not only constitutional, but also proper, to deny prisoners the right to counsel while the police interrogated defendants for whatever reasonable time might be necessary to induce a confession—with what is reasonable depending, not upon the character of or evidence against the suspect, but rather upon the gravity of the offense under investigation.

Jackson agreed with Felix Frankfurter about the desirability of controlling publicity concerning judicial proceedings. Newspapers (in Jackson's day; today it is TV[7]) posed a threat to the legal profession's monopolistic control over the prosecution and trial of crime: not only did the press broaden the channels of communication for attempts to influence the discretion of both prosecutors and judges; publicity might also bias the jury by informing jurors about other aspects of the case (as a social problem and political issue), thereby shifting the focus from the tunnel vision that the building of the legal record was supposed to impose.

Jackson's position in regard to juries was that they should of course be stacked—it is their function to provide variation in the representation of differing constellations of interests in the decisions of trial courts—but stacked in the proper direction. He had no objection to the use of "blue-ribbon" juries,[8] packed with upper-middle class jurors to assure higher rates of conviction, because it was the upper-middle class (with which he himself identified)[9] whose interests were threatened by socially dangerous defendants such as burglars, embezzlers, and arsonists—or at least, so Jackson thought. Similarly, guilty Negroes were appropriately brought to trial on the indictment of grand juries that consisted exclusively of the defendants' poor white neighbors, thus forming, at a lower level of caste, the same kind of superordinate class bias as the blue-ribbon panel system. Juries packed with government employees were unfair when corruptible bureaucrats (a social class for which Jackson entertained considerable negative deference) convicted taxpayers (desirable middle-class defendants); but the same kind of jury was acceptable when placed in opposition to a more obnoxious defendant, namely, a Communist.

---

[7] *Billie Sol Estes* v. *Texas,* 381 U.S. 532 (1965).

[8] *Fay* v. *New York,* 332 U.S. 261 (1947); *Moore* v. *New York,* 333 U.S. 565 (1948).

[9] "His concern for the minority of the wealthy, of which he was a member, contrasts with his comparative lack of concern for other minorities to which he did not belong." Fred Rodell, "Justification of a Justice," *Saturday Review,* XXXVIII (July 16, 1955), 18.

His concern in so-called Fourth Amendment cases was not with the violation of personal privacy, as one might have expected in view of his expression of strong concern for freedom of belief. It was only when both personal *and property* rights were invaded in a search that Jackson sometimes objected. His stated objective in *Brinegar*, for example, was to extend the concept of curtilage to include the home in transit that the automobile constitutes, much of the time, for many Americans. In so doing, he proselyted for the very type of legal fiction against which, in other contexts and as against other propounders, he railed most vigorously. (It seems banal, but necessary, to observe that both the lord's manor and the freeman's cottage could be expected to remain rooted while the police consulted a magistrate, laying before him evidence sufficient to justify his issuing a search warrant; but Everyman's Ford often would be out of the realm, in the jurisdiction of some other magistrate and police, while consultation was taking place.) But this seeming anomaly can be explained by the circumstance that a more important goal for Jackson was to utilize this case for a rhetorical attack upon the libertarian position: to be consistent, he argued, they should be more sympathetic to the economic rights associated with the Fourth Amendment, or less sympathetic to the political rights associated with the First, or both. Hence his advocacy of equalization in constitutional rights was a two-edged sword, and quite consistent with his general position of strong support for property, and moderate support for political and religious liberty.

5

Jackson's support of property rights, over the four decades of his professional career, can best be described as curvilinear. For the first two decades, his practice became increasingly integrated with the business life of the city and section of the state in which he resided; and his published speeches and articles of this period define a conservative economic position. Then for the seven odd years of his bureaucratic career, he was thrust on the other side of the fence; and like the shifting hues of a chameleon, Jackson's advocacy of economic ideology became perfectly adjusted to his new role. Certainly all of the public commentators at the time of his appointment to the Court,[10] and possibly President Roosevelt as well,

---

[10] Typical comments were: "He believes deeply in the liberal tradition of American democracy, which is not [sic] rugged individualism," (Karl Shriftgeisser, "Career Man of the New Deal—Robert H. Jackson," *North American Review*, CCXLVIII [1939], 343); and "Jackson is a left winger by conviction" ("Jack the Giant Killer—Heir Apparent?" *Business Week*, No. 545 [February 10, 1940], 24). Jackson had encouraged such perceptions in then recent speeches such as his "Call for a Liberal Bar," *National Lawyers Guild Quarterly*, I (1938), 88-91.

thought Jackson to be an economic liberal in 1941. He quickly demonstrated that they were wrong; but it was only after Nuremberg that his identification with the defense of the rights of property, business, and management became obvious and was so perceived. His modal position on the Court, in regard to property rights, was proentrepreneur (tradesmen), promanagement (masters), antilabor (servants), probusiness monopoly, and antiunion monopoly.

The three cases in Chapter 5 that deal with fiscal claims against the government well illustrate his position. Jackson defended the claims of affluent ranchers whose property had been—at least so far as concerns its economic function—in effect condemned by withholding the water needed to feed their stock; and he rejected claims in behalf of destitute Indians who had been denied all use of their former lands and had asked compensation the better to feed themselves and their children. Cowboys, yes; Indians, no. Jackson upheld also the tort claimants injured by the government's exploding fertilizer; and here his conditioned inclination to support the individual victims (and their heirs at law) against the government was reinforced by a strong antibureaucracy bias, which also permeates his opinions.

Jackson was quick to support an embezzling entrepreneur who became entangled in the coils of appellate judicial administration; and was equally quick to reject claims of coal miners, to be paid for their underground travel to get to work, apparently on the exquisitely appropriate but archaic ground that Congress—which "can" do so, because the contract clause applies on its face only to states—had not authorized the government to change in labor's favor the terms of labor-management contracts. In two of the remaining three cases in this chapter, Jackson voted to support patent (business) monopolies, although he argued opposite positions in the cases; but he protested in the most passionate language a labor monopoly. Jackson's individualism was obvious in the rhetoric of his opinions concerning the "third party" to unionization conflicts and collectively bargained contracts—the hard-headed and poor-but-honest workingman whom Jackson portrayed as a pawn in the disputes of his "betters."[11] But these arguments for the free worker invariably coincided with the interests of the employers, for whom Jackson voted in these cases.

6

Except during his New Dealer days, a strong and persistent theme in all of Jackson's writing was hostility toward big government and its minions. The national government constituted the greatest, and local govern-

---

[11] So far as I know, Jackson never called him this in print.

ments the least, threat to individual liberty and freedom; and within the national government, the "Executive Branch" was most dangerous, next the regulatory commissions, then Congress, and least the judiciary. Officials were preoccupied with routine, small-minded tasks which they invariably pursued with great zeal, riding roughshod over the property and personal rights of the citizenry. It is easy to relate such parochial, stereotyped views to the rural individualism of the environment in which Jackson was raised. Mail carriers were doubtless about the only federal civil servants with whom he came in contact prior to reaching his majority.

But motives are rarely unmixed; and it seems apparent that Jackson's anti-bureaucratic bias was reinforced, in the cases in Chapter 6, by other considerations. In the Steel Seizure, he was presented with an opportunity to help damage politically the man who was F.D.R.'s successor, and who was, therefore, in the very role that Jackson thought was rightfully his own. Moreover, the Steel Seizure was an invasion of the property rights of mill owners, and it was (just as *Jewell Ridge* had been) an effort to substitute governmental fiat for the free processes of collective bargaining.

Similarly, in the next two cases dealing with regulatory commissions, the zeal of the bureaucrats was directed toward interfering with the property rights of the defendant corporations. And the persistent and extraordinarily passionate tone[12] that permeates Jackson's discussion of a rather complicated point of administrative law[13] betrays the concern that he had long felt for the economic threat that the administrative process made against the profession of law. Jackson's orthodox solution to this problem was to give lawyers the same dominant control over and vested interest in administrative decision making that they had come to acquire over judicial decision making.

The two cases involving aliens both tapped stages of Jackson's own career in Washington. "I have had some personal experience in handling questions of this sort," he reminded the audience assembled in the Supreme Court chamber during oral argument of Ellen Knauff's case.[14] Not only had he functioned in the role of an appellate tribunal in his own relationship to the Immigration and Naturalization Service; he had also

[12] But not without notorious precedent, as when James Clark McReynolds departed from his prepared script, in reading his opinion in a case dealing with monetary devaluation, to declare with utmost fervor on February 18, 1935, that: "As for the Constitution, it does not seem too much to say that it is gone."

[13] Whether under legislative delegation of authority, administrative policy can be made by processes of adjudication as well as by rule-making.

[14] I happened to be present on the occasion.

had to deal with Army intelligence as a rival administrative agency to his own cadre of legal eagles in his Nuremberg operation. So in these two cases involving the expulsion of aliens, his normal hostility toward federal bureaucracy was buttressed by his sense of personal involvement in events closely analogous to those at hand. He was, in short, his own expert in the facts that he believed to be true in these cases.

But to be consistent with the policy position that he was soon to advocate at Nuremberg,[15] and for which he had been laying the ground for several years previous,[16] Jackson ought to have urged that *all* military war criminals should answer to legal authority for their offenses. Surely if it was an offense against international morality for Nazi generals to put disloyal and non-German citizens in concentration camps, it was an offense against the Constitution of the United States for an American general to put loyal American citizens in concentration camps. If Nazi civilians should be tried before an ad hoc tribunal of military victors, then American General De Witt should be deemed responsible to the United States Supreme Court for deprivations of the civil liberties of American citizens. But Jackson left DeWitt and the American military to be responsible "to the political judgment of their contemporaries and to the moral judgment of history." If he had taken the same approach toward the Nazis, he could never have associated himself with the war crimes trials. Certainly Nuremberg was not "the moral judgment of history," coming as it did close upon the heels of the events at issue. It probably did represent "the political judgment of contemporaries" of the Nazis, but to accept this is to reject the entire rationale of legal justification for which Jackson purported to stand in regard to Nuremberg. The upshot of Jackson's position seems to be that zealous civilian bureaucrats should be held responsible to the ultimate policy direction of the civil courts, while zealous military

15 Wesley McCune has reported that "some who remembered Jackson from World War I, or even those who read his dissent in the Japanese relocation case, might well wonder how Jackson got into this particular [the Nuremberg] legal job. He was accused bitterly of being pro-German in World War I for opposing the use of American troops overseas. Later, he vigorously attacked the Versailles Treaty as starting the next war. He was a 100 per cent isolationist." *The Nine Young Men* (New York: Harper & Row, Publisher, 1947), p. 185.

16 For example, his address to the Inter-American Bar Association meeting in Havana which was read for him—his plane was grounded by bad weather in New York—on March 27, 1941: "International Order," *American Bar Association Journal*, XXVII (1941), 275-279; or his "The Challenge of International Lawlessness," *ibid.*, 690-693. In the latter speech he felt impelled to enter this caveat: "I share the public disappointment at the renewal of war as a means of settling the problems *of Europe,* because I also shared some of the choice illusions of my time." *Ibid.*, 690. (Emphasis added.)

bureaucrats are responsible only to their own political superiors, or to the superior force of their conquerors. *Inter arma silent leges.*

7

When we turn to values that correspond more closely to legal modes of conceptualization, we find a more prominent manifest ambivalence in his argumentation. The reason, of course, is clear: legal concepts relating to following precedent authority, and to modes of interpreting documents (such as constitutions, statutes, and wills), have no direct substantive value content. Rather, they refer to techniques for advocating one among various alternative substantive meanings. Hence, we must look for patterns of consistency in Jackson's position regarding political, social, and economic rights rather than to expect him to maintain (other than coincidentally) a position in voting and in his opinions that reflects his attitude toward, say, *stare decisis.*

In the first case in this chapter, for example, Jackson's attitude toward following precedent (if we may call it that, for present purposes only) was one of contempt. His interest was in keeping both workmen's compensation awards small and the acquisition of divorces difficult, because, he thought, the former strengthens the economic security of the businessman and the latter helps to maintain social stability. Nevertheless, having recently lost a round on the former issue, Jackson argued that he was duty-bound to follow *stare decisis* (and a bad precedent which justified *easy* divorce, when he could by so doing justify a parsimonious compensation award for an injured workman) until a majority of his colleagues would agree *not* to follow *stare decisis* on the divorce issue. Tit for tat.

His argument in the next two cases was simpler. In each, he found himself in the happy position of having new colleagues who joined with him and other former dissenters to reestablish conservative policies with which Jackson agreed. But the others were content to bring about a reversion in the result, without openly advocating what they were doing; Jackson took the more radical position that the recent, and more liberal, precedents should be flatly repudiated and overruled. Such, incidentally, is a very common use of the *stare decisis* argument. Legal commentators usually assume that proponents of *stare decisis* favor stability in public policy, whereas their opponents are out to remold society. Quite to the contrary, as exemplified by Jackson's behavior in these three cases, the judge who advocates departure from precedent often is a conservative who seeks to reverse recent policy changes which are in closer accord than he with contemporary political preferences.

The technique of statutory interpretation presents a similar and equally false dichotomy. Any judge worth his salt can find just as much room for semantic maneuver in the manifest language of any long and complex document which is itself the verbalization of a heterogeneity of political compromises, as he can discover by roaming at large among the fragmentary by-products, that have been reduced to writing, of the legislative process. Interpreting the major purpose of Congress often is a quest for an utterly fictitious (and often quite unholy) grail that provides judges with a rationale for supporting, in the name of the Congress, policy results that they deem wise. And equally so is the eschewal of the quest a means whereby judges can hide behind the express words of the statutes into which they have poured a fresh semantic content, and, therefore, a rhetorical device for covering up the tracks of judicial policy makers. Jackson, naturally, was on both sides of this fence, sometimes (7D) favoring the letter, and sometimes (7E) the spirit, of the statute; and sometimes (7G, 7H) delving into legislative history and sometimes (7F) not. It all depended upon the instrumental value of the approach as an aid in justifying the arrival at a preferred outcome.

8

The combination of Jackson's New Deal and Jamestown experiences tended to cancel out each other's effects upon his beliefs regarding centralization. The New Deal days were more recent, but the country lawyer years were of much longer duration. He favored an orthodox concept of federalism, but that image reflects an ambiguous as well as a static structure, and hence provides little guidance for resolving questions concerning dynamic conflicts about governmental functions.

Very seldom is the Supreme Court confronted with what lawyers describe as a direct conflict between the national and state "governments" (or between their instrumentalities, as in 7H, supra). The usual question is one of conflict between action taken in the name of governmental authority, either national or state-and-local, and a "private" defendant who asserts some political or economic right to be free from public control. The so-called federal question then is raised as one of his defenses: regulation may be proper, but not by *this* (whichever one it may be) level of political authority; if it is national regulation of commerce, it should be state; if it is state control of the closed shop, it should be national; and so on. The real conflict in these situations is about economic, social, and political rights; "federalism" is only a legal spook.[17] Given enough such

17 See Martin Landau, *"Barker* v. *Carr* and the Ghost of Federalism," in *Reapportionment,* ed. Glendon Schubert (New York: Charles Scribner's Sons, 1965), pp. 241-248; and my "Jackson's Judicial Philosophy," 951.

cases over a long enough period of time, we would expect a judge's votes and opinions to reflect his attitudes toward the substantive issues of personal and property rights, and to find him ambivalent, as Jackson was, in his expressions of favor and disfavor toward *both* the national and state-and-local governments.

Chapter 8 samples Jackson's opinions regarding three facets of what he considered to be federal relationships: interstate commerce, interstate litigation, and the nationalization of state adjudication. The core economic issue with which the Supreme Court had worked during the second and third decades of this century was state regulation of business; and although the question had been largely resolved in favor of public authority before Jackson reached the Court, this was the problem that he defined as crucial in both *Edwards* and *Duckworth*. He sought unsuccessfully to invoke more specialized constitutional language to provide justifications in lieu of the more general commerce clause rationale accepted by the Court's majorities in these decisions. Jackson sought to minimize the doctrinal expansion, that is, the extension of the norm system, favorable to state regulation of business enterprise.

Jackson talked about a nebulous *national* legal system. How this would differ from the then extant version of the federal legal system he never made clear. Presumably a *national* system would entail both greater homogeneity in the structure of legal norms and greater centralization in the authority to pronounce them. Neither did he ever explain how Supreme Court insistence upon "full faith and credit" would bring unity out of diversity in the patterning of state norms of law. It is clear, however, that in the three cases relating to Nevada divorces (8C-E), as elsewhere in his behavior as a judge, Jackson maintained no consistent position on this issue. While pouring acid criticism upon his colleagues for *their* inconstancy, he himself waxed and waned like the fickle moon on which star-crossed young lovers forbear to swear. But I do not suggest (as he often did about others, and the law) that the reason, which best explains his variant responses, is "confusion." Rather, he was responding to such questions as whether the Court should attempt to maintain societal stability by making divorce more difficult and expensive to obtain, and how a decedent's property should be apportioned among his several surviving and former wives.

Only when the issue could be sharply defined as one of conflict between national and state judges did Jackson assume a more consistent stance. Here he favored judicial decentralization.[18] The widow could

---

[18] In regard to the related question of whether the Supreme Court should extend its policy control over lower courts (*either* national or state), Jackson tended to argue in favor of deference, by a ratio of about 4–1. *Ibid.*, 949.

sue the railroad,[19] but only in the courts of states that would permit her suit. Similarly, it is demoralizing to state judges for their decisions convicting criminals to be placed under the continuing threat of collateral attack by subordinate federal judges. Here Jackson argued for a *minimal* federal supervisory role, and a complete reversal of the Court's continuing policy trend throughout the period beginning shortly after Stone became Chief Justice.

9

Jackson's favorite subject was his profession. The law was his life-long passion in a special way that was different from its function for his colleagues. For Black, law was a body of norms to be manipulated in order to help bring about or, in his latter days on the Court, to forestall social change. For Frankfurter, law was a set of institutional restraints upon human passions. But for Jackson, law was a *modus operandi*, a set of skills by means of which impassioned technicians could manipulate decision-making processes in order to advance whatever might be the interests of patrons. At thirty-five years of age, Jackson was an armed knight at the crossroads awaiting a joust with the next stranger who came along; at forty-five, he was a legal gun for hire, a temporary mercenary of F. D. R.'s New Deal; at fifty-five, he was Lasswell's *homus politicus*, the power seeker who displaces his private motives upon public objects which he then rationalizes in the public interest.[20] He was the complete advocate.

Jackson found it easy to empathize with old knights of the law who, as their labors neared a close, were singled out for persecution by vindictive bureaucrats or by his own more puritanical colleagues. As the Court's reputed leading non-ghost writer, Jackson was in a strong moral position to defend what he viewed as ordinary lawyerlike ways of doing business (as on the part of Dorsey) ; and as for old Communist rapists, what lawyer had not sowed a few wild seeds in his youth, or argued too vehemently in defense of his client in the heat of legal battle?

But Jackson's pristine model of the judicial process in trial courts, the legal arena with which he was most familiar, was that of the dominant, decorous, dispassionate, decision-making judge surrounded (and pursued) by active, antagonistic, agnostic advocates. The advocate's job was to outwit, outtalk, and outmaneuver his competitors; the trial judge's job was to see that the better man won. And the authority of judges to maintain discipline in the conduct of trials should be upheld, irrespective whether

---

[19] A position consistent with the individualistic faith of "Jack the Giant Killer" in Washington, who had earlier fought and beaten the Bell system in Jamestown.

[20] Harold D. Lasswell, *Power and Personality* (New York: W. W. Norton & Company, Inc., 1948), pp. 38, 62-93.

overt criticism of the judge comes from within or without the courtroom. Jackson therefore sided with Medina over Isserman, even though he was dealing with an exceptionally passionate judge; and similarly, when the question was one of choosing between an orderly trial and freedom of the press, Jackson staunchly supported the right—even of a judge who was not a lawyer—to punish his journalist critics.[21] But even Jackson's hostility for Communism was a lesser consideration than the right of a lawyer, who already had been punished for his overenthusiasm, to continue to practice his profession.

Supreme Court justices themselves are placed in an exceptionally difficult role. "It is not easy," he remarked wistfully as his own days on the Court drew to a close, "for one to shift from the warm partisanship of advocacy to the cold neutrality which is supposed to express itself so circumspectly as to give the impression that the author never warmed to his subject."[22] Of course, he never really did; and it is doubtful that he ever tried very hard to do so. The image of the dispassionate judge, he once observed, is a child's myth, on the same level of intellectual credulity as Santa Claus and the Easter Bunny.[23] And the trouble with fictions is that they are most often apt to mislead those who invoke them. The adult judge, at least as a member of a political institution like the Supreme Court, uses political symbols, such as the concept of the dispassionate judge, to build the kind of public image necessary for the courts to carry out their policy-making function with minimal interference from such competitive outsiders as governmental agencies and newspapers. But the adult advocate does not hesitate, when it suits his immediate purposes, to attack the public image of dispassionate justice;[24] and the adult Supreme Court justice does not hesitate to continue to employ his skills as an advocate to advance the policy goals for which he competes as such a justice. His clientele, in the latter role, has at long last become the set of beliefs that he has been in the process of acquiring and remolding throughout his life.

War, it has been said, is diplomacy carried on by other means; for Jackson, judging was advocacy carried on by only slightly different means —the written opinion instead of the brief, or argument with judges in conference instead of in the courtroom. His identification of the two roles is seen most clearly in the *Hirota* decision, where he exposed to public gaze

---

[21] He did vote the other way (but without an independent expression of his own views) by joining the majority in *Bridges* v. *California,* 314 U.S. 252 (1941).

[22] *Syracuse Law Review,* VI (1955), 223.

[23] *United States* v. *Ballard,* 322 U.S. 78, 94 (1944), and Chap. 2B, *supra.*

[24] Robert H. Jackson *The Struggle for Judicial Supremacy: A Study of a Crisis in American Power Politics* (New York: Alfred A. Knopf, Inc., 1941).

the whole scenario, both for himself and for his colleagues. It was as desperately political a plot as one can imagine. Nor should we be misled by the jovial good humor of Jackson's much-quoted and evidently widely appreciated opinion in *McGrath* v. *Kristensen*. The point of that opinion, after all, was to disavow personal responsibility for an earlier legal opinion that, by his own post hoc testimony, not only was ghost-written for him, but he had not even bothered to read before it was foisted, over his signature, upon an unsuspecting political world. His apologia is a most graceful piece of advocacy in his own behalf. It is also an example which surely comports better with the common understanding of what is meant by political, rather than by judicial, behavior.

EPILOGUE

Jackson's career at law and in politics, and his ideology which these events both shaped and subserved, suggest a romantic parable about the relationship between passionate lawyers and judges and the dispassionate justice which they create. Once upon a time there was a lawyer who was fearless, independent, and successful in the exercise of his craft, in a democratically Republican little riding that we may call (following excellent authority) Erewhon. The constituents of this advocate included the entire community; they loved and respected him because he was their champion when they got into trouble. The people rewarded their hero with fame, money, and respect, all of which he richly deserved. His was truly an idyllic existence.

But such an outstanding lawyer might well be called upon to display his talents at a distant royal court, in company with other knights of the realm from distant shires. And so it came to be that Sir Robert Jackson journeyed to Camelot. There he entered the lists with fellow legal Lancelots and jousted for favor in the tournaments, took part in several crusades, and was in due course given a place at the great Round Table. But he pined for action, and was granted permission to undertake one great and final quest. He traveled to lands far away, across the sea, where he slew many dragons and won great fame. But jealous rogues led by a fierce Black Knight plotted against him, and he lost favor with Harry, the pretender, who in those days was temporarily ensconced on the throne of power. Sir Robert returned to his homeland, still a hero to some, but disgraced in the eyes of many of his countrymen. Unfortunately, by this time, there were few worthy dragons left to slay, at least around Camelot. And so he languished away the remainder of his allotted days, still at the Court, a grizzled old warrior who loved to exercise his singing blade, Excandor, as he recounted the exploits of his youth in opinions which he gave freely to all who liked to hear a tale well told.

INDEX